Jesus Christ

Jesus Christ

Source of Our Salvation

Ave Maria Press AVE Notre Dame, Indiana

The Subcommittee on the Catechism, United States Conference of Catholic Bishops, has found that this catechetical high school text, copyright 2018, is in conformity with the *Catechism of the Catholic Church* and that it fulfills the requirements for Course III of the *Doctrinal Elements of a Curriculum Framework for the Development of Catechetical Materials for Young People of High School Age.*

Nihil Obstat: Reverend Monsignor Michael Heintz, PhD
Censor Librorum

Imprimatur: Most Reverend Kevin C. Rhoades
Bishop of Fort Wayne–South Bend

Given at: Fort Wayne, Indiana, on 17 May 2017

The *Nihil Obstat* and *Imprimatur* are official declarations that a book or pamphlet is free of doctrinal or moral error. No implication is contained therein that those who have granted the *Nihil Obstat* or *Imprimatur* agree with its contents, opinions, or statements expressed.

Catechetical Writing Team
Michael Pennock
Christine Schmertz Navarro
Michael Amodei

Theological Consultant
Troy Stefano, PhD
Associate Professor of Systematic and Historical Theology
St. Vincent de Paul Regional Seminary
Boynton Beach, Florida

Pedagogical Consultant
Michael J. Boyle, PhD
Director, Andrew M. Greeley Center for Catholic Education
Loyola University Chicago

Theology of the Body Consultant
Sr. Helena Burns, F.S.P.

Founded in 1865, Ave Maria Press is a ministry of the United States Province of Holy Cross.

Engaging Minds, Hearts, and Hands for Faith® is a trademark of Ave Maria Press, Inc.

www.avemariapress.com

Paperback: ISBN 978-1-59471-627-0

E-book: ISBN 978-1-59471-628-7

Cover images © Alamy, Super Stock.

Cover design by Andrew Wagoner.

Text design by Christopher D. Tobin.

Printed and bound in the United States of America.

ENGAGING MINDS, HEARTS, AND HANDS FOR FAITH

An education that is complete is the one in which hands and heart are engaged as much as the mind. We want to let our students try their learning in the world and so make prayers of their education.

Bl. Basil Moreau
Founder of the Congregation of Holy Cross

In this text you will:

learn methods for investigating and understanding all that God has done for the world through his Son, Jesus Christ, and the description of redemption that is accomplished through the Paschal Mystery.

receive suggestions for answering God's call to each person for an intimate relationship with him through the deepening practice of prayer.

find ways to practice discipleship, including adherence to all that Christ taught, service to the poor and marginalized, and fulfilling the responsibility for the mission of evangelization.

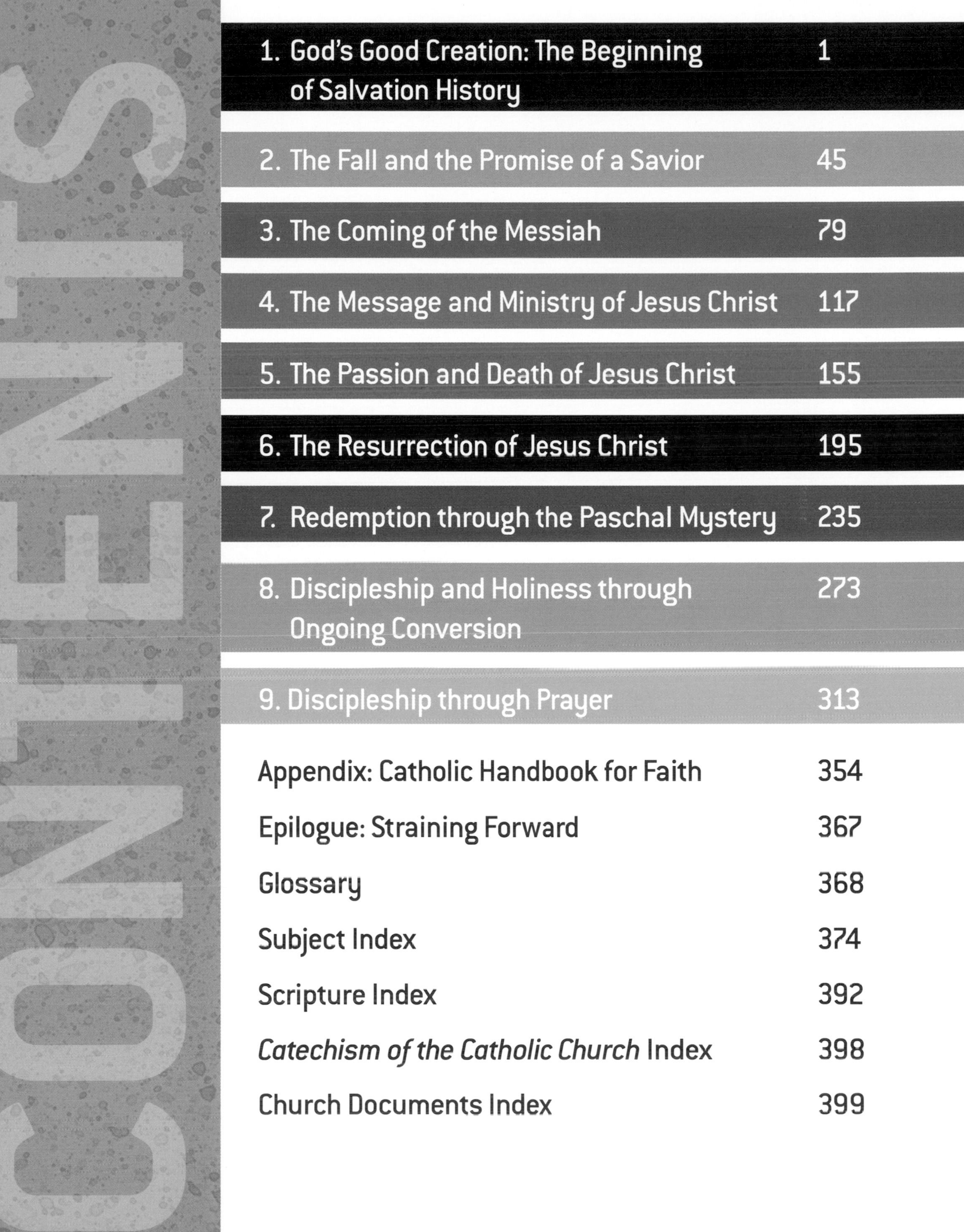

CONTENTS

GOD'S GOOD CREATION

THE BEGINNING OF SALVATION HISTORY

GOD'S GIFTS: CREATION and the SACRAMENTS

At age fifteen, Annie Powell dreamed of having a summer camp for teens in the Colorado Rockies so that they could enjoy the beauty of her state and encounter God through creation. After she married, Annie and her husband, Scott, founded Camp Wojtyla. They named the camp after St. John Paul II, using his given name, Karol Wojtyla. As a young priest, Karol Wojtyla himself had spent a great deal of time leading teens and young adults to perceive God through hiking and skiing; he had a strong passion for inviting youth to encounter Christ through creation.

Camp Wojtyla now serves middle-school and high-school teens and provides opportunities for encountering God in exploration of the natural world. During each week-long session, participants rock climb, raft, zip line, and hike through the Rockies as well as attend daily Mass and Eucharistic Adoration and have opportunities for Confession. In the evenings, campers reflect on their various outdoor and spiritual experiences, making connections with their day-to-day lives.

The teens emerge with a profound sense of God's love as experienced in creation. "Camp not only gave me a sense of courage and strength in myself, it gave me long-lasting friendships with young Catholics who want the same thing I do: a friendship with Jesus Christ. Every morning, I woke up to God's beautiful creation, and that was enough to remind me how much he truly loves us," one camper said at the end of the experience.

Annie Powell also notices growth in the college students who serve as staff members. They too seem to strip off their false selves and truly come alive during their summer work.

FOCUS QUESTION

What does **GOD'S CREATION** tell you about his **PLAN FOR SALVATION**?

Chapter Overview

INTRODUCTION

God Created Humans to Share in His Own Life

MAIN IDEA

God created humans to share, by knowledge and love, in his own life. His creation reveals the type of relationship that he wanted with humanity. After sin entered the world, the only way this relationship would be possible was through the saving actions of Christ.

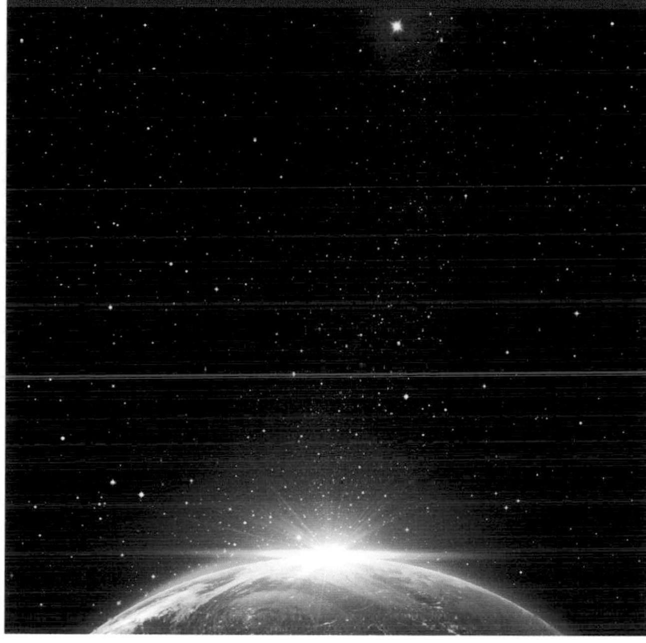

Creation reveals God and his mystery. Having a simple, rosy picture of creation, however, is naïve: camping in a tent during a Sierra Nevada blizzard can broaden your perspective! The natural world has many dimensions, so it stands to reason that its Creator does too.

This book will familiarize you with the Paschal Mystery—that is, the Good News that Jesus freely suffered, died, rose from the dead, and ascended to heaven to save you from sin and give you the opportunity to be with him eternally in heaven. Like creation and God, the Paschal Mystery also has many dimensions. On one level, its truth can be summarized in a sentence. On a deeper level, the Paschal Mystery sheds light on all of history, especially the mission of Jesus Christ on earth. The Paschal Mystery explains how you are destined for heaven and teaches you that life is stronger than death. The *Catechism of the Catholic Church* highlights the importance of the Paschal Mystery:

> The Paschal Mystery of Christ's cross and Resurrection stands at the center of the Good News that the apostles, and the Church following them, are to proclaim to the world. God's saving plan was accomplished "once for all" by the redemptive Death of his Son Jesus Christ. (*CCC*, 571)

The story of God's redeeming activity in human history, which reaches its completion in the Lord's Passion, Death, and Resurrection, starts at the very beginning of creation, both the creation of spiritual beings known as angels and the creation of the first humans, named in Genesis as Adam and Eve. Adam and Eve's fall from grace, known as Original Sin (see Chapter 2), ruptured their relationship with God, but God did not abandon them or their descendants to sin. The story of humankind is the story of salvation

NOTE TAKING

Synthesizing Information. Print the following quotation in your notebook. Write your own sentence explaining its meaning. As you read this section, list relevant points pertaining to God's creation that support and enrich St. Bonaventure's words.

God created all things "not to increase his glory, but to show forth and communicate it" (St. Bonaventure, quoted in *CCC*, 293).

history, a history that reaches its climax in Jesus Christ, the Savior of the world.

Why Did God Create?

Creation is the common work of the Trinity: Father, Son, and Holy Spirit. St. Bonaventure, who lived in the thirteenth century, once said that God can freely create the world out of his love only because he is a Trinity. What he meant by this is that humans can only understand how God can freely create the world from nothing when they see God as an eternal communion of love. The Father, for all eternity, loves his Son and gives life to his Son. The Son, in receiving the Father's love, returns his love to his Father. From their mutual love, the Holy Spirit comes forth as the bond of love between the Father and the Son.

It is within this intimate and eternal exchange of love between Father, Son, and Holy Spirit that creation takes place. The Father creates the world and gives his love to it in a similar way that he has always loved his beloved Son. The Son, receiving the Father's love and expressing his love in return, impresses the image of the Father's love on all of creation. The New Testament teaches that the Father created everything by the eternal Word, his beloved Son. In Jesus "were created all things in heaven and on earth . . . all things were created through him and for him. He is before all things, and in him all things hold together" (Col 1:16–17; cf. Jn 1:1–3). Likewise, the Holy Spirit, who is the bond of love between the Father and the Son, breathes life into creation (see Gn 2:7). The Church confesses the Holy Spirit as the "giver of life" in the Nicene Creed. The Father, Son, and Holy Spirit worked together as one to create the world.

Understanding the world as created by the Blessed Trinity explains something about *why* God created the world. God did not need to create the world, nor does God need anything from the world; that would imply that God was imperfect and needed to become better or more perfect. Rather, the Blessed Trinity is a perfect communion of love, overflowing with goodness and perfection. God created the world freely to manifest his glory and share it with humans. God wants you to share in his truth, goodness, and beauty—and above all, in his love. God the Father created the world so that humans could become sons and daughters through Jesus Christ (see *CCC*, 294) and share in the Father's love for his beloved Son.

God created human beings in a state of **original holiness and original justice**. This means that the first human beings were created good and established friendship with God. In particular, *original justice* means that they were in harmony with God, themselves, and creation. *Original holiness* means that they shared intimately in God's divine life. Human beings lost this sense of harmony and this intimate share in God's life by rejecting God. Although original holiness and original justice were lost, these aspects of creation reveal that God's intention from the beginning has been to share his life with humans.

In the face of sin, God did not abandon humanity. He gradually revealed his love over the thousands of years leading to the coming of his Son, Jesus Christ, into the world. God's purpose for his creation is most fully revealed in the Paschal Mystery. By his Death, Christ liberated the world from sin. By his Resurrection, he opened for you and all people a way to a new life as a son or daughter of the Father. The Sacrament of Baptism restores original holiness but not original justice (*CCC*, 400).

original holiness and original justice The state of man and woman in paradise before sin. The grace of original holiness was to share in the divine life (see *CCC*, 375). "The inner harmony of the human person, the harmony between man and woman, and finally the harmony between the first couple and all of creation, comprised the state called 'original justice'" (*CCC*, 376). "From [Adam and Eve's] friendship with God flowed the happiness of their existence in paradise" (*CCC*, 384).

Knowing God through Natural Revelation

There are two main orders of knowledge of God. You can learn about God through *natural revelation*—by looking at the world around you and at human beings and by thinking about them, you can come to know the one personal God as the Creator of all things. But there is another order of knowledge that you cannot arrive at by your own powers: the order of *Divine Revelation*. "Through an utterly free decision, God has revealed himself and given himself to [us]. . . . God has fully revealed [his plan for us] by sending us his beloved Son, our Lord Jesus Christ, and the Holy Spirit" (CCC, 50).

As human beings, we can come to know God by looking at the world around us and at other human beings. We are by nature and vocation religious beings. We have a longing in our hearts for communion with God, in whom we find our happiness. God filled our hearts with a longing for him and gave us inquisitive minds. Albert Einstein had this to say about natural human inquiry:

> The important thing is not to stop questioning. Curiosity has its own reason for existing. One cannot help but be in awe when he contemplates the mysteries of eternity, of life, of the marvelous structure of reality. It is enough if one tries merely to comprehend a little of this mystery every day. Never lose a holy curiosity.
> (Message for a Ben Scheman dinner, March 1952)

Einstein was not a particularly religious man, but he saw asking questions as a process that can lead humans to seek God.

As you look to your future, you likely share similar questions with people your age from across the world:

- What can I do with my life so that I will be happy and make a difference?
- Will I succeed in my chosen career?
- Will I meet the love of my life and have close friends?

Questions about where you came from and where you are going are critical because the answers you arrive at will affect the meaning and orientation of your life and actions. Through the ages, men and women have tried to make sense out of reality and to seek meaning in the world around them, a quest that helps explain the existence of **philosophy**. Many people who think deeply about these kinds of questions have concluded that, behind the life you see and experience, there is a Source—something or someone greater than human beings, someone who brought life into existence and who sustains it. By means of reason, human beings can come to know God as the one personal source of reality, and they can recognize him as the end for which they were made. Furthermore, you can recognize something of the Creator through your conscience, which he has inscribed on your heart.

philosophy The human attempt to provide rational explanations for why things are the way they are and for how people should conduct their lives.

Knowing God through Divine Revelation

Scientists have spent years enriching your understanding of the world's origins and dimensions, the

Trying to Comprehend God's Love

It is easy to say that you know God loves you without giving this truth much thought. In fact, in human terms, God's love pursues you and does not easily take no for an answer. He gives you many chances to accept his love, as he has done for humans throughout history. Review from your previous study of salvation history some of these opportunities God provided for humans to accept his love:

- God created human beings in his image and likeness (Gn 1:27). Of all God's creatures, it is human beings alone that are "called to share, by knowledge and love, in God's own life" (*CCC*, 356).

- God manifested himself to the first humans, Adam and Eve, and offered them his first covenant. God "invited them to intimate communion with himself and clothed them with resplendent grace and justice" (*CCC*, 54; cf. 374). "From their friendship with God flowed the happiness of their existence in paradise" (*CCC*, 384). But because they turned away from God, they lost paradise and their friendship and intimacy with God. They also lost their harmony within themselves, with each other, and with all of creation (see *CCC*, 397–400). Sin, suffering, and death made their entrance into human history (see *CCC*, 400–406). Human beings stood in need of salvation.
- God's manifestation of himself to humans was not broken off by the sin of Adam and Eve. "'After the fall, [God] buoyed them up with the hope of salvation, by promising redemption'"; and despite the escalation of sin, he has never ceased to show his care for humans. "'For he wishes to give eternal life to all those who seek salvation by patience in well-doing.'" (*CCC*, 55, quoting *Dei Verbum*, 3).
- "After the unity of the human race was shattered by sin, God at once sought to save humanity part by part" (*CCC*, 56). He formed a series of covenants as solemn commitments between himself and human beings, beginning with Noah. His covenant with Noah offered humans a chance to have a relationship with him through living uprightly (see *CCC*, 58).

- "In order to gather . . . scattered humanity, God call[ed] Abram from his country, his kindred, and his father's house, and [made] him Abraham, that is, 'the father of a multitude of nations'" (*CCC*, 59). God made a promise to Abraham that would be preserved by his descendants, the patriarchs and the Chosen People, and which would be fulfilled one day through Christ, when God gathered all his children into the unity of the Church (see *CCC*, 59–60).
- "After the patriarchs, God formed Israel as his people by freeing them from slavery in Egypt. He established with them the covenant of Mount Sinai and, through Moses, gave them his law so that they would recognize him and serve him as the one living and true God, the provident Father and just judge, and so that they would look for the promised Savior" (*CCC*, 62).
- God appointed judges, kings, and prophets to remind the people of ancient Israel about his promise of salvation, and to call them to a more faithful relationship with him. "Through the prophets, God form[ed] his people in the hope of salvation, in the expectation of a new and everlasting covenant intended for all, to be written on their hearts" (*CCC*, 64).
- God sent his Son to the Jewish people: this was the pinnacle of human history. There remained division among Jewish groups at the time, and many Jewish leaders failed to recognize Jesus as God's Chosen One. Many other Jews and Gentiles did indeed recognize that Jesus was Lord, and some became his first disciples. Jesus Christ, the Messiah spoken of by the prophets, was put to death. He rose from the dead three days later.
- Jesus sent the Holy Spirit to assemble believers into the community of the Church as part of his promise to remain with us forever. This Church persists to this day. The Church has always consisted of sinners in various stages of holiness.

Given this history of God's interaction with humans, what might your reaction be to the way God has been treated? Would you say something like:

- God, I hate to see people treat you like this.
- God, I question your taste in friends.
- God, if you stop treating them so lovingly, these people will get the message and do what you say.
- God, I understand why you might give people a few chances, but this many? People are taking advantage of you!

While it is often unhealthy for people to stay in human relationships with those who ignore or take advantage of them, it is God's nature to love the people he created unconditionally. Because God creates people, he knows them. He understands human tendencies and behaviors. When people ignore him, their attitudes do not diminish him. While he unconditionally loves everyone and offers forgiveness to all, in the end, he does not force people to know and love him. People can freely choose to be with him forever or not. Through the prophet of the Book of Isaiah, God points out:

> For my thoughts are not your thoughts,
> nor are your ways my ways—oracle of
> the Lord. (Is 55:8)

JOURNAL REFLECTION

Write your responses to the following questions:

- Why would a person not choose God?
- What do you think God wants for your life?
- What keeps you from fully following God's will?

way life came to be, and the appearance of human beings. Fantastic discoveries about rock formations, genes, and different species of life give you further reason to admire God the Creator. You can give thanks for the knowledge and wisdom God has granted to scholars and researchers. You might be one of these scientists ten years from now!

But the natural sciences have limits. They cannot discover the meaning of creation or answer questions such as *why* evil exists. Scientists can study *how* creation unfolded over time, but they cannot answer *why* the world exists in the first place.

- Why is there something rather than nothing?
- Why did God create, and what is creation's meaning?
- Why is there evil in the world, and how should we understand it?

These questions are beyond the scientific domain. Christians answer these questions based upon God's Revelation. Humans receive through Divine Revelation truths about which science and history can only speculate.

Divine Revelation, as you recall from earlier courses, is the way God communicates who he is to humankind: a self-communication realized by his actions and words over time, most fully realized by the sending of his own Son, Jesus Christ. You learned in earlier courses how God's self-Revelation in Jesus is handed on in the Church through Scripture and Tradition, under the inspiration and guidance of the Holy Spirit. The Church has been entrusted by God to preserve, guard, and hand on his Revelation for every generation. The Church invites us to enter into communion with God as Father, Son, and Holy Spirit and with the whole Church by professing the Creed. The *Catechism* describes the Creed as the "treasure of our soul" (*CCC*, 197) because it unites all believers in professing what God has done for us in Jesus Christ.

Catholics profess the Nicene-Constantinopolitan Creed at Mass each Sunday and on holy days of obligation. The Creed begins:

> I believe in one God,
> the Father almighty,
> maker of heaven and earth,
> of all things visible and invisible.

To say these statements is to profess, together with the whole Church, that only God is Creator and that everything that exists came from him and depends on him. The Creed also makes clear that Christians believe that God is the source of both the "visible" and the "invisible" world. As a matter of faith, we understand that God has created spiritual realities beyond what is scientifically observable through our senses. The next subsections explore these themes in more depth.

Things Visible

This chapter focuses primarily on those aspects of God's creation that are perceptible to the human senses or visible. You will learn about the two creation accounts at the beginning of the Book of Genesis. You will also learn about how these accounts tell us not just about the beginning of the world but also about the kind of relationship God wants to have with us. Seen from the perspective of what God has revealed to us in Jesus Christ, creation is the beginning of God's plan of loving goodness. God's plan for us begins with creation and continues through the Paschal Mystery, up to our heavenly communion with the Father, through Christ, in the Holy Spirit. "Creation is the foundation of 'all God's saving plans,' the 'beginning of the history of salvation' that culminates in Christ. . . . From the beginning, God envisaged the glory of the new creation in Christ" (*CCC*, 280, quoting the *General Catechetical Directory*, 51).

Every year, the Easter Vigil liturgy reminds Catholics of God's plan: the very first Scripture reading is the creation account, while the essence of the celebration is the Paschal Mystery, new creation through Christ. The first three chapters of Genesis present you with a good deal of information about why God created the universe, answers that cannot be found through scientific study.

Things Invisible

So what are the "invisible" things God created that are mentioned in the Creed? God is Creator of "heaven and earth," which means that God created the universe and all that exists. Heaven is properly God's domain, as Jesus indicated in his prayer: "Our Father in heaven, hallowed be your name" (Mt 6:9). It is also the "place" where the angels and saints live, and it is where the redeemed experience eternal life in its fullness.

You may have learned from Sacred Tradition and Sacred Scripture about angels. During the Fourth Lateran Council, convened by Pope Innocent III in the thirteenth century, the Church's **Magisterium** articulated a revealed truth about creation that had been held by Christians since the beginning and, before them, by many Jewish people. They taught that God created three types of creatures out of nothing: fully spiritual creatures such as angels, fully bodily creatures such as animals, and human beings, who are both body and spirit.

Angels are purely spiritual creatures. The word *angel* comes from a Greek word, *aggelos*, which generally means "a messenger from God." *Angel* describes what these spiritual creatures do as God's servants and messengers. As purely spiritual creatures, angels possess intelligence, will, and personality. They are greater than any visible creature. They, like you, are also immortal spirits. They glorify God without stopping and serve him by assisting in his saving plan for human beings.

Angels belong to Christ in a special way because they were created through him and for him. They are *his* angels:

> For in him were created all things in heaven
> and on earth,
> the visible and the invisible,
> whether thrones or dominions or principalities or powers;
> all things were created through him and
> for him. (Col 1:16)

Magisterium The bishops, in communion with the pope (the successor of St. Peter), who are the living and teaching office of the Church. The Magisterium is entrusted with guarding and handing on the Deposit of Faith and with authentically interpreting God's Revelation, in the forms of both Sacred Scripture and Sacred Tradition.

Angels belong to Christ still more because he has made them messengers of his saving plan. Angels have been active throughout salvation history. They announce God's plan of salvation near and far and serve God by helping his plan of salvation. See if you can remember their roles in these biblical situations before the birth of Jesus:

- at the Garden of Eden after God expelled the humans (Gn 3)
- with Hagar and Ishmael, after Abraham expelled them (Gn 16)
- with Lot, leaving the city (Gn 19)
- at the call of Moses (Ex 3)
- with Tobit, when God answered the prayers of this righteous man (Tb 3)
- with Mary, when she learned what God wanted of her (Lk 1)

In addition, angels announced other births and callings, and they assisted the prophets.

Angels also played an important role in Jesus' earthly life, serving him in his mission to save humanity. They praised God at his birth, served him in the desert, strengthened him during his agony in the garden, proclaimed his Resurrection, and explained his Ascension to his disciples. They will also be with him at the **Parousia**, when he returns to judge the world.

Angels help the Church as a whole in mysterious and powerful ways, and the Church *venerates* them—that is, honors them with special devotion—as together humans and angels worship God. Prior to the Eucharistic Prayer at Mass, you join the angels as you sing:

Holy, Holy, Holy Lord God of hosts.
Heaven and earth are full of your glory.
Hosanna in the highest.
Blessed is he who comes in the name of the Lord.
Hosanna in the highest.

Angels also play a role in your life today. Psalm 91:10–12 refers to angels who guide you toward good thoughts, works, and words, protecting you from evil. Your **guardian angel** protects you and helps to lead you toward God.

Like humans, angels were created by God; unlike humans, angels are purely spiritual creatures.

Parousia The Second Coming of Christ, when the Lord will judge the living and the dead.

guardian angel The name for a messenger with free will and naturally superior intellect to humans. Since the third century, the Church has maintained, though not officially, that all the baptized have guardian angels who personally watch out for them. The Feast of the Guardian Angels is October 2.

Humans: Body and Spirit

Created by God in his own image, you are at the same time *corporeal* (having a physical, material body) and spiritual. The second creation account illustrates this fact: "Then the LORD God formed the man out of the dust of the ground and blew into his nostrils the breath of life, and the man became a living being" (Gn 2:7). God willed that you be both body and spirit.

These are some implications of being both body and soul:

- You possess great dignity as a person. You are *someone* rather than *something*. You can know yourself, and you can love other people and your Creator.
- The God of love is a communion of Three Divine Persons: Father, Son, and Holy Spirit. Because God made humanity in his own image, he calls men and women to love and be in communion with each other and with him.
- Though made of body and soul, you are a unity. Together, spirit and matter form in you a single nature because the soul takes on the "form" of the body. Your soul allows your material body to live.
- Your body is part of what makes you in the image of God.

- Your body is a temple of the Holy Spirit.
- In your body, you encompass the elements of the material world and bring them to perfection so as to praise God the Creator.

- In the Bible, the terms *spirit* and *soul* are both used to show that you are ordered toward a supernatural end. In the spiritual tradition of the Church, the word *heart* also describes the depth of a person's being.
- You must view your body as good and honor it because God created it and will raise it up on the last day. Your soul is immortal, which means that it will not die when it is separated from your body in death, and it will be reunited with your body at the final resurrection.
- Your parents did not "produce" your soul; rather, God created your soul immediately when you were conceived.

This final truth is represented in the story about an unborn baby under the heading "God Creates the Human Soul" on page 12.

GOD CREATES THE HUMAN SOUL

When they heard that Micah was pregnant, her parents said that they would support her with any plan that did not include abortion. Both Micah and her boyfriend, Kyle, already wanted to keep the baby.

Micah and her parents prepared for teen pregnancy and college. Her parents asked her to pray about adoption, but they could see that she wanted to raise the baby herself, as Micah's mother had wanted to do when she was a teenager pregnant with Micah. The family began to get excited about the new baby.

The eighteen-week ultrasound revealed that the baby was a girl and that she had anencephaly, a condition where a great part of a baby's brain and skull do not develop properly, making it impossible for her to live long after birth if she makes it that far. The parents named her Ambra Storm. Micah's first instinct, when the doctor offered abortion as an option, was to refuse.

She did struggle with this option because she wondered if abortion would save her a good deal of heartache. Micah articulated her final reasons for deciding to bring the baby to term:

> Because no matter what, she was my daughter. There was a life inside of me and I couldn't just take that away from her. She didn't choose to have this happen to her, so how could I choose to end her life just to save myself from more heartache?

Micah's parents also asked themselves whether they should encourage her to terminate the pregnancy. When their pastor supported Micah's decision to continue the pregnancy, they began to research the condition on the Internet and found no accounts of moms in similar situations who regretted bringing their babies to term.

Micah and her parents shifted gears, preparing her no longer for motherhood but for letting go of a baby. They found that laughing and crying together helped them to handle this. Micah began to enjoy her pregnancy and her very active baby. She was amazed, however, at how insensitive people were. They made rude comments about her as a woman pregnant with a baby headed for death. They asked, "Why don't you just abort?"

The doctor induced labor at thirty-five weeks because an excess amount of amniotic fluid was making it hard for Micah to breathe. Micah and Kyle's daughter was stillborn. The two of them spent three-and-a-half hours with her. They identified traits that she had inherited from both of them and their families. It was difficult to let the baby go when it was time for her to go to the funeral home. Micah said, "I got to meet my daughter, to hold and kiss her. I couldn't imagine not being able to share those few hours with her." Her mother added, "Treasure the short time these precious babies are with us. Remember them. Use the journey to strengthen relationships and experience the blessing of family" (Rebekah O'Brien, "Pregnant at 17 with a Baby Doomed to Die at Birth, She Chose Life," LifeSiteNews.com, June 5, 2013).

REFLECTION

- How do you think the title of this story describes Micah's experience?

SECTION ASSESSMENT

NOTE TAKING

Use the notes you made related to the St. Bonaventure quotation to help you answer the following questions.

1. Why did God create the world?
2. God created the world out of the love shared by the Divine Persons of the Blessed Trinity; what does this imply about the relationship between creation and the Paschal Mystery?

VOCABULARY

3. How does the existence of the intellectual discipline of *philosophy* shed light upon what humans can know about God based on creation?

COMPREHENSION

4. Why did God start something in creation that would not be fulfilled for thousands of years?
5. Why is it important to give thanks for the knowledge and wisdom God has granted to scholars and researchers?
6. What did God want to reveal about himself in addition to his role as Creator?
7. Who lives in heaven?
8. Name a biblical passage that includes an angel, and explain the importance of that angel.

CRITICAL ANALYSIS

9. Explain the meaning of the Albert Einstein quotation on page 5.

REFLECTION

10. Which of the questions on page 5 has the most meaning for you? Explain.

SECTION 1

Understanding How to Read Scripture

MAIN IDEA

Basic scriptural scholarship can help you understand the lessons the Church draws from the Book of Genesis.

The first three chapters of Genesis reveal important theological truths about the origins of creation, humans, and sin (see, for example, Gn 1:31). Sacred Scripture is the inspired Word of God. To discover its theological truths, you must be aware of the Church's teaching on Scripture as taught by the Magisterium. The Church reads Genesis (and all of Scripture) in a *typological* manner that recognizes the unity of the Old and New Testaments. This means that what God did in Genesis and the other books of the Old Testament prefigures what he would do in the fullness of time in the Divine Person of his Son, Jesus Christ. Only by keeping this typological and *Christological* focus in mind can you understand the essential truths of these sacred readings. St. Augustine is famously credited with saying that "the New Testament lies hidden in the Old, and the Old Testament is unveiled in the New." A typological reading of Scripture recognizes the movement toward the fulfillment of God's plan in Christ.

Any examination of a particular text must be from this unified typological and Christological perspective. You can then employ other historical-critical and literary-theological methodologies to get a better glimpse at what the biblical authors intended in their writing. Reading the Bible with understanding requires recognizing that the Bible deals with a time, people, and culture foreign to people today. The *Catechism of the Catholic Church* explains:

> In Sacred Scripture, God speaks to man in a human way. To interpret Scripture correctly,

NOTE TAKING

Prioritizing Information. Number a notebook page with a list from one to three. After you read this section, write three important points (criteria) to keep in mind when reading the creation stories in the Book of Genesis. For example: *The form a biblical text takes is important for understanding its meaning.*

the reader must be attentive to what the human authors truly wanted to affirm and to what God wanted to reveal to us by their words.

In order to discover *the sacred authors' intention,* the reader must take into account the conditions of their time and culture, the literary genres in use at that time, and the modes of feeling, speaking, and narrating then current. (*CCC,* 109–110)

One way to access the sacred authors' intention is through applying certain critical methods or theories to Scripture to aid our understanding of what the text meant *in the context of its time.* Some of the methods you will learn about in this section are called *source criticism, redaction criticism,* and *form criticism.*

But these methods only tell you about what the biblical text meant *at that time.* They don't tell you what the Bible means to you now, as containing and revealing the living Word of God. Since Sacred Scripture is divinely inspired, the historical understanding of the sacred authors' intention must be brought to life and given meaning for people today by interpreting the Scripture "'in the light of the same Spirit by whom it was written.' The Second Vatican Council indicates three criteria for interpreting Scripture in accordance with the Spirit who inspired it" (*CCC,* 111, quoting *Dei Verbum,* 12):

1. Pay attention to the content and unity of all of Scripture as a whole, not just as individual books of the Bible or individual passages.
2. Read Scripture in light of the Church's entire living and Sacred Tradition. The Holy Spirit inspires the Church to interpret the spiritual meaning of Scripture.
3. "Be attentive to the analogy of faith" (*CCC,* 114), which means setting the truths of faith both among themselves and in the context of God's entire Revelation.

Keeping these three criteria in mind, under the direction of the Magisterium of the Church, you can employ certain methods that allow an understanding of the Book of Genesis in its original context. Then, guided by these three criteria, you can ask what those biblical passages mean for people today.

The Study of Scripture

To study Sacred Scripture, biblical scholars work according to the rules established by the Church toward "a better understanding and explanation of the meaning of Sacred Scripture in order that their research may help the Church to form a firmer judgment" (*CCC,* 119, quoting *Dei Verbum,* 12). According to an ancient tradition, Sacred Scripture can be distinguished between two *senses*: the literal and the spiritual.

The *literal sense* is what the words mean at the surface level and, as it was understood at the time, how things actually happened. The *spiritual sense,* or *mystical sense,* refers not just to the words themselves but rather to what is signified by the words. Three further divisions explain the spiritual sense more clearly. The *allegorical sense* recognizes the significance of Christ in scriptural events. The *moral sense* seeks instruction for living and behaving—what a person is to do. The *anagogical sense* derives heavenly matters—that is, the eternal life we are awaiting—from earthly matters described in the narrative. For example, the Church on earth is a sign of your destiny in heaven.

Consider this example: the Exodus of the Chosen People from Egypt in the Old Testament. The

Exodus was literally a historical event; allegorically, it represented Jesus' salvation of the world; morally, it symbolized the individual's conversion to God; anagogically, it embodied, in death, a person's departure from this life to the eternal life of heaven.

Applying these rules, biblical scholars have used methods that have yielded different theories for reading and understanding Sacred Scripture. It's important to underscore that these are only theories, not definitive practices. For example, one *source criticism* theory proposes that the two creation accounts in Genesis may have had different origins. One theory based on *redaction criticism* suggests that people who edited Genesis may have thought that it was important to keep both accounts.

The first creation account is from Genesis 1:1 to 2:4a, and the second is from Genesis 2:4b to 2:25. Although they may come from different sources and emphasize slightly different points, they both belong to the divinely inspired Sacred Scriptures, and they complement rather than contradict one another. Here are the main differences between the two accounts:

- The first creation account portrays creation as dramatic, orderly, and awesome. God is glorious and majestic.
- The second creation account shows the close relationship between God and his people (which was unique at the time, since most ancient peoples feared their gods). Out of compassion, God gave Adam a lush garden and different creatures, allowing him to name them.

To interpret the Bible correctly, you need to have some background information on the text so you can distinguish between different forms of writing. This is what *form criticism* helps to do: provide context and background. It searches into the history of how most biblical books took shape as oral tradition before being written down. Form criticism also identifies literary genres, or types of writing, so that you can better understand the human author's intention and actual meaning.

In this twelfth-century manuscript, the stages of creation are depicted.

Reading the Bible in the Spirit in Which It Was Written

Once you have made the best literal sense of the text, you are then ready to search for the spiritual meaning. What did God want to say to his people then, and what does he want to say to his people now? *Dei Verbum* (*Dogmatic Constitution on Divine Revelation*), a Second Vatican Council document that discussed Revelation in Scripture and in Church Tradition, states:

> But, since Holy Scripture must be read and interpreted in the sacred Spirit in which it was written, no less serious attention must be given to the content and unity of the whole of Scripture if the meaning of the sacred texts is to be correctly worked out. The living tradition of the whole Church must be taken into account along with the harmony which exists between elements of the faith. (12)

Reading the Bible in this way means that you cannot take a biblical passage out of its overall context. To understand what is meant by interpreting the Bible in the Spirit in which it was written, according to the three criteria described above, consider the following verse from the first chapter of the Book of Genesis as an example:

> God blessed them and God said to them: Be fertile and multiply; fill the earth and subdue it. Have dominion over the fish of the sea, the birds of the air, and all the living things that crawl on the earth. (Gn 1:28)

This passage, taken out of context and apart from Scripture as a whole and the living Tradition of the Church, could be interpreted in a variety of ways. For example, someone could interpret the command to "subdue" the earth and to "have dominion" over all of the earth's animals as meaning that humans can do whatever they want with the created world, including wasting natural resources or eliminating species. This interpretation would be mistaken, and this example serves as a warning that picking and choosing verses can lead to very misleading results! If the passage is interpreted in the Spirit in which it was written, then you must look at other biblical passages that are in proximity and the teachings of the Church to authentically understand this passage's meaning. You would have to take into account, for example, the following passages from Sacred Scripture and teachings from Sacred Tradition:

- The second creation account says that God created everything for man and man was to cultivate and care for the Garden of Eden and offer everything back to God (Gn 2:15).
- The later account of Noah and the Ark conveys the Israelites' understanding that God cared for animals, birds, and so on, not just for Noah and his family (see Gn 6:5–9:17).
- "Whether believers or not, we are agreed today that the earth is essentially a shared inheritance, whose fruits are meant to benefit everyone. For believers, this becomes a question of fidelity to the Creator, since God created the world for everyone" (*Laudato Si'*, 94).

After consideration of these other passages, it becomes evident that the passage cannot be interpreted as saying that people can do whatever they want with creation. The point of this example is that understanding the Scriptures correctly involves trying to see every passage in reference to the Church's full and entire faith in Jesus.

The best way to read a passage in the spiritual sense is by uniting ourselves to the heart of the Church. The Church carries "the living memorial of God's Word" in her heart (*CCC*, 113). When you are united to the Church by faith and love, you encounter the living Word of God who dwells there and who comes to meet us. The Holy Spirit who inspired the Sacred Scriptures (see *CCC*, 105; 107) is the very same Spirit who was poured into your heart to draw you to Christ (see *CCC*, 737; cf. Rom 5:5). This same Holy Spirit is poured out into the Church and "*makes present* the mystery of Christ" at the heart of the Church, "supremely in the Eucharist, in order to reconcile [you and God], to *bring [you] into communion* with God" (*CCC*, 737).

Reading Genesis in the Spiritual Sense

Once you have a literal sense of the creation accounts, you also want to read them in a specifically spiritual sense, which includes three approaches:

1 *The allegorical sense* seeks to understand Scripture by recognizing its connection and significance to Christ. For example, the creation account of God breathing life into the first humans foreshadows Christ bringing all humans to new life through the Paschal Mystery.

2 *The moral sense* seeks to understand how Scripture teaches people to act more justly. The Genesis creation accounts teach, for example, that one gender should not be viewed as superior to the other. They also teach that all humans should be stewards of creation.

3 *The anagogical sense* reminds you that the sacred words are intended to lead you to eternal life. You might think, "If I want to go to heaven, what do I need to do to treat men and women fairly and to respect God's gift of the earth?" Scripture provides answers to this and other similar questions.

Although it is possible for you to achieve a fairly good literal and spiritual understanding of biblical passages on your own, it is the task of the Magisterium of the Church to help Christians to read, interpret, and judge a biblical text according to these senses of Scripture. The Magisterium is responsible for watching over and interpreting God's Word.

Other Literary Forms in the Bible

In a previous course, you learned about some of the literary forms used in the Bible, including allegory, biography, creed, fable, history, law, and prophecy. Listed below are five other literary forms from the Old Testament. Read the examples cited. Write one sentence for each example, explaining how the passage fits the definition of the form.

- *Anthropomorphisms* attribute human characteristics or experiences to God. Example: 2 Chronicles 16:9.
- *Chronicles* are accounts of events in the order of time. Example: Ezra 1.
- *Contracts* are binding legal agreements between two parties. Example: Ruth 4:1–12.
- *Hyperboles* are deliberate exaggerations as a figure of speech to make a point. Example: Psalm 119:136.
- *Riddles* are thought-provoking questions or statements. Example: Judges 14:12–18.

EXTRA CREDIT

Read 2 Samuel 12:1–4. Identify its literary form.

SECTION ASSESSMENT

NOTE TAKING

Use the list you prepared to help you answer the following question.

1. What are three criteria for interpreting Sacred Scripture to keep in mind when reading the creation stories in Genesis?

COMPREHENSION

2. Explain the differences between two senses for reading Scripture: literal and spiritual.
3. How must a reader of Sacred Scripture discover the intentions of a biblical author?
4. Explain the three approaches of the spiritual sense of reading Scripture.
5. Who is ultimately responsible for biblical interpretation in the Catholic Church?

CRITICAL ANALYSIS

6. Why is it important to read Scripture "in the light of the same Spirit by whom it was written"?
7. Which two of the three spiritual senses do you think most people use when reading the Bible? Explain your answer.

SECTION 2

The First Creation Account (Genesis 1:1–2:4a)

MAIN IDEA

The first creation account reveals God's power and majesty as he creates the earth and its inhabitants from nothing in six days.

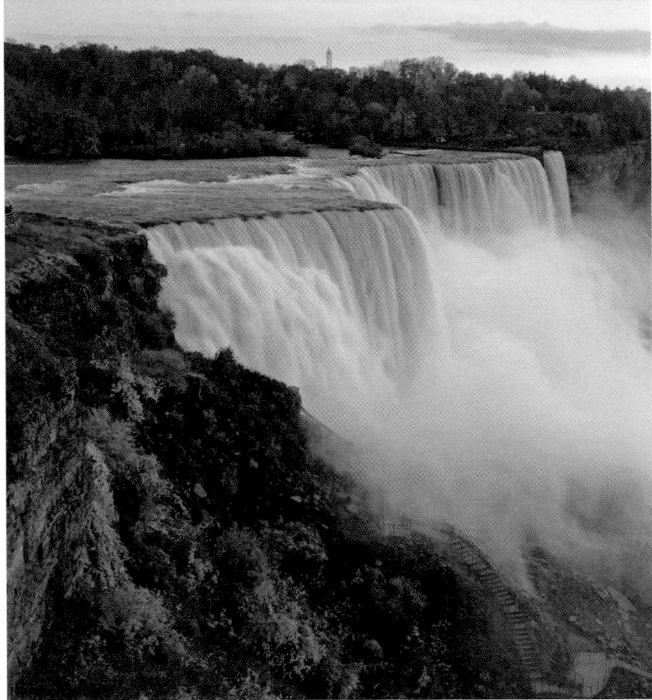

Both creation accounts in Genesis 1 and 2 are part of **primeval history**. Recall that in Sacred Scripture, God speaks to human beings in a human way. This means that biblical authors oftentimes use stories, symbols, or other devices from the culture of their time to express deep religious truths to their contemporaries in a meaningful way. The Israelites, inspired by the Holy Spirit, used some of the traditional stories and symbols of their neighbors while correcting them to convey their belief in the one, true God—YHWH—who entered their history in a radical new way. Despite the symbolic nature of the creation accounts, they do describe an actual event that occurred at the beginning of human history, whether or not the event occurred exactly as narrated in Genesis.

primeval history The accounts humans have told and recorded about the origins of the earth, humans, other creatures, languages, and cultures.

It is important to ask what the intention of the biblical authors was in writing these kinds of accounts. Some readers expect the Bible to contain the kind of information you would find in scientific journals today, so they compare the Bible's account of creation to current scientific research about the theory of evolution. It is important to ask what the intention of the biblical authors was in writing these kinds of accounts. Today, scientific questions and scientific writing are very widespread. But if you look at the creation accounts, you find that their question and intent was not trying to provide a primitively scientific account of the beginning of the world but rather to express something much deeper. The biblical authors were

NOTE TAKING

Identifying Concepts. The first creation account in the Book of Genesis communicates many truths. As you go through this section, identify at least four of these truths. Organize them in a numbered list.

Truths

1. *There is only one God.*
2.
3.
4.

Michelangelo's The Creation of Adam *depicts God breathing life into the first human.*

not much concerned with *how* creation happened scientifically—in fact, the Bible spends no time on that question since it has little to no importance for our salvation. Rather, the biblical authors were primarily concerned with expressing their understanding of God and the meaning of creation. In particular, you see the biblical authors using language, myths, stories, and other devices from the religious beliefs of their neighbors in order to distinguish their understanding of God and to make it meaningful for the people of their time and place.

Among the world's early human civilizations, the Hebrews (Israelites) were one of the few to believe in one God. For example, the Babylonians, a nearby people who took the Israelites into captivity after conquering the southern kingdom (Judah), were polytheists. The Babylonian creation story, the ***Enuma Elish***, is the oldest creation myth discovered to date.

Both the *Enuma Elish* and the creation accounts in Genesis have the literary form of a myth. Here, *myth* does not mean "false story," as it can in everyday language. In the literary sense, a myth is a narrative that seems to relate actual events but is primarily symbolic, often associated with religious beliefs. Ancient peoples used myths to express spiritual truths and basic cultural beliefs. Many of these ancient stories used common themes and symbols like creation near or from water, battles between heavenly powers, and the creation of humans from the earth. In a Christian context, the Genesis creation accounts reveal spiritual truths of who God is, how God interacts with human beings, the nature of God's creation, the interaction between good and evil, and so on. They are not intended to convey scientific truth or historical truth in the way people think of those categories today.

When you read a myth, you should look for the symbolism within the story rather than focusing on its historical or scientific accuracy. God inspired the writers of the creation accounts in Genesis to use myth as the best way to communicate religious truths to their audience.

Enuma Elish The Babylonian epic or myth of creation.

The FIRST CREATION ACCOUNT AND THE *ENUMA ELISH*

The Babylonian *Enuma Elish*, an ancient pagan creation myth, was the prevalent creation myth among the contemporaries of the biblical authors. It is the creation account that the first readers would likely have been familiar with. By incorporating language and concepts from this pagan creation myth, the biblical authors are able to accentuate the uniqueness of God and the meaning of his creation. This point serves to stress that these creation accounts are not a replacement for or competitor with scientific or historical accounts. Rather, they reveal to us in the humble vessels of human language the mystery of God's love for humans as he created the world.

Below is a comparison of the first creation account in Genesis 1:1–2:4a with the Babylonian *Enuma Elish*. The *Enuma Elish* is a much longer text. Note the obvious theological differences between the two.

CONTRASTING THE BABYLONIAN CREATION STORY (*ENUMA ELISH*) WITH THE FIRST CREATION ACCOUNT FROM GENESIS

ENUMA ELISH	IMPLICATIONS FOR BABYLONIAN RELIGION	IMPLICATIONS FOR JEWISH RELIGION	BOOK OF GENESIS
"When of the gods none had been called into being . . ."	There are multiple gods. **For you:** Praying means praying while only hoping that one or another god will respond.	There is only one God. **For you:** Praying means praying to the one, true God who desires a relationship with you and who has the power to grant the relationship.	"In the beginning, when God created the heavens and the earth . . ." (1:1)
"Tiamat made weighty her handiwork, Evil she wrought against the gods her children. To avenge Apsu, Tiamat planned evil." (Apsu and Tiamat were the gods who first existed.)	The gods commit evil acts. They are both constructive and destructive. **For you:** You awake each day wondering whether the gods are in a constructive or destructive mood and what that means for you.	God makes only good things. He is creative and not destructive. **For you:** When destructive events come along, you can feel confident that God did not cause them, though he will accompany you through them.	"God looked at everything he had made, and found it very good. Evening came, and morning followed—the sixth day." (1:31)

ENUMA ELISH	IMPLICATIONS FOR BABYLONIAN RELIGION	IMPLICATIONS FOR JEWISH RELIGION	BOOK OF GENESIS
"Let then thy host be equipped, let thy weapons be girded on! Stand! I and thou, let us join battle!"	The gods fight one another. **For you:** If the gods are violent toward one another, will they use violence against you?	The communion of Divine Persons that makes up the Blessed Trinity is at peace. After creation, God can rest on the seventh day. **For you:** God is not violent. God never desires anything harmful for you.	"God blessed the seventh day and made it holy, because on it he rested from all the work he had done in creation." (2:3)
"[He] devised a cunning plan. He split her up like a flat fish into two halves; One half of her he established as a covering for heaven."	The gods form the world out of a dead god who lost in battle. **For you:** The world results from a cunning plan. Is the world good? How powerful are these gods?	God forms the world from nothing. **For you:** If God can create the world out of nothing, how much more can he protect and love you? The world is good.	"And the earth was without form or shape, with darkness over the abyss and a mighty wind sweeping over the waters." (1:2b)
"I will create man who shall inhabit the earth, That the service of the gods may be established, and that their shrines may be built."	The gods created humans for the purpose of serving the gods and establishing their shrines. **For you:** If serving gods is your purpose, do you have free will? Is anyone looking out for your well-being?	God created humans so that they could join him forever in love. **For you:** God created you to share in his own nature, and he gives you responsibilities regarding creation.	"Then God said: Let us make human beings in our image, after our likeness. Let them have dominion over the fish of the sea, the birds of the air, the tame animals, all the wild animals, and all the creatures that crawl on the earth." (1:26)

Religious and Theological Truths of the First Creation Account

Now that you have studied the *textual form* of the first account of creation in Genesis, pay more attention to its *theological significance*. Always keep in mind that the Bible is inspired text and God is its true author. The first creation account is not a scientific explanation of the beginning of the universe. God inspired the Bible's human authors to reveal important *spiritual and theological* truths about creation that are necessary for salvation. These truths are revealed without error. The first creation account reveals the following truths:

- ***There is only one God.*** While the ancient Babylonians and others believed in multiple gods, the biblical authors affirmed that there is only one God, who is eternal. He created out of nothing all that exists outside of himself. He made all things by himself, with the Son and the Holy Spirit; creation is the common work of the Blessed Trinity (see *CCC*, 292).
- ***God planned creation.*** God created the world in an orderly way to share his own self, wisdom, and goodness with humanity (see *CCC*, 295). Creation did not result from chaotic forces, warring gods, fate, or chance.
- ***God created the world out of nothing.*** Human artists can create incredible things. Advances in human technology also demonstrate the incredible capacities of humans to make new things. These things shed light upon God's creation in a special way. When a person makes things, he or she always uses preexisting materials, such as metal, chemicals, and so forth. But when God created the universe, he created it from *nothing*. God did not take preexisting "stuff" and make the world out of it; rather, he made all things *out of nothing*.
- ***God ordered the world and made it good.*** Ancient peoples believed that much of material reality was evil and constantly at war with spiritual elements in the universe. In contrast, Jews and Christians see in Genesis a positive view of created reality: material creation is good, not the result of magic or of the workings of false gods. God is pleased with everything he made, especially human beings.
- ***God created humans in his own image, male and female.*** Humans are unique among all creatures for this reason. Made in God's own image and likeness, humans alone are called to share, by knowledge and love, in God's own life. It was for this end that humans were created, and this is the fundamental reason for your own uniqueness (see *CCC*, 356). Humans are entrusted with responsibility for the rest of creation.

Aspects of Your Uniqueness

- You possess great dignity, value, and worth. A human is "the only creature on earth that God has willed for its own sake" (*CCC*, 356, quoting *Gaudium et Spes*, 24).
- You are able to participate "in the light and power of the divine Spirit" (*CCC*, 1704). By your intellectual abilities, you can understand the order of things established by God. You can hear God's voice in your conscience, urging you to do what is right and to avoid what is evil (see *CCC*, 1706). By your free will, you can choose to direct your life toward the good (see *CCC*, 1704). Your obligation to follow God's law "is fulfilled in the love of God and neighbor" (*CCC*, 1706).
- You—and every other person on earth—reflect the divine image. Your gender is part of your identity.

The Sabbath

By saying God rested on the seventh day, the biblical author reminds God's Chosen People of their own obligation to worship God on the Sabbath (from sundown on Friday to sundown on Saturday). God's actions are a model for human action. The Sabbath is a day of rest, when people pause from their everyday work in the world to worship God. For the Israelites, "the Sabbath is for the Lord, holy and set apart for the praise of God, his work of creation, and his saving actions on behalf of Israel" (*CCC*, 2171). When the Jews were in captivity, the Sabbath observance also helped them distinguish their identity as God's Chosen People among a foreign people, the Babylonians.

The Sabbath, as described in the Book of Genesis, represents the completion and fulfillment of creation—the goal for which creation was made; namely, the glory of God. Jesus' Resurrection took place on the "first day of the week," the day after the Sabbath. This "eighth day" symbolizes the new creation ushered in by Christ's Resurrection (see *CCC*, 2174). Catholics (and most other Christians) observe Sunday as the Lord's Day, which fulfills the Sabbath obligation.

ASSIGNMENT

Analyze how you spent the past two Sundays. In your journal, note what you did to show that you take "Sabbath rest" and the "Sunday obligation" seriously. If your review shows that you struggle to "keep holy the Lord's day," write out some plans to help you observe it more faithfully this coming weekend.

Importantly, the Eucharist is celebrated on Sunday as the memorial of the Paschal Mystery—that is, of the work of salvation accomplished by the life, Death, and Resurrection of Christ. Christ himself, along with this work of salvation, is made present in the Eucharist. Sunday is the preeminent day for the worship of God, when the faithful gather "to listen to the word of God and take part in the Eucharist, thus calling to mind the Passion, Resurrection, and glory of the Lord Jesus, and giving thanks to God" (*CCC*, 1167). Catholics also rest from regular work and activity on Sundays.

The first creation account tells us that land-dwelling animals were created on the sixth day and that God created humans immediately afterward.

You have been created male or female. Both genders are equal, with inalienable dignity—that is, dignity that cannot be changed or taken away. Physical, moral, and spiritual difference and complementarity between genders are oriented toward the goods of marriage and the flourishing of family life.

- Your human nature is a unity of the spiritual and material worlds. You have a body and a soul. Every soul is created at the moment of conception by God and is immortal. God willed you to be whole and entire, comprising body and soul. Your soul is endowed with intellect and free will, reflecting the image of God. Your human nature is a reflection of Christ, who revealed what it means to be in the image of God, as he is God's Revelation.
- You have been given a place of honor in creation. God has placed humans, created in his image and likeness, at the summit of creation. You are responsible for taking care of and developing the many gifts of creation God entrusted to you. You are a steward of God's creation.
- From the moment of your conception, you were "destined for eternal beatitude" (*CCC*, 1703).

- ***God blessed the Sabbath and made it holy.*** The writer of the first account tells how God rested on the seventh day of creation. Obviously, God does not need to rest. The inspired words in this passage show the meaning of creation. They tell how the world was created "with a view to the sabbath and therefore for the worship and adoration of God" (*CCC*, 347). (See "The Sabbath" on page 27.)

All these truths emerged from the first creation account. They highlight the Church's belief in the one, powerful, good, wise, and loving God who shares his life with his creatures.

SECTION ASSESSMENT

NOTE TAKING

Use your notes to help you complete the following item.

1. Choose one of the truths you identified in this section, and write two or three sentences about what it means to you.

VOCABULARY

2. Define *primeval history*.
3. Use the word *myth* appropriately in a sentence.

COMPREHENSION

4. What are three differences between the Babylonian gods and the God of Israel?
5. What type of unity exists in human nature?
6. Why do most Christians worship God on Sundays?

CRITICAL ANALYSIS

7. How would your worldview be different if you had grown up in ancient Babylon?

REFLECTION

8. What are some of the benefits of the use of figurative and symbolic language in Genesis as opposed to scientific language?
9. What are some challenges you and your peers encounter when trying to keep Sunday holy?

SECTION 3

The Second Creation Account (Genesis 2:4b–25)

MAIN IDEA

The second creation account reveals the care and concern that God feels for his newly created people and shows what he wanted to provide for them.

The second creation account is written in what might be described as a more "down-to-earth" style and portrays God with human qualities. Many biblical scholars have dated its origin to sometime in the tenth century BC.

In this creation account, God focuses on people. God resembles a human potter, molding Adam's body like a delicate sculpture and breathing his spirit, the breath of life, into his creation. This intimate picture reveals the loving relationship between YHWH and the first human beings. In the first creation account, God creates humans last, while in this second account, YHWH creates humans before any other creatures.

The author describes a compassionate God who cares for Adam by creating a garden and sending him animals for companionship. God puts Adam in charge of creation by permitting him to name the animals. (In the ancient world, the power to name something gave one control over what was named.) Animals, however, do not fulfill Adam's basic human need for companionship.

The author narrates Eve's creation from Adam's rib. This image highlights women's dignity and equality with men. This second account provides

NOTE TAKING

Finding Parallels. Create a chart like the one below. At the top on the left, print "First Account," and on the right, "Second Account." As you go through this section, identify three words or phrases from the second creation account that describe God and list them in the right column of your chart. Then list three characteristics of God from the first creation account in the left column. Connect them with a green line if they are mostly similar, a yellow line if they are somewhat similar, and a red line if they are dissimilar.

First Account	Second Account
God talks with the first humans.	*God interacts with the first man.*

an **etiology** of marriage—that is, a causal explanation of why men and women leave their own families "and the two of them become one body" (Gn 2:24), entering into a close relationship that mirrors God's own relationship with them. The love between a man and a woman reflects the love between God and humanity. In Catholic theology, a sacramental marriage reflects Christ's love for his Church.

With this knowledge, you can better understand why the final editor of Genesis was inspired by God to include two different creation accounts. Together, they reveal very important truths about God: the awe-inspiring sole Creator of the universe (first account) is intimately concerned with the man and woman who are the jewels of his creation (second account).

Truths of the Second Creation Account

These are some truths you can glean from the second creation account:

- ***Humans are created both equal and different.*** God willed that there be men and women. Each possesses inalienable and equal dignity as a person, "'since both were created in the image and likeness of the personal God'" (*CCC*, 2334, quoting *Mulieris Dignitatem*, 6).
- ***Adam and Eve were born in a state of original holiness and original justice.*** Recall that this describes the harmony within the human person, between humans and God, between man and woman, and between people and all of creation.
- ***God willed that man and woman be for each other.*** Men and women were created for each other, for companionship, to be helpmates to each other, and to share in God's work of creating new life.
- ***God is not in the image of humans.*** This is an important distinction. It means that God is neither male nor female. God is pure spirit, and he is beyond embodied gender such as humans and animals have. This does not mean, however, that men, especially as fathers and husbands, and women, especially as mothers and wives, do not uniquely reflect something of God's infinite perfection.

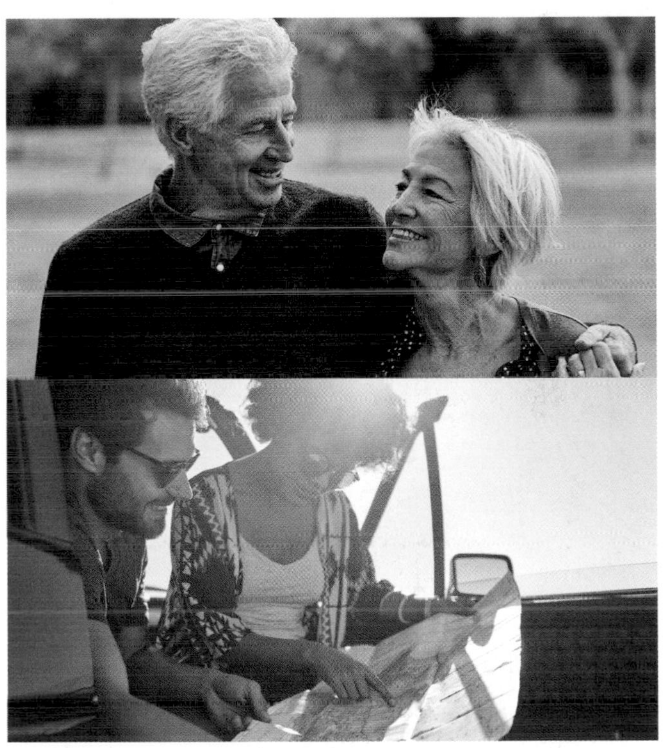

When God created human beings, he willed that men and women be equal. He intentionally created the two sexes, communicating that each gender is good. Men and women possess an inalienable dignity that comes to them directly from God the Creator. Each sex has equal significance. "In their 'being-man'

etiology An explanation of the cause of something. In the Bible, etiology appears as narrative, typically reaching back to the distant past to describe the core meaning of something that we experience universally. For example, although Genesis attributes the origin of sin to Adam and Eve in the past, it is also an explanation of humanity's rejection of God at all times, even today.

and 'being-woman,' they reflect the Creator's wisdom and goodness" (*CCC*, 369).

God made man and woman and willed them "for each other." God says, "It is not good for the man to be alone. I will make a helper suited to him" (Gn 2:18). After God creates the woman, the man says,

"This one, at last, is bone of my bones
and flesh of my flesh." (Gn 2:23a)

God created man and woman to form a "communion of persons" in which each can help the other specifically as masculine and feminine. In marriage, God designed man and woman to participate in his creative work by transmitting human life and by imitating the Creator's generosity. God shows that this union is not to be broken. "What God has joined together, let not man put asunder" (*CCC*, 2336, quoting Mt 19:6). Physical and spiritual differences between men and women help spouses support each other's strengths and balance out each other's weaknesses. This complementarity makes for a healthier marriage and family life.

Through Catholic theology, you also come to understand more deeply the significance of the intimacy shared by Adam and Eve as described in the second creation account. They are two persons, and yet they "become one" (Gn 2:24). The Catholic faith holds that God is an eternal communion of love between Father, Son, and Holy Spirit. In a way infinitely greater than and different from human beings, the Father, Son, and Holy Spirit are different and unique Persons, and yet they are one, united in love, power, and being. God created man and woman to express something of his inner life, and so that we would be capable of sharing in the Blessed Trinity's communion of love. The differences between man and woman ("the two") become an expression of God's intimate communion when man and woman "become one" (Gn 2:24).

SECTION ASSESSMENT

NOTE TAKING

Use the chart you created to help you answer the following question.

1. Which pair of descriptive words or phrases presented the greatest contrast between the first and second creation accounts? Why?

VOCABULARY

2. Define *etiology*. How does this term relate to the second creation account from the Book of Genesis?

COMPREHENSION

3. What evidence is there from the second creation account that God is compassionate and that he cared for Adam?
4. Why is God without gender?

CRITICAL ANALYSIS

5. What is the value of including both creation accounts in the Book of Genesis?
6. Explain the meaning of the following: "God did create man and woman in his own image, but God is neither in man's nor in woman's image."

REFLECTION

7. Does one of the two creation accounts present God in a way that more closely resembles your own image of him? Explain.

Section Summaries

Focus Question

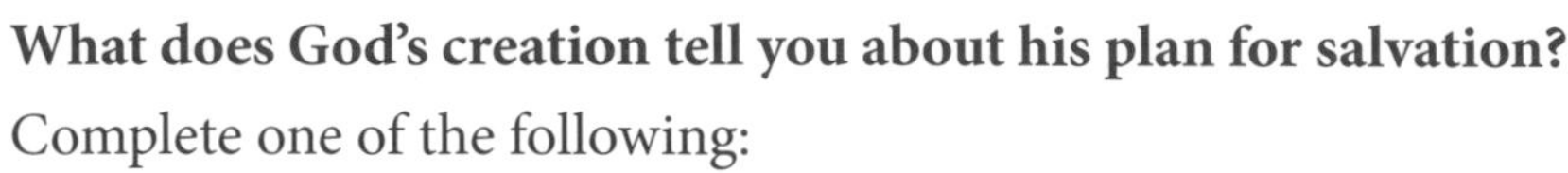

What does God's creation tell you about his plan for salvation?

Complete one of the following:

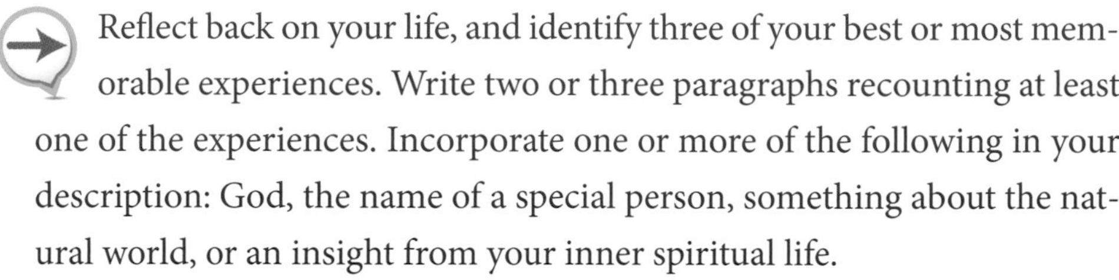

Reflect back on your life, and identify three of your best or most memorable experiences. Write two or three paragraphs recounting at least one of the experiences. Incorporate one or more of the following in your description: God, the name of a special person, something about the natural world, or an insight from your inner spiritual life.

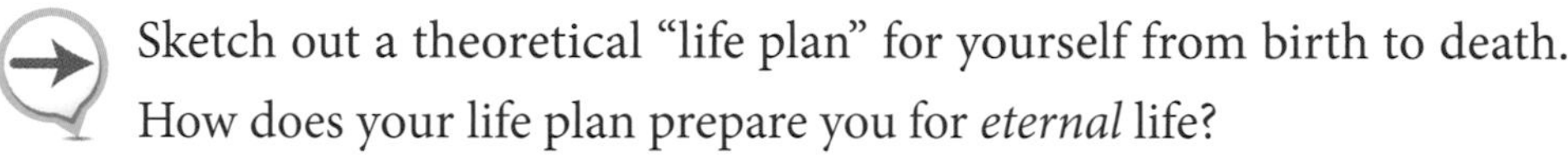

Sketch out a theoretical "life plan" for yourself from birth to death. How does your life plan prepare you for *eternal* life?

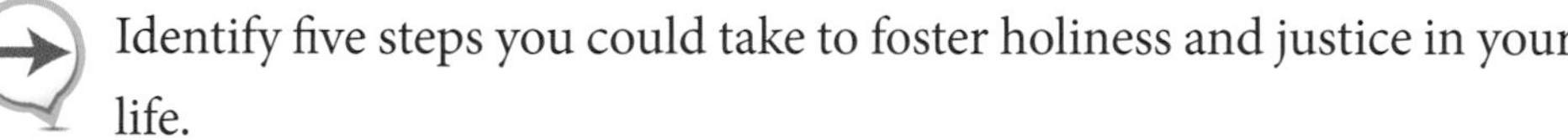

Identify five steps you could take to foster holiness and justice in your life.

INTRODUCTION (PAGES 3–14)

God Created Humans to Share in His Own Life

God created humans with the intention that they would be happy in an eternal, loving relationship with him. After sin entered the world, this relationship would only be possible through the Paschal Mystery. God sent his beloved Son, Jesus Christ, to become one with humanity, to express the Father's love for the world, and to offer his life to reconcile the world with his Father. His life, Death, and Resurrection reveal the mystery of God's love for humanity—the very love out of which God created the world. The first three chapters of the Book of Genesis present the mystery of creation. These texts present information about *why* God created the world and the *meaning* of creation, rather than *how* he did so, providing answers that cannot be found through scientific study.

God is the Creator of all things, both spiritual and material. Angels are also part of God's creation. These creatures, who are invisible yet present, belong to Christ and are used in his saving mission of bringing us into communion with the Father. The Book of Genesis sheds light upon our uniqueness and awesome dignity. Both material and spiritual, we were created in the "image of God," endowed with reason, freedom, and the desire for communion with God. Humans were created by God as male and female, who are equal yet different, reflecting the loving communion of Divine Persons that is God. Human beings—and through us all of creation—are destined for the glory of God (see *CCC*, 353).

Read paragraphs 293–294 of the *Catechism of the Catholic Church*. Based on this reading, write one paragraph that answers the question: Why did God create the world?

SECTION 1 (PAGES 15–21)

Understanding How to Read Scripture

There are several ways to read and understand the Book of Genesis. Biblical study involves understanding the literal sense of the text in order to have a better grasp of its spiritual sense. Because the Bible is divinely inspired, the main purpose of your study is to find out about God and what he is revealing about himself, the world, and you. Since God speaks to us in a human way in Sacred Scripture, we must be attentive to what God wants to reveal to us through the words of the biblical authors. Methods of biblical criticism help to uncover the sacred authors' intention by taking into account the conditions and culture of their time, literary genres, and modes of feeling, speaking, and narrating at that time. By understanding these things and by uniting ourselves to the Church, we can better understand what God wants to reveal to us through Sacred Scripture.

Review the two senses of Scripture—literal and spiritual—from paragraphs 115–119 of the *Catechism of the Catholic Church*. Answer: What is the task of biblical criticism?

SECTION 2 (PAGES 22–29)

The First Creation Account (Genesis 1:1–2:4a)

God created the earth and its inhabitants from nothing in six days. The first creation account reveals God's power and majesty. Written in the form of a myth, the first creation account should be read primarily for its religious truth rather than its historic or scientific truth. The section compares a Babylonian creation story with the first creation account from Genesis and highlights ways God's Chosen People explained creation in light of their belief in the one, true God. The first creation account ends with God's rest on the seventh day, indicating that all of creation is oriented toward the worship of God.

Perhaps you have seen a crime-scene investigation show where the detectives ask, "What is the evidence *not* showing us?" (i.e., "What would we expect to find at this scene that is missing?") If you were a detective tasked with uncovering the truths of creation, what, if any, pieces of evidence not present in the first creation account would you require?

SECTION 3 (PAGES 30–33)

The Second Creation Account (Genesis 2:4b–25)

The second creation account reveals the care and concern that God feels for humans and tells more about what he wanted to provide for them. The biblical author describes a God who lovingly creates Adam, breathes the spirit of life into him, and gives him intimate companionship. This creation account presents a picture of Adam and Eve's original holiness and original justice, describing a person's original inner harmony, as well as harmony with others and creation and in relation to God.

In a poem, story, song, drawing, painting, or video, depict the harmony and connectedness of original holiness and original justice.

Chapter Assignments

Choose and complete at least one of the following three assignments to assess your understanding of the material in this chapter.

1. Food Production and the Environment

Familiarize yourself with several of the subjects and related documents presented on the "Agriculture, Nutrition, and Rural Issues" page of the United States Conference of Catholic Bishops' website (www.usccb.org). Produce a unique chart or infographic that illustrates how issues surrounding agriculture, poverty, nutrition, and the environment are related. Note any suggestions you found for how Catholics can offer support for people affected by these issues. Arrange a shareable media form of your presentation so that you can present it both to your teacher and to your classmates.

2. Your Ecological or Environmental Footprint

Human activities consume products and produce waste. An assessment of these activities is often called an *ecological* or *environmental footprint*. Make a visual representation that charts the goods you consume during a week and what happens to them after you are done with them (e.g., reused, recycled, trashed). Describe the goods both by type and by weight. Research environmentally acceptable totals of consumed waste per person, and compare those numbers to your total. Write a reflection telling how you might lessen your ecological footprint and how your community might practice better stewardship of its resources. Write a concluding prayer for the environment.

3. Creation Accounts in Other Religious Traditions

Write a two-page report that details how a non-Christian religious tradition describes the creation of the world and creation of the first humans. Note some or all of these points in your report:

- presence of one God or gods: the divine
- relationship between the divine and creation
- relationship between the divine and the world after creation
- relationship between matter and spirit
- nature of human relationships with the divine

Add a two-column chart that details some of the similarities and differences between the creation account you researched and the creation accounts in Genesis. See pages 24–25 for a model of the type of chart you might use.

Faithful Disciple

St. Isidore the Farmer

St. Isidore the Farmer

St. Isidore grew up a poor day laborer near Madrid, Spain, toward the end of the eleventh century. He worked on a large farm owned by a rich man named Juan de Vargas.

Isidore's fellow workers complained about him to the owner; it seems he was arriving late to work each day. Isidore did not deny the claim when he was brought before Juan de Vargas, explaining that he was late because he went to Mass before work, adding, "I do my utmost to make up for a few minutes snatched for prayer." He told de Vargas that if he looked at the amount of work that Isidore completed, he would find it far surpassed the others' work. If it did not, Isidore said, de Vargas could dock his pay.

Juan de Vargas accepted this story but remained suspicious of Isidore. One morning near the time that Mass ended, de Vargas hid outside the church. Sure enough, Isidore was there. The owner followed him to the fields and watched him take up his plow. Then de Vargas swore he saw another sight: a second plow drawn by white oxen moving up and down the crop rows. A legend developed that an angel assisted St. Isidore with his plowing. When questioned by de Vargas, Isidore responded, "I work alone and know of none save God to whom I look for strength."

St. Isidore also cared greatly for nature and the environment. One winter day, he found a flock of wood pigeons searching for food beneath a thick snow cover. Isidore emptied half of his sack of corn on the ground for the birds. Passersby mocked him for doing so. But when Isidore brought what was left of his corn to the mill, he found the bag full. The milled corn also produced double the normal amount of flour.

St. Isidore's wife, Bl. Maria Torribia, is under study for canonization. She is known for her care of the poor and is today venerated in Spain during times of drought. The couple's son once fell into a well. After they prayed, the water rose miraculously to ground level and the boy was saved.

St. Isidore died in 1130. Forty years after his death, his body was moved near the church of St. Andrew, his home parish in Madrid. There he was said to have appeared to Alfonso VIII, the king of Castile, showing him a way to victory in battle over the Moors. St. Isidore was canonized by Pope Gregory XV in 1622 along with Sts. Ignatius, Francis Xavier, Teresa of Ávila, and Philip Neri. St. Isidore is the patron saint of farmers and farm laborers and of Catholic Rural Life.

Reading Comprehension

1. What was causing St. Isidore to be late to work?
2. What did the landowner witness when he saw Isidore take up his plow?
3. Name one of the other miracles associated with St. Isidore.

Writing Task

- Research information about Catholic Rural Life. Write two paragraphs that summarize its history and mission.

Explaining the Faith
What does the Church teach about evolution?

The word *evolution* means many different things to different people. The term has been applied to the origin of the universe, to the origin of life, and to the origin of humans.

Your biology textbook might define evolution simply as "change over time." This definition applies to any sequence in the events of nature. People explain these changes in various ways. An atheist might explain them as part of an unguided, materialistic process of random variation and natural selection. Believers, however, view evolution as part of God's ongoing, providential action in his creation of life and of human beings. Another understanding of evolution refers to the idea that a group of organisms are descended from a common ancestor. Some people hold that all organisms have come from a common ancestor.

In light of Divine Revelation, what can Catholics believe about evolution? The Church teaches that scientific truth and truths of the faith that come from Divine Revelation cannot contradict each other, as they are complementary paths to one truth. The *Catechism of the Catholic Church* explains:

> Though faith is above reason, there can never be any real discrepancy between faith and reason. Since the same God who reveals mysteries and infuses faith has bestowed the light of reason on the human mind, God cannot deny himself, nor can truth ever contradict truth. (*CCC*, 159, quoting *Dei Filius*, 4)

Concerning the origin of the universe, the Book of Genesis reports that God created the entire universe—both material and spiritual aspects of it—out of nothing at the beginning of time. The Church does not take a position on whether the stars, nebulae, and planets were all created at once or developed (evolved) over time. However, if they did evolve and are evolving over time, it is according to God's plan.

Turning to biological evolution, the Church has not taken an official position on whether life forms developed over the millennia. However, if various life forms have developed over time, it is because God guides their development. He is the one who ultimately created them.

Concerning human evolution, the Church permits belief that the human body developed from previous life forms but still teaches that God creates each human soul. The human soul, your spiritual nature, does not evolve from matter, nor is it inherited from your parents the way your body is.

However the "six days of creation" are interpreted—either literally or symbolically—the biblical text specifies that the universe did not always exist. The infinite and eternal God created the universe, and that is when time began. The *Catechism* puts it this way:

> *Nothing exists that does not owe its existence to God the Creator.* The world began when God's word drew it out of nothingness; all existent beings, all of nature, and all human history are rooted in this primordial event, the very genesis by which the world was constituted and time begun. (*CCC*, 338)

In 2014, Pope Francis commented on the creation accounts in the Book of Genesis in relation to the topic of evolution. He said:

> When we read about creation in Genesis, we run the risk of imagining God was a magician, with a magic wand able to do everything. But that is not so. He created human beings and let them develop according to the internal laws he gave to each one so they would reach their fulfillment.
>
> God is not . . . a magician, but the Creator who brought everything to life. Evolution in nature is not inconsistent with the notion of creation, because evolution requires the creation of beings that evolve.

Further Research

- Investigate why Pope Francis's teaching on evolution is not a new Catholic teaching. See, for example, Pope John Paul II's October 22, 1996, "Message to the Pontifical Academy of Sciences on Evolution." Craft a brief response based on a summary of St. John Paul II's words.

Prayer

The Canticle of the Sun

Most High, all powerful, good Lord,
yours are the praises, the glory, the honor,
and all blessing.

To you alone, Most High, do they belong,
and no man is worthy to mention your name.

Be praised, my Lord, through all your creatures,
especially through my lord Brother Sun,
who brings the day; and you give light through him.
And he is beautiful and radiant in all his splendor!
Of you, Most High, he bears the likeness.

Praised be you, my Lord, through Sister Moon
and the stars: in heaven you formed them
clear and precious and beautiful.

Praised be you, my Lord, through Brother Wind,
and through the air, cloudy and serene,
and every kind of weather through which
you give sustenance to your creatures.

Praised be you, my Lord, through Sister Water,
which is very useful and humble and precious and chaste.
Praised be you, my Lord, through Brother Fire,
through whom you light the night, and he is beautiful
and playful and robust and strong.

Praised be you, my Lord, through Sister Mother Earth,
who sustains us and governs us and who produces
varied fruits with colored flowers and herbs.

Praised be you, my Lord,
through those who give pardon through your love,
and bear infirmity and tribulation.

Blessed are those who endure in peace
for by you, Most High, they shall be crowned.

Praised be you, my Lord,
through our Sister Bodily Death,
from whom no living man can escape.

Woe to those who die in mortal sin.
Blessed are those whom death will
find in your most holy will,
for the second death shall do them no harm.

Praise and bless my Lord,
and give him thanks
and serve him with great humility.

Amen.
—St. Francis of Assisi

2

THE FALL AND THE PROMISE OF A SAVIOR

A COURAGEOUS FIGHT against ANOREXIA

For Kaitlyn Bowman, a junior in a Catholic high school outside Philadelphia, eating had become an inner battle. She would hide food so her parents would think that she had eaten it when she really had not. Kaitlyn had begun this pattern in middle school, when she was already underweight for her height and age. Her self-perception, however, was that she was overweight. Her parents tried to increase her caloric intake, but she resisted. Finally they sought medical advice.

As a freshman in high school, Kaitlyn received in-patient treatment for anorexia at the Renfrew Center in Philadelphia. She did not put her heart into the seven-week program and regressed to her old habits after she left. She did, however, form a significant friendship there with another patient named Julia. The two stayed in touch after leaving the center.

Tragically, it took Julia's suicide to make Kaitlyn realize just how serious her condition was and resolve to get better. She reentered the program at Renfrew and engaged in it much more seriously.

Now, with a healthy diet, Kaitlyn has gained weight. She has spoken in several parishes as well as her own high school about the signs of potential eating disorders. She has also founded a support and awareness organization for those affected by eating disorders and named it after her friend: J.U.L.I.A. (Just Understand Life Is Amazing).

(Lou Baldwin, "After Battle with Anorexia, Teen Educates Peers," CatholicPhilly.com, January 26, 2011.)

FOCUS QUESTION

Why are YOU in need of SALVATION?

Chapter Overview

INTRODUCTION
Original Sin

MAIN IDEA
The consequences of Original Sin, the fallen state of human nature in which all people are born, remain part of human life today.

In Chapter 3 of the Book of Genesis, the description of Adam and Eve's sin, you see that Adam and Eve had it all: inner peace, a close intimate relationship with God, the ability to enjoy the natural world, and a loving relationship with each other. While Adam and Eve obeyed God's commands, they had the greatest human paradise possible. They did not suffer. They would not die. Work was creative and not a burden. Love of God and neighbor was alive. The two practiced self-mastery.

Then along came cunning **Satan**, disguised as a snake, who lied to them about the fruit of the tree of knowledge of good and evil, saying:

> "You certainly will not die! God knows well that when you eat of it your eyes will be opened and you will be like gods, who know good and evil." (Gn 3:4–5)

Notice that Satan suggested that it was God who was lying when he said that they would die if they ate the fruit.

Placing their trust in Satan rather than God, Adam and Eve chose to disobey God and follow their own will over God's, and so they ate of the forbidden fruit. They rejected a God-centered life and chose a self-centered life. Immediately after, Adam and Eve realized that they were naked, clothed themselves, and then hid from God. When God asked Adam whether he had eaten from the forbidden tree, Adam blamed Eve, who then blamed the snake.

In a modern context, you can almost imagine Satan whispering into Kaitlyn's ear that she needs to lose weight, or saying to someone else who is feeling lonely, "Did the Bible say that God loves you? People just made that up. No one even likes you."

Satan A fallen angel or the devil; the Evil One (see *CCC*, 391, 395, 2851).

NOTE TAKING

Adding Details. Record the consequences of Original Sin listed below. For each consequence, write one sentence explaining its implications for humans.

- Loss of the grace of original holiness

  People do not relate to God as a friend. Rather, they are afraid of God.

- Loss of original justice
- Loss of inner harmony
- Loss of harmony between man and woman
- Loss of harmony with creation

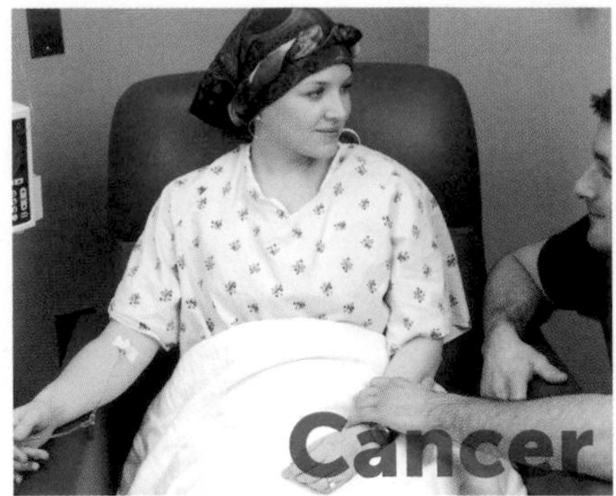

No doubt you have experienced inner battles. You may have to fight against critical thoughts such as "I am not beautiful" or "No one likes me." You have possibly observed family and friends go up against various adversaries such as alcoholism, overeating, cancer, or depression. Some of your loved ones may have been able to conquer their adversaries, while others were defeated by them.

Free Will and Evil

These types of struggles and the great suffering witnessed in the world every day lead many to wonder, "If Satan still has so much power, how can we believe that God can save us?" Unfortunately, there are no easy answers to questions about evil. While there may be persuasive rationales for the existence of evil in a good world and tools to fight it, these explanations and potential solutions do not always provide immediate help to those in the grip of suffering.

Thinking about evil requires thinking about free will. God is a loving communion of Three Divine Persons—the Blessed Trinity. Humans are limited beings created by God with the ability to freely receive his love and to enter into communion with him and one another. But this also means that you are free to refuse God. While there is no evil in God, he allowed for the reality of sin and evil when he created limited beings and gave them free will to choose him or refuse him. If there were no freedom and opportunity to choose, you would be like a puppet or action figure that God manipulated. Both angels and humans, because they are intelligent and free, have to choose their destinies by free will. Because of this free will, they can choose to move toward God or away from him. When you turn away from God—like a plant that leans away from sunlight—you move away from the source of goodness, truth, life, and love and toward ignorance, darkness, suffering, lies, and death.

The Fall of the First Angels

God created angels as intelligent and free spiritual creatures. Because of this freedom, some of the angels chose their own path away from God. *Devils* and *demons* are names for angels who reject God radically and choose evil. Satan, a main figure in the Fall of human beings, was created a good angel; he chose to disobey God and go his own way. Satan is the "prince of darkness" among all of the fallen angels. His lie that eating the fruit would make Adam and Eve like God is one reason he is also called "the father of lies" (Jn 8:44). In rejecting God, Satan and other demons made a choice that they could not take back.

Even though Satan tried to use his power and cunning to tempt and distract Jesus from his mission, Satan is not equal to God in power, nor is he

While free will gave the first humans the chance to reject God and his commands, it also gives you the opportunity to love God and choose to follow his commands.

infinite. Satan is only a creature; he cannot destroy the establishment of God's Kingdom. Certainly, his actions injure people physically and spiritually. God permits this because it is the price for making free and intelligent creatures. Also, it allows God to show his mercy, power, and goodness by bringing even greater good out of evil, without making evil into good. "From the greatest moral evil ever committed—the rejection and murder of God's only Son, caused by the sins of all men—God, by his grace that 'abounded all the more' brought the greatest goods: the glorification of Christ and our redemption" (*CCC*, 312, quoting Rom 5:20).

The First Humans Fall

God had created Adam and Eve to be his friends, giving them paradise with only one restriction. God told Adam, "You are free to eat from any of the trees of the garden except the tree of knowledge of good and evil. From that tree you shall not eat; when you eat from it you shall die" (Gn 2:16b–17). By restricting that one tree in the garden, God made Adam *free*. He was free to love God or reject God, to put God first or to put himself first. Thus warned, Adam and Eve fell for the snake's lie and disobeyed God anyway.

As you learned in Chapter 1, human beings were destined for eternal beatitude. However, seduced by the devil, Adam and Eve wanted to "be like God" but *without* God and *without* his help. Their sin consisted first and foremost in disobeying God and preferring themselves to God—that is, in choosing a self-centered life rather than a God-centered life. God gave them freedom so that they could love him and each other *freely*. Instead they abused their freedom, dishonored their Creator, and disobeyed him.

By rejecting God, Adam and Eve acted against their creaturely status and against their own good.

Since paradise reflected Adam and Eve's state of original holiness and original justice, God expelled them from the garden after they had sinned. This expulsion from paradise reflects the tragic consequences that their disobedience had on their intimate relationship with God and on their harmony within themselves, with each other, and with all of creation. Adam and Eve's intimacy with God was the source of their life and happiness; having lost the intimacy of that relationship by betraying God's trust and command, they lost everything that derived from the intimacy they shared with God: their place in paradise, original grace, original holiness, and original justice.

The Nature of Original Sin

"Scripture portrays the tragic consequences of this first disobedience. Adam and Eve immediately lose the grace of original holiness" (*CCC*, 399). After the first sin, the world was overrun by sin. Although only Adam and Eve personally sinned, all of their descendants have been implicated in this sin by inheriting their fallen state. Adam and Eve's personal sin affected human nature, and that wound has been passed down through the generations. St. Paul taught that "through one person sin entered the world, and through sin, death, and thus death came to all, inasmuch as all sinned" (Rom 5:12). **Original Sin** is "contracted" rather than "committed." It is a state, not an act (see *CCC*, 404).

In the fifth century, the famous convert and theologian St. Augustine of Hippo refined the teaching about the transmission of Original Sin in response to the heresy of **Pelagianism**. Pelagius, a highly educated fourth-century monk who lived an austere life, believed that people could lead morally good lives without God's help because of their

St. Augustine of Hippo

natural powers of free will. If this were really true, then Adam and Eve's sin would not really affect their descendants except by setting a bad example. St. Augustine disagreed with this heresy and affirmed that, because of Original Sin, humans needed God's grace for the forgiveness of their sins,

Original Sin "The sin by which the first human beings disobeyed the commandment of God, choosing to follow their own will rather than God's will. As a consequence they lost the grace of original holiness, and became subject to the law of death; sin became universally present in the world. Besides the personal sin of Adam and Eve, Original Sin describes the fallen state of human nature which affects every person born into the world, and from which Christ, the 'New Adam,' came to redeem us" (*CCC*, Glossary).

Pelagianism The heretical belief that people, because of their natural powers of free will, can lead morally good lives without God's help. Associated with this view is the belief that Original Sin is passed on only through example, but is not "contracted" as such. This system of beliefs derives from Pelagius (AD 354–420), who disputed with St. Augustine of Hippo on the question of grace.

The final session of the Council of Trent took place on December 4, 1563. It would be more than three hundred years until the next ecumenical council, Vatican I, was convened.

for the healing of their relationship with God, and for the elevation of men and women to the status of sons and daughters of God.

Centuries later, on the other end of the spectrum, some of the first Protestant teachers—such as Martin Luther and John Calvin—taught that Original Sin had so radically destroyed human freedom that it was impossible for humans to overcome it. At the Council of Trent (1545–1563), which was dedicated to meeting the challenge of Protestantism and reforming the inner life of Catholicism, the Church's Magisterium opposed this teaching. Catholic teaching holds that Original Sin has wounded human nature but has not completely corrupted it. Even with Original Sin, humans still bear the "image of God," and you can engage in a life of healing and progress toward holiness through God's grace.

Recall from previous courses that the Book of Genesis chronicles the spread of personal sin due to humanity's weakened state from Original Sin following the Fall of Adam and Eve. Most of the Old Testament is an account of Israel's struggle with temptations to stray from covenants—especially the Law of Moses—that God established with his people in his tireless efforts to help them. The full meaning of the doctrine of Original Sin is revealed only in light of the Death and Resurrection of Jesus, through which he has restored in humans what sin had damaged (see *CCC*, 1708). To offer an analogy: humanity had run up a debt through its betrayal of God, and Christ paid that debt for all people. You find out how much debt humanity had amassed only when you see the price Christ had to pay to free them from this debt: the cost of forgiveness of sin and freedom from sin is Christ's own life.

Recovering CREATION

In his encyclical *Laudato Si'* (*Praise Be to You*): *On Care for Our Common Home*, Pope Francis contrasted the experience of young adults today who have experienced the effects of unbridled consumerism and have been at the forefront of both awareness of environmental damage and work caring for God's creation. Pope Francis wrote that "young people have a new ecological sensitivity and a generous spirit, and some of them are making admirable efforts to protect the environment. At the same time, they have grown up in a milieu of extreme consumerism and affluence which makes it difficult to develop other habits" (*Laudato Si'*, 209).

ASSIGNMENT

Cite and detail three recent efforts young adults have made to care for the environment. Write one additional, unique idea of your own for caring for God's creation. How would you go about implementing this idea?

Consequences of Original Sin

It's important to note that Kaitlyn's battle with anorexia had nothing to do with her personal sin. However, even conditions such as the anorexia Kaitlyn suffered through can be traced to Original Sin. Anorexia is a psychiatric disorder; like any illness, it reflects the loss of original holiness and original justice in the human race. All life-threatening and life-reducing aspects of human existence are due to Original Sin; this includes physical, emotional, and spiritual illnesses; injustices of all types; and natural disasters.

Following Adam and Eve's sin, all humans have experienced the following consequences:

- Humans have lost the grace of original holiness and have become afraid of God. Now, rather than perceiving God as a beloved friend and loving Creator, we perceive God in a distorted way, as jealous about his power and place.
- Humans are "subject to ignorance, suffering, and the dominion of death" (*CCC*, 405). With Original Sin, "*death makes its entrance into human history*" (*CCC*, 400; cf. Rom 5:12).
- Humans are in need of salvation. Because of Adam and Eve's sin, all human beings are born with a wounded human nature. Therefore, we could not live eternally with God unless we were redeemed (see *CCC*, 402–406). God the Father allowed Jesus Christ, his Son, to suffer and die the way he did because of his love for all human beings; because of that love, he wants us to live eternally with him in heaven. Christ's Passion reveals the depth of the Father's love and desire to save all people from being overcome by evil, sin, and death. Through Jesus' sacrifice, the power of sin has been destroyed and our friendship with God has been restored.
- Humans have also lost original justice, which has shattered our harmony within ourselves, between man and woman, and with creation:
  - *Loss of our inner harmony.* Human nature is weakened. Your soul's control over your body is shattered. You are now inclined to commit personal sin (this inclination is called *concupiscence*). St. Paul describes this experience firsthand: "For I do not do the good I want, but I do the evil I do not want. Now if [I] do what I do not want, it is no longer I who do it, but sin that dwells in me" (Rom 7:19–20).
  - *Loss of harmony between man and woman.* This relationship is now filled with tensions and marked by lust and domination. Rather than seeking only to love their spouses as God has loved them, men and women tend to seek partners for our own gratification and use.
  - *Loss of harmony with creation.* Visible creation has become hostile and alien to humans, and humans, in return, are inclined to master and abuse creation rather than being stewards of it.

"After that first sin, the world [was] virtually inundated by sin" (*CCC*, 401). Sin became present everywhere in human history. By the sin of Adam and Eve, the devil acquired a certain power over humans, even though they remained free. Remember that it was by trusting Satan over God—forming some sort of bond with him by believing his words over God's—that Adam and Eve turned away from God and brought death into the world. "Original sin entails 'captivity under the power [of the devil] who thenceforth had the power of death'" (*CCC*, 407, quoting the Council of Trent). The First Letter of John states that "the whole world is under the power of the evil one" (1 Jn 5:19b).

You can see all around you the consequences of Original Sin, which the Gospel of John calls "the sin of the world" (Jn 1:29). There remains in everyone a struggle to do what is right, sometimes at great cost. You find yourself placed in a battle against the powers of evil. With God's grace, you can remain a person of integrity and avoid sinfulness.

SECTION ASSESSMENT

NOTE TAKING

Use the notes you made to help you to answer the following question.

1. Write one paragraph summarizing the overall implications of Original Sin on humankind today.

VOCABULARY

2. Explain *Pelagianism*.

COMPREHENSION

3. Who is Satan?
4. Describe Adam and Eve's sin and its consequences for them.
5. What does it mean to be in a fallen state?
6. What does it mean to say that humans "contract" Original Sin?

CRITICAL ANALYSIS

7. Name one similarity and one difference between God the Creator and his human creatures.

REFLECTION

8. Comment on this statement: "There are no easy answers to questions about evil."

SECTION 1

Sin Multiplies

MAIN IDEA
God remains faithful to his people in spite of their sinfulness.

It is fortunate for you and the rest of the human family that God did not stop revealing himself and caring for us after Adam and Eve's sin. Instead, God promised redemption and gave your ancestors the hope of salvation after their expulsion from the garden.

The *Protoevangelium*

God did not abandon Adam and Eve or their descendants after Original Sin. Immediately after Adam and Eve offered their excuses for disobedience, the Lord God revealed his plan of salvation as he expelled the couple from the garden. God said to the serpent (Satan) who deceived Adam and Eve:

> I will put enmity between you and the
> woman,
> and between your offspring and hers;
> They will strike at your head,
> while you strike at their heel. (Gn 3:15)

This verse, known as the *Protoevangelium* (meaning "first Gospel"), predicts a future Messiah and Redeemer who will battle with evil and emerge victorious. The Church understands this passage to be the announcement of the **New Adam**, Jesus Christ. The First Letter of John teaches that "the Son of God was revealed to destroy the works of the devil" (1 Jn 3:8). Jesus Christ did this by "becoming obedient to death, even death on across" (Phil 2:8). His obedience made up in a superabundant way for Adam's disobedience. Several *Church Fathers*—early Christian writers who defended the core teachings of the faith—have identified the woman in this passage as the Blessed Mother, Mary, whom they see as the new Eve. Her offspring, of course, is Jesus Christ.

Have you ever thought that without sin, the world would not have known Jesus Christ? What

New Adam A name for Jesus Christ, who, through his obedience in his Life and Death, makes amends for the disobedience of the first Adam.

NOTE TAKING

Drawing Parallels. The scriptural accounts of Adam and Eve, Cain and Abel, Noah, and the Tower of Babel share parallels. Use arrows as shown below to indicate parallels between various accounts, characters, and topics.

Example
Adam and Eve➔ sinners➔ Cain and Abel

need would there have been for a Redeemer without the presence of sin? At the Easter Vigil, the Church proclaims in the Exsultet:

> O happy fault
> that earned so great, so glorious a Redeemer!

Likewise, other Scripture passages and words of the great saints of the Church echo the same sentiment:

- Where sin increased, grace overflowed all the more (Rom 5:20b).
- Christ's inexpressible grace gave us blessings better than those the demon's envy had taken away (St. Leo the Great).
- There is nothing to prevent human nature's being raised up to something greater, even after sin; God permits evil in order to draw forth some greater good (St. Thomas Aquinas).

Reading the *Protoevangelium* in this way—identifying persons, events, or things in the Old Testament that prefigure and serve as a prototype of the fulfillment of God's plan in the Person of Christ—is known as **typology**. Because the Old Testament retains its own importance as God's Revelation, a typological reading does not mean that an Old Testament passage is important *only* in light of Christ. But it does mean that the Old Testament speaks about Christ by anticipation, and that the promise of redemption found throughout the Old Testament is fulfilled in Christ, who is the fullness and completion of God's Revelation for us. The Gospels recognize Jesus as the fulfillment of the promise of redemption.

typology A method of biblical interpretation in which persons, events, places, or things in the Old Testament are seen to prefigure ones found in the New Testament. The initial one is called a *type*, and its fulfillment is called its *antitype*. By showing how Old Testament types are fulfilled in God's plan in the Person of Christ, typology points to the unity of God's salvific work.

The Genesis accounts detailed in the next subsections explain that sin spread quite rapidly after Adam and Eve's initial transgression. The author stressed God's judgment on sinners but also his mercy. This theme is brought to fulfillment in Jesus' own attitude toward sinners.

Cain and Abel (Gn 4:1–16)

Adam and Eve's son Cain's jealousy of his brother Abel led to *fratricide* (the killing of a sibling). Beforehand, God had told Cain that he could master his sinful urges (see Gn 4:7), but Cain did not resist the temptation to express his jealousy with violence by killing his brother.

God is just and loving. He banished Cain from the land and condemned him to a life of wandering. But even though there were consequences for Cain's act, God continued to protect him. He "put a mark on Cain, so that no one would kill him at sight" (Gn 4:15).

Noah and the Flood (Gn 6:5–9:29)

In the story of the great flood, God chose Noah, "a righteous man and blameless in his generation" (Gn 6:9), to build an ark and put representatives of every living creature on it. The Great Flood prefigures Christ's saving us from our sins in the waters of Baptism.

> When the Lord saw how great the wickedness of human beings was on earth, and how every desire that their heart conceived was always nothing but evil, the Lord regretted making human beings on the earth, and his heart was grieved. (Gn 6:5–6)

Afterward, God showed his love for Noah and his descendants by pledging that a flood would never again destroy the earth or the entire human race. The rainbow was the symbol of God's covenant with Noah, an everlasting covenant between God and humanity. Remember that a covenant is a binding and solemn agreement between God and human beings in which each side is held to a particular course of action. The rainbow is also a reminder to everyone that God continues to love human beings, though their sins really merit correction and punishment.

Noah was a Gentile. God's covenant with him and the Gentiles remained valid until Jesus came. God honored several other Gentiles who are mentioned in the Bible, such as Daniel, Job, Ruth, and Melchizedek.

The Tower of Babel (Gn 11:1–9)

The Tower of Babel was a *ziggurat*—a temple that the Babylonians constructed to worship their god, Marduk. The Scripture account illustrates the continued proliferation of sin and the pride that humans had in their own achievements without giving credit to God. When the people became unable to understand one another's speech, they had to cease building the ziggurat. This account makes it clear that human beings cannot fully succeed in their work without the providence of God. As the Book of Genesis teaches over and over, the sin of "going it alone" apart from God ultimately leads to sorrow and evil.

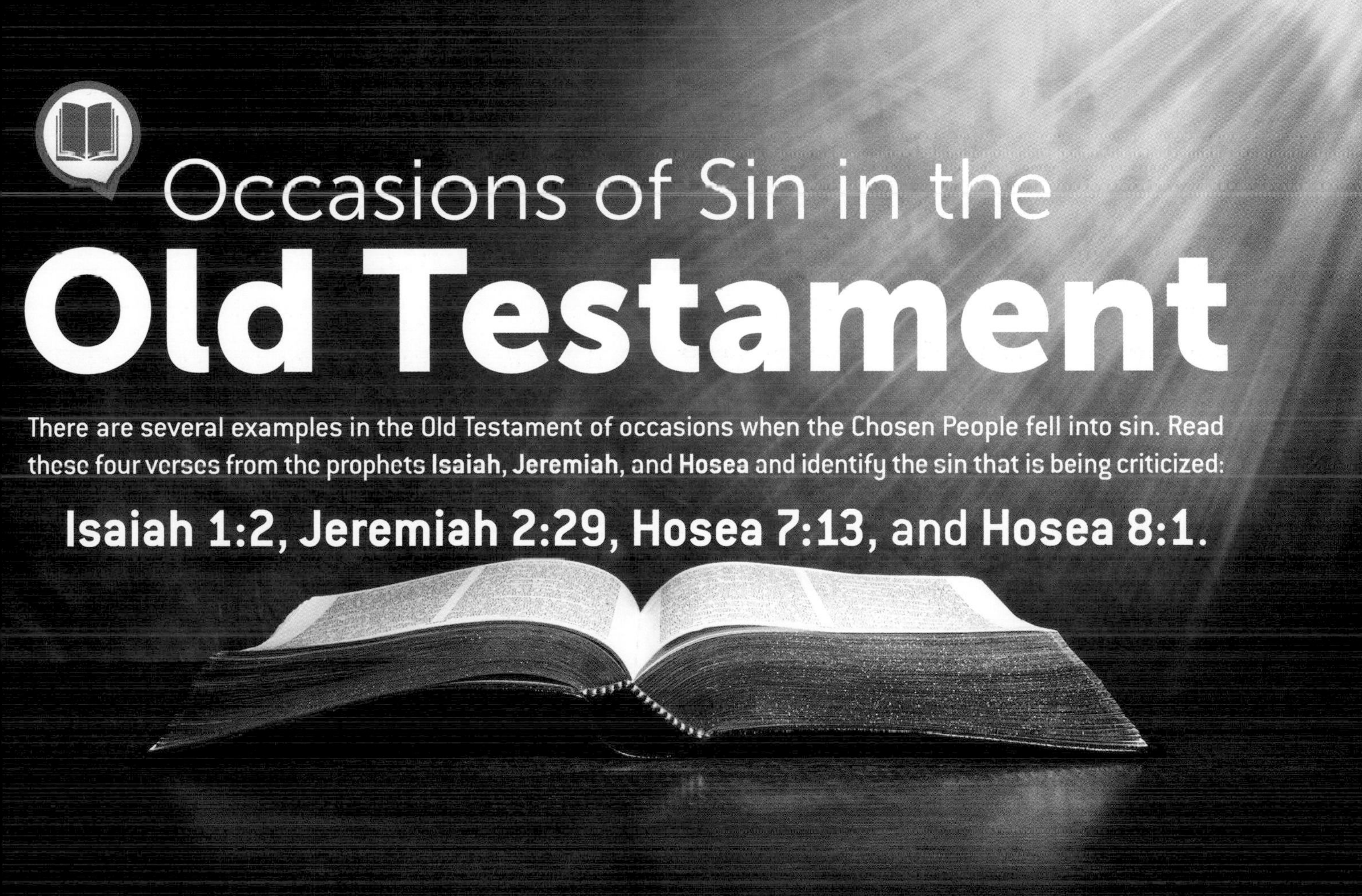

Occasions of Sin in the
Old Testament
There are several examples in the Old Testament of occasions when the Chosen People fell into sin. Read these four verses from the prophets Isaiah, Jeremiah, and Hosea and identify the sin that is being criticized:
Isaiah 1:2, Jeremiah 2:29, Hosea 7:13, and Hosea 8:1.

SECTION ASSESSMENT

NOTE TAKING

Use the notes you took to help you answer the following question.

1. What is the most important parallel that you found between the Genesis accounts mentioned in this section? Explain.

VOCABULARY

2. Define *typology*.

COMPREHENSION

3. How can Original Sin be thought of as a "happy fault"?
4. How does the *Protoevangelium* indicate that someone in the future will conquer evil?
5. Who is the "New Adam," and why is this an appropriate title for him?
6. Explain the meaning and symbolism of the first covenant between God and humanity.
7. How does the Tower of Babel passage teach that going it alone apart from God ultimately leads to sorrow and evil?

SECTION 2

Covenants in the Old Testament

MAIN IDEA

God's covenants reveal his desire to draw humans to himself.

God reached out to his people through covenants. Old Testament covenants foretold a New Covenant (see Jer 31:31–34) that would be written on the hearts of humankind (see also Is 42:6, 49:8). God entrusted the people of ancient Israel with knowledge of his promise. As recognized in the Gospels, this promise is fulfilled in the Person of Jesus Christ.

Three Covenants Explained

The covenant between God and Noah was the first Old Testament covenant. God made three other covenants with the Chosen People that are recorded in the Old Testament:

- The covenant with Abraham, in which God blessed Abraham's family, promising to give them the land of Canaan and make him a blessing to the nations (Gn 15:18).
- The covenant with Moses on Mount Sinai, in which God selected Israel as his Chosen People (Ex 19:3–6).
- The covenant with David, in which God announced that the Messiah and Savior would come from David's dynasty (2 Sm 23:5).

NOTE TAKING

Identifying Common Elements. Create your own version of this chart. As you read through this section, fill out these elements for each of the covenants mentioned.

Covenant	God's Promise	Conditions for the People	Outcome
Abraham	*Blessing for Abraham's family, Promised Land, blessing to nations*	*Circumcision*	*God did eventually allow Abraham's descendants into the Promised Land*

Biblical covenants have two sacred parts: the promise God made *and* the conditions God asked the person or group entering into the covenant to fulfill. In the covenant with Abraham, for example, one condition was that Abraham and all of his descendants were to be circumcised.

Old Testament covenants foretold a New Covenant (Jer 31:31–34) which would be written in the hearts of humankind (see Is 42:6, 49:8). God entrusted the people of ancient Israel with knowledge of his promise. As recognized in the Gospels, this promise would be fulfilled in the Person of Jesus Christ.

Other Key Elements of Old Testament Covenants

Hearing, believing, and obeying God are other key elements of the Old Testament covenants. For example, the migrant herder originally named Abram heard God's words to him to move from his ancestral land of Ur (today's southern Iraq) with his family to the land of Canaan. God promised that he would give this new land to Abraham and his descendants (see Gn 12:2–3). Abraham became a patriarch of the Chosen People, the "Father of Faith" (cf. Rom 4:16).

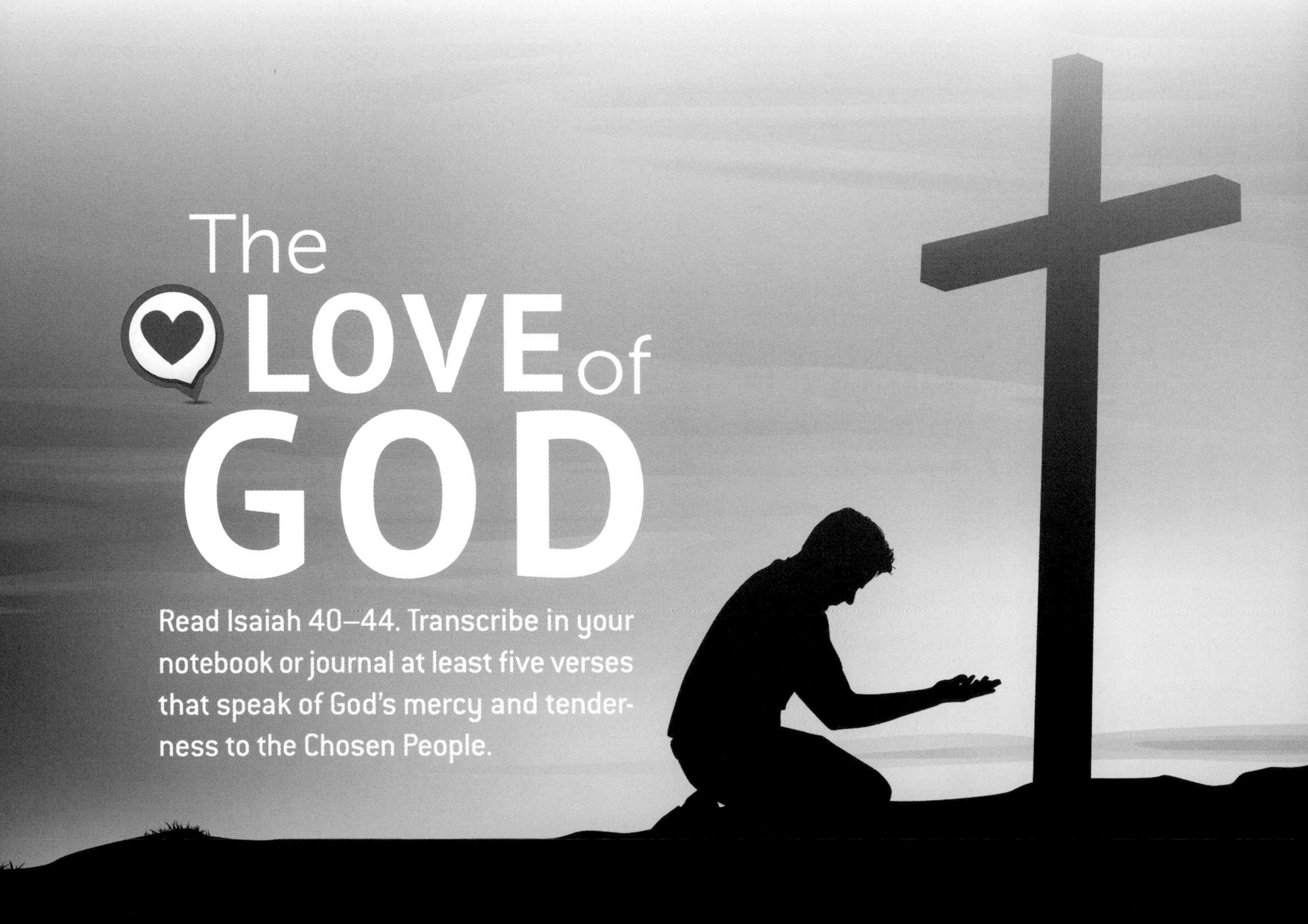

The LOVE of GOD

Read Isaiah 40–44. Transcribe in your notebook or journal at least five verses that speak of God's mercy and tenderness to the Chosen People.

When God gave Moses the Law on Mount Sinai, all of the Chosen People were required to obey its statutes so they would know how to serve him. The **Decalogue** summarizes the Law of Moses and expresses what humans know in their hearts, and deduce by reason, to be right or wrong. The Law of Moses also encompassed many ceremonial laws of the Old Testament. It regulated rituals, the priesthood, sacrifices, and many other things. The Law foreshadows the Paschal Mystery, pointing forward to Christ's sacrifice. The people of Israel were God's priestly people, the people he loved, the first to hear his Word. By worshipping the Lord alone as the true God and by living a life conformed to the Law, the Chosen People were meant to be a beacon of God's Revelation to the whole world.

Failing to heed the warnings of judges (tribal chieftains) and prophets to remain faithful to the Law of Moses, the Israelites requested a king. David was Israel's greatest king. The key promise of God's covenant with David was that Israel would be a royal dynasty, a promise that led to the Israelites' belief in the Messiah (God's "anointed one"), who would save the Chosen People from their enemies. The prophet Nathan told David:

> Moreover, the LORD also declares to you that the LORD will make a house for you: when your days have been completed and you rest with your ancestors, I will raise up your offspring after you, sprung from your loins, and I will establish his kingdom. (2 Sm 7:11–12)

Decalogue Literally, "ten words," it describes the Ten Commandments given by God to Moses.

God made many covenants with the Chosen People, and his promises are fulfilled in Christ's Passion, Death, and Resurrection.

God not only blessed Abraham and his descendants but he also formed a people from them, gave them the Law to guide them, and asked them to worship him in truth and love. God further promised that the future Messiah, the Savior of all humanity, would descend from the house of King David. For their part, the Chosen People were to live the Law as a beacon to the nations of the one, true, and saving God. Despite the infidelities of the people and even of kings like David, God always remained faithful to his promises.

SECTION ASSESSMENT

NOTE TAKING

Use the chart you made to help you complete the following item.

1. Summarize the covenants God made with Abraham, Moses, and David.

VOCABULARY

2. What is another term for the *Ten Commandments*?

COMPREHENSION

3. What are the two sacred parts of biblical covenants?
4. Why is Abraham called the "Father of Faith"?
5. Name three components of the Law of Moses.
6. What was the key promise of God's covenant with David?

CRITICAL ANALYSIS

7. Why is it important for Catholics today to understand the relationship between the covenants of the Old Testament and the New Covenant?

REFLECTION

8. How does Abraham's status as an immigrant compare to the experiences of immigrants in the world today?

SECTION 3

God Prepares the World for a Savior

MAIN IDEA

Through the Old Testament prophets and kings, God makes regular efforts to call his people away from sin to a relationship with him and to give them hope of a Savior.

The last judge and prophet, Samuel, appointed Saul to be the first Israelite king. Although he was an effective leader at first, Saul began to disobey God and take on religious roles reserved for the priests. So God asked Samuel to anoint his successor, David, while Saul still reigned.

In many ways, the reign of King David was a golden period in Israel's monarchy. He brought peace, culture, and prosperity to the land. He made Jerusalem its capital. King David sinned, however, most notably by committing adultery with Bathsheba, the wife of a soldier named Uriah. To conceal that he had conceived a child with Bathsheba, he sent Uriah to the front line of a battle to ensure his death. When confronted by the prophet Nathan, David repented (see 2 Sm 11–12 and the image at left). However, the rest of his reign was beset with various hardships and rebellions.

Idolatry and Excess Split the Kingdom and Lead to Captivity

David's son Solomon succeeded his father as king. Solomon, who reigned in the tenth century BC, was known for his wisdom (see 1 Kgs 3). He supervised the building of the Temple in Jerusalem, a center of worship and pilgrimage for the Chosen People.

NOTE TAKING

Citing Examples. Draw a circle, and label it "Ways God Helps." Then, as you read through this section, identify the different ways God helped the Israelites remain faithful to their covenants with him. Write each way on a spoke you draw radiating out from the circle. Add as many spokes as necessary.

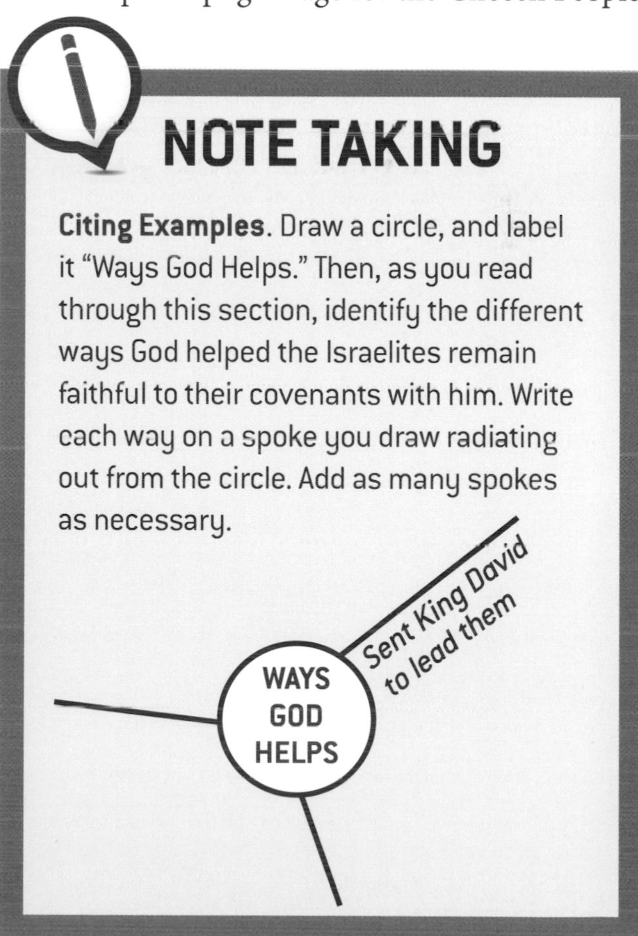

After Solomon's death, the unified kingdom of Israel split in two.

Unfortunately, Solomon's building projects severely taxed the people, and his many foreign wives led him to worship their idols. After Solomon's death, the kingdom divided into the northern kingdom of Israel, which consisted of ten of Israel's twelve tribes, and the southern kingdom of Judah, which consisted of the tribes of Benjamin and Judah and had Jerusalem as its capital.

The northern kingdom chose idolatry from the beginning, as the king tried to create new worship sites that would rival the Temple in Jerusalem. Although God sent prophets to the north to warn the leaders that idolatry would lead to their downfall, they did not change, and the kingdom fell to Assyria in 722 BC. The southern kingdom had a few faithful kings, but most succumbed to idolatry. Despite the warnings of God's prophets, the southern kingdom was overrun by the Babylonians in 587 BC, and many of the Jewish people were taken to Babylonia as captives.

During the time of political turmoil and religious backsliding prior to these invasions, God had sent prophets to both the north and the south to remind people of his covenant with them. The prophets spread God's message to the people in the following ways:

The Prophets' Messages

- proclaiming the need for the Chosen People to worship the one, true God in fidelity and truth
- warning the people of their need to repent
- urging the people to live according to the Law
- asking the people to look out for the needs of the poor and powerless

Prophets Preach Repentance and Hope

The Assyrian conquest effectively wiped out the northern kingdom of Israel. A number of the Jews from the southern kingdom, Judah, continued to worship God and tried to live according to the covenant while in captivity. When they had the opportunity to leave, though, many stayed in Babylon since they had become accustomed to that culture.

Because the Jews were suffering the consequences of many years of infidelity and sin in Babylon, God sent prophets not to warn them about coming disaster but rather to give them hope for their future. The prophet Jeremiah told this to the people:

> See, days are coming—oracle of the LORD—when I will make a new covenant with the house of Israel and the house of Judah. It will not be like the covenant I made with their

> ancestors. . . . I will place my law within them, and write it upon their hearts; I will be their God, and they shall be my people. They will no longer teach their friends and relatives, "Know the LORD!" Everyone, from least to greatest, shall know me—oracle of the LORD—for I will forgive their iniquity and no longer remember their sin. (Jer 31:31–34)

This message clearly shows God once again reaching out to his people. The Law would no longer be written only on tablets of stone or in law books. Rather, God would touch people's hearts so that he might live within them. Jesus Christ would fulfill this prophecy when he established the **New Covenant** through his life and the events of the Paschal Mystery.

The prophet Ezekiel also preached a hopeful message. He predicted a time when God would restore Israel. In a prophetic dream, Ezekiel stood in a field of dry bones—symbolizing the house of Israel—which the Lord promised to raise from the dead (see Ez 37:11–14). Ezekiel's vision prophesied that the people would return to the Promised Land. Their despair would be turned to hope. God would bring them back to life.

Prediction of the Messiah

By foretelling the coming of a Messiah, the prophets brought hope to the Jewish people. The Book of Isaiah (which may contain the words of three different

New Covenant The covenant established by God in Jesus Christ to fulfill and perfect the Old Covenant. The New Covenant, also called the Law of the Gospel, is the perfection here on earth of the natural law and the Law of Moses. The New Covenant is the law of love, grace, and freedom. The New Covenant, made in the Blood of Jesus, is the climax of salvation history and is God's eternal covenant with human beings.

prophets) predicted much about the Messiah, including a sign that God would give: "the young woman, pregnant and about to bear a son, shall name him Emmanuel" (Is 7:14). These words also apply to Jesus Christ:

> For a child is born to us, a son is given to us;
> upon his shoulder dominion rests.
> They name him Wonder-Counselor,
> God-Hero,
> Father-Forever, Prince of Peace.
> His dominion is vast
> and forever peaceful. (Is 9:5–6)

The prophet also proclaimed that God was coming to save his people and that his love is enduring, like that of a mother for her baby (see Is 49:15–16).

A second part of the Book of Isaiah includes the *Servant Songs*, which also apply to Jesus. These describe an individual, "the servant," whom God will use to usher in a glorious future. These Servant Songs present more prophetic images of Jesus, the Suffering Servant whose sufferings redeemed all people. Jesus was familiar with these passages and applied them to himself. He interpreted the messianic way to salvation as a path of suffering and service, not one of earthly glory and domination.

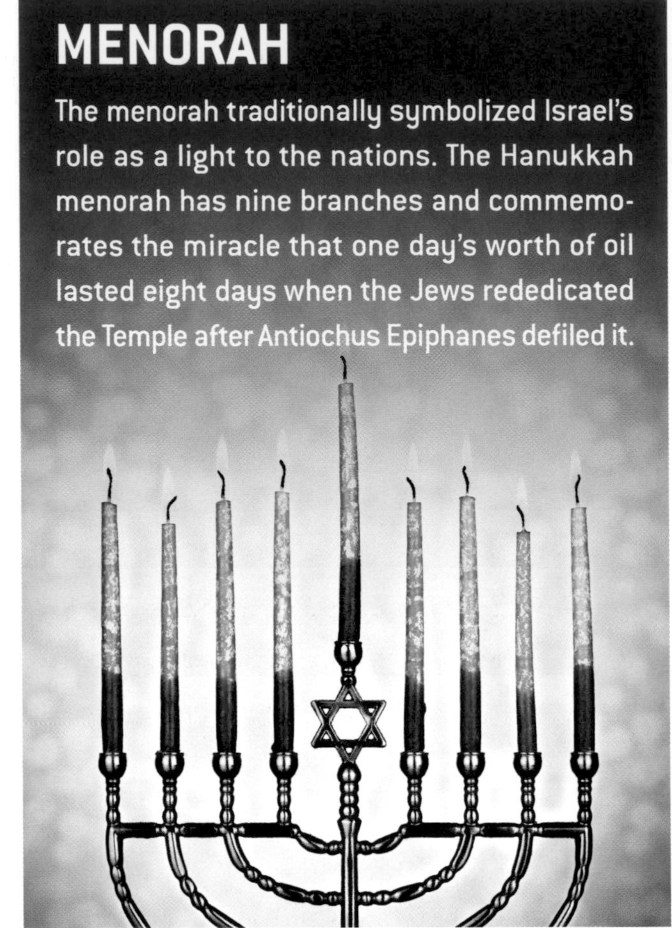

MENORAH

The menorah traditionally symbolized Israel's role as a light to the nations. The Hanukkah menorah has nine branches and commemorates the miracle that one day's worth of oil lasted eight days when the Jews rededicated the Temple after Antiochus Epiphanes defiled it.

Israel's Role in Salvation

In 538 BC, King Cyrus of Persia permitted the Jews held captive in Babylon to return home. Isaiah's prophecies reminded the Israelites that God called them to draw other nations to the worship of the one, true God:

> I will make you a light to the nations,
> that my salvation may reach to the ends of the earth. (Is 49:6)

Isaiah 56–66 contains another promise that, in coming days, God's light would shine brightly on the Jewish nation and attract all people to God (see Is 60:1–5). These verses express the belief that God's salvation is meant for all, not just the Chosen People. The people of ancient Israel were entrusted with knowledge of God and his promise.

The Centuries before Jesus' Birth

In the centuries before the birth of Christ, Persian rule gave way to the Greeks under Alexander the Great, then to the Seleucid dynasty, and finally to the Romans. God's Chosen People fought efforts to *Hellenize* them—that is, to impose Greek culture on their way of life and religion. Faithful Jews kept their religion alive through Temple worship and by meeting in prayer houses called *synagogues*.

The Seleucid ruler Antiochus Epiphanes tried to obliterate Judaism. In 165 BC, he desecrated the Temple, an action that led to a revolt by the Maccabees, a family that helped preserve the Jewish religion from pagan influence. For a time, Israel had some political independence, but disagreement among Jewish leaders and priests divided Judaism into different sects, including the Pharisees, Sadducees, Essenes, and Zealots mentioned in the Gospels.

In 63 BC, the Romans imposed their rule on Israel. They appointed Herod the Great, who was half-Jewish, to govern in Palestine. Herod was a great builder and was responsible for the reconstruction of the Temple. He was also a cruel, heavy-handed, and vindictive ruler. Shortly before Herod's death, Jesus was born in Bethlehem. It is now estimated that his birth took place in the year 4 BC.

As recognized in the Gospels, God's covenant with the Jews and God's plan for all of humanity would reach its perfect fulfillment in Jesus' Passion, Death, and Resurrection.

SECTION ASSESSMENT

NOTE TAKING

Use your notes to help you complete the following item.

1. Name three ways God helped the Chosen People remain faithful to their covenant with him prior to the birth of Christ.

VOCABULARY

2. Define the *New Covenant*.

COMPREHENSION

3. Why did the kingdom split in two?
4. Which outside powers conquered the northern and southern kingdoms?
5. After the Babylonians had conquered the Jews, what did God send the prophets to do?
6. What do the Servant Songs describe?
7. What is the Jewish nation's (Israel's) role in salvation?
8. How did the prophets describe the Messiah?
9. Which foreign nations ruled over Israel in the centuries before Christ's birth?
10. What did the Seleucid ruler Antiochus Epiphanes do that inspired the Maccabees to revolt?

CRITICAL ANALYSIS

11. Why do you think it was the northern kingdom that turned to idol worship rather than the southern kingdom?
12. Compare and contrast God's covenant with Moses with the New Covenant as described by the prophet Jeremiah.

Section Summaries

Focus Question

Why are you in need of salvation?

Complete one of the following:

After centuries of showing his love, God still reaches out to people today. Do you take God's love for granted? Explain.

From the time of Original Sin, God desired salvation for the world. What do you find to be the strongest evidence for this statement?

Name two ways you are conscious of your need for salvation.

INTRODUCTION (PAGES 47–54)

Original Sin

God, who is a loving communion, created human beings and angels with freedom so that they can freely choose to love and serve him or freely choose to reject him. God allows you the freedom to reject him in order to ensure that you have the freedom to love him truly, for love that is not free is not love. Adam and Eve, trusting Satan and his lies, chose themselves over God. They tried to become God but without God's help. As a result, the couple lost the grace of original holiness and original justice and were expelled from paradise; the consequence of Original Sin applies not just to them but to all of their descendants as well. We, as their descendants, have received a fallen human nature. We experience suffering, death, a tendency toward sin (concupiscence), and the need for salvation.

Name a movie or television program that portrays a battle between good and evil. Write down at least two moral choices between good and evil faced by a major character. How did the script portray the decision-making process? What was the result?

SECTION 1 (PAGES 55–58)

Sin Multiplies

Though God witnessed the sins of his people, he remained faithful to them. After discovering Adam and Eve's sin, God promised he would save humanity and defeat the devil (Gn 3:15). This is the *Protoevangelium*, the first announcement of the Good News. The Exsultet is a reminder that the "happy fault" of sin "earned so great, so glorious a Redeemer" as Jesus Christ. God's promise endures despite the spread and escalation of sin, as seen in the murder of Abel, the Tower of Babel, and the Great Flood.

Describe a situation you have witnessed (personally or in the media) in which someone denied the need for God. What were the results of this choice?

SECTION 2 (PAGES 59–62)

Covenants in the Old Testament

God's covenants with the Old Testament peoples reveal his desire to draw humans to himself. Covenants are solemn commitments between God and human beings. God has truly entered into these covenants, and as St. Paul tells us, "the gifts and the call of God are irrevocable" (Rom 11:29). Three Old Testament covenants God made with his Chosen People were through Abraham, Moses, and David. Although the Old Testament retains its own intrinsic value, each of these covenants foreshadows the Paschal Mystery and is fulfilled in it.

Research more about the Jewish feast of Passover. How do Passover and Easter both celebrate liberation?

SECTION 3 (PAGES 63–67)

God Prepares the World for a Savior

Before Jesus' time, God made regular efforts to call his people away from sin to a relationship with him. First, God appointed judges to rescue the Israelites when they drifted away from him. God then agreed to let the people have kings to rule them. King David represents the best of Israel's monarchs, though his life was also marred by sinfulness. Subsequent kings strayed from worshipping God. God sent prophets to remind them about repentance and about the need to worship him, to live according to the Law, and to care for the poor. The message of the prophets changed to one of hope when the people were in exile. Prophets also told about the coming Messiah. In each of these stages, judges, kings, or prophets were appointed to remind the people of ancient Israel about God's promise and his fidelity to his promises.

The Old Testament describes leaders who set both good and bad examples for moral living. Name a local, national, or world leader from the last forty years who you think used his or her power morally, giving several examples. Then name a leader from this time period who abused his or her power, also giving several examples. Identify three qualities that you think are essential for moral leadership, using biblical leaders and your researched leaders as resources.

Chapter Assignments

Choose and complete at least one of the following three assignments to assess your understanding of the material in this chapter.

1. Examining Three Other Biblical Covenants

Read the following selected passages of three other biblical covenants. Two are from the Old Testament; the other is from the New Testament. Answer the questions that accompany each.

1 Samuel 18:1–5

- Why was this covenant made?
- What was the sign of the agreement?

Ezra 10:1–5

- What was the agreement made as part of this covenant?
- How was this covenant made?

Hebrews 9:11–22

- Who is the mediator of this covenant?
- What is the role of the mediator of this covenant?
- How is this covenant like the Mosaic covenant?

2. Angels and Demons in Art

Although there is no consistent portrayal of either angels or demons in Western art, certain characteristics or items are associated with each group when they are depicted. For example, Satan and the demons are often portrayed as "modified" humans—humans with horns or a tail, for example—while angels share human features. Research at least four specific pieces of art that portray angels and Satan or other demons. Write a brief background summary for each piece that identifies its title, subject, artist, and time period. For each piece, describe how the artist portrayed the theme of good versus evil. Finally, compare all four pieces. In three to five paragraphs, note similarities and differences in the ways angels, Satan, demons, and the subject of good and evil were represented. You may wish to narrow your art selection to a specific time period or region.

3. Women of the Faith

Read and report on one of the wives of the Old Testament patriarchs: Sarah, Rebekah, Rachel, or Leah. Use a biblical concordance to identify relevant Scripture passages that refer to the woman you choose. Write a two-page essay about the matriarch, including as much detail about her biography as possible. Use biblical commentary notes to help you fill in the details. Make sure your essay addresses the following questions:

- What role does this woman play in salvation history?
- How is her role different from her husband's?
- How does she complement her husband's role?
- How is this woman like Mary, the Mother of Jesus?
- What can her story teach you that her husband's story might not?

Faithful Disciples

The Archangels Gabriel, Raphael, and Michael

Archangel is a name for angels of a chief rank. Scripture names only three angels—Gabriel, Raphael, and Michael—who have been given this title. The Church's feast day for archangels is September 29. More information about each of the archangels follows.

St. Gabriel

Gabriel

You may be most familiar with the archangel Gabriel, who came to Mary and told her that she would be the Mother of God's Son. A few months earlier, he had visited Zechariah, the father of John the Baptist, and instructed him on what to name his son, even though John was not a family ancestral name. Gabriel also interacted with Daniel in the Old Testament. The name *Gabriel* means "might and power."

Raphael

Raphael, whose name means "God has healed," appears in the Book of Tobit. Tobit was an Israelite who had been captured and taken to Nineveh in the land of the Assyrians. While he was sleeping outside, bird droppings fell on his eyes and blinded him without a cure. He prayed for death.

Meanwhile, in a different town, a woman named Sarah had been given in marriage to seven husbands who all died by the hand of a demon, Asmodeus, before they could spend their wedding night with her. She also prayed for death.

God heard both of their prayers and sent Raphael to heal them both. Tobit told his son Tobiah about some money that he had left

St. Raphael

with a trusted kinsman in Media, the place where Sarah lived. Tobiah went to retrieve it, and the archangel Raphael was his companion on the journey. Along the way, while Tobiah bathed in the Tigris River, a fish attacked Tobiah and tried to swallow his foot. Raphael told Tobiah to capture the fish and keep its insides for medicine. In Media, Tobiah met Sarah and asked for her hand in marriage.

On Tobiah and Sarah's wedding night, Tobiah smoked the fish's liver and heart to repulse the demons and drive them away. Later, when he returned home to Nineveh, Tobiah applied the fish gall to his father's eyes and cured his blindness.

After this second miracle, the archangel Raphael revealed his identity, saying "I am Raphael, one of the seven angels who stand and serve before the Glory of the Lord" (Tb 12:15).

St. Michael

Michael

A prophetic passage from the Book of Daniel says that in a time of distress "there shall arise Michael, the great prince, guardian of your people" (Dn 12:1).

The archangel Michael is mentioned in the New Testament as well. The Letter to Jude portrays Michael battling with evil, saying that Michael had fought with the devil over the body of Moses (see Jude 1:9). In the Book of Revelation, when a dragon is poised to devour the woman in labor "clothed with the sun, with the moon under her feet, and on her head a crown of twelve stars" (Rv 12:1), Michael and other angels battle the dragon, who is thrown down to earth with the evil angels.

In 1886, Pope Leo XIII introduced the Prayer to St. Michael the Archangel (page 76) to be recited at the end of Mass. Though it is no longer recited as part of the Eucharistic liturgy, later popes have encouraged people to recite it frequently. Pope John Paul II urged Catholics to pray the Prayer to St. Michael "to obtain help in the battle against forces of darkness and against the spirit of this world."

Reading Comprehension

1. What is the meaning of the term *archangel*?
2. What two problems did the archangel Raphael address in the Book of Tobit?
3. Which book of the Bible reveals St. Michael's role as a "guardian of the people"?

Writing Task

- Read 1 Thessalonians 4:13–18. Explain how the term *archangel* is used in this passage. Refer to the commentary notes in your Bible to help you complete the assignment.

Explaining the Faith

What are the capital sins?

The Church refers to seven "deadly sins." They are also called *capital sins* because they can easily lead to other sins. As the *Catechism of the Catholic Church* teaches:

> Sin creates a proclivity to sin; it engenders vice by repetition of the same acts. This results in perverse inclinations which cloud conscience and corrupt the concrete judgment of good and evil. Thus sin tends to reproduce itself and reinforce itself, but it cannot destroy the moral sense at its root. (*CCC*, 1865)

The capital sins are as follows:

- *Pride* is undue self-esteem or self-love that seeks attention and honor and sets the self in competition with God.

- *Avarice* is a passion for wealth and the power it brings.
- *Envy* is resentment or sadness at another's good fortune and a desire to have it for oneself.
- *Wrath* is strong and vengeful anger.
- *Lust* is a disordered desire for or inordinate enjoyment of sexual pleasure.
- *Gluttony* is overindulgence in food or drink.
- *Sloth* is an irresponsible lack of physical or spiritual effort, often simply called laziness.

Further Research

- The Church also teaches that there are "sins that cry to heaven." What are those sins? See paragraph 1867 of the *Catechism of the Catholic Church*.

Prayer

Prayer to St. Michael the Archangel

St. Michael the Archangel, defend us in battle.
Be our protection against the wickedness
and snares of the devil.
May God rebuke him, we humbly pray;
and do Thou, O Prince of the Heavenly Host—
by the Power of God—
cast into hell Satan and all the evil spirits
who roam throughout the world seeking the
ruin of souls.
Amen.

CHAPTER REVIEW

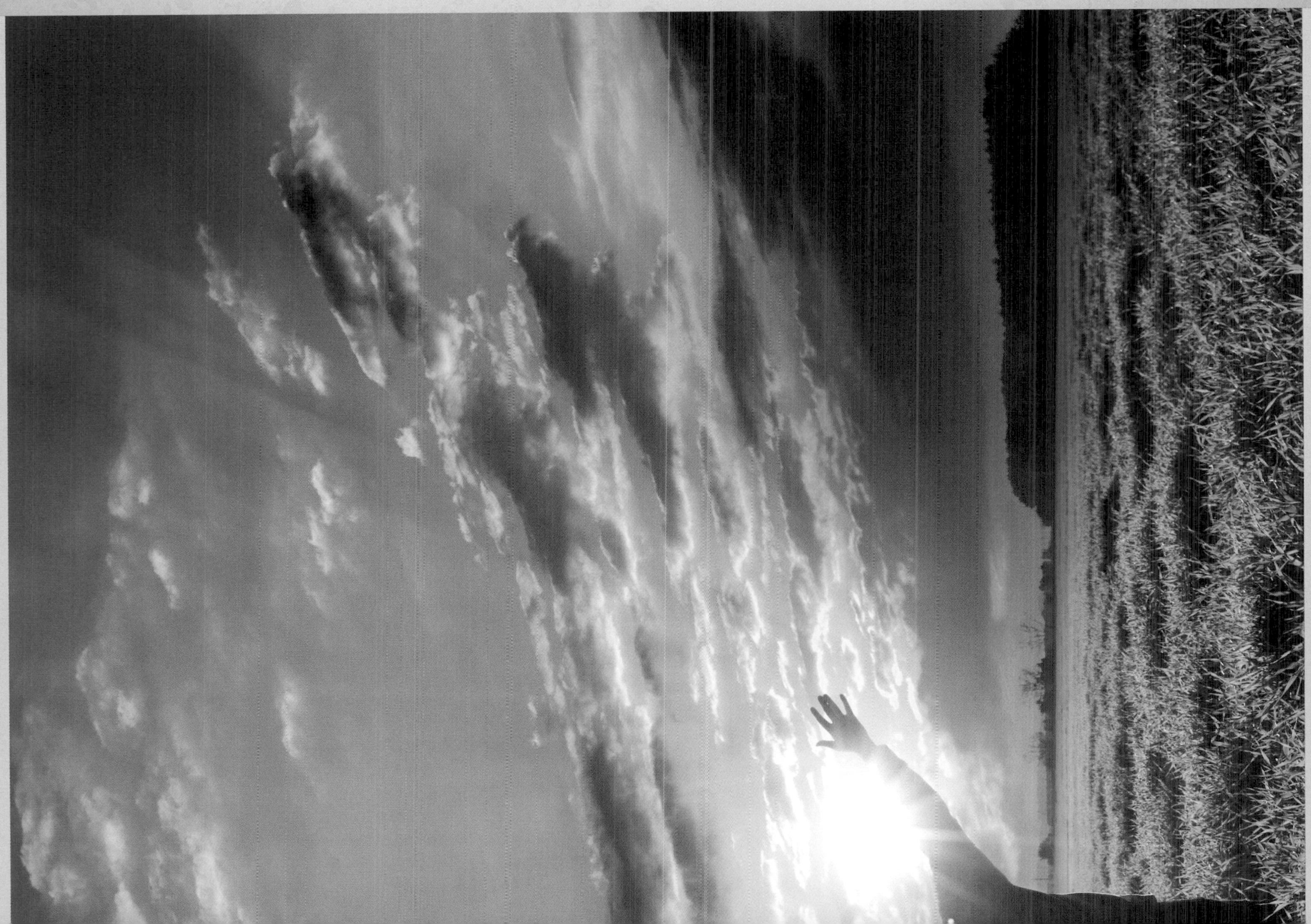

3

THE COMING OF THE MESSIAH

GIVING BACK

Jon Lester, a major league baseball pitcher and graduate of the Catholic high school Bellarmine Prep in Tacoma, Washington, can make things happen both on and off the field. When he was a rookie with the Boston Red Sox in 2006, Lester found out that he had lymphoma, a rare blood cancer. At the time, nothing seemed good about that situation. Looking back, however, Lester sees that positive things happened because of the cancer: for example, he bonded more closely with his parents. Because of the illness, the Red Sox sent Lester down to Greenville, South Carolina, in early 2007 to rehabilitate with a minor league team. It was there that he met his future wife—another very good thing.

Just one year after his diagnosis, Lester was back with the Red Sox and won the clinching game of the 2007 World Series. Even more good things were to come: Lester and his wife, Farah, became parents to two children. But only when his father was also diagnosed with cancer did Lester begin to think about ways he could help others.

Lester began to visit children at cancer hospitals when he traveled to different cities with the team. He saw that his own presence and experience helped the kids he met. He and his wife partnered with the Pediatric Cancer Research Foundation to form the NVRQT (short for "Never Quit") campaign. The campaign supports kids who are fighting cancer and funds research on pediatric cancer. As part of his work with the foundation, Lester invites children to the stadium to watch games as his guest as well as continuing his hospital visits. Jon and Farah also hold larger fund-raising events to support cancer research.

Jon Lester's World Series success wasn't finished, either. He won two games for the Red Sox against the St. Louis Cardinals in the 2013 World Series. In 2014 he signed a new long-term contract to pitch for the Chicago Cubs.

(Jon Lester, "MLB Pitcher Battles Cancer, Never Quits," CNN.com, July 17, 2013.)

FOCUS QUESTION

How did **CHRIST'S BIRTH** and early years reveal the **PRESENCE OF GOD**?

Chapter Overview

INTRODUCTION

Jesus Christ: Son of God, Son of Mary

MAIN IDEA
Jesus' name and titles reveal different aspects of his identity as fully divine and fully human.

Jon Lester used his experience as a cancer patient, his desire to give back, and his financial resources and contacts to follow Jesus' example of being a healing presence in the world. This chapter will lead you, too, to reflect more deeply on how Jesus has come to heal the world.

In Chapter 2, you considered how God constantly reached out to his Chosen People in the Old Testament, reminding them of his promise at every stage. After sending patriarchs, judges, kings, and prophets, God sent his Son, Jesus Christ, to redeem his Chosen People and the whole human race. God not only fulfilled his promises to Abraham and his descendants but he also did so in a way that no one could have imagined. God himself, as the Second Divine Person of the Blessed Trinity, entered human history in the birth of Jesus, the Son of Mary.

Basic information from the Gospels can tell you some things about who Jesus really is. Exploring his name and his titles can deepen your knowledge and lead you to want to know him better. It is also necessary to learn about Jesus' birth and his early years in order to find out what God is like. Looking at how the Gospel writers refer to passages from the Old Testament can show you both how they understood Jesus as the fulfillment of God's promises to the people of Israel and how they understood Jesus in relation to the God of Israel.

NOTE TAKING

Summarizing Key Points. Using the format below, write summary sentences that explain each of the titles of Jesus.

Jesus	*The angel Gabriel's instruction to Mary about her Son's name sums up his whole life's work: Jesus saves.*
Christ (Messiah)	
Son of God	
Lord	
Son of Mary	

Religious Education or Catechesis

Have you ever helped to teach a religious education class to young children? Have you recently prepared to receive Confirmation with other teens your age? Have you attended school retreats? These three examples and your current theology class are all forms of **catechesis**.

At the heart of catechesis is the proclamation of the Good News of Jesus Christ so that others can come to have faith in him. All that you have learned through your parish and schools, from your family, and from your own spiritual searching is intended to lead you to more knowledge about Jesus Christ in order that you might form a true personal friendship with him. When you have a relationship with the one who offers you salvation, you are naturally led to want to share your knowledge of and love for Jesus with others. And when you share this kind of information about Christ, you are fulfilling some of the roles of a catechist yourself. Since this is true, you should know that catechesis also means the following (see *CCC*, 426):

catechesis The education of children, adolescents, and adults in the faith of the Church through the teaching of Christian doctrine in an organic and systematic way to make them disciples of Jesus Christ. Those who perform the ministry of catechesis in the Church are called *catechists*.

- revealing the whole of God's eternal design as reaching fulfillment in the Person of Christ
- seeking a deeper understanding of Christ's words and actions as well as his miracles
- putting people in communion with Jesus Christ and, through him, leading them to participate in the life of the Blessed Trinity

To be a catechist, you should know Christ intimately and value him above all things. Your desire to evangelize should spring from a loving knowledge of him. When you teach others about Christ, he teaches through you. You become his spokesperson.

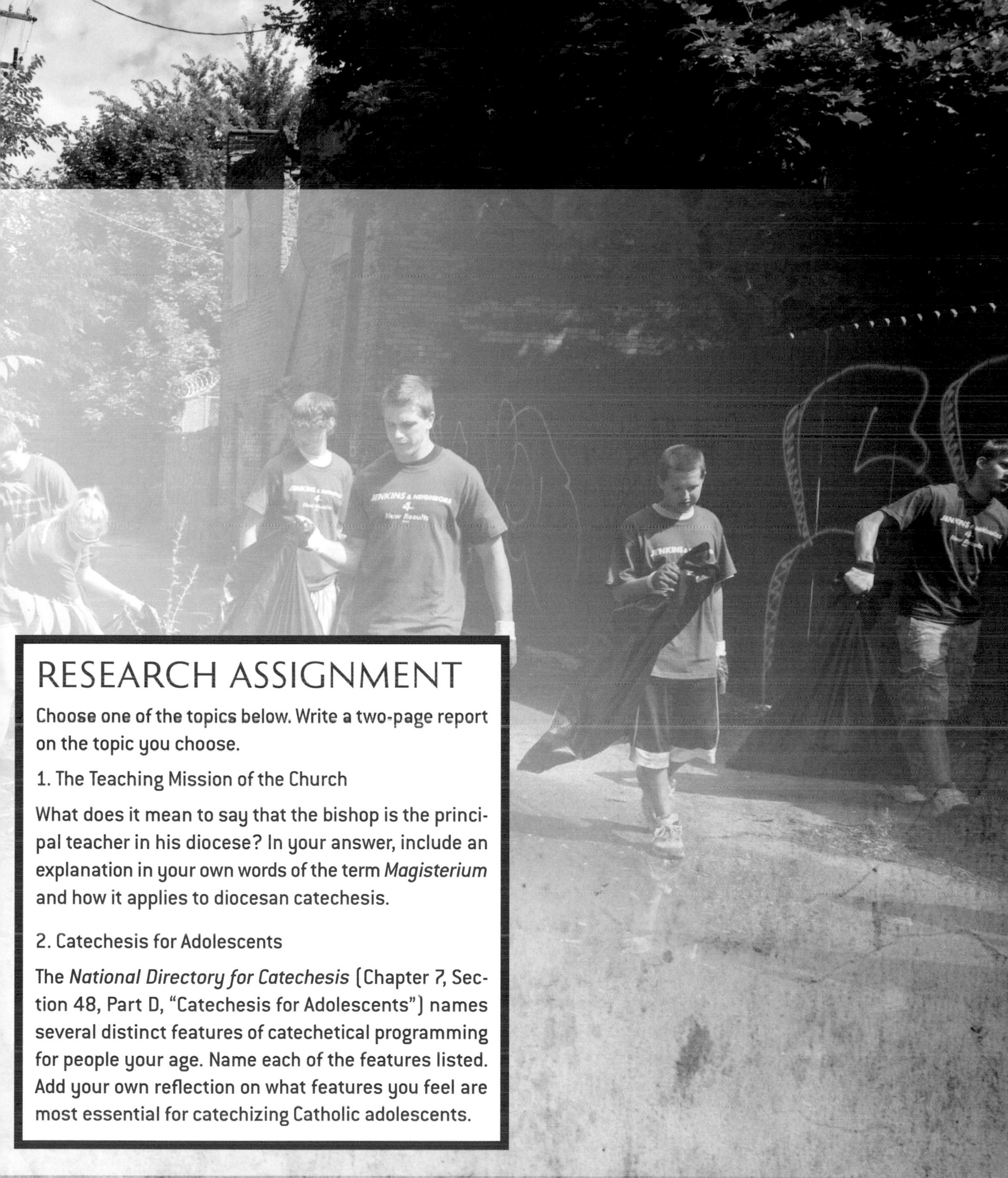

RESEARCH ASSIGNMENT

Choose one of the topics below. Write a two-page report on the topic you choose.

1. The Teaching Mission of the Church

What does it mean to say that the bishop is the principal teacher in his diocese? In your answer, include an explanation in your own words of the term *Magisterium* and how it applies to diocesan catechesis.

2. Catechesis for Adolescents

The *National Directory for Catechesis* (Chapter 7, Section 48, Part D, "Catechesis for Adolescents") names several distinct features of catechetical programming for people your age. Name each of the features listed. Add your own reflection on what features you feel are most essential for catechizing Catholic adolescents.

Jesus

Jesus means "God saves." Jesus' name sums up his identity and his mission to rescue humans from sin. Mary and Joseph did not choose Jesus' name themselves; it was the angel Gabriel (see page 73) who told Mary to name her Son Jesus. St. Paul wrote that Jesus' name is powerful and is above all other names:

> [Christ Jesus], though he was in the form of
>   God,
>   did not regard equality with God some-
>   thing to be grasped.
>   Rather, . . . he humbled himself,
>   becoming obedient to death, even death
>   on a cross.
> Because of this, God greatly exalted him
>   and bestowed on him the name
>   that is above every name,
>   that at the name of Jesus
>   every knee should bend,
>   of those in heaven and on earth and
>   under the earth. (Phil 2:6, 8–10)

The Incarnation made Jesus an ally with human beings so that people could call out to him in their need for salvation. Here are some other essential points to remember about his name:

- Scripture reveals that evil spirits feared the name of Jesus and that Jesus' disciples performed miracles in his name.
- Jesus' Resurrection glorified his name.
- Jesus' name is central to Christian prayer. Even repeating Jesus' name meditatively is prayer.

It was evident that no matter how God guided them throughout history, the people of Israel could not save themselves from sin. God freed them from sin through Jesus as he had freed them from slavery in the Exodus.

Christ (Messiah)

The Hebrew word *Masiah* (Messiah) translates to the Greek word *Christos* (Christ); both mean "anointed one." "Christ" is not a last name or family name of Jesus. In the Old Testament, priests, prophets, and kings were anointed prior to their missions. It is fitting, therefore, that the Messiah would be anointed by the Holy Spirit as priest, prophet, and king.

The hope for a messiah became especially strong among the Jews after the kingdom was divided into the north and the south and, eventually, the office of king was lost. Both Matthew's and Luke's Gospels note that Joseph, the husband of Mary, came from the messianic line of David.

Jesus' role as Messiah was publicly shared at his Baptism when God the Father declared that Jesus was his Son. God the Father commissioned this anointing, God the Son received the anointing, and the anointing itself was the work of God the Holy Spirit. Many Jews and some Gentiles recognized early in his ministry that Jesus possessed the attributes of the Messiah.

However, Jesus was careful when using the title "Messiah" because many Jews understood it to be a political title. When Peter professed that

Jesus was the Messiah (see Mk 8:29), Jesus immediately explained that his mission as Messiah was his redemptive suffering and Death. Jesus' Crucifixion definitively revealed that he was not a political messiah.

Son of God

Traditionally, the Jews did not understand the title "son of God" to mean that the "son" was divine. Rather, in the Old Testament, "son of God" describes an "adoptive" son who had a special relationship with God. The Old Testament also uses the title "son of God" to describe angels, kings, and the Chosen People as a whole. This means that "son of God" as used in the Old Testament was not necessarily a claim of Jesus' divinity.

Jesus' divine identity is a matter of Divine Revelation, recorded in the New Testament. As Jesus' public ministry went on, more people connected the title "son of God" with Jesus' divinity. When Simon Peter professed, "You are the Messiah, the Son of the living God" (Mt 16:16), Jesus told him that he could only have learned his true identity from the Father. In his preaching, Jesus referred to himself as God's Son multiple times. There were two key moments in Jesus' life when God the Father clearly revealed it: at Jesus' Baptism and at his Transfiguration. The truth of his divinity and of his words and teaching is confirmed by his Resurrection. "The Resurrection of the crucified one shows that he was truly 'I AM,' the Son of God and God himself" (*CCC*, 653).

Lord

Jews to this day do not pronounce the sacred name of God, YHWH, aloud. They have always used other names for God out of reverence. In the Old Testament, the term *LORD* is often substituted for YHWH.

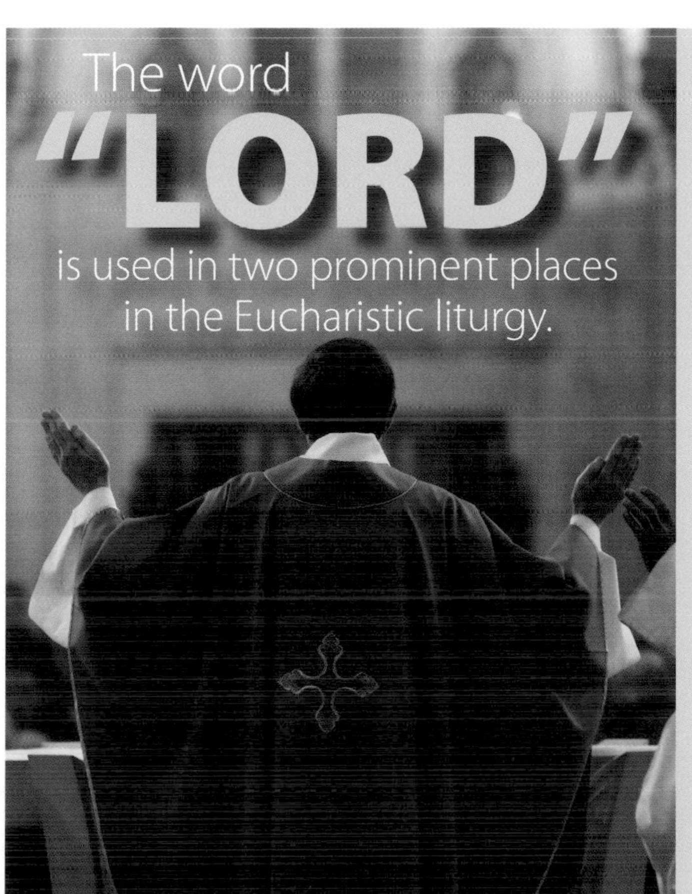

The word
"LORD"
is used in two prominent places
in the Eucharistic liturgy.

The formula of the prayer, "Lord, have mercy" (accompanied by "Christ, have mercy") is part of the Penitential Rite at the beginning of Mass. This prayer is the only prayer in the Latin rite of the Mass with Greek origins. In fact, the Greek version of the prayer is often recited or sung today at Mass:

Kyrie eleison.	**Lord, have mercy.**
Christe eleison.	**Christ, have mercy.**
Kyrie eleison.	**Lord, have mercy.**

As part of the Communion Rite, the word *Lord* is also spoken by the assembly as they express their unworthiness to receive Holy Communion. These words resemble the words spoken by the centurion to Jesus and recorded in Matthew 8:8 and Luke 7:6:

"Lord, I am not worthy that you should enter under my roof, but only say the word and my soul shall be healed."

In the New Testament, *Lord* has two meanings: it is used both for God the Father and for Jesus.

Initially, Jesus' disciples referred to him as "Lord" out of respect, as one would call someone "sir." But as time passed, more understood that Jesus was "Lord" in a divine sense. The Holy Spirit prompted some to recognize Jesus' divinity this way. By using this title for Jesus, the earliest Christians expressed that the power, honor, and glory due to God the Father were also due to God the Son. They also affirmed that humans should not submit themselves to any earthly powers but only to the divine Lord.

Today, the title "Lord" is used frequently in Christian prayer, including in the Church's liturgy, with a clear understanding that the title expresses Jesus' divinity. In the Mass, for example, prayers are offered "through Christ our Lord."

Son of Mary

The angel Gabriel's Annunciation to Mary initiated the fulfillment of God's promises. From the moment of her Immaculate Conception, Mary was graced by God to become the Mother of the Savior. At the Annunciation, the angel Gabriel salutes Mary as "favored one." The Holy Spirit came upon Mary, not only helping her to say yes to the angel's request that she be the Mother of God but also confirming her holiness so that she could conceive God's Son by the Holy Spirit.

The Blessed Virgin Mary played a vital role in Jesus' life. The Catholic Church reveres her above all of the saints. Her greatest title is "Mother of God." This means that one of Jesus' most important titles is "Son of Mary." Below are several key teachings about Mary:

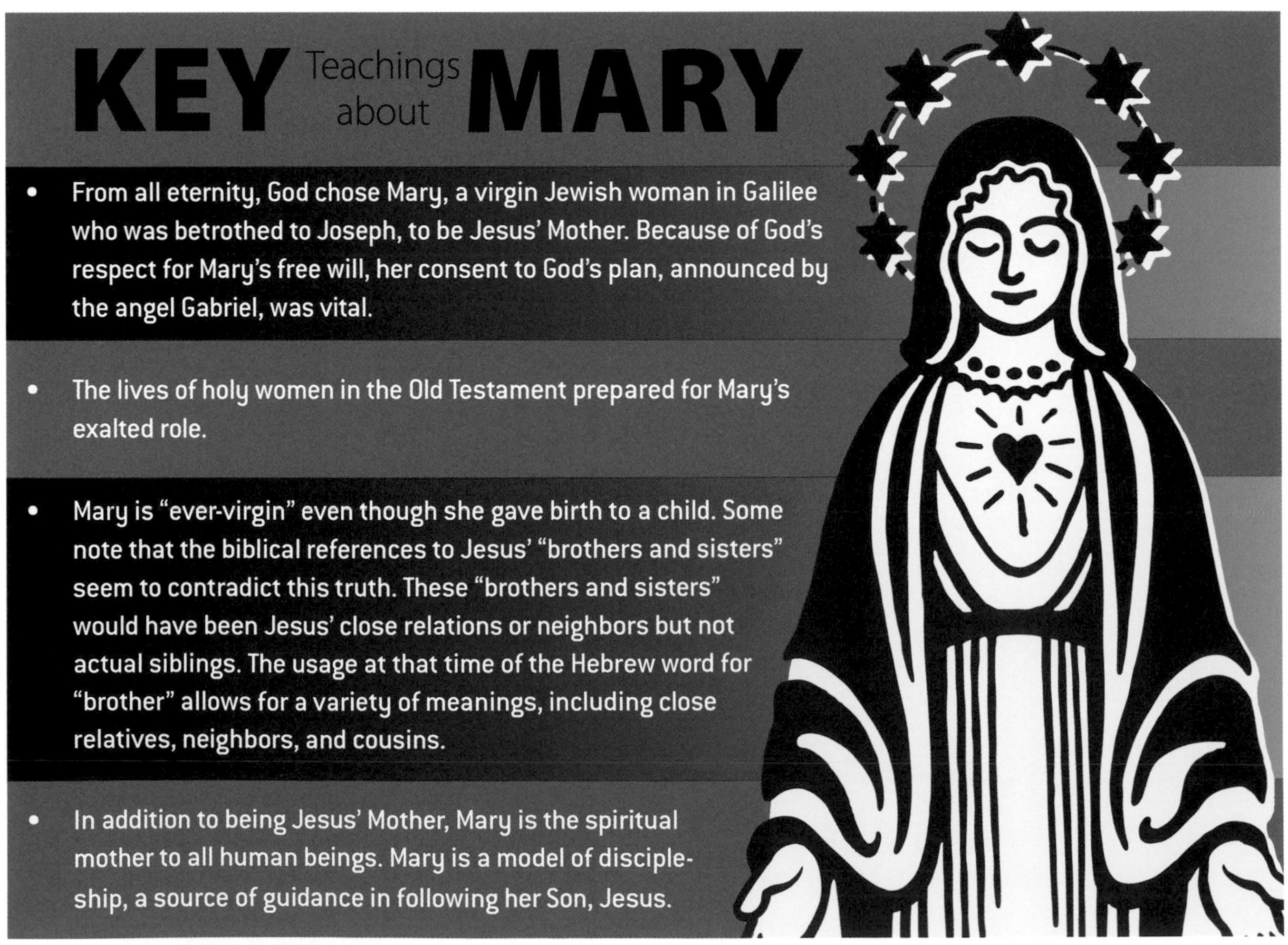

KEY Teachings about MARY

- From all eternity, God chose Mary, a virgin Jewish woman in Galilee who was betrothed to Joseph, to be Jesus' Mother. Because of God's respect for Mary's free will, her consent to God's plan, announced by the angel Gabriel, was vital.
- The lives of holy women in the Old Testament prepared for Mary's exalted role.
- Mary is "ever-virgin" even though she gave birth to a child. Some note that the biblical references to Jesus' "brothers and sisters" seem to contradict this truth. These "brothers and sisters" would have been Jesus' close relations or neighbors but not actual siblings. The usage at that time of the Hebrew word for "brother" allows for a variety of meanings, including close relatives, neighbors, and cousins.
- In addition to being Jesus' Mother, Mary is the spiritual mother to all human beings. Mary is a model of discipleship, a source of guidance in following her Son, Jesus.

SECTION ASSESSMENT

NOTE TAKING

Use the statements you wrote summarizing key points in this section to help you answer the following question.

1. Which name or title do you believe best captures Jesus' identity? Why do you think this is true?

VOCABULARY

2. What is the meaning of the name *Jesus*?
3. What is the meaning of the title *Christ*?

COMPREHENSION

4. How was Jesus' anointing Trinitarian?
5. Why was Jesus careful when using the title *Messiah*?
6. When did God the Father claim Jesus as his Son?

CRITICAL ANALYSIS

7. What does the statement "no matter how God guided them throughout history, the people of Israel could not save themselves from sin" imply about human nature?

SECTION 1

Jesus' Birth and Early Years

MAIN IDEA
The Gospels show that Jesus' life mission was apparent from his earliest years.

After centuries of preparation during Old Testament times, God himself entered salvation history. St. Paul wrote in his Letter to the Galatians: "But when the fullness of time had come, God sent his Son, born of a woman, born under the law, to ransom those under the law, so that we might receive adoption" (Gal 4:4–5). Jesus Christ our Lord, the Son of God, is God made flesh.

The Gospels of Matthew, Mark, and Luke are called the *synoptic Gospels* because of their similar flow and content. They each bring a unique focus to the different parts of Jesus' life story. Mark's Gospel does not mention Jesus' birth or Jesus' family life, beginning instead around the time of Jesus' Baptism. Mark highlights the connection between Old Testament prophecies and John the Baptist, the Messiah's messenger. The infancy narratives of Matthew and Luke include details about Jesus' birth and early years. They have differences, but they also agree on several points:

- Jesus' identity is highlighted.
- An angel foretells Jesus' birth.
- Jesus is conceived by the action of the Holy Spirit.
- Jesus is born of the Virgin Mary, as was prophesied.
- Joseph, Jesus' foster father, is his legal father. Joseph is from the house of David; therefore, Jesus is truly a descendent of King David, as promised.
- Jesus is born in Bethlehem, as prophesied in Micah 5:1 (the photo at left marks the site today).

NOTE TAKING

Evaluating People of Importance. When you finish reading this section, go back and count the number of times the text mentions the names listed below. If the book is your own, you may also want to shade each of the names in a different color in your text for comparison.

Person	Number of Times Mentioned
John the Baptist	
Joseph	
Mary	

Reviewing and reflecting on Jesus' birth and early years brings new insight into God's great gift of salvation. The next subsections provide an overview of the infancy narratives of Matthew and Luke.

The Infancy Narratives in Matthew's Gospel (Mt 1–2)

The Gospel of Matthew was written around AD 80–85 for a predominantly Jewish-Christian audience. One of Matthew's major concerns was to show that Jesus fulfilled God's promises to the Jews. His infancy narratives accomplish this aim.

Genealogy (Mt 1:1–17)

Matthew's genealogy connects Jesus' lineage to Abraham, the father of the Jews, and to King David, from whose dynasty the promised Messiah was to come. These links communicate to the reader that Jesus is the fulfillment of Jewish hopes.

Matthew includes some known sinners and Gentiles in his genealogy, such as Rahab (see Jos 2), Ruth (see Ruth), and Bathsheba (see 2 Sm 11). By including sinners in the genealogy, Matthew shows that God can accomplish his plan of salvation even with less-than-perfect people. By including Gentiles, he shows that all of humanity—not just the Chosen People—is important to God. The genealogy emphasizes the marvelous way God accomplishes his plan of salvation.

Jesus' Birth (Mt 1:18–25)

Jesus' birth results from the power of the Holy Spirit working in Mary. Jesus is both fully divine and fully human. Matthew quotes the prophecies (Is 7:14) that speak of the Messiah's arrival:

> "Behold, the virgin shall be with child and
> bear a son,
> and they shall name him Emmanuel,"
> which means "God is with us." (1:23)

Matthew quotes four other Old Testament prophecies in his infancy narrative:

- Matthew 2:6 cites the prophet Micah's prediction (Mi 5:1) that the Messiah would be born in Bethlehem.
- Matthew 2:15 refers to Hosea's prophecy (Hos 11:1) about God's Son being called out of Egypt, as was the Holy Family.
- Matthew 2:18 recalls Rachel's weeping over her exiled descendants (Jer 31:15) as a prophecy of Herod's slaughter of the infants.
- Matthew 2:23 connects the town of Nazareth to prophetic statements in the Old Testament.

Joseph plays a key role in Matthew's genealogy, in part because Joseph is David's descendant. Joseph accepted the angel's message, sent in a dream, that Mary conceived Jesus by God's power. A righteous man, Joseph took Jesus as his own son, making him legally a son of David. Joseph named his child "Jesus," as the angel requested.

Joseph was warned by an angel in a dream to take his family and flee to Egypt. The Holy Family would stay there until the death of Herod.

The Magi's Visit (Mt 2:1–12)

"The *Epiphany* is the manifestation of Jesus as Messiah of Israel, Son of God and Savior of the world" (*CCC*, 528). The Church celebrates the Feast of the **Epiphany** to remember the main events by which Jesus' identity was revealed to the world: the adoration of Jesus by the wise men from the East, together with his Baptism in the Jordan River and the wedding feast at Cana in Galilee. The Magi were visitors from the East who brought gifts of gold, frankincense, and myrrh to the Holy Family. The presence of the Magi represents God's willingness to accept Gentiles among those who worshipped Jesus: "Their coming means that pagans can discover Jesus and worship him as Son of God and Savior of the world only by turning toward the Jews and receiving from them the messianic promise as contained in the Old Testament" (*CCC*, 528).

Epiphany The *manifestation* to the world of the newborn Christ as Messiah, Son of God, and Savior of the world. The Feast of the Epiphany celebrates the adoration of Jesus by the wise men (Magi) from the East, together with his Baptism in the Jordan River and the wedding feast of Cana in Galilee.

The Holy Family's Flight into Egypt (Mt 2:13–18)

Matthew links Jesus to Moses. God asked Moses to lead his people to freedom in the Exodus and to give the Law to the people on Mt. Sinai. Similarly, Jesus liberates people from the slavery of sin and gives the New Covenant or New Law.

Jesus' narrow escape from death at the hands of a jealous and evil leader, Herod, brings to mind Moses's own narrow brush with death as an infant when the pharaoh ordered the death of all Hebrew males (Ex 1:22). The Holy Family's flight into Egypt reveals that the forces of darkness opposed Jesus from the beginning of his life—Jesus, who in himself is the "light of the world" (Jn 8:12; cf. Jn 1:4–5, 9).

The Return to Nazareth (Mt 2:19–23)

"Jesus' departure from Egypt recalls the Exodus and presents him as the definitive liberator of God's people" (*CCC*, 530). As commanded by the angel in a dream, Joseph settled his family in the small town of Nazareth in Galilee.

Matthew's infancy narrative is consistent with Jesus' mission of salvation. The genealogy and the visit of the Magi emphasize that God ultimately wanted to extend salvation to the Gentiles through the Jews. The quotations from Old Testament prophecies and the parallels between Moses and Jesus highlight the link between Jewish hopes for liberation and the Messiah.

The Infancy Narratives in Luke's Gospel (Lk 1–2)

St. Luke was a skilled writer and a careful historian. He also wrote the Acts of the Apostles as "part two" of his Gospel. Luke, who wrote around AD 85, and Matthew, writing in the same decade, probably did not know of each other's efforts. This helps explain why they feature different accounts of the events surrounding Jesus' birth. Luke wrote for an audience of Gentile converts to Christianity.

Announcement of John the Baptist's Birth (Lk 1:5–25)

Luke masterfully interweaves the announcements and births of Jesus and his cousin John the Baptist. In his narrative, however, Luke clearly shows that it is Jesus who is the Messiah, not John. John the Baptist is described as a bridge between the Old Testament and the New Testament. He is a new Elijah, announcing the coming of the promised Messiah (Lk 1:17). He is Jesus' immediate forerunner, the one to prepare the way.

Announcement of Jesus' Birth (Lk 1:26–38)

Six months after announcing the birth of John the Baptist, the angel Gabriel appears to Mary, who is engaged to Joseph. The angel greets Mary with the words "Hail, favored one! The Lord is with you" (Lk 1:28). The angel tells Mary she will conceive Jesus by the power of the Holy Spirit. With great humility and faith, Mary believes the angel and says, "Behold, I am the handmaid of the Lord. May it be done to me according to your word" (Lk 1:38). Mary, a humble daughter of Israel, says yes to God's plan to bring Christ into the world.

Mary cooperated with God's plan, even knowing that her yes might bring her ridicule and condemnation. God singled out Mary among women and gave her the graces necessary to cooperate with his plan. Mary's mother conceived her without Original Sin, a miracle called the **Immaculate Conception**. By his special and singular divine intervention, God applied to Mary the merits that Jesus would earn on the Cross from the moment of her conception so that she could be truly free to say yes to God. Being preserved from sin was the condition for her freedom; and her freedom was the condition for her absolute and entire response of yes to God. Although humans still suffer from the effects of Original Sin,

Immaculate Conception "The dogma proclaimed in Christian Tradition and defined in 1854, that from the first moment of her conception, Mary—by the singular grace of God and by virtue of the merits of Jesus Christ—was preserved immune from original sin" (*CCC*, Glossary).

God likewise gives each person the grace he or she needs to flourish in life despite trials. As it was with Mary, it is your choice whether or not you cooperate with God's plan.

Mary's Visit to Elizabeth (Lk 1:39–56)

Mary's compassionate concern for her aged relative prompts her to visit Elizabeth. After Mary greets Elizabeth, Elizabeth joyfully acknowledges that Mary is indeed the Mother of God:

> Most blessed are you among women, and blessed is the fruit of your womb. And how does this happen to me, that the mother of my Lord should come to me? (Lk 1:42–43)

Mary's response to Elizabeth is the famous *canticle* (little song) called the **Magnificat** (see page 114). Mary's words echo those of the prophet Samuel's mother, Hannah, who recited similar words after Samuel's miraculous birth (see 1 Sm 2:1–10). In humility, Mary praises God as the source of blessedness. She praises his mercy for reversing normal human expectations, for raising up the lowly, and for overthrowing proud and powerful people:

> The hungry he has filled with good things;
> the rich he has sent away empty. (Lk 1:53)

John the Baptist's Birth (Lk 1:57–80)

Zechariah loses his ability to speak because he does not believe the angel who came to announce John's birth. When Zechariah receives his speech back

Mary, free from the stain of sin, is blessed among women.

at John's birth, the Holy Spirit inspires him to sing God's praises in a prayer known as the *Benedictus* (Latin for "blessing," the first word in the prayer). In it, Zechariah praises God for remembering the promises he made to David to save the Jews. In the last part of the prayer, Zechariah speaks to his newborn son:

> And you, child, will be called prophet of the
> Most High,
> for you will go before the Lord to prepare
> his ways,
> to give his people knowledge of salvation
> through the forgiveness of their sins. (Lk 1:76–77)

Magnificat Named for its first word in Latin, the Blessed Virgin Mary's song of praise to the Lord found in Luke's Gospel. It is also known as the Canticle of Mary.

Jesus' Birth (Lk 2:1–20)

Because Bethlehem was the birthplace of his ancestor David, Joseph takes the pregnant Mary there to enroll in a census. Mary gives birth to Jesus in a manger because there are no suitable lodgings.

The angel announces to shepherds the coming of the Savior who will be both Messiah and Lord. He will bring "peace to those on whom his favor rests" (Lk 2:14). The first people to visit Jesus are shepherds.

A major theme in Luke's Gospel is that Jesus comes to preach to the lowly and outcast. The shepherds are the first to broadcast the news of salvation to the Jews. Later in Luke's Gospel, Jesus invites humble fishermen and other outsiders to be his disciples and spread his Good News.

When Mary hears all the good things being said about her Son, she keeps them in her heart, reflecting on their meaning (see Lk 2:19). Her heartfelt reflection on God's Word is a model for all who want to learn how to pray.

Jesus' Circumcision and Presentation in the Temple (Lk 2:21–38)

Jesus' circumcision on the eighth day after his birth signifies his incorporation into the Jewish people. It prefigures Jesus' lifelong submission to the Law and his willingness to worship in the faith of his ancestors.

After forty days, Mary and Joseph take the infant Jesus to the Temple in Jerusalem for the rite of purification as specified by the Mosaic Law (see Lv 12). His parents offer two turtledoves, or young pigeons, for a sacrifice rather than the more expensive year-old lamb; this shows that they most likely were poor.

At the Temple, the prophets Simeon and Anna recognize Jesus as the long-expected Messiah, the firstborn Son who belongs to the Lord. They bless God for being allowed to see him. They also predict the perfect sacrifice that the adult Jesus will endure for the salvation of humanity, and say to Mary, "and you yourself a sword will pierce" (Lk 2:35).

Finding Jesus in the Temple (Lk 2:41–52)

When Jesus is twelve years old, he goes to the Temple in Jerusalem with his parents for the Passover feast. When he is found missing from the caravan on the way home, his distraught parents search for him. They eventually find Jesus astounding the teachers in the Temple by his brilliant responses to their questions.

When Mary asks why he remained in the city, Jesus replies, "Did you not know that I must be in my Father's house?" (Lk 2:49). Mary and Joseph do not fully understand the meaning of Jesus' words, but again Mary keeps his words in her heart, prayerfully reflecting on their significance (see Lk 2:51c).

The finding of Jesus in the Temple

Luke ends his infancy narrative by reporting that Jesus returned with Mary and Joseph to Nazareth, where he lived in obedience to them (see Lk 2:51). The Holy Family provides people today with an example of holiness that should be emulated. Jesus' obedience contrasts with Adam's disobedience to God: "For just as through the disobedience of one person the many were made sinners, so through the obedience of one the many will be made righteous" (Rom 5:19). Jesus' life as an ordinary Jew of his time reveals the mystery that God became flesh in order to enter into solidarity with humans.

Some of the events in Luke's infancy narratives connect directly with Jesus' mission of salvation. Jesus' ministry would be focused on the lowly and poor, the Gentiles, and other outcasts. Jesus was born in a very humble stable and was welcomed by shepherds. As he grew up from infancy, to childhood, to adulthood as a true Jew who would not do away with the Law, Jesus fulfilled God's covenant with the people of Israel perfectly (see Lk 16:17), and he pointed out how, beginning with Moses and all the prophets, the entire Old Testament spoke of him (see Lk 24:27, 44–47). But he would take the Law a step further when he redeemed people from their sins and introduced the New Covenant (cf. Lk 22:20). It was through his obedience, even in his hidden life, that he atoned for our disobedience.

In summary, the birth and early life of Jesus teach that Jesus of Nazareth, born of Mary in Bethlehem at the time of Caesar Augustus and King Herod, is the eternal Son of God. The eternal Son of God became a man and lived among human beings prior to his Crucifixion and Resurrection. Called by God the Father and inspired by the grace of the Holy Spirit, the Church echoes St. Peter's confession that Jesus is the "Son of the living God" (Mt 16:16).

SECTION ASSESSMENT

NOTE TAKING

Use the tally you kept to complete the following question.

1. How many times are John the Baptist, Joseph, and Mary each mentioned in this section? Write a sentence for each that explains his or her significance in the early life of Jesus.

VOCABULARY

2. What does the *Epiphany* celebrate?
3. Does the term *Immaculate Conception* describe Mary's conception or Jesus'? Explain.
4. Who sang the Magnificat?

COMPREHENSION

5. Give the approximate dates for the writing of the Gospels of Matthew and Luke.
6. How does Mark's Gospel begin?
7. How did Matthew suggest that God could still accomplish his plan of salvation with less-than-perfect people?
8. Explain the relationship between the Magi and the Gentiles.
9. How does Matthew's Gospel link Jesus to Moses?
10. What is the *Benedictus*, and why did Zechariah sing it?
11. How can a reader of the Gospel of Luke tell that Mary and Joseph were poor?

CRITICAL ANALYSIS

12. Which one of the messianic prophecies quoted in Matthew do you think best describes Jesus? Why?

SECTION 2

The Incarnation in John's Prologue

MAIN IDEA

John's Gospel begins by stating that the Word of God participated in creation and was born into the world to destroy evil and save his people.

Matthew and Luke begin their Gospels with the birth of Christ, and Mark, with his Baptism. The Gospel of John, on the other hand, opens at the beginning of creation, well before the life of Christ on earth. The Gospel of John retells the Genesis accounts of creation by showing that creation came about through the Word of God:

> All things came to be through him,
> and without him nothing came to be.
> What came to be through him was life
> and this life was the light of the human race. (Jn 1:3–4)

The Incarnation

John's Gospel introduces the foundational teaching on the **dogma** of the Incarnation: the earth-shaking truth that the very Word of God became human in the Divine Person of Jesus Christ. John emphasizes that at the appointed time, the only Son of the Father, the eternal Word, assumed human nature—both body (flesh) and soul—and became a man in order to accomplish human salvation.

The source of the dogma of the Incarnation is Divine Revelation. You can believe it to be true because God has revealed it himself:

> In the beginning was the Word,
> and the Word was with God,
> and the Word was God.
> He was in the beginning with God. . . .

dogma A revealed teaching or set of revealed teachings of Christ proclaimed by the fullest extent of the exercise of the authority of the Church's Magisterium. The faithful are obliged to believe the truths or dogmas contained in Divine Revelation and defined by the Magisterium.

NOTE TAKING

Identifying Descriptors. Create a block letter design for ***WORD*** as shown to the right. As you read the text, note other words or phrases that describe the Word of God both from the section and from Scripture.

And the Word became flesh
and made his dwelling among us,
and we saw his glory,
the glory as of the Father's only Son,
full of grace and truth. (Jn 1:1–2, 14)

The Incarnation means that Jesus Christ, who is the Son of God and the Second Person of the Blessed Trinity, is both truly God and truly human. "He is truly the Son of God who, without ceasing to be God and Lord, became a man and our brother" (*CCC*, 469).

The Significance of the Incarnation

The masterful prologue to John's Gospel includes many marvelous truths of faith. The *Catechism of the Catholic Church* explains more fully what John's Gospel reveals about why God became human—why the Word became flesh:

- *To save you by reconciling you with God,* "who loved us and sent his Son to be the expiation for our sins" (*CCC*, 457, quoting 1 Jn 4:10). Jesus came to be the Savior who takes away the sins of the world.
- *So that you might know God's love* (see *CCC*, 458). In one of the most famous verses in the entire Bible, John proclaims: "For God so loved the world that he gave his only Son, so that everyone who believes in him might not perish but might have eternal life" (Jn 3:16). This verse has been called the "Gospel in miniature" because it proclaims that God is a God of love. God showed his love by sending his Son to reconcile people with him and to be an expiation for the sins of the world, thus saving humanity. Those who believe in him will not perish; instead, he offers his people eternal life. Indeed this is Good News—truly great news.
- *To be your model of holiness* (see *CCC*, 459). By his taking on flesh, Jesus, the Second Divine Person of the Blessed Trinity, gave you the opportunity to imitate him and become more like him. Jesus said, "I am the way and the truth and the life. No one comes to the Father except through me" (Jn 14:6). By his Life, Death, and Resurrection, Jesus has shown you the deepest meaning of love. He instructs you to imitate him.
- *To make you a partaker of the divine nature.* Christ became human to adopt you into the divine family by the power of the Holy Spirit. St. Athanasius expressed it this way: "For the Son of God became man so that we might become God" (*On the Incarnation*, 54, 3). You are not to become God himself, but you are to share in God's nature. Through his divine power, the Son of God has conferred on humans precious promises and gifts "so that through them you may come to share in the divine nature, after escaping from the corruption that is in the world because of evil desire" (2 Pt 1:4).

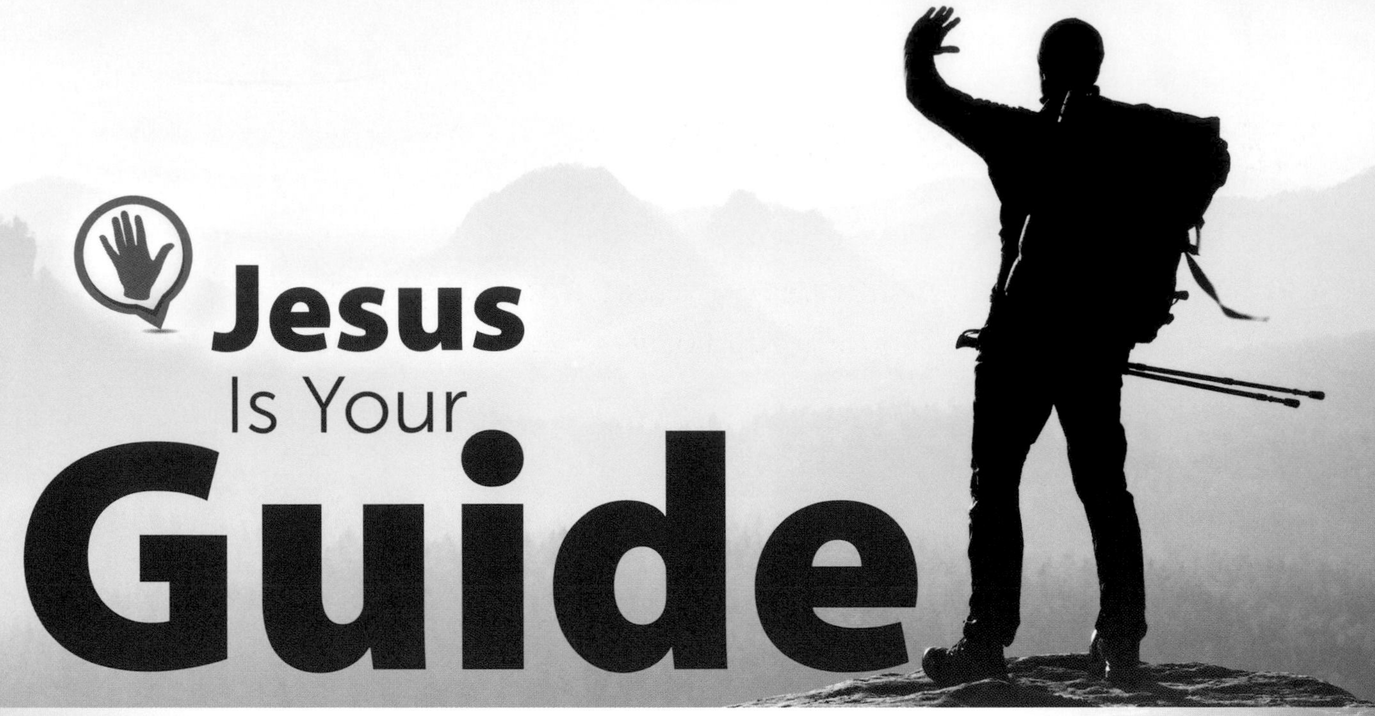

Jesus Is Your Guide

It is said that when Michelangelo was working in his studio one day, a young boy entered the studio and saw the famous sculptor hammering away at a large, shapeless block of granite. The boy asked what he was doing. Michelangelo picked up the child, stood him on his workbench, and said, "Can't you see? There is an angel hidden in this rock. I am chipping away all the pieces that are not the angel to set it free."

Likewise, God sees hidden beauty in each person. He sent his Son Jesus Christ to free you, to unleash your hidden possibilities. The Lord's chisel is his Gospel that frees you and calls you to be what he created you to be.

John 6 is known as the "Bread of Life Discourse." Read John 6, then take the following personal inventory to help you explore how much you look to the Lord as the source of your life. Write down whether each statement is very true, somewhat true, or not very true in your life.

- ***Possessions*** I enjoy the good things that come my way, but I know that they can never be the true source of my happiness.
- ***Scripture*** I derive spiritual nourishment from the scriptural Word of God, which I read regularly.
- ***Eucharist*** I attend Mass every Sunday and holy day of obligation and frequently receive Holy Communion.
- ***Prayer*** I ask the Lord for help when I need it, talking to him as my best friend.
- ***Gratitude*** I take time to thank the Lord for the life he has given me, for my family, friends, health, education, and talents.
- ***Bread for Others*** Just as the Lord is bread for me, I try to be a source of life for others. For example, I try to listen to their needs and respond to them.

ASSIGNMENT

Reflect on one of these statements. Which needs most improvement in your life? Write out a specific plan of action for how you can begin to improve over the next two weeks. Each night, write down one or two sentences about your progress.

SECTION ASSESSMENT

NOTE TAKING

Use the notes you created to help you complete the following question.

1. Write three words or phrases that describe the Person of the Word of God in the Gospel of John.

COMPREHENSION

2. At what point in time does the narrative of John's Gospel begin?
3. How did the Divine Word participate in creation?
4. How is Jesus fully divine and fully human?
5. What are two reasons that the Word of God became flesh?

CRITICAL ANALYSIS

6. How does John 3:16 explain why God gave his only Son?
7. How do you understand St. Athanasius's quotation, "For the Son of God became man so that we might become God"?

REFLECTION

8. Which aspects of Jesus' life are the easiest to imitate? Which are the most difficult?

SECTION 3

Jesus' Early Public Life

MAIN IDEA

Jesus' Baptism and his temptation in the desert reveal the nature of his sacrificial mission.

Modern biographies seem to treat every imaginable aspect of a person's life story. The Gospels are not like that. For example, the Gospels do not provide Jesus' physical description. Furthermore, the Gospels reveal little about Jesus' hidden life—that is, the years from his birth and early childhood until he entered the public scene at his Baptism—except for one incident when Jesus was twelve years old (see Lk 2:41–52). The Gospels focus on Jesus' three years of public ministry that began when he was around thirty years of age.

Every aspect of Christ's earthly life—his words and deeds, silences and sufferings, way of being and speaking, fidelity and obedience—is a Revelation of the Father. Even the least particulars of the mysteries of Jesus' life manifest God's love among us. As God the Father instructed Peter, James, and John on the mountain at the time of Jesus' Transfiguration, "This is my chosen Son; listen to him" (Lk 9:35). Or, as Jesus told Philip at the Last Supper, "Whoever has seen me has seen the Father" (Jn 14:9b). Because the eternal Son of God became a human being so that you might come to know the depth of God's love for you, *everything* about Christ's life has profound meaning. From the smallest detail to the most awe-inspiring miracles, the Gospels reveal God's great love for you in his Son, Jesus Christ.

This mystery of Christ's redemptive love and suffering is at work throughout his life (see *CCC*, 517):

- *He enriches the world by his poverty.* By emptying himself of his infinite riches, power, and glory in order to become a humble and poor human being, Christ enriches us. He lived his life of

NOTE TAKING

Identifying Key Information. From the material in this section, list three ways Jesus' Baptism and temptation foreshadow his suffering and Death on the Cross.

1. *Jesus perfectly submitted to the will of his Father at both his Baptism and his Crucifixion.*
2.
3.

self-emptying solidarity with us not for himself but *for humanity.*

- *He atones for disobedience through his obedience.* By his faithful obedience to the Father, Jesus, called the "Second Adam," is able to atone for the disobedience of the first Adam. He is able to fix people's relationship with God by following the will of the Father, even to the point of Death on a Cross (cf. Phil 2:5–8).
- *He purifies by his Word.* In his preaching, he purifies the human conscience. His Word serves as a mirror that leads people to examine themselves deeply and challenges all to follow him faithfully.
- *He bears our infirmities and diseases.* In his healings and exorcisms, by which "he took away our infirmities and bore our diseases" (Mt 8:17), he offered signs of his victory over sin, death, suffering, and the devil, who is "the ruler of this world" (Jn 12:31). He showed that the Kingdom of God was inaugurated in his very Person.
- *He offers us **justification**.* The Word became flesh to save the world by reconciling people with God. Through his Cross and Resurrection, he justified the world. Through faith in Christ and the Sacrament of Baptism, you receive a share in the justice and holiness of God. In Baptism, you are cleansed of your Original Sin and all personal sins. You become a member of Christ's Body, the Church. Justification is accomplished through the Death and Resurrection of Christ. By his Death, you are liberated from your sins. By his Resurrection, new life is open to you. "This new life is above all justification that reinstates us in God's grace" (*CCC*, 654).

Christ's whole life, therefore, is a mystery of redemption (see *CCC*, 517). The *Catechism of the Catholic Church* reminds us that all Christ's words, deeds, and sufferings had one purpose: to restore humanity from the separation caused by sin to the original closeness and intimacy God desired to share with us (see *CCC*, 518).

justification God's gracious action freeing a person from sin through faith in Jesus Christ and the Sacrament of Baptism. Justification not only frees a person from sin, but also brings sanctification and deep interior renewal.

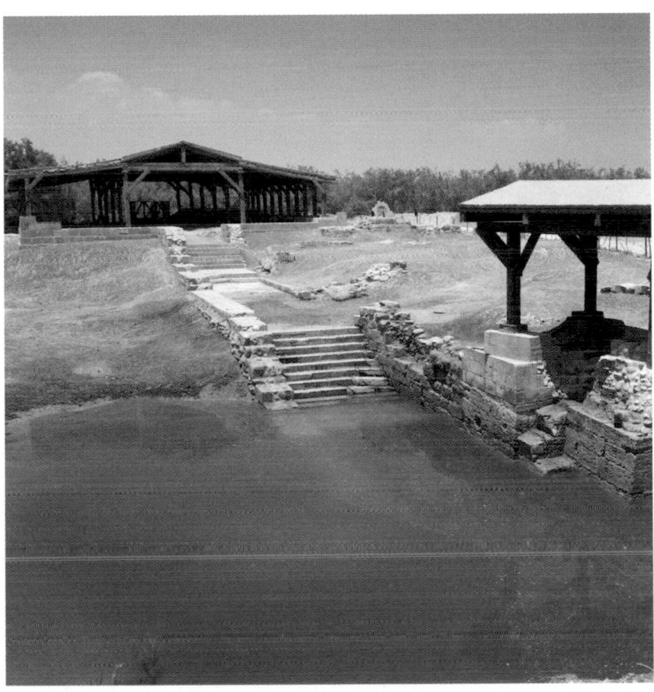

The River Jordan at the place of Jesus' Baptism.

Jesus' Baptism (Mt 3:1–17, Mk 1:2–11, Lk 3:1–22, Jn 1:19–34)

Jesus' Baptism is linked to the figure of John the Baptist. Jesus himself heard of John's preaching and traveled from Galilee to the Judean wilderness to hear John for himself and to be baptized. John proclaimed a Baptism of repentance for the forgiveness of sins. His Baptism was for sinners who, repenting of their sins, would be baptized and try to live more faithfully to God. By submitting to John's Baptism,

Jesus—though perfect and sinless—identified himself with sinners (that is, the entire human race). Jesus displays his humility through his Baptism by allowing himself to be numbered among sinners. He places himself in solidarity with sinners, "in the likeness of sinful flesh" (Rom 8:3). From the beginning of his mission of preaching and healing, the Lord accepted the role of God's Suffering Servant.

While the Gospel accounts are not identical, all four Gospels mention the following phenomena at Jesus' Baptism:

- *The sky opens.* At his Baptism, "'the heavens were opened'—the heavens that Adam's sin had closed—and the waters were sanctified by the descent of Jesus and the Spirit, a prelude to the new creation" (*CCC*, 536, quoting Mt 3:16). The opening of the heavens reveals that it is God himself who has come to meet his people. Jesus was sent to make us partakers of the divine nature.

- *A dove descends from the sky.* The dove represents the Holy Spirit. "The Spirit whom Jesus possessed in fullness from his conception comes to 'rest on him.' Jesus will be the source of the Spirit for all [human beings]" (*CCC*, 536, quoting Jn 1:32–33). Humanity will receive the Holy Spirit when Jesus sends it upon the Church as part of his promise to remain with humanity forever (see Mt 28:20).

- *A voice proclaims, "You are my beloved Son; with you I am well pleased"* (Mk 1:11). "The Father's voice responds to the Son's acceptance of his mission, proclaiming his entire delight in his Son" (*CCC*, 536).

Two Old Testament prophecies were fulfilled in the Baptism of Jesus. Psalm 2 promised the coming of the anointed king, the Messiah (see pages 84–85); and the prophet Isaiah foretold the Servant who would suffer on behalf of the human race:

> I will proclaim the decree of the LORD,
> he said to me, "You are my son;
> today I have begotten you." (Ps 2:7)

> Here is my servant whom I uphold,
> my chosen one with whom I am pleased.
> Upon him I have put my spirit;
> he shall bring forth justice to the nations.
> (Is 42:1)

> Yet it was our pain that he bore,
> our sufferings he endured. . . .
> But he was pierced for our sins,
> crushed for our iniquity.
> He bore the punishment that makes us whole,
> by his wounds we were healed. (Is 53:4a–5)

The Baptism of Jesus reveals important theological truths:

- It shows Jesus' perfect submission to his Father's will.
- It illustrates Jesus' acceptance of his role as Suffering Servant.
- It foreshadows Jesus' Death for the remission of sins.
- It serves as a model for the Sacrament of Baptism.

Through the Sacrament of Baptism, you are sacramentally united with Christ. You share in Christ's humility as you go down in the water, repenting of your sins. You then rise with Christ to become an adopted child of God the Father.

The Devil's Temptation of Jesus (Mt 4:1–11, Mk 1:12–13, Lk 4:1–13)

The synoptic Gospels all report that Jesus retreated to the Judean wilderness after his Baptism, prior to embarking on his public ministry. As Mark's Gospel states, "At once the Spirit drove him out into the desert, and he remained in the desert for forty days, tempted by Satan. He was among wild beasts, and the angels ministered to him" (Mk 1:12–13). Matthew and Luke fill in the details of Mark's brief statement by explaining that Satan tempted Jesus three times.

1 Satan first tempted Jesus to turn stones into loaves of bread. Jesus' hunger from fasting would not turn him away from doing God's will. He said,

> One does not live by bread alone,
> but by every word that comes forth from the mouth
> of God. (Mt 4:4)

2 Next, Satan challenged Jesus to throw himself down from the Temple's pinnacle. The devil wanted Jesus to reveal his power. Jesus' faithful answer to the devil was "You shall not put the Lord, your God, to the test" (Mt 4:7).

3 The third temptation was about power and wealth. The devil offered Jesus the kingdoms of the world if he would worship him, but Jesus was committed to being faithful to God at all times. Jesus rebuked Satan by saying,

> The Lord, your God, shall you worship
> and him alone shall you serve. (Mt 4:10)

Jesus' temptations in the desert prefigured certain temptations he would face in his public ministry. In preaching the Gospel, however, his heart was undivided. He put his Father's will above everything as he lived a life of poverty and rejected any effort to make him a worldly king.

You can turn to Jesus when you are tempted because he can identify with you. Jesus, the Suffering Servant, has conquered Satan, the one who tempts you to reject your own salvation. The Letter to the Hebrews reminds you:

> For we do not have a high priest who is unable to sympathize with our weaknesses, but one who has similarly been tested in every way, yet without sin. So let us confidently approach the throne of grace to receive mercy and to find grace for timely help. (Heb 4:15–16)

Notice that the temptations took place *after* Jesus' Baptism. This means that Jesus identified himself with fallen humanity, with all who bear the sin of Adam. In the desert, the devil comes to tempt Jesus as he once tempted Adam in the garden. Jesus, rather than trusting the devil and choosing himself over his Father, loves his Father and remains faithful to his Father to the very end. "Jesus is the new Adam who remained faithful just where the first Adam had given in to temptation" (*CCC*, 539).

Jesus resisted the political and self-serving roles suggested by the devil and revealed himself as God's Servant, entirely obedient to the Father's will. Jesus' decisive victory over Satan in the desert foreshadowed the ultimate victory he would win through his Passion, Death, and Resurrection. Jesus faced these temptations and set his ministry on the path of gentle, compassionate service to others.

Plan for Avoiding Temptation

Think about some of the temptations you and your peers face today. These may be temptations to instant gratification, to power, or to worshipping something other than God (e.g., fame, money, prestige). Read and practice the following steps for avoiding temptation. Answer each question. Then add two additional steps of your own. Include a Gospel example with each new step.

1. *Stay true to your mission*. Jesus stayed true to his mission. He offered his life for every human being. He taught that God cares about everything (see Mt 10:29–31) and does not want a single person to be lost (see Mt 18:10–14).

    - How do you treat others when you meet them—more as strangers or as brothers and sisters in Christ?

2. *Always keep in mind what is important*. Jesus came to do God's will. Nothing would deter him (see Lk 9:62 and Mt 6:19–24).

    - How are your life goals aligned with serving and loving God the Father? What can you imagine derailing this goal? How can you avoid any roadblocks to reaching your goal?

SECTION ASSESSMENT

NOTE TAKING

Use the list you made to help you answer the following question.

1. How do Jesus' Baptism and temptations foreshadow his ultimate conquest of Satan on the Cross?

COMPREHENSION

2. Why did Jesus search out John the Baptist?
3. How did Jesus' Baptism show his humility?
4. What events do all four Gospels include in their accounts of Jesus' Baptism?
5. How did Jesus' Baptism connect to two Old Testament prophecies?
6. What are three theological truths revealed by Jesus' Baptism?

CRITICAL ANALYSIS

7. Draw a connection between two of the temptations Jesus faced and the challenges of his earthly ministry.

REFLECTION

8. What is your reaction to the statement in the Letter to the Hebrews that Jesus' temptations make it easier for you to ask Jesus for help?

Section Summaries

Focus Question

How did Christ's birth and early years reveal the presence of God?
Complete one of the following:

Name a person you know at each of these levels—high school, college, young professional, and successful adult—who models Jesus' steadfast commitment to following God's will. What do these people share in common?

As part of salvation history, God the Son became man at a particular time and place in history chosen by God. What unique opportunities to come to know Christ have been given to you at this time and place in history?

Develop a slogan to encourage people not to give in to temptation. Write a paragraph explaining why your slogan is effective.

INTRODUCTION (PAGES 81–87)

Jesus Christ: Son of God, Son of Mary

Jesus' name and other titles reveal different aspects of his identity as fully divine and fully human. The title "Christ" communicates that people believed him to be the anointed one spoken of in the Old Testament. Jesus used the description "Messiah" (Christ) carefully, though, because many people believed that the Messiah would be a military leader rather than the Suffering Servant. The title "Son of God," when connected with Jesus, differs from earlier understandings of the term and conveyed his *unique* and *eternal* relationship with the Father. The title "Lord" also conveys a realization that Jesus was divine. The title "Son of Mary" stresses that Jesus was truly human and highlights Mary's special role in God's plan for your salvation.

Research the meaning of *Messiah* from the Jewish perspective. How does this understanding differ from the Christian definition of the term?

SECTION 1 (PAGES 88–95)

Jesus' Birth and Early Years

The Gospel accounts indicate that Jesus' mission was evident from his earliest years. Although Mark does not tell of Jesus' birth, he does make the connection between one of Isaiah's prophecies and John the Baptist's preparation for Jesus' birth. Matthew's audience consisted of Jews who were Christian disciples, so he emphasized how God's promises to the Jews foreshadowed the life of Jesus. For example, he compared the Exodus of the Chosen People from Egypt with the Holy Family's first traveling to and then emigrating from Egypt. Luke's Gospel also tells of Mary's visit to Elizabeth, Jesus' birth in a stable, and the angels announcing the Good News to shepherds.

Read 1 Kings 11:40 and Jeremiah 26:21. How do these passages relate to the Holy Family's flight to Egypt?

SECTION 2 (PAGES 96–99)

The Incarnation in John's Prologue

The dogma of the Incarnation is that the Word of God—who is the eternal Son, the Second Divine Person of the Blessed Trinity—became human in the Person of Jesus Christ. Jesus is fully human and fully divine. The Gospel of John begins by describing how the eternal Word of God, who participated in creation, was sent into the world by the Father to become one with humanity and reveal the Father's love and glory. The eternal Son was entrusted with the task of destroying the power of the devil and reconciling the world with the Father. The purpose of the Incarnation was to reconcile you with God, reveal God's love, model human holiness, and enable you to partake in God's divine nature.

Imagine you are explaining the Incarnation to a third-grade religious education class. How would you construct a lesson to help them better understand the meaning of the term *Incarnation*?

SECTION 3 (PAGES 100–105)

Jesus' Early Public Life

Every aspect of Christ's earthly life is a Revelation of the Father. Because Jesus became a human being to do his Father's will, *everything* about Christ's life has profound meaning and reveals God's great love for you. Jesus' Baptism reveals his solidarity with sinners and his faithfulness to his Father's will. It also foreshadows his Death for the remission of sins and serves as a model for Christian Baptism. After his Baptism, Jesus was tempted by the devil in the desert. Jesus, as the second Adam, remained faithful to the Father just where the first Adam had given in to temptation, thereby revealing himself as God's Servant, obedient to the Father. Having faced temptations, Jesus empathizes with you and invites you to call upon him when you face temptations.

Jesus was sinless and perfect (see Heb 4:15, 1 Pt 1:18–19). He did not need to be baptized to remove Original Sin. Why do you think he chose to be baptized?

Chapter Assignments

Choose and complete at least one of the following three assignments to assess your understanding of the material in this chapter.

1. An Autobiography of St. John the Baptist

Using all four Gospel accounts of John the Baptist and the biblical commentaries that accompany them, write a biographical sketch about his life. Your narrative should have an introduction, five body paragraphs, and a conclusion. Quote plenty of Gospel passages that refer to John. Also quote information from biblical commentaries. Fully and properly cite each reference. Your body paragraphs should focus on the following events in the life of St. John the Baptist:

Announcement of the Birth of John the Baptist

- Luke 1:5–25

Birth of John the Baptist

- Luke 1:57–80

Preaching of John the Baptist Near the Time of Jesus' Baptism

- Matthew 3:1–17
- Mark 1:1–8
- John 1:19–34

Jesus' Teaching about John the Baptist

- Matthew 11:1–19

Death of John the Baptist

- Matthew 14:3–12
- Mark 6:17–29

2. Survey of the Basilica of the National Shrine of the Immaculate Conception

Dedicated to Mary, the Mother of God, under her title "The Immaculate Conception," the Basilica of the National Shrine of the Immaculate Conception in Washington, DC, is patterned after the great cathedrals of the world. It is a centerpiece of the Catholic Church in America.

Research and view information on the Basilica of the National Shrine of the Immaculate Conception. Then do all of the following:

- Write a one-page history of the basilica.
- Create a floor plan of either the Upper Church or the Lower Crypt Church, listing all of the separate chapels and oratories.
- Choose three of the chapels or oratories from your map. Write a two-paragraph description of each, including its name, history, and religious meaning.

3. Exploring Early Events in the Life of Christ through Church Art

Catholic churches are often dedicated to a particular aspect of the life of Christ or to Mary or a saint. Research the history of two churches in your diocese associated with these names or topics:

- St. John the Baptist
- Immaculate Conception
- Annunciation
- Nativity
- Incarnation

Write a one-page report on each church. Include the following: (1) the meaning of the church's title; (2) the founding and history of the church; (3) the mission of the parish today; and (4) ways the parish commemorates its name (e.g., art, architecture, mission, feast day celebration). If possible, visit the church. Include photos to support your written work. If your diocese does not have two churches that fit these profiles, you may complete the assignment with churches outside your diocese.

Faithful Disciple

St. John the Baptist

St. John the Baptist, Jesus' forerunner and relative, lived an *ascetic* life (one of simple living and few pleasures) and preached in the region surrounding the Jordan River that Israel's judgment was at hand. He presented the basic message of earlier Jewish prophets, adding the idea of a Baptism for the repentance of sins. This Baptism symbolized the washing away of their sins. When Jesus arrived at the banks of the river for Baptism, John humbled himself and acknowledged Jesus as the Messiah. Jesus counted John as the last and among the greatest of the prophets. Though most of John's followers became disciples of Jesus, some broke away on their own. Disciples of John are cited in Acts of the Apostles 19:1–4.

What were the origins of John's ministry? At the time of Christ there were several branches of Judaism in addition to the Sadducees and the Pharisees, two branches mentioned often in the Gospels. The Dead Sea Scrolls, for example, helped to shed light on an apocalyptic group known as the Essenes, who believed that God would usher in his Kingdom through a dramatic, even catastrophic, event. The Essenes withdrew to live in the Qumran area near the northwest shore of the Dead Sea. As celibates who did not marry, they shared goods in common and tried to be ritually pure, washing frequently throughout the day. It is possible that John the Baptist was part of the Essene community or another similar Jewish group.

St. John the Baptist

The Jordan River

It is certain that John the Baptist understood his role in relationship to Christ. When he saw Jesus coming toward him at the river, John said,

> Behold, the Lamb of God, who takes away the sin of the world. He is the one of whom I said, "A man is coming after me who ranks ahead of me because he existed before me." I did not know him, but the reason why I came baptizing with water was that he might be made known to Israel. (Jn 1:29b–31)

John had already told his disciples, "One mightier than I is coming after me. I am not worthy to stoop and loosen the thongs of his sandals" (Mk 1:7). The respect between John and Jesus was mutual. Jesus said of him, "Among those born of women there has been none greater than John the Baptist" (Mt 11:11).

Herod Antipas had John arrested and imprisoned at Machaerus fortress (a fort originally built by Hasmonean king Alexander Jannaeus on the Dead Sea a century earlier) after John criticized Herod's adulterous marriage. Matthew and Mark tell us that John was beheaded at the request of the daughter of Herodias, Herod's wife.

In her Advent readings, the Church highlights the prophetic readings from the Old Testament and the New Testament passages of John the Baptist. Catholics remember the expectant waiting of the Chosen People for the Messiah and look themselves to the Second Coming of Christ.

The Feast of St. John the Baptist is June 24. The feast of his beheading is August 29. St. John the Baptist is the patron saint of Baptism, converts, and innkeepers.

Reading Comprehension

1. What does it mean to say that St. John the Baptist led an ascetic life?
2. What was distinct about the Jewish religious group the Essenes?
3. How is it clear that St. John the Baptist understood his role in relationship to Christ?

Writing Task

- Read a profile of the Old Testament prophet Elijah. How is his role similar to that of St. John the Baptist? Read 2 Kings 1:8 for evidence of similarity in the clothing of the two prophets.

Explaining the Faith

Why is Jesus' birth celebrated on December 25?

Neither of the infancy narratives in the Gospels of Matthew or Luke names the day or year of Jesus' birth. There is no way to be exactly sure of the date on which he was born. However, we do know that by AD 336, the Church officially marked the birth of Christ on December 25. It may have been celebrated on that date for years before. The tradition certainly spread after 336 throughout the Church and the world.

How was December 25 established as the date of Christ's birthday? One reason is that December 25 is near the winter solstice. The Romans observed a solstice holiday called Saturnalia from December 17 to 23. A birth date of December 25 offered a good chance to counter this pagan festival with an important religious celebration.

Also, by the fourth century, March 25 had already been established as the date of the Annunciation, the conception of Jesus. Celebrating the birth of Jesus nine months later followed logically.

Further Research

- Read Pope Francis's Christmas Midnight Mass homily from a recent year (see the Vatican website, www.vatican.va). Report on its message about the historical significance of Christ's birth.

Prayer

The Magnificat

My soul proclaims the greatness of the Lord;
    my spirit rejoices in God my savior.
For he has looked upon his handmaid's lowliness;
    behold, from now on will all ages call me blessed.
The Mighty One has done great things for me,
    and holy is his name.
His mercy is from age to age
    to those who fear him.
He has shown might with his arm,
    dispersed the arrogant of mind and heart.
He has thrown down the rulers from their thrones
    but lifted up the lowly.
The hungry he has filled with good things;
    the rich he has sent away empty.
He has helped Israel his servant,
    remembering his mercy,
according to his promise to our fathers,
    to Abraham and to his descendants forever.
—Luke 1:46–55

CHAPTER REVIEW

THE MESSAGE AND MINISTRY OF JESUS CHRIST

Living Differently

Maryknoll Lay Missioners are single and married adults who serve the poor of the world in Africa, Asia, and South America for a period of three-and-a-half years. The missioners live and work side by side with the people they serve, with a special focus on education and healthcare ministries.

Their core mission statement proclaims that missioners are "nourished by God's revelation in the world, . . . inspired by the rich tradition of Catholic social teaching, and . . . grounded in the history and spirit of our Maryknoll mission family." The life of Jesus inspires the missioners to work to create a more just and compassionate world. The missioners tell many different stories. Consider these two examples:

- Melissa and Peter Altman are a married couple working to teach children from a parish center in a small rural village, La India, in El Salvador. "Ours is the only game in town," the Altmans explain, "so if the children are not with us, they are on the streets." Recently, in an art workshop they sponsored, they discovered a timid eleven-year-old boy who had never painted before. Given the chance, he showed a great gift for painting.
- Kim Fischer and her family are ministering in Brazil. She recently gave birth to a daughter while living in mission. She found great support from the refugee women she worked with; they watched her son while she was in the hospital. She calls children a "common denominator" in her ministry. With the other mothers, "we pass along clothes, diapers, and advice. We form new networks of women helping women."

Maryknoll Lay Missioners were founded in 1975 by the efforts of the Maryknoll priests, nuns, and brothers. Since that time, more than seven hundred lay Catholics from the United States have served in missions in some of the world's poorest communities. The minimum age to be a Maryknoll missioner is twenty-two. Search out more information on being a Maryknoll missioner on their website (www.mklm.org) under the label "Become a Missioner."

FOCUS QUESTION

How do **JESUS' MESSAGE** and **MINISTRY** influence the way you **LIVE YOUR LIFE**?

Chapter Overview

INTRODUCTION

Jesus Begins His Ministry

MAIN IDEA
Jesus faced both acceptance and rejection as he began his ministry and formed a community of followers that was the foundation of the Church.

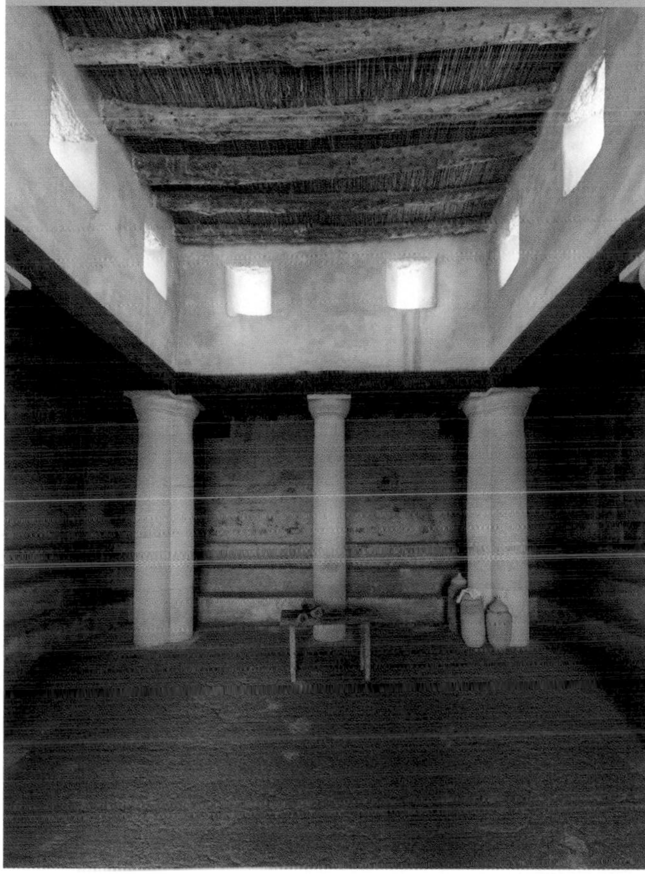

Jesus said, "For where your treasure is, there also will your heart be" (Lk 12:34). Society often sends the message that wealthy people are more valuable than poor people, but this is not God's perspective. Jesus clearly taught that "one's life does not consist of possessions" (Lk 12:15). He came to tell you that God loves you and that your focus in life should be not on what you have but on who you are as the Father's beloved child. People who choose to simplify their lives and make God's love their true treasure—whether dramatically, as missioners in another country, or simply within their day-to-day lives at home—usually find that they gain peace and contentment that outweigh any loss of possessions.

Jesus' ministry was aimed at all people, all sinners—from the wealthy and influential people in Palestine to the marginalized, the outsiders, the poor, and the despised. Jesus called on the wealthy and influential to rethink the meaning of their true life's treasure and at the same time sought out those who weren't prestigious or accepted—those whom society considered "nobodies." Luke reports that Jesus began his public ministry by teaching in the **synagogues** of Galilee (see example at left) and recruiting his disciples.

Jesus as a "Sign of Contradiction"

From the beginning of his public ministry, Jesus was a figure who was embraced and rejected. He was a *sign of contradiction* (cf. Lk 2:34–35, 1 Cor 1:23)—that is, one who provoked people to either follow

synagogues Meeting places for Jews to study and pray.

NOTE TAKING

Naming Actions. As you read through this section, look for steps Jesus took to begin his ministry and found the Church. In your notes, list several action verbs that describe his efforts.

Taught (priorities)

Fulfilled (prophecies)

him or reject him. Certain Pharisees and partisans of Herod, along with some priests and scribes, agreed together to destroy him. These religious Jews interpreted some of Jesus' words and actions as opposing the Jewish religion *as they understood it*. They expected a Messiah who would be a military leader and who would once again establish Israel as a leading nation in the world. For them, the Messiah could not be the Suffering Servant of God that Jesus revealed himself to be.

This might explain the reactions some of the Jews had toward Jesus during his public ministry. Their misunderstanding of Jesus' identity reveals an important theme throughout Jesus' public ministry: you cannot understand Jesus—his words or his deeds—unless you believe in him and follow him. The Jews, like people today, were looking for a Savior who would be important in all of the prestigious categories. He would be politically powerful, a "man of means," a leader in this world. The Gospel writers take great pains to show how Jesus fulfills the true understanding of the promised Savior by quoting prophecies that apply to him.

When God chose to reveal himself in the Divine Person of Jesus, he concealed himself in a cloak of humility. The eternal Son of God humbled himself by stripping himself of his divine glory and majesty and becoming a human being. And not just any human being, but a poor man, living in a small and poor city—in other words, someone whom society would consider a "nobody."

What this means is that in order to *see* Jesus, you first need to remove your pride. You need to *convert*, which means to receive God's offering of love and forgiveness by turning away from your sins and darkness and toward God and his light. You can only learn to see Jesus and understand his significance by becoming humble the way he did, and following him. We must undergo a mysterious kind of death to our prideful selves and receive a new "birth from above" (*CCC*, 591; cf. *CCC*, 428).

As you journey through Jesus' public ministry in this chapter, you find Jesus gathering twelve disciples around himself and proclaiming "the gospel of God" (Mk 1:14) through preaching, parables, and miracles. Throughout Jesus' public ministry, you find a pattern: as people follow him, they come to see and understand who he is more and more; and as people reject him, they progressively misunderstand who he is. At the end of Jesus' life, this pattern reaches a peak of intensity: "Whoever does not take up his cross and follow after me is not worthy of me" (Mt 10:38). Jesus calls his disciples—and you, too—to take up your cross and follow him.

Jesus Calls Many Disciples and Twelve Apostles

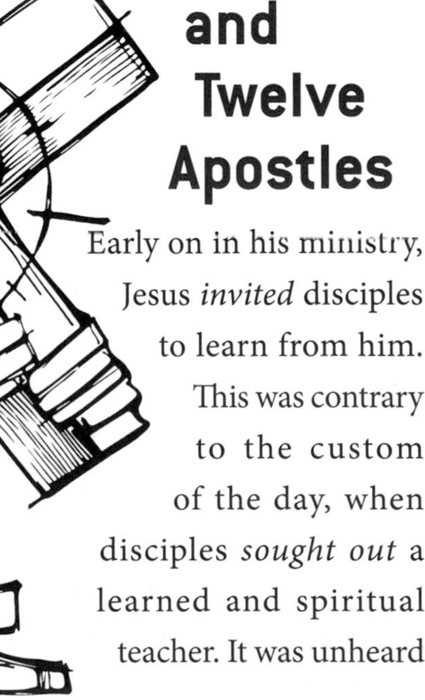

Early on in his ministry, Jesus *invited* disciples to learn from him. This was contrary to the custom of the day, when disciples *sought out* a learned and spiritual teacher. It was unheard

After his Resurrection, Jesus commissioned his disciples to "make disciples of all nations, baptizing them in the name of the Father, and of the Son, and of the Holy Spirit, teaching them to observe all that I have commanded you" (Mt 28:19–20).

of for teachers to go out and seek students, but that is exactly what Jesus did.

Jesus chose twelve men to be with him and to participate in his mission. "He gives the Twelve a share in his authority and 'sent them out to preach the kingdom of God and to heal'" (*CCC*, 551, quoting Lk 9:2). Specifically, he invited the fishermen Simon and his brother Andrew to follow him. Then he saw James, the son of Zebedee, and his brother John in a boat, and he called them too. In Capernaum, he asked Levi (Matthew) to leave his customs post and follow him. Later, after spending all night praying on a mountain, Jesus appointed twelve men to be the disciples who would travel with him and whom he could send out as Apostles to preach and drive out demons.

Note that the twelve disciples left their occupations and families to follow Jesus. Being Jesus' follower means that you must leave something behind. While following Jesus doesn't have to mean picking up and moving to a new nation, it should mean leaving behind your old way of life and embracing a new way of life with Christ at the center, in which you put others in touch with Christ through what you say and the way you live.

Also note that in the New Testament there is a distinction between those who are *disciples* and those who are *apostles*. *Disciple* means pupil, learner, or follower; it is a term that describes those who have accepted Jesus' Revelation about the Kingdom of God and have followed him. Oftentimes in the Gospels, the term *disciple* is used in a broad sense to refer to people who follow Jesus and not solely to the Twelve (cf. Mt 8:19–22; Lk 6:13, 17, 20; 19:37; Jn 4:1; 6:66; 8:31; 9:28; Acts 6:1–7). But the term *disciple* is also used to refer to the Twelve specifically when Jesus called them to follow him (cf. Mt 10:1, 11:1, 20:17). The word *apostle* means "one who was sent forth" and describes those whom Jesus sent to preach the Gospel to the whole world. One must first be a disciple (a student of the teacher) before one can be sent out as an apostle (a representative of the teacher). Although the term *apostle* is used in several places in the New Testament to refer to people other than the Twelve, it typically refers to the Twelve whom Jesus gathered around him early in his ministry and, after his Death and Resurrection, sent to proclaim the Gospel to the ends of the earth (see Mk 16:15).

Apostleship carried more responsibility than discipleship, since Jesus expected the Twelve Apostles not only to follow and learn from him but to share his Good News and baptize people of all nations. St. Paul was uniquely called to be an Apostle of Jesus Christ, though he was not one of the original Twelve Apostles. He is an Apostle because the resurrected Jesus appeared to him and sent him forth to serve as his representative and to preach the Gospel (cf. 1 Cor 9:1–2).

Peter the Rock

Among the Apostles, Simon Peter had the first place because Jesus entrusted a special mission to him. Through a special Revelation from the Father, Peter confessed that Jesus was the Messiah and the Son of the living God (see Mt 16:13–20). Jesus then declared that Peter would be the rock, or foundation, upon which he would build his Church. Peter's role would be to keep his extraordinary faith, strengthen his fellow Apostles, and pass the Catholic faith down to his successors.

Jesus also gave Peter the power of arbitration: "I will give you the keys to the kingdom of heaven. Whatever you bind on earth shall be bound in heaven; and whatever you loose on earth shall be loosed in heaven" (Mt 16:19). This "power of the keys" meant that Peter had the authority to govern the house of God, the Church. Later, after his Resurrection, Jesus confirmed this assignment when he asked Peter to feed his sheep (see Jn 21:15–19).

The power to "bind and loose" meant that Peter had authority to absolve people of their sins, make judgments about doctrine, and make disciplinary decisions in the Church. Peter shared these responsibilities with the other Apostles. They, in turn, passed on this leadership to other men who led local churches. These successors to the Apostles were the first bishops. Because St. Peter's ministry and his life ended in Rome, the bishop of Rome took on the same primacy of leadership that Peter had in his lifetime. The bishop of Rome is the pope.

This etching of Christ giving the keys to the kingdom to St. Peter is modeled after a fifteenth-century painting in the collection of the Sistine Chapel at the Vatican.

SECTION ASSESSMENT

NOTE TAKING

Use the action words you listed to help you complete the following item.

1. Write one sentence that summarizes the beginning of Jesus' ministry, using at least three verbs.

VOCABULARY

2. What is a *sign of contradiction*?
3. Distinguish between a *disciple* and an *apostle*.

COMPREHENSION

4. What kind of Savior were the Jews expecting?
5. What special role did Jesus give Peter?
6. What is the title of the successor of Peter?
7. What does it mean that Peter had the "power of the keys"?

CRITICAL ANALYSIS

8. What does it mean that God became a "nobody" for you?
9. Why must you undergo a mysterious kind of death to your prideful self and receive a new "birth from above" in him in order to understand Jesus' life and words?
10. Why do you think Jesus called laborers rather than religious leaders to be his disciples?

REFLECTION

11. How do you live Jesus' statement, "For where your treasure is, there also will your heart be" (Lk 12:34)? Explain.

SECTION 1

Jesus Announces the Kingdom of God

MAIN IDEA

Jesus preached the coming of the Kingdom of God and described several of its characteristics.

Jesus is the Messiah. He is God's only Son, *Emmanuel*—"God-with-us." He is the one who announced the coming of God's Kingdom: God's reign of peace, justice, truth, and goodness. He asked people to prepare for God's rule by turning from their sins and believing in the Gospel.

Jesus' contemporaries understood the expression "Kingdom of God" to be a time in the future when God would show his power, pass judgment, and establish his divine rule over all of creation. In this understanding, every creature would recognize the one, true God—the God who revealed himself to the Chosen People. When God's Kingdom was fully established, the will of God would then be accomplished in "a new heaven and a new earth" (Rev 21:1; cf. Is 65:17).

Jesus' description of the Kingdom of God differed in some respects from Jewish expectations. One main difference is that he himself would usher in the Kingdom and, through his Death and Resurrection, open the gates to heaven. And Jesus' description of the Kingdom of God had a present dimension as well as a future dimension. Jesus also taught about the meaning of the Kingdom of God in much more depth and detail than the Old Testament provided.

The *Catechism of the Catholic Church* (541–546) expands on the announcement of the Kingdom of God and on some of its characteristics.

The Kingdom of God Is at Hand

Jesus announced the Kingdom of God through parables and miracles from the beginning of his public

NOTE TAKING

Naming and Summarizing Content. Use a model like the one below to help you list characteristics of the Kingdom of God that are named in this section. Add at least one key detail for each characteristic.

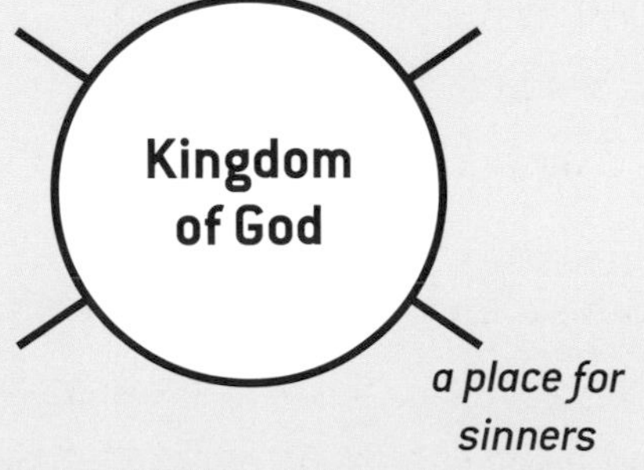

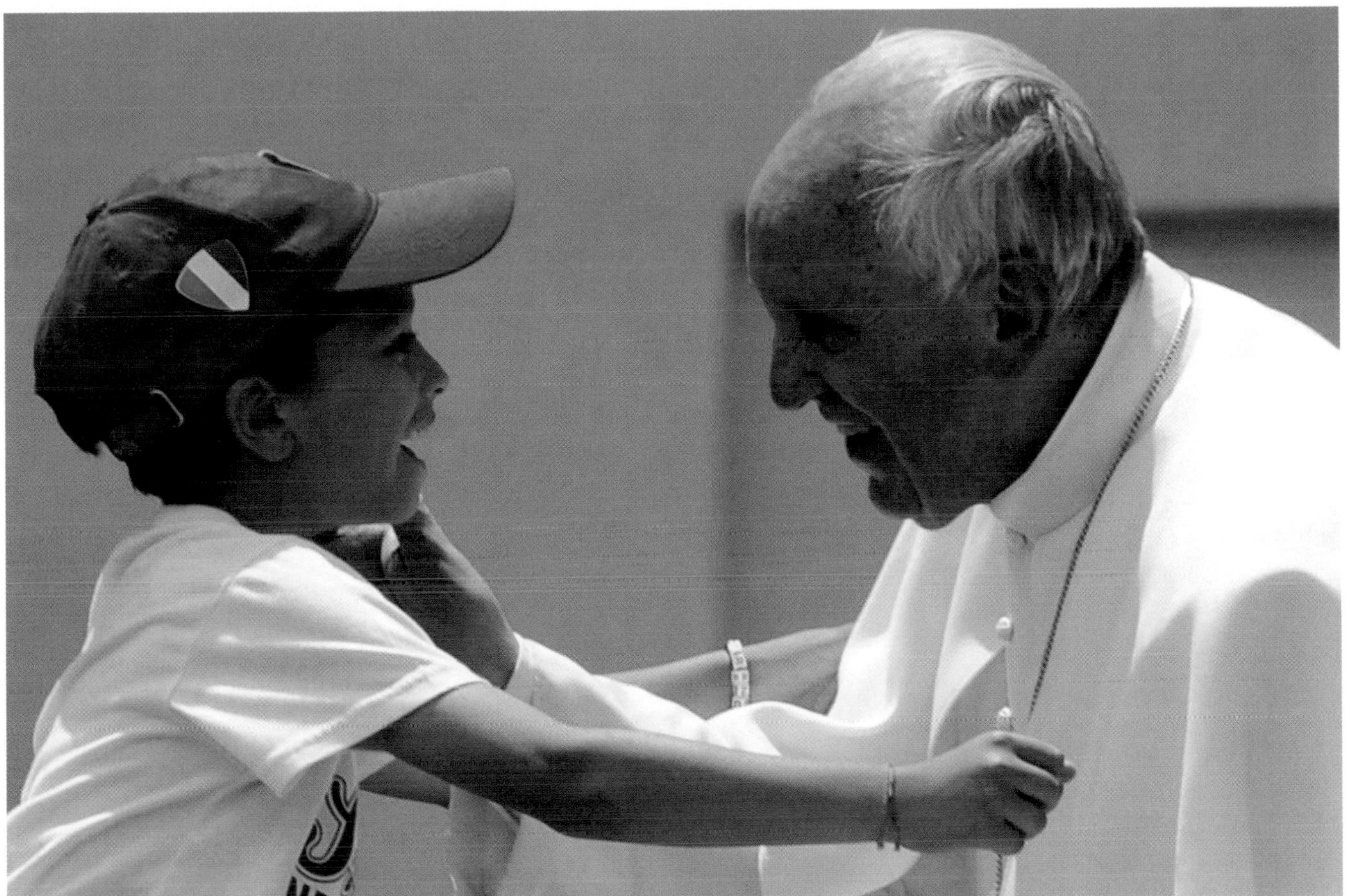

After being asked to pray over children, Jesus told his disciples that "the kingdom of heaven belongs to such as these" (Mt 19:14).

ministry. In Galilee, Jesus preached, "This is the time of fulfillment. The kingdom of God is at hand. Repent, and believe in the gospel" (Mk 1:15). As the Gospel writers make clear, Jesus not only announced the coming of God's Kingdom but also inaugurated it in his own Person.

Jesus stands at the center of the gathering of all people into this "family of God" (*CCC*, 542). As the Father's Son, Jesus continues to call and gather all human beings into this family. "By his word, through signs that manifest the reign of God, and by sending out his disciples, Jesus calls all people to come together around him" (*CCC*, 542). God's love excludes no one. Jesus gave up his life as a ransom for every person. It is in the Paschal Mystery—his Death on the Cross and his Resurrection—that he ultimately accomplishes the coming of his Kingdom.

The Invitation to the Kingdom of God

Although Jesus first announced the coming of the Kingdom to the Chosen People, this invitation was extended to all people. The message was emphasized in the parable of the sower (see Mt 13:1–9, 18–23). Jesus emphasized that the poor and the lowly—those who have accepted the Kingdom of God with humble hearts—are most eligible to enter. Jesus himself shared the life of the poor, from his humble birth in a stable to his Death on the Cross, stripped of his clothing. He knew hunger and thirst. He had no possessions. "Foxes have dens and birds of the sky have nests, but the Son of Man has nowhere to rest his head" (Mt 8:20).

Examining Prejudice

Prejudice is an attitude that goes against Jesus' declaration that everyone should look on others as brothers or sisters in the Lord. Prejudice involves forming preconceived opinions about others without consideration of known factors and usually based on erroneous knowledge. Prejudice is a mindset that continues to exist in society today. It diminishes people and leads to behaviors such as talking behind people's backs, avoidance of others, discrimination, and even violence.

ASSIGNMENT

- Write a short summary of a situation in your local community in which prejudice against an individual or group has been exhibited. Then add a reflection of your own ideas for concrete actions you and others in your community could undertake to prevent this type of behavior in the future.

The eternal Word of God emptied himself of his power and glory (that is, his "richness") in order to enter into solidarity with human beings (that is, he became "poor"). Even if the eternal Word of God had become a prestigious and wealthy king in the Incarnation, he would have lived in abject poverty in comparison to his divine state. However, he did not become a royal or rich human being but a poor carpenter who grew up in solidarity with the poor and marginalized and who reached out to the poor as his own.

Jesus calls you to reflect his act of self-emptying in the way you approach the poor. Thus, in the same way God became poor for you so that you could benefit from his riches, he calls you to empty yourself of your pride and to join the poor in solidarity and with a humble heart that they may become enriched. Jesus taught that you must respond to the needs of the poor by feeding the hungry, giving drink to the thirsty, welcoming the stranger, clothing the naked, caring for the sick, and visiting the imprisoned (see Mt 25:31–46). He preached that love in action toward those in need is the condition for entering the Kingdom of God.

The invitation to *everyone* to enter to the Kingdom of God also extends to sinners. Jesus said, "Those who are healthy do not need a physician, but the sick do. I have not come to call the righteous to repentance but sinners" (Lk 5:31–32). By his association with sinners and his care for their welfare, Jesus showed that God's mercy is a sign of the coming of the Kingdom. This mercy is the same quality that Jesus requires of you: to love even your enemies.

How is the invitation to the Kingdom of God extended? "Jesus' invitation to enter his kingdom comes in the form of *parables*, a characteristic feature of his teaching" (*CCC*, 546). For example, Matthew 13 contains a number of short **parables** about the present and future dimensions of the Kingdom of God. Writing for his Jewish and Christian audience, Matthew used the expression "Kingdom of Heaven" rather than "Kingdom of God" out of reverence because Jews typically avoided saying God's holy name. Examples of some of the parables that express God's invitation to the Kingdom and the characteristics of the Kingdom are shared in the next section.

parables Simple images or comparisons that confront the hearer or reader with a radical choice about Jesus' invitation for us to enter the Kingdom of God. Parables are a characteristic feature of the teaching of Jesus.

SECTION ASSESSMENT

NOTE TAKING

Use the model you made to help you complete the following questions.

1. Name three characteristics of the Kingdom of God. Rank these characteristics in order from least to most challenging or difficult for you to keep.
2. What can you do to better enact the *most* challenging or difficult characteristics on your list? How can Catholics best live out their belief in the Kingdom of God in the modern world?

VOCABULARY

3. Define *Emmanuel.*
4. What are *parables*?

COMPREHENSION

5. How did Jesus' contemporaries understand the expression "Kingdom of God"?
6. How did Jesus share the life of the poor?
7. Why did Matthew use the term "Kingdom of Heaven" rather than "Kingdom of God" in his Gospel?

CRITICAL ANALYSIS

8. Explain in your own words the present and future dimensions of the Kingdom of God.

REFLECTION

9. Think about three different people: for example, a sibling, a classmate, a parent, a teacher, or a teammate. For each person, write one sentence describing how you would like them to treat *you*. Then, in light of what you wrote, list a specific thing you can do for each person you wrote about.

SECTION 2

Jesus Teaches about the Kingdom of God in Parables

MAIN IDEA

Jesus' parables were a masterful means of communicating the nature of the Kingdom of God using everyday subjects and surprising twists.

Jesus regularly used parables to reveal what the Kingdom was like, and he asked his listeners to make a radical choice to give up everything in order to enter the Kingdom. "Words are not enough; deeds are required" (*CCC*, 546). In his preaching, especially the parables, Jesus challenges his followers to purify their consciences, to examine their own lives, to ask themselves hard questions based on the nature of the parables. The parables are like mirrors by which you can examine yourself: Will you be the hard soil or the good earth in which God's Word is planted? What use have you made of the talents God has given you? To enter the Kingdom of God, you must become Christ's disciple.

The Importance of Parables

In general, a parable is an analogy in which the storyteller compares an unfamiliar or new reality (such as the Kingdom of God) with a familiar reality from daily life. Using images and real-life examples that his listeners knew well, Jesus was able to expand their understanding of the Kingdom of God.

Some of the familiar objects and people Jesus used in his parables were connected with fishing, farming, and wedding celebrations. His parables incorporated seeds, bread, and wine. Many of his

NOTE TAKING

Identifying Key Meanings of the Parables. Create a chart like the one to the right for any three parables discussed in this section. For each parable, list the title and Scripture reference in the left column. In the middle column, identify the ordinary elements (e.g., people, events, nature) that Jesus uses in the parable. In the right column, explain the allegorical message of the parable for your life today.

Parable	Ordinary Elements	Allegorical Message for Today
The Good Samaritan (Lk 10:25–37)	*People on a journey, road, robbers, religious figures, injured man*	*Think beyond legalities and customs to treat everyone with love and respect, even "enemies."*

parables featured landowners, stewards, and servants, but they also included widows, shepherds, fathers, and children. Jesus' parables are important for several reasons, including the following:

1. *They convey the heart of his message.* To learn from them is to learn much about the Kingdom of God.
2. *They show that Jesus was an outstanding teacher.* Parables like the good Samaritan and the prodigal son contain lessons that are very memorable. They are easy to remember and successfully bring to mind important points in Jesus' teaching.
3. *They give you a good sense of Jesus' ability to defend himself against opponents.* For example, when asked why his disciples do not fast the way the disciples of John the Baptist or the Pharisees do, Jesus compares himself to a bridegroom at a wedding. Because he is present, it is a time for celebration and feasting. The point of the parables is that the Gospel is new and revolutionary. The Kingdom of God is an entirely new way of believing and living.
4. *They engage listeners at a deeper level and challenge them to conversion.* Jesus' parables assist the hearer to think deeply about principles in a concrete way.
5. *They purify the consciences of their hearers.* The stories hold up a mirror to those who hear them, challenging them to examine their lives.

You must become a disciple of Christ in order to understand the parables. They are like little treasure chests whose only key is Christian discipleship. Those who open the treasure chest find Christ and his Kingdom at the heart of the parable.

A CLOSER LOOK AT THREE PARABLES

Evaluate the three parables in this feature according to these three criteria:

1. **How does the parable convey the heart of Jesus' message about the Kingdom of God?**
2. **How does the parable exemplify Jesus' skill as a teacher?**
3. **How does the parable show Jesus' ability to defend himself against his opponents?**

THE GOOD SAMARITAN (LK 10:25-37)

Jesus and a scholar of the Law had already agreed that in order to inherit eternal life, a person must "love the Lord, your God, with all your heart, with all your being, with all your strength, and with all your mind, and your neighbor as yourself" (Lk 10:27). Jesus responds with this parable when the scholar asks, "Who is my neighbor?" (Lk 10:29).

Jesus tells a story about three people who encounter a man who was robbed, stripped, beaten, and left on the road. A priest and Levite see the injured man but pass him by, walking as far away from him as possible. These two represent law-abiding Jews, the same group to which the scholar probably belonged. They likely feared that if they helped the injured man (or even walked too close to him), they might become ritually impure according to the judgment of Jewish law.

The parable of the good Samaritan is depicted in this twelfth-century stained-glass window in Chartres Cathedral, France.

The third person to see the injured man is a Samaritan. Samaria was a region between Judea and Galilee west of the Jordan River. Samaritans and Jews were bitter enemies due to religious and ethnic differences. But in this parable, it is the Samaritan who stops, is moved to compassion, bandages up the injured man, takes him to an inn, and puts him up while he recovers.

When Jesus asks the scholar to identify the best neighbor of this injured man, the scholar says that it is the one who treated him with mercy. Jesus tells him, "Go and do likewise" (Lk 10:37).

Jesus taught that you should model yourself after the good Samaritan in caring for others who need your help. The priest and the Levite were supposed to model holiness to others, but the rigidity of their view of the Law got in their way. Jesus prioritized love over legalism. Even a Gentile like the Samaritan was able to follow the essence of God's law better than the priest and the Levite, who supposedly knew the Law so well. Luke's non-Jewish readers would have understood this story to mean that non-Jews can also be saved. A more important lesson is that so-called enemies are always to be treated as neighbors—with love.

THE GREAT FEAST (LK 14:7-24)

Luke sets this parable around a conversation Jesus has with guests at a Sabbath meal hosted by one of the leading Pharisees. Jesus speaks to the guests about their desire to sit in places of honor. In some ways, in addition to illustrating what humility is, Jesus really offers some commonsense etiquette guidelines to these guests.

Like the good Samaritan, St. Teresa of Calcutta cared for those most in need, regardless of their nationality, race, or religion.

It is embarrassing to sit in a place of honor and then have a host ask you to move because a more important guest has arrived. If, on the other hand, you sit first in a lower spot, then the host or hostess may invite you to move to a more significant place at the table. Jesus says, "For everyone who exalts himself will be humbled, but the one who humbles himself will be exalted" (Lk 14:11).

Jesus provides the banquet's host with an additional tip by asking him not to invite guests who considered themselves honorable to his dinners, but rather to invite the poor, the crippled, the lame, and the blind. This latter group cannot repay the host, so the host would be repaid at the resurrection.

Then Jesus tells a parable in which all of the guests invited to a great banquet refuses the invitation, giving a variety of excuses. The giver of the banquet then orders his servants to "go out to the highways and hedgerows and make people come in that my home may be filled" (Lk 14:23). The parable emphasizes that God's invitation to his Kingdom has been rejected by those he initially invited, so the invitation has been extended to others.

THE WORKERS IN THE VINEYARD (MT 20:1-16)

In this parable of the workers in the vineyard, Jesus compares God to a landowner who hires laborers for his vineyard. He hires workers at dawn, nine, noon, three, and five o'clock. The foreman first pays the group last hired a full day's wage. The workers who had labored for a longer time then expect higher payments and are surprised to receive the same amount, even though they agreed to work for this daily wage. The landowner responds that he has not cheated them and that he is free to use his money as he chooses. He suggests that the grumbling laborers may be envious of his generosity.

Jesus concludes this parable by saying, "Thus, the last will be first, and the first will be last" (Mt 20:16). In his generosity, the landowner violated no rule of justice, and neither does God. It is not important when a person begins his or her relationship with Christ, only that a person does eventually repent of sin and begin to help Jesus to build up his Kingdom.

St. Augustine and the Good Samaritan

The basic message of the parable of the good Samaritan (Lk 10:25–37) is that you need to love all your neighbors, including your enemies. But this parable has a richer meaning as well. For example, St. Augustine of Hippo (AD 354–430) saw this parable as an allegory and interpreted it this way:

- Jerusalem = heaven
- Jericho = the world
- robbers = Satan and the bad angels
- wounded man = Adam
- priest = the Law (Torah)
- Levite = the prophets
- Samaritan = Jesus
- the inn = the Church
- Samaritan's return = Jesus' return at the end of time

ASSIGNMENT

Using the allegorical elements from St. Augustine, rewrite the parable of the good Samaritan.

The Messages of the Parables

The synoptic Gospels contain a total of forty-one parables. The parables contain the heart of the Good News and reveal lessons about God and about how to live. The following infographic is a summary of some of the most important lessons of the parables and what they teach about the Kingdom of God.

The Kingdom is here, yet it also has a future dimension.

Jesus ushers in the Kingdom of God just as spring brings leaves to the fig tree (Mt 24:32–35). Like a mustard seed, the Kingdom begins small but will grow (Mk 4:30–32) according to God's own design (Mk 4:26–29). Eventually the Kingdom of God will reach a great harvest (Lk 8:5–8).

You cannot earn the Kingdom of God; it is fully God's gift.

The heavenly banquet is for everyone (Mt 22:1–14). Jesus invites everyone into the Kingdom, even people you might consider unworthy (Lk 14:15–24). God is like the vineyard owner who freely dispenses his gifts, far beyond what one has earned (Mt 20:1–16). For your part, you are like the servant who can only joyfully and gratefully accept his master's love (Lk 17:7–10).

God loves sinners and calls them to his Kingdom.

God is like a good shepherd who seeks out the lost sheep (Lk 15:3–7), the woman who searches frantically for her lost coin and rejoices when she finds it (Lk 15:8–10), and the merciful father who welcomes back a lost son and deals gently with another son who harshly judges his brother (Lk 15:11–32). God's joy over the returned sinner is great. He asks in return only that you forgive others as you have been forgiven (Mt 18:23–35).

The Good News of God's Kingdom demands repentance.

Having repented or accepted the gift of the Kingdom, you must live a life full of good deeds (Mt 22:1–14). You must remain faithful (Mt 21:28–32). You must ask for God's mercy, as did the sinful tax collector (Lk 18:9–14). You must forgive others (Mt 5:25–26). You must pray without ceasing, like the friend begging for bread at midnight (Lk 11:5–8) or the widow badgering the unjust judge (Lk 18:1–8). Above all else, you must love everyone, even your enemies, following the example of the good Samaritan (Lk 10:25–37).

The Good News about the Kingdom of God requires an urgent response.

You must be ever watchful for God's return (Lk 12:35–40) because the bridegroom (Jesus) can come at any time (Mt 25:1–13). Some people will refuse to respond to God, like tenants in a vineyard who refuse to give the owner his proper share (Mt 21:33–46). The Kingdom of God is like finding a pearl or a hidden treasure; you must give your all in order to gain it (Mt 13:44–46). You need to accept and live the grace of redemption by practicing the virtues of faith, hope, and love and by praying for the coming of the Kingdom of God and working toward that goal.

Following Jesus may bring suffering.

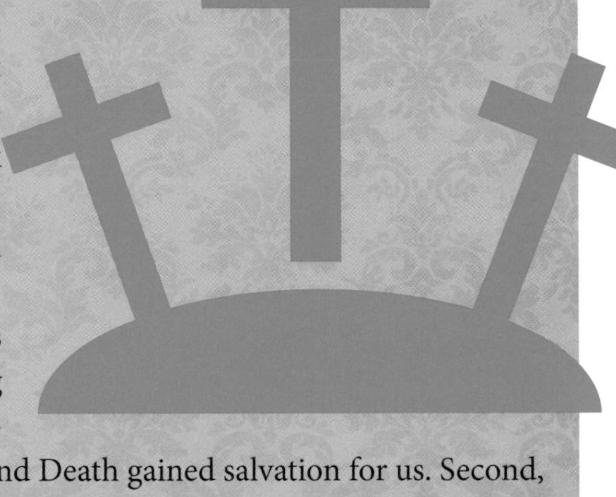

If you respond to the "least of these," you respond to Jesus and will enter into the fullness of God's Kingdom for eternity (Mt 25:31–46). Those who suffer for Jesus will be rewarded, while those who ignore the suffering of others will be punished (Lk 16:19–31). Jesus calls you to put his moral and spiritual teaching into practice and to show your response to God's call in your way of life.

As a follower of Jesus, you must be willing to bear witness to the Lord by making sacrifices and undergoing suffering patiently for a number of reasons. First, you would be following the example of Jesus Christ, who through his suffering and Death gained salvation for us. Second, Jesus predicted that people would suffer for their faith and promised that he would be with them in their suffering. Third, followers of Jesus Christ know that suffering is never in vain because it can help you move toward heaven and eternal life. In your suffering, you can help make up to some degree for the hurt and harm you cause by your sin. Finally, the suffering, Death, Resurrection, and Ascension of Jesus teach you to look beyond the sufferings of this world to the promise of eternal life with God in heaven.

In the end, you will be judged.

Christ himself will separate the good from the evil just as wheat is separated from the weeds (Mt 13:24–30) and bad fish are tossed out of the net (Mt 13:47–50).

The essence of the parables and of the Good News is that God loves sinners (which all people are). He desires repentance so that everyone can share in the fruits of his Kingdom. The time for choosing is now!

SECTION ASSESSMENT

NOTE TAKING

Use the chart you made to help you complete the following items.

1. Summarize the allegorical meaning of one of the parables you read in this section.
2. How do the ordinary elements of the parable help you to understand its meaning?

COMPREHENSION

3. What makes a parable different from other types of stories?
4. What are three reasons that Jesus' parables are important?
5. How does Jesus define *neighbor* in the parable of the good Samaritan?

CRITICAL ANALYSIS

6. Why does the Kingdom of God require an urgent response?
7. How does the parable of the good Samaritan show that religious people could be blinded by legalism?
8. What did Jesus mean by saying, "For everyone who exalts himself will be humbled, but the one who humbles himself will be exalted"?
9. How can the parables associated with God's love and call to sinners also be understood as God's search and rescue of sinners?

REFLECTION

10. How would you explain to a nonbeliever that God's Kingdom is both here in the present and will arrive in the future as well?
11. What does "praying without ceasing" look like for you in your life today?

SECTION 3

Jesus' Miracles Are Signs of God's Kingdom

MAIN IDEA
Jesus' miracles are signs that the Kingdom of God is at hand. In his miracles, Jesus shows his divine power over illness, evil, nature, and death.

To support his teachings about the Kingdom of God, Jesus performed works and signs that could not be explained naturally; these are also known as *miracles*. They were signs that the messianic age had dawned, and they also invited people to believe that Jesus was the Christ, the Son of God, sent by the Father. Jesus' miracles were always accompanied by his own faith in God the Father and also the faith of those around him. In fact, there were times, such as when he visited his hometown of Nazareth, when "he was not able to perform any mighty deed" because of the "lack of faith" of the people around him (see Mk 6:5–6).

When Jesus did perform a miracle, he responded to the faith of those around him by granting what they asked, though he *never* responded simply to satisfy people's curiosity or desire for magic. Both then and now, the intention of miracles is to strengthen a person's faith in God.

The marvelous signs Jesus performed, however, did not automatically cause people to believe in him. His opponents could not deny that he healed people and performed other miracles. But they

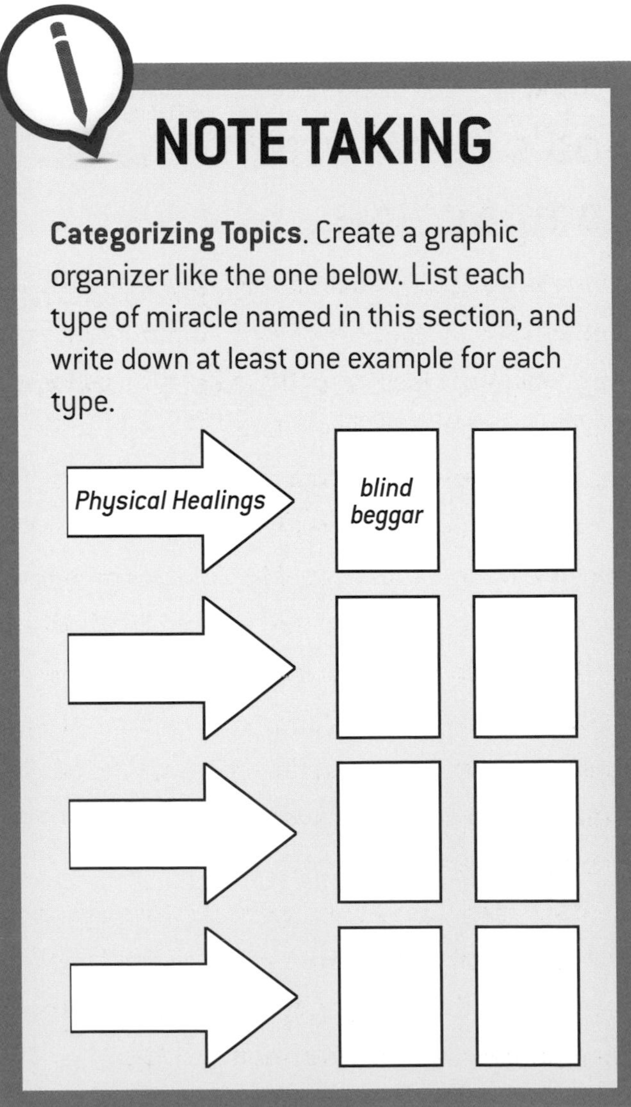

NOTE TAKING

Categorizing Topics. Create a graphic organizer like the one below. List each type of miracle named in this section, and write down at least one example for each type.

questioned the source of his power; sometimes they even said that it came from the devil. This happened when Jesus drove a demon out of a mute person, who was then able to speak. But Jesus knew that their charge was absurd. The coming of God's Kingdom meant Satan's defeat. Satan's work was about darkness and evil, so it made no sense for Jesus to work on behalf of Satan. Jesus challenged his critics by saying:

> Every kingdom divided against itself will be laid waste and house will fall against house. And if Satan is divided against himself, how will his kingdom stand? (Lk 11:17–18)

Jesus clearly showed that his works and signs pointed to the coming of God's Kingdom.

Jesus' Miracles Showed God's Power and Compassion

Jesus' miracles mirrored his teachings on the Kingdom of God in that they freed vulnerable people from earthly problems and the evils of hunger, injustice, illness, and even death. Jesus' mission, however, was not to abolish all human suffering on earth but to bear human infirmities in order to free people from the worst slavery: sin. His miracles prefigured the victory of the Paschal Mystery, which would abolish Satan's power, defeat sin and death, and win for humankind eternal life with God. Jesus' miracles are announcements about the Kingdom of God. The signs and wonders anticipate the Kingdom that Jesus himself inaugurated.

Jesus' miracles fall into four categories: physical healings, exorcisms, nature miracles, and raisings from the dead. Each type of miracle reveals something unique about the Kingdom of God:

- When Jesus *healed* people of their illnesses, he revealed his divine nature and the nature of the Kingdom of God, where there would be no more suffering. Luke's Gospel gives several accounts of physical healings performed by Jesus. Some examples are the healing of Simon Peter's mother-in-law of a severe fever (see Lk 4:38–39), the cleansing of a leper (see Lk 5:12–16), and the healing of a blind beggar who recognized Jesus as the Son of David (see Lk 18:35–43).

- Through miracles of *exorcism*, Jesus expelled the evil spirits that plagued people, demonstrating that he had power over Satan and his demons. Some examples are his expulsion of a demon from a man at the Capernaum synagogue (see Lk 4:31–37) and the healing of the Gerasene demoniac (see Lk 8:26–39). Only in Satan's defeat would the Kingdom of God reach its fullness.

- Through *nature* miracles, Jesus showed his mastery over the elements. It is not surprising that Jesus had power over the forces of nature, since all creation came about through him. When Jesus calmed the storm at sea (see Lk 8:22–25), the experience invoked Old Testament passages in which God commands the seas (see Pss 65:8, 89:10, 93:3–4, and 107:29). Even his disciples asked the question, "Who then is this, who commands even the winds and the sea, and they obey him?" (Lk 8:25). The miracle of the loaves and fishes (see, for example, Lk 9:10–17 and the image on page 138) is recorded in all four Gospels. The language and actions in this miracle resemble Jesus' language and actions at the Last Supper in his institution of the Eucharist.

- In *raisings from the dead*, Jesus demonstrated that he has mastery over life and death. There are three occasions in the Gospels when Jesus raised a person from the dead: the raising of the widow of Nain's son (see Lk 7:11–17), the raising of Lazarus (see Jn 11:1–44), and the raising of the synagogue leader's daughter (reported in all the synoptic Gospels). All of these raisings from the dead were clear signs that the Messiah had come, that it was the time Isaiah had prophesied about: "The blind regain their sight, the lame walk, lepers are cleansed, the deaf hear, the dead are raised, the poor have the good news proclaimed to them" (Lk 7:22). They also foreshadowed Jesus' own Resurrection.

Jesus' miracles accomplished many things. They showed that God's power had broken into human history through his Son. They were performed as messianic signs—that is, signs that the Kingdom of God had begun in Jesus' very Person. As signs of God's Kingdom, Jesus' miracles demonstrate in a remarkable way the love and compassion that God has for you.

SECTION ASSESSMENT

NOTE TAKING

Use the graphic organizer you made to help you complete the following item.

1. Write the name, the definition, and an example of each type of miracle performed by Jesus.

COMPREHENSION

2. What was the purpose of Jesus' miracles?
3. What did Jesus' miracles accomplish?
4. Why did Jesus perform exorcisms?

CRITICAL ANALYSIS

5. Explain the meaning of Jesus' statement, "Every kingdom divided against itself will be laid to waste and house will fall against house. And if Satan is divided against himself, how will his kingdom stand?" (Lk 11:17–18).
6. Explain in greater depth two things that Jesus' miracles accomplished.

REFLECTION

7. Jesus accompanied his words with "many 'mighty works and wonders and signs'" that let people know that the Kingdom was present in him (*CCC*, 547–549). Jesus asked the blind man this question: "What do you want me to do for you?" (Lk 18:41). Name one thing you need in your life right now. Write a note to Jesus telling him what you think he can do for you. Then write down what you think you can do for Jesus.

SECTION 4

Three Luminous Mysteries

MAIN IDEA

The wedding at Cana, the Transfiguration, and the institution of the Eucharist revealed both Jesus' identity and his power as the Son of God.

In 2002, Pope John Paul II introduced a new set of mysteries to accompany the praying of the Rosary. To the joyful, sorrowful, and glorious mysteries (see pages 363–364) that have been part of the Rosary since the sixteenth century, he added the *luminous mysteries*, or mysteries of light. They highlight these events in the life of Jesus:

- The Baptism of Jesus
- The Wedding at Cana
- The Proclamation of the Kingdom of God
- The Transfiguration
- The Institution of the Eucharist

Chapter 3 discusses Christ's Baptism (pages 101–102), and this chapter covers his proclamation of the Kingdom of God (pages 124–127). This subsection focuses on the Gospel sign of the wedding at Cana, the Transfiguration, and the institution of the Holy Eucharist.

The Wedding at Cana (Jn 2:1–12)

Jesus' first sign or miracle took place at a wedding feast in the town of Cana (see the image at left) before he began his public preaching. Mary, Jesus' Mother, informed him that the hosts had run out of wine. Mary was likely sensitive to the importance of

NOTE TAKING

Identifying Important Actions. This section describes three important luminous mysteries in the life of Jesus using vivid action words. After you read the section, write three sentences that summarize the material. Use at least one of the following action verbs in each sentence.

- reveal
- celebrate
- transform
- prefigure
- institute

Example: *The Transfiguration* revealed *the presence of all Three Persons of the Blessed Trinity.*

hospitality and the great shame that the hosts would feel if they were unable to provide refreshment for their guests. Mary displayed simple and confident faith that Jesus would help the hosts even though he told her that it was not yet time for him to manifest himself openly.

In this first sign, there are clear references to three sacraments.

1. Jesus' attendance at a feast showed that he was in touch with ordinary people and enjoyed a good celebration. But this particular celebration was a wedding, which celebrates spousal love and new life. The Lord's attendance at this wedding blessed marriage as a sacrament of divine love. The *Sacrament of Matrimony* represents the union of Christ and the Church, and it gives spouses the grace to love each other with the love Christ has for the Church (see Eph 5:21–33).

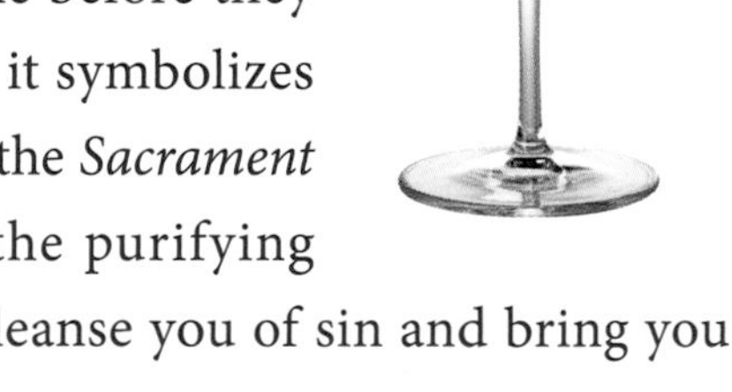

2. The miracle Christ performed at Cana involved transforming water into wine. The water was used to cleanse people before they ate the meal; it symbolizes the waters of the *Sacrament of Baptism*, the purifying waters that cleanse you of sin and bring you new life in Christ.

3. Finally, the transformation of water into wine—which, at the Last Supper, Jesus changes into his own Blood—points to the *Sacrament of the Holy Eucharist*. The Eucharist brings spiritual life—that is, communion with Jesus, who is Lord and Savior.

This first of seven signs in the Gospel of John reveals a caring Jesus who has power over nature. It also shows his mother's influence with him.

Jesus' Transfiguration (Mt 17:1–8, Mk 9:2–8, Lk 9:28–36)

One of the most dramatic and important events in Jesus' life was his **Transfiguration**. The disciples Peter, James, and John witnessed the event that took place after Peter's confession of Jesus as the Messiah (see Lk 9:18–21); Jesus gave Peter, James, and

Transfiguration The glorious transformation of Jesus that manifested his divine identity to Peter, James, and John on a high mountain, probably Mount Tabor. The event, reported in all three synoptic Gospels, also involved the appearance of Moses and Elijah.

John a glimpse of his divine glory as God's beloved Son. He took them on a high mountain, and "he was transfigured before them; his face shone like the sun and his clothes became as white as light" (Mt 17:2). Moses and Elijah appeared and spoke with him. In addition, a voice came from the cloud and said, "This is my beloved Son, with whom I am well pleased; listen to him" (Mt 17:5). Through this manifestation, Jesus gave his disciples a foretaste of God's Kingdom.

In his book *Jesus of Nazareth*, Pope emeritus Benedict XVI observed that the Transfiguration happened while Jesus was praying. He wrote, "In his oneness with the Father, Jesus is himself 'light from light.'" The Transfiguration also revealed all Three Persons of the Blessed Trinity: the Father (in the voice), the Son (in his radiant glory), and the Holy Spirit (in the shining cloud). Two important Old Testament figures—Moses and Elijah—also appeared at Jesus' Transfiguration, their presence testifying that Jesus is the fulfillment of both the Law and the prophets.

The Transfiguration affirmed both Peter's confession of faith that Jesus was God's Chosen One and Jesus' explanation of what it means to be Messiah. Jesus instructed Peter, James, and John not to discuss the Transfiguration with others "until the Son of Man has been raised from the dead" (Mt 17:9).

The Transfiguration prefigured Jesus' Passion, Death, and Resurrection. Jesus' mention of his suffering is a reminder that though he was the Son of God, he did not come as an earthly king. He came to preach the Good News of God's love. This preaching led him to Jerusalem and his own Death at the hands of the authorities.

Jesus shared his Body and his Blood with his disciples at the Last Supper.

The Institution of the Holy Eucharist (Mt 26:26–30, Mk 14:22–26, Lk 22:14–20, Jn 6:22–59)

In the Eucharist, Christ shares the gift of himself. When you accept this gift, you are nourished by the **Real Presence** of Jesus in your life.

At the Last Supper, a celebration of the Jewish Passover, Jesus understood that his hour had come and that he would soon to return to his Father. But he made sure not to abandon his disciples: he gave

Real Presence The Real Presence of Jesus Christ means that he himself is truly present under the appearances of the consecrated bread and wine.

his disciples his Body and his Blood in the form of bread and wine. Jesus instituted the Eucharist as a memorial of his love for his disciples and of his Death and Resurrection. The Eucharist meant that he would never be apart from his disciples and made them sharers in his Passover. Jesus also commanded his disciples to celebrate the Eucharist until he returned again.

> Then he took the bread, said the blessing, broke it, and gave it to them, saying, "This is my body, which will be given for you; do this in memory of me." And likewise the cup after they had eaten, saying, "This cup is the new covenant in my blood, which will be shed for you." (Lk 22:19–20)

Jesus spoke directly to his disciples, but he speaks to you as well. He gave them and you a way to share in his Passover and to come to you under the appearance of bread and wine. Jesus is the Bread of Life, come down from heaven (see Jn 6:48–51). The *Catechism of the Catholic Church* explains that Jesus gave the Passover its definitive meaning because he would "pass over" to his father by his Death and Resurrection, fulfilling the Jewish Passover (see *CCC*, 1340).

From her very beginnings, the Church has faithfully carried out Jesus' command to celebrate the Eucharist, especially on Sunday, the day of the Lord's Resurrection. The Eucharistic celebration occurs daily in the biggest cathedrals and the most humble churches. Catholics recognize in the Holy Eucharist the very center of the Church's life in Christ. The Eucharist recalls his Life, Passion, Death, and Resurrection and his intercession for you before the Father. It allows the People of God to advance on the spiritual journey, "'following the narrow way of the cross' toward the heavenly banquet" (*CCC*, 1344, quoting *Ad Gentes*, 1). The Eucharist is the "source and summit" of the life of the Church through which Jesus Christ lives in and transforms you and every other person who participates in it.

SECTION ASSESSMENT

NOTE TAKING

Use the notes you made to help you answer the following questions.

1. How is *transformation* at the heart of any miracle?
2. Why is it important that Jesus *celebrated* specifically at a wedding feast?
3. How did the wedding at Cana *prefigure* the institution of the Eucharist?

VOCABULARY

4. What is the *Transfiguration*?
5. Describe the *Real Presence*.

COMPREHENSION

6. Explain how the Rosary came to have a fourth set of mysteries.
7. What are the five luminous mysteries?
8. Who asked Jesus to perform a miracle in Cana?
9. What aspects of Jesus' divine glory did Peter, James, and John glimpse?
10. Who appeared with Jesus at the Transfiguration?
11. How was the Transfiguration Trinitarian?
12. Why did the Church, from the beginning, celebrate the Eucharist on Sundays?

CRITICAL ANALYSIS

13. What are the differences between an earthly king and Jesus the Messiah?

REFLECTION

14. Because Jesus is present in the Blessed Sacrament, it deserves reverence. What are two things you can do in order to show reverence to Jesus in the Blessed Sacrament?

Section Summaries

Focus Question

How do Jesus' message and ministry influence the way you live your life? Complete one of the following:

Read a news article, blog post, or promotional material on the Maryknoll Lay Missioners' website that shows how another person or family has answered the Focus Question above.

Besides parables, Jesus also taught with *paradoxes*—statements that, at first glance, seem self-contradictory but that in reality present a deeper truth. Read one such example in Luke 9:24. What is the meaning of this paradox for your own life?

Skim through the pages of Luke 4:31–21:38. Which is your favorite miracle? Which miracle of Jesus impresses you the most? Explain both of your answers.

INTRODUCTION (PAGES 119–123)

Jesus Begins His Ministry

Jesus begins his ministry, preaching "the gospel of God" (Mk 1:14). He is a sign of contradiction (see Lk 2:34), provoking people to either follow him or reject him. Despite the Jewish expectation for a military leader as Messiah, Jesus showed himself to be the Suffering Servant of God, calling others to follow him on a path of humility and service. He gathered the Twelve around himself as the "seed and beginning" of the Kingdom of God on earth (*CCC*, 541). These men, plus St. Paul, are forever associated with Christ's Kingdom, for through their successors he continues to be present in the world and directs the Church (see *CCC*, 551). They, in turn, passed on this leadership to other men who led local churches. These successors to the Apostles were the first bishops. The bishop of Rome, the pope, is the successor to Peter and continues Peter's primacy of leadership.

Jesus seemed to connect with ordinary people throughout his ministry but often came into conflict with those in power. How do you think this style of relating to others would play out if Jesus lived in the world today?

SECTION 1 (PAGE 124–128)

Jesus Announces the Kingdom of God

God calls all people to be part of his Kingdom. Jesus taught that preparation for God's Kingdom begins with faith and repentance. The Kingdom has a present and future dimension, and it is meant for all people, especially the poor and lowly. Jesus invites sinners to his Kingdom and requires that believers follow him, leaving behind their old lives, and live according to his commands. Jesus also taught that those who suffer now for doing what is right will rejoice later.

Read the Sermon on the Plain (Lk 6:17–49), and name three things that Jesus requires of his followers.

SECTION 2 (PAGES 129–137)

Jesus Teaches about the Kingdom of God in Parables

The parables convey the heart of the Good News. Jesus' parables were a masterful means of communicating the nature of the Kingdom of God using everyday subjects and surprising twists. Although they might have seemed only to be simple stories, the parables challenge Jesus' listeners to examine their own lives. They remind people that God's Kingdom is a pure gift for sinners, but that it demands repentance and an urgent response.

Read the parable of the barren fig tree (Lk 13:6–9). Identify the everyday subject Jesus used and the parable's surprising twist. Read a biblical commentary that explains more about the parable's meaning. Summarize what you read in one paragraph.

SECTION 3 (PAGES 138–140)

Jesus' Miracles Are Signs of God's Kingdom

In demonstrating his divine power over illness, nature, and death, Jesus communicated the arrival of God's Kingdom. While Jesus' miracles proved that he was the Messiah, the Son of God, Jesus' enemies attempted to attribute Jesus' works to Satan—a charge that Jesus easily refuted. Jesus healed people physically, called demons out of them, demonstrated power over nature, and even raised people from the dead. Jesus' miracles verified his teachings about himself and the Kingdom of God.

Research a miracle that has been attributed to a saint. Describe the miracle. Explain how it was similar to miracles performed by Jesus. Summarize the main message of the saint's miracle.

SECTION 4 (PAGES 141–145)

Three Luminous Mysteries

Three miracles—the wedding at Cana, the Transfiguration, and the institution of the Eucharist—especially reveal Jesus' identity and power as the Son of God. Jesus' first miracle, recorded in John's Gospel, was at the wedding at Cana. While Jesus initially hesitated, his Mother, Mary, was able to convince him to turn water into wine for the wedding hosts. In his Transfiguration, Jesus revealed his divine glory to three disciples. Jesus instituted the Eucharist at a Jewish Passover to show that he was freeing people from sin in a new Passover. In the Eucharist, the Church is able to remember his sacrifice, be with him always, and share in his Paschal Mystery.

Interview three people to find out who they think Jesus is. Then write a reflection comparing and contrasting their views about Jesus with your own views.

Chapter Assignments

Choose and complete at least one of the following three assignments to assess your understanding of the material in this chapter.

1. Interpreting Jesus' Miracles

Write a report that summarizes three of Jesus' miracles. Each miracle you choose must appear in at least three of the four Gospels. Use the titles of the miracles as headings for your report. Follow all of these directions to complete the assignment:

1. Read all of the versions of each miracle you choose.
2. Note what has taken place on the surface level.
3. Decide which of the four categories of miracles each one belongs to.
4. Interpret the deeper meaning of each miracle. How do they show God's *power*? What *significance* do they have?

2. Parables in Depth

Choose and complete *two* of the three options listed below:

- Choose a parable from Luke's Gospel not covered in depth in this chapter. Research and cite three commentaries explaining what this parable means. Write a one-page report summarizing your findings.
- With at least two other classmates, act out and record a video presenting one of the parables. Provide a working Internet link to the video so that your teacher can view your completed work.
- Read the parable of the rich man and Lazarus (Lk 16:19–31). Write three to five sentences in response to each of the following questions: (1) What is Jesus' view of wealth according to this parable? Explain. (2) What does Jesus want you to do with the "riches" you have been given?

3. Adding Your Own Parable about God's Kingdom

Read the short parables in Matthew 13:44–50 that begin with "The kingdom of heaven is like . . ." Use a digital camera to take photos that illustrate these descriptions of God's Kingdom. Create a slideshow or video matching each passage with a photo. Then write one short parable of your own that begins with Jesus' words "The kingdom of heaven is like . . ." Illustrate your own words with a photo and include it in your presentation. *Optional*: You may draw your own illustrations instead of taking photos.

Faithful Disciple

St. Josephine Bakhita

Born in Sudan in 1869, St. Josephine Bakhita was kidnapped from her family by Arab slave traders before she was ten years old. Before gaining her freedom, Bakhita was sold several times to abusive masters and endured the humiliation and suffering of slavery. When an Italian consul, Callisto Legnani, bought Bakhita and allowed her to live with his family, it was the first time since childhood she had been with people who treated her lovingly. When Legnani needed to return to Italy, Bakhita asked if she could accompany him. She was brought to Italy and given to another Italian family, the Michielis. Bakhita became the primary caretaker and friend of the Michielis' only daughter.

St. Josephine Bakhita

Eventually, when both Michieli parents needed to return to Africa, they entrusted Bakhita and their daughter to the care of the Canossian Sisters of the Institute of Catechumens in Venice. Members of this religious order taught Bakhita about God, Jesus, and the Gospel. She recalled that before she had been taken a slave she had looked lovingly at the sun, moon, and stars and wondered, "Who is the Master of these beautiful things?" and had "a great desire to see him, and know him, and worship him." Bakhita entered the Catholic Church and was baptized with the name Josephine. Though the Michielis later wanted to bring Bakhita to Africa to live with them, she asserted herself and said that she wanted to stay with the sisters. This was her right under Italian law. After staying with the sisters for a time, she realized that God was calling her to join their community. On December 8, 1896, she was consecrated to God, whom she continued to refer to as "Master."

Sr. Josephine spent fifty years living in the Canossian community doing simple tasks such as answering the door, sewing, and cooking. She encouraged children and people who were poor and suffering who came to the door. Sr. Josephine was loved and admired by the other sisters as well as by the people outside of the community. She was humble, simple, and constantly smiling. She had a great desire to make God known to all, saying, "Be good, love the Lord, pray for those who do not know him. What a great grace it is to know God." She died in Italy in 1947 after a difficult illness.

To St. Josephine, God was always "Master." Having known cruel masters, she appreciated God's goodness all the more. St. Josephine Bakhita was beatified in 1992 and canonized on October 1, 2000.

Reading Comprehension

1. Where was St. Josephine Bakhita born and enslaved?
2. Whom did St. Josephine care for when she moved to Italy?
3. How did St. Josephine learn about God?
4. What was St. Josephine's role in her community of sisters?

Writing Task

- Describe St. Josephine's understanding of God as "Master." Compare her understanding of God under this title with your own experience of God.

Explaining the Faith

Do miracles happen today?

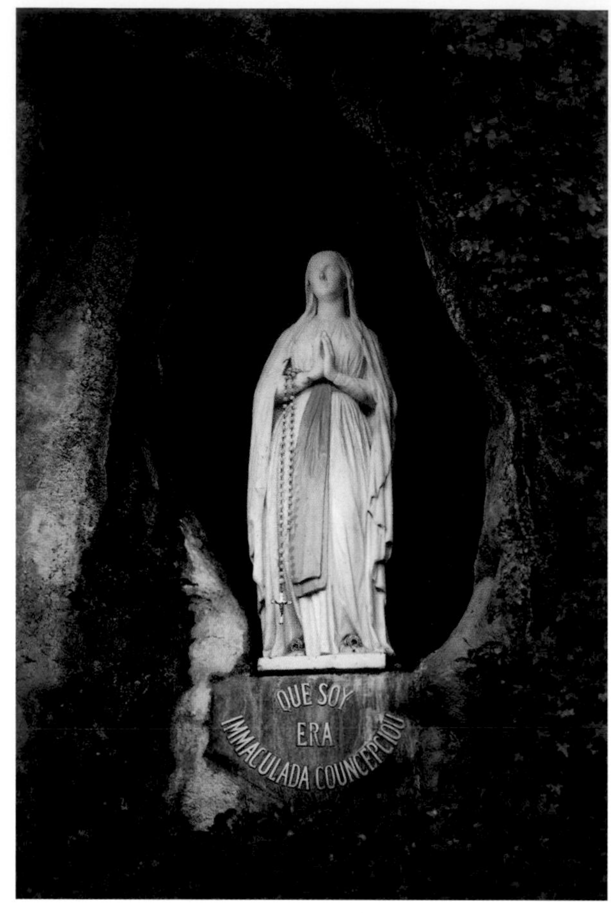

During his public ministry, Jesus accompanied his words with many "mighty deeds, wonders, and signs" (Acts 2:22), which manifest that the Kingdom is present in him and attest that he is the promised Messiah. His miracles invite belief in him; they bear witness that he is the Son of God. God continues to work in the world today and to use miracles to build faith and invite people to believe in him. Miracles are not intended to satisfy people's curiosity or desire for magic; rather, they are special gifts of God's grace intended to build up love and faith in the Church.

Church history is full of examples of God offering miracles as a sign of his ongoing presence in the world. For example, it is possible to view the *incorrupt*—that is, undecayed and miraculously preserved—bodies of some saints. Science cannot explain this phenomenon. At Fátima, Portugal, where Mary appeared in 1917, more than seventy thousand people saw the sun "dance" and appear to plummet to earth. At Lourdes, France, where Mary appeared to St. Bernadette Soubirous in 1858, more than seven thousand people have reported cures to the medical bureau.

Many miracles are attributed to saints. St. Pio of Pietrelcina bore the *stigmata* (wounds of Christ) and cured many people during his lifetime, including curing a woman of blindness. The Church conducts a very thorough investigation to determine whether a candidate for *canonization* (sainthood) has worked a miracle of healing. A doctor must offer a judgment that science cannot explain the medical wonder. The Magisterium then determines whether a miracle has occurred.

Modern skeptics, influenced by the belief that it is impossible for God to intervene in the natural world, claim that miracles do not happen. But this opinion does not square with the facts. Thanks to the Good News of Jesus Christ, the world is full of grace, and wonders truly happen.

Further Research

- Research how the Vatican determines the validity of miracles during the canonization process. Cite two specific miracles credited to two different saints who were canonized within the last twenty years.

Prayer

Prayer for Growth and Understanding

Creator of all things,
true source of light and wisdom, lofty origin of all being,
graciously let a ray of your brilliance
penetrate into the darkness of my understanding
and take from me the double darkness in which I have been born,
an obscurity of both sin and ignorance.
Give me a sharp sense of understanding,
a retentive memory,
and the ability to grasp things correctly and fundamentally.
Grant me the talent of being exact in my explanations
and the ability to express myself with thoroughness and charm.
Point out the beginning, direct the progress,
and help the completion;
though Christ our Lord.
Amen.
—St. Thomas Aquinas

5

THE PASSION AND DEATH OF JESUS CHRIST

Thomas Vander Woude SAVES HIS SON

Thomas Vander Woude, a retired Vietnam veteran and commercial pilot, was working on his family farm on the morning of September 8, 2008, after returning from early morning Mass. He was accompanied by Josie, his youngest of seven sons. Josie has Down syndrome and was almost always at his father's side.

While Thomas was working, Josie moved to a different part of the yard and slipped into a hole measuring only two square feet. The hole opened to an eight-foot drop into a septic tank filled with sewage. Thomas rushed to the hole to find his son submerged.

Thomas jumped into the muck and dove deep to find his son. It took several tries before he was able to lift Josie onto his shoulders and push him to the top of the tank, where rescuers who had arrived were able to get ahold of him and pull him out. The process took twenty minutes. Thomas had saved his son's life, but Thomas himself did not survive. Josie was in a coma for a few days and suffered from double pneumonia, but he is healthy now and living with his mother.

A few years later, one of Thomas's other sons—Fr. Thomas Vander Woude Jr., pastor of Queen of Apostles Catholic Church in Alexandria, Virginia—reflected on his father and what he had done that day in early September: "If that was the only time Dad ever sacrificed for any of us, this would be a very sad story. But his devotion to us was constant. He went down there in peace. This is what he did. This is who he was. This is where his life was taking him."

Another of Thomas's sons, Chris, added, "My dad knew what God wanted of him, and God wanted him to be a father."

FOCUS QUESTION

How did JESUS' DEATH ON THE CROSS bring about YOUR SALVATION?

Chapter Overview

INTRODUCTION

Dying for Love

MAIN IDEA

When you are open to God's love and aware that all people are made in his image, you are more likely to sacrifice yourself for another.

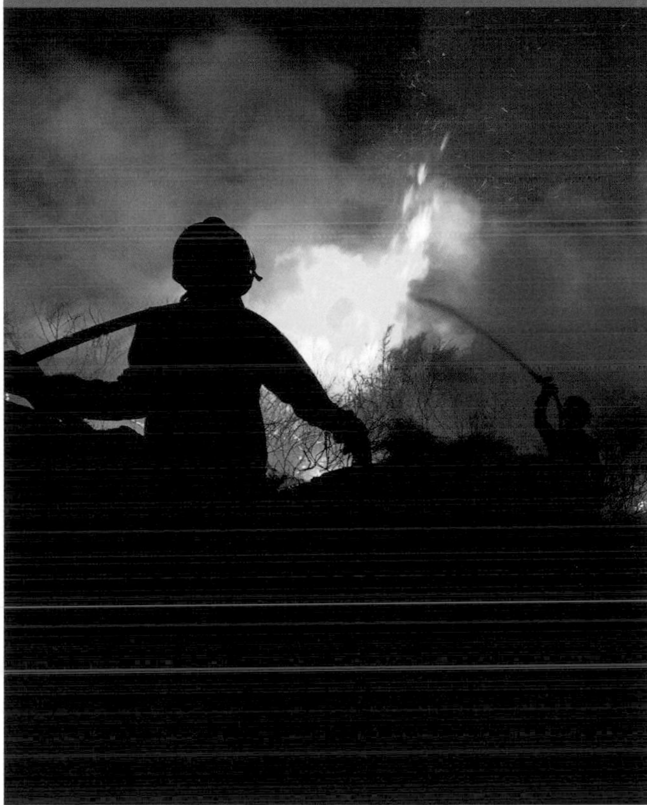

The story of Thomas Vander Woude parallels the greatest story ever told—God's willingness to give up the life of his only Son to save humanity from the darkness of sin and the pains of death.

You can gain significant insight into how much God loves you and others through examples of deep human love, such as the story of Thomas and his son Josie. Thomas's prayer life, deep faith, and daily love for Josie led him to make the greatest sacrifice—his own life for another. When Thomas found himself faced with a life-or-death decision, it was only natural for him to act with greater care for his son's well-being and survival than for his own.

You probably know many other stories of great heroism arising from love:

- A priest gives a kidney to one of his parishioners.
- A pregnant woman forgoes cancer treatment until after she has given birth, no matter what the outcome.
- A soldier throws himself on a grenade to protect other soldiers.
- First responders jump into a burning building or gunfight and try to protect other lives.
- A husband in an inevitable head-on collision angles the car so that he receives the fatal brunt of the accident and thereby saves his wife and unborn child.

Many people take these risks for loved ones and strangers in part because their worldview values love and includes God. They know that God loves all people and gives them the infinite value of being made in his image. Realizing that someone else's life is just as sacred and valuable as your own develops the virtue of humility. In addition, believing in God enables you to see your own life on earth from the perspective of eternal life. This is not all there is!

In fact, this is not all there is because Jesus died on your behalf. If people who believe in God are able to die on others' behalf, how much more would God, who is love, die for his own people?

NOTE TAKING

Discerning Personal Significance. As you read about people who sacrificed themselves for others, which of the examples in this section strikes you most powerfully? Why? Write a description of this person and why you find his or her example the most inspiring.

Fullness of Life in Following Christ

Following Christ leads to fullness of life, even when following Christ means you must embrace death. This paradox is true because "life" implies being joyful, hopeful, loving, and faithful in all circumstances—not negative, fearful, self-centered, or cynical. St. Jerome said, "One is rich enough who is poor with Christ," meaning that a person who is in relationship with Christ is not rich because of material things but is alive with Christ, who is the source of real treasure.

ASSIGNMENT

Take some time to brainstorm the names of people (famous or not) you believe have found fullness of life by following Jesus. Think especially of friends, relatives, neighbors, teachers, and acquaintances who reflect a spirit of having found fullness of life in Jesus Christ. Make a list of five to ten names, and then answer the questions that follow:

- What is a wise quotation about faith in Jesus or life in general that you have heard someone on your list say?
- How has someone on your list incorporated sacrifice into his or her life, such as giving up some pleasures in order to develop the self-discipline of following Jesus?
- What have you learned from those on your list about how you should treat others, including your enemies?
- Who on your list do you think would be willing to give up his or her life for another? Explain why you chose that person.
- Is there anyone you would be willing to die for? Describe a possible scenario in which you might be willing to be a martyr.

SECTION ASSESSMENT

NOTE TAKING

Use the description you wrote to help you answer the following question.

1. What do you find most inspiring about the person you selected? Explain.

COMPREHENSION

2. How does human love teach you about God's love?
3. What kind of worldview enables people to make heroic sacrifices?
4. What realization develops the virtue of humility?

REFLECTION

5. How do human love stories help you better understand God's willingness to sacrifice his Son for his people?

SECTION 1

The Events Leading Up to Jesus' Passion

MAIN IDEA

The events leading up to Jesus' Passion and Death help to provide understanding of why Jesus suffered.

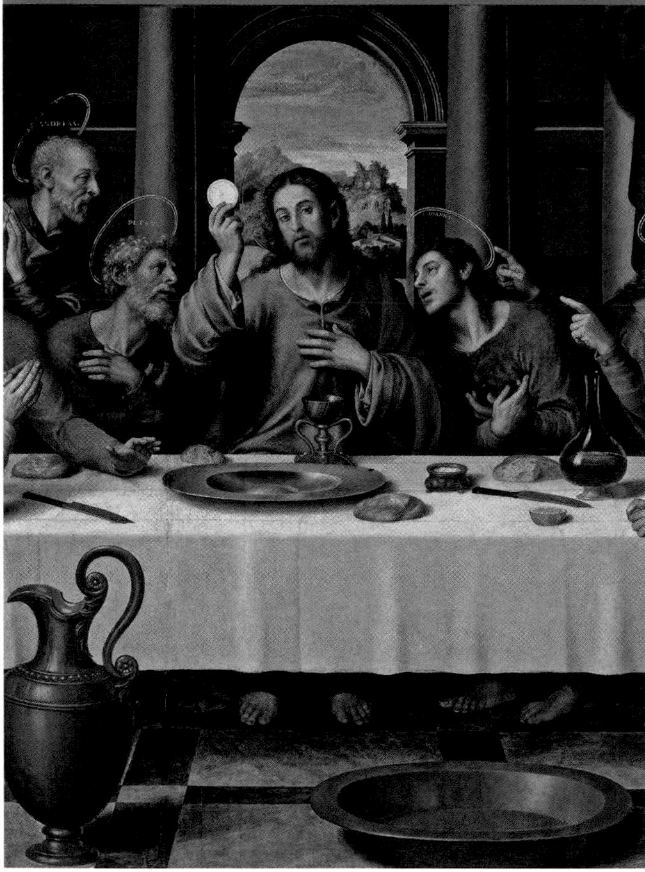

Several key events led up to Jesus' Passion and Death. As difficult as it is to believe that humans killed Jesus, he knew that this would be the path to accomplishing his Father's will. Jesus said that "the Son of Man did not come to be served but to serve and to give his life as a ransom for many" (Mk 10:45). He also described himself as the Good Shepherd who "lays down his life for the sheep" (Jn 10:11).

The **passion narratives** of the Gospels are probably the oldest accounts about Jesus proclaimed by the early Church. They were all formed and added very quickly to the liturgy of the early Church. They include many references to Old Testament prophecies that allude to the Death of the Messiah, especially as the Suffering Servant of God referenced in the Book of Isaiah, in order to show Jesus as the fulfillment of the promise of redemption. The evangelists agree on essential details in the passion narratives, but each wrote from unique perspectives with different points of emphasis. They shaped the events of Christ's Passion in order to emphasize certain

passion narratives Four separate accounts of the Passion of Christ in the four Gospels. The passion narratives of the synoptic Gospels follow a similar literary and thematic plan. The passion narrative of John's Gospel provides an independent account of these Paschal events.

NOTE TAKING

Charting Highs and Lows. Create your own graph like the one below that illustrates the highs and lows that Jesus experienced leading up to his Passion and Death. For example, Jesus' entrance into Jerusalem began on a high note when the people waved palms to welcome him as they would a king. Graph other events from this section in the same way. Are they high points or low points?

Jesus' triumphal entry into Jerusalem is remembered on Palm Sunday, the Sunday before Easter and the beginning of Holy Week.

theological points. For example, the Gospels of Matthew and Mark stress how the disciples abandoned Jesus but were vindicated in the end. Luke's Gospel presents the disciples more favorably; for example, they fall asleep only once in the Garden of Gethsemane, not three times, and only then because they are sorrowful at Jesus' impending fate.

The next subsections provide a summary of how the events leading up to Jesus' Passion and Death unfolded, including how these events fulfilled several Old Testament prophecies and prophecies made by Jesus himself.

Jesus' Entrance into Jerusalem Fulfills a Prophecy of Zechariah

Jesus' saving mission was destined to culminate in Jerusalem. When Jesus and his disciples reached the small villages of Bethpage and Bethany, near the Mount of Olives just east of Jerusalem, he told two of his disciples where to find a colt and its mother, and they went off to retrieve them. Jesus then rode into Jerusalem on the colt, thus fulfilling one of the Old Testament prophet Zechariah's prophecies (see Zec 9:9).

> Say to daughter Zion!
> "Behold, your king comes to you,
> meek and riding on an ass,
> and on a colt, the foal of a beast of
> burden." (Mt 21:5)

The crowds spread out their cloaks as a sign of respect for Jesus and waved palm branches as they enthusiastically shouted:

> **Hosanna** to the Son of David;

hosanna A Hebrew word meaning "(O Lord) grant salvation," but the invocation became a shout of joy and welcome.

blessed is he who comes in the name of the Lord;
hosanna in the highest. (Mt 21:9)

The people who welcomed Jesus were the ones who came to him for healing and the poor. They greeted Jesus as a prophet. He was their humble king, and they were his subjects.

Jesus Speaks Out against the Hypocrisy of Sin

If you have ever worked very hard on a project only to have someone else ruin it, you have a small sense of what Jesus must have felt when he saw the Temple, his Father's house, used as a marketplace.

> Jesus entered the Temple area and drove out all those engaged in selling and buying there. . . . And he said to them, "It is written:
> 'My house shall be a house of prayer,'
> but you are making it a den of thieves."
> (Mt 21:12–13)

This incident intrigues some scholars, because the business conducted at the Temple was religious in nature and occurred in the court of the Gentiles, the outermost court in the Temple area. Regardless, Jesus' charge that the Temple had become a den of thieves showed his disciples and others that he had authority over the religious practices of Israel, a reality that angered the religious leaders. Immediately after his interaction with the merchants at the Temple, Jesus cured blind and lame people in the Temple area, attracting a following of children who shouted "Hosanna to the Son of David" (Mt 21:15), further offending the chief priests and scribes.

Through the early years of the Church, many Jewish converts to Christianity (the primary audience of Matthew's Gospel) continued to experience conflicts with Pharisaic Judaism. These later tensions may have been related to the intensity of Jesus' speech against the scribes and Pharisees about the use of the Temple for business. However, Jesus was speaking out mainly against the hypocrisy of sin to which all people are vulnerable. Matthew 23 records several sayings of Jesus against hypocrisy. For example, Jesus said,

- "Woe to you, scribes and Pharisees, you hypocrites. You pay tithes of mint and dill and cumin, and have neglected the weightier things of the law: judgment and mercy and fidelity." (Mt 23:23)
- "You are like whitewashed tombs, which appear beautiful on the outside, but inside are full of dead men's bones and every kind of filth." (Mt 23:27)
- "Even so, on the outside you appear righteous, but inside you are filled with hypocrisy and evildoing." (Mt 23:28)

Jesus is the opposite of hypocrisy. He is the "whole of God's truth" (*CCC*, 2466). To follow Jesus is to live in the spirit of truth.

JERUSALEM AT THE TIME OF JESUS' CRUCIFIXION

After sharing the Last Supper with his disciples in the Upper Room (lower left), Jesus walked with his disciples to the Mount of Olives. Because it was Passover, and Passover typically is celebrated on the night of the first full moon of spring, there would have been a full moon lighting the way. He had to pass through the Kidron Valley ①, situated to the east of the old walled city of Jerusalem. At this time, the east side of the Kidron Valley was a large cemetery. Their destination was the Garden of Gethsemane near the base of the Mount of Olives (upper right), a two-mile ridge that rises some two hundred feet above the level of the city. The word *Gethsemane* means "oil press." The Garden of Gethsemane likely contained an olive grove and a press to crush the olives. It was here that Jesus prayed and the soldiers came to arrest him.

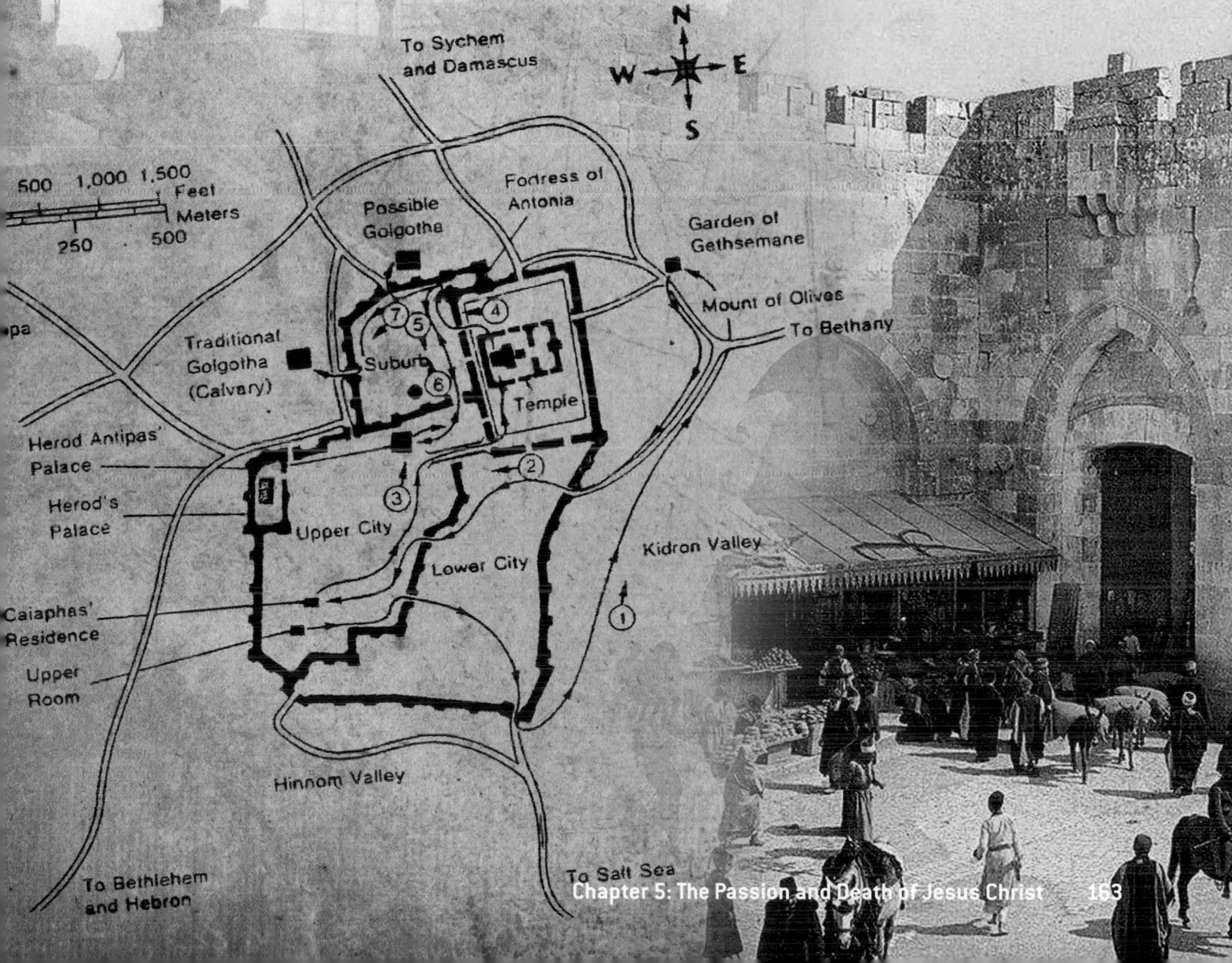

After his arrest, Jesus was taken first to Annas ② and then to the high priest Joseph Caiaphas's residence where there was a hearing. Next, Jesus had a more formal hearing before the Sanhedrin, the Jewish court, most likely at the Temple ③. From there, he was taken to Pontius Pilate, who resided at the Antonia fortress ④. Pilate sent Jesus to Herod Antipas ⑤. Herod returned Jesus to Pilate, who finally handed Jesus over for scourging ⑥ and ordered his Crucifixion. Jesus then carried his Cross to the site of execution at Golgotha outside of one of Jerusalem's west gates ⑦. Pilgrims entering the city would have been able to read the inscription on Jesus' Cross as they passed by.

Garden of Gethsemane

Jesus Meets Resistance from Religious Leaders

Jesus was opposed by several Jewish groups. The Pharisees and Herodians (see Mk 12:13–17) questioned the source of his teaching authority, his views on beliefs like the resurrection of the dead, and whether it was lawful or not to pay taxes to Rome. Jesus upset the Sadducees, who saw him as a threat to the civil order and a danger to their positions of leadership: "If we leave him alone, all will believe in him, and the Romans will come and take away both our land and our nation" (Jn 11:48).

The religious leaders likely felt that Jesus threatened their position. They may also have believed that Jesus was straying from key tenets of Judaism. Although he showed submission to the written Law, he did not always interpret the oral tradition connected to the Law in the same way as the Pharisees. Ironically, as Son of God, Jesus was the only Jew who could perfectly keep the Law. Unfortunately, in their extreme zeal to keep the Law, the Pharisees invited the danger of hypocrisy (see page 162).

Jesus asked the religious leaders of his time to believe in him because he accomplished his Father's works. When Jesus claimed that he was greater than Jewish leaders such as Solomon and Abraham, his listeners had to make a leap in understanding to comprehend that Jesus was the Son of God. Grasping Jesus' identity would have involved a real conversion from the religious leaders' belief system. Those whose hearts remained hardened to Jesus as Savior instead identified him as a blasphemer. As Christian evangelists, the Apostles would later encounter similar resistance from Jewish leaders when they went out to preach the Gospel (see Acts 2:14–4:22).

The religious leaders conspired among themselves to kill Jesus. The chief priests and the elders assembled in the high priest's palace and conferred about how to arrest Jesus and put him to death.

Joseph Caiaphas, the **high priest**, is quoted in John 11:50 saying that it was better for Jesus to die than for the whole nation to perish. Their plan—not to arrest Jesus "during the festival, that there may not be a riot among the people" (Mt 26:5)—changed for an unexplained reason. The authorities actually arrested Jesus on the night of the Preparation Day for the Passover, and put him to death the next day.

Jesus Is Recognized as the Anointed One

Jesus' Death was foreshadowed when a woman in Bethany anointed him in what turned out to be a preparation for his burial. In the Gospels of Mark and Matthew, the woman's identity is anonymous. John's Gospel identifies the woman as Mary, the sister of Lazarus. Some of Jesus' followers questioned the waste, observing that the costly ointment could have been sold and its proceeds given to the poor. But Jesus commended the woman's generous action, saying, "The poor you will always have with you, and whenever you wish you can do good to them, but you will not always have me" (Mk 14:7). The woman of simple faith by this gesture also recognized Jesus to be the Christ, the "anointed one," when so many others did not. She recognized the unique worth of his presence with her—a worth that exceeds any worldly value.

high priest In Jewish history, the priest in charge of Temple worship. The high priest shared in the general priestly duties; however, he was the only one allowed to enter the holy of holies, and then only on the Day of Atonement. Jesus is the High Priest of the New Covenant. Christ fulfilled everything that the priesthood of the Old Covenant prefigured (cf. Heb 5:10, 6:20). He offered himself once for all (cf. Heb 10:14) in a perfect sacrifice upon the Cross. His priesthood is made present in a special way in the Church through the ministerial priesthood, conferred through the Sacrament of Holy Orders.

Jesus Is Betrayed by One of His Own Disciples

Judas Iscariot's betrayal of Jesus is a separate tragic part of the passion narratives. Jesus was aware of the betrayal before it occurred. At the Last Supper, Jesus said, "And behold, the hand of the one who is to betray me is with me on the table" (Lk 22:21). Judas betrayed Jesus for thirty pieces of silver. His motive of greed fits the description in John's Gospel of Judas as the one who kept the treasury of the Apostles and who stole from it (see Jn 12:6). Judas is willing to "hand him over," the same Greek verb used to describe how Jesus is handed over to death. The Gospels of Luke and John mention that Satan influenced Judas to betray his friend (see Lk 22:3–6).

Afterward, Judas regretted what he had done and went back to the religious leaders, trying to return the money because he had sinned by participating in the arrest and death of an innocent man. Then he committed suicide (see Mt 27:3–5).

Many people would despair if they had done something as horrific as betraying Jesus, the Messiah and Son of God. Perhaps you have encountered a person who believes that he or she has committed an unforgivable sin. The tragedy in Judas's life is that Jesus was about to save all human beings, including Judas, from *all* of their sins. Though people may commit very serious sins, Jesus can redeem them all from the sins' eternal consequences. The Sacrament of Baptism and the Sacrament of Penance are the paths to divine forgiveness.

Called a "second Baptism," the Sacrament of Penance is a path to divine forgiveness.

Only God knows Judas's heart and only Christ, the judge of the living and the dead, can make a judgment about Judas's ultimate fate at the moment of his death. "Everyone is responsible for his or her life before God who has given it to [them]" (*CCC*, 2280). Suicide is often a choice made by people who are suffering from great psychological distress, anguish, or chemical imbalances. Jesus himself cautioned his listeners from making assumptions about others' sins. "By ways known to him alone, God can provide the opportunity for salutary repentance" to anyone (*CCC*, 2283), and "the Church prays that no one should be lost" (*CCC*, 1058). On the Day of Judgment, Judas—along with the rest of humanity—will appear in his own resurrected body before Christ, who is both merciful and just, to render an account of his deeds.

Jesus and His Disciples Celebrate the Last Supper

Jesus carefully planned the Passover meal with his disciples, an indication that he was very much in control of the events. At this Last Supper, he showed the disciples how they should recall his selfless gift of sacrificing his life through the perpetual celebration of the Holy Eucharist. The sacrifice he would make on behalf of all was truly a free choice.

During the Passover meal, Jesus took bread, blessed it, broke it, and gave to his disciples, saying, "Take and eat; this is my body" (Mt 26:26). He then took a cup, gave thanks, and gave it to his disciples, saying, "Drink from it, all of you, for this is my blood of the covenant, which will be shed on behalf of many for the forgiveness of sins" (Mt

26:27–28). With these words, Jesus instituted the Sacrament of the Holy Eucharist, a memorial of his Passover from death to new life. At the Eucharist, Jesus is truly present in the forms of the consecrated bread and wine.

Jesus Prays in the Garden before His Arrest

After the meal, Jesus and the disciples made their way to the Mount of Olives to a garden called Gethsemane, where Jesus prayed in great sorrow. Jesus then predicted that Peter would deny knowing him three times, though Peter proclaimed, "Even though I should have to die with you, I will not deny you" (Mt 26:35).

Jesus' sorrow at his impending Death was very human. From the depths of his soul, Jesus prayed that his Father would take away his cup of pain and death, which also involved his battles with Satan and sin. ("Drinking the cup" is a metaphor in the Old Testament for accepting God's plan.) But Jesus remained obedient to his Father unto death, praying: "My Father, if it is possible, let this cup pass from me; yet, not as I will, but as you will" (Mt 26:39).

Meanwhile, the disciples could not stay awake to comfort Jesus during his time of trial. Three times he needed to tell them to stay awake to prepare for the coming test. He said them, "Watch and pray that you may not undergo the test. The spirit is willing, but the flesh is weak" (Mt 26:41).

The experience of the disciples is common to people today. In spite of an outward willingness to follow Jesus and be loyal to him, distractions and weakness of the spirit can often be overwhelming. You too must call on God the Father to lead you through such tests of faith.

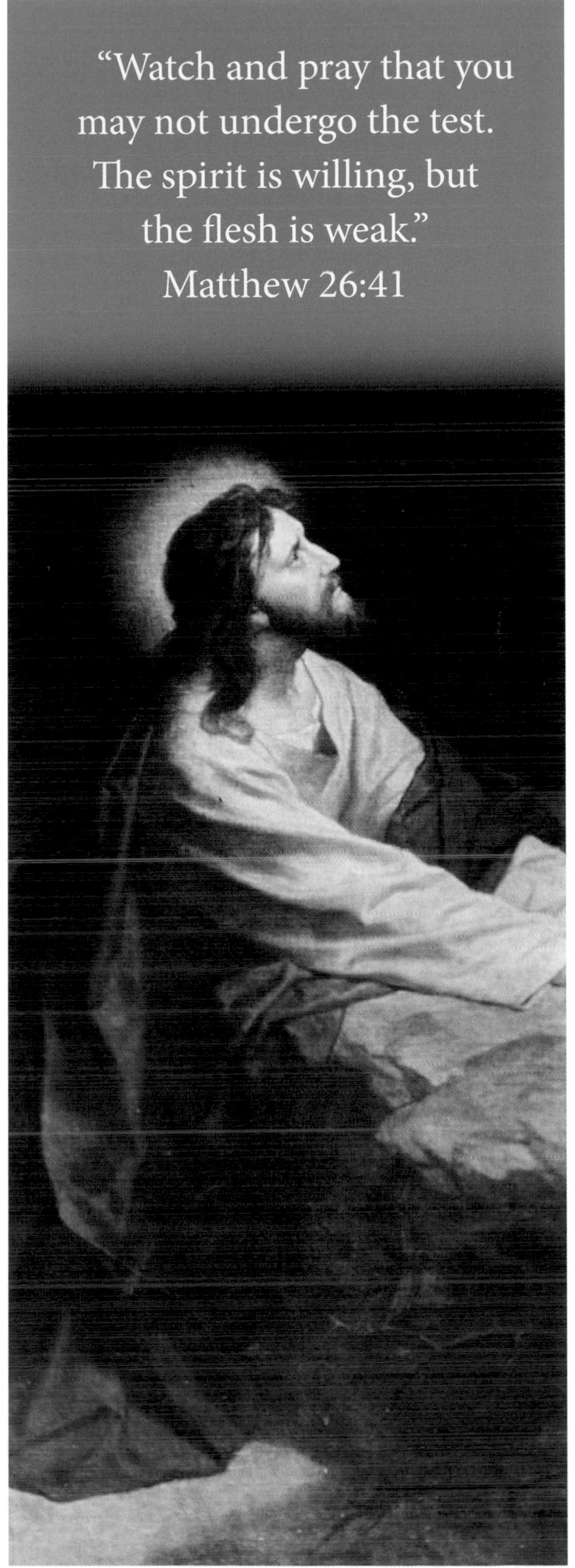
"Watch and pray that you may not undergo the test. The spirit is willing, but the flesh is weak."
Matthew 26:41

SECTION ASSESSMENT

NOTE TAKING

Use the graph you created to help you answer the following question.

1. What do you think was Jesus' darkest moment among the events prior to his Crucifixion?

VOCABULARY

2. Define *hosanna.*
3. What are the differences in the *passion narratives* among the synoptic Gospels?

COMPREHENSION

4. Why did the religious leaders initially decide to wait until after the Passover celebration to arrest Jesus?
5. What were two problems that the Pharisees and Herodians had with Jesus?
6. What type of meal was Jesus' Last Supper?

CRITICAL ANALYSIS

7. Who did the Jewish religious leaders understand Jesus to be?
8. How are each of the names given to Jesus in the Book of Zechariah and the Gospel of Matthew regarding his entrance into Jerusalem accurate descriptions of him?
9. Explain what "the poor you will always have with you" means in its original context.
10. Give a modern example of "the spirit is willing, but the flesh is weak."

SECTION 2

Jesus' Passion and Death

MAIN IDEA

Some religious leaders and Pontius Pilate unjustly condemned Jesus to an agonizing Death on the Cross.

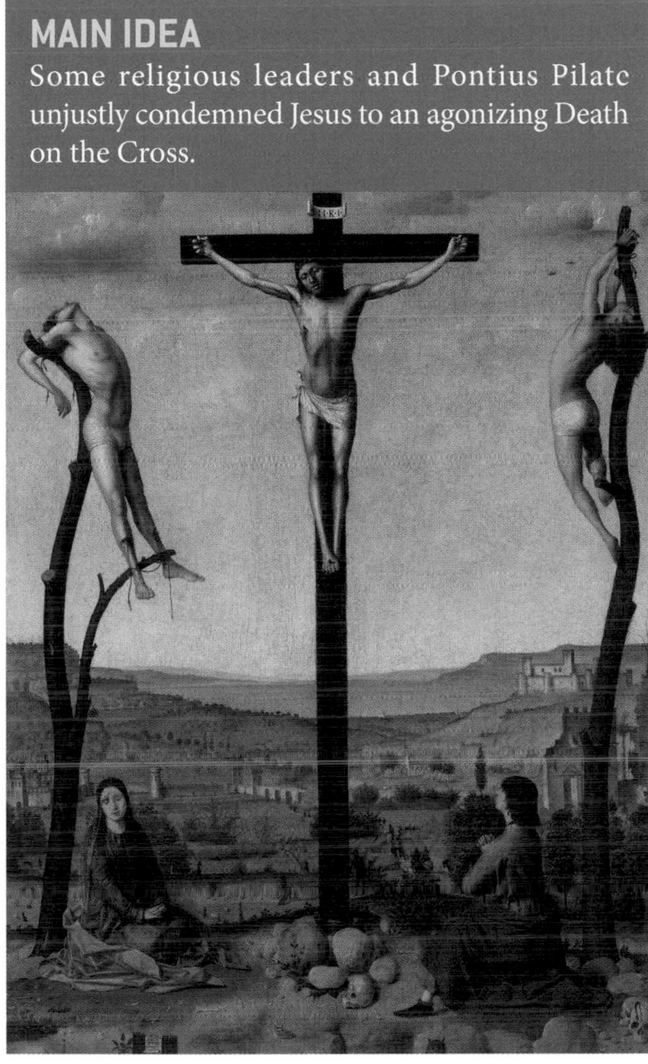

After Jesus prayed in the Garden of Gethsemane, he was arrested. From there the events leading to his suffering and Crucifixion moved at a rapid pace. John 18 provides the details that Jesus had a hearing before the former Jewish high priest Annas as well as the current high priest, Joseph Caiaphas. The exact sequence of events is not clear, although the text beginning at Matthew 26:57 provides many details. This hearing and other events of Jesus' Passion and Death are described in this section.

Jesus Goes before the Sanhedrin

Matthew 26:57–68 states that after Jesus' arrest there was a night trial before Caiaphas involving scribes, elders, priests, and members of the Sanhedrin. At this hearing, the Jewish leaders obtained false evidence and brought in false witnesses so that they could sentence Jesus to death. Finally, Caiaphas asked Jesus if he were the Messiah, the Son of God. Jesus said,

> You have said so. But I tell you:
> From now on you will see "the Son of Man
> seated at the right hand of the Power"
> and "coming on the clouds of heaven."
> (Mt 26:64)

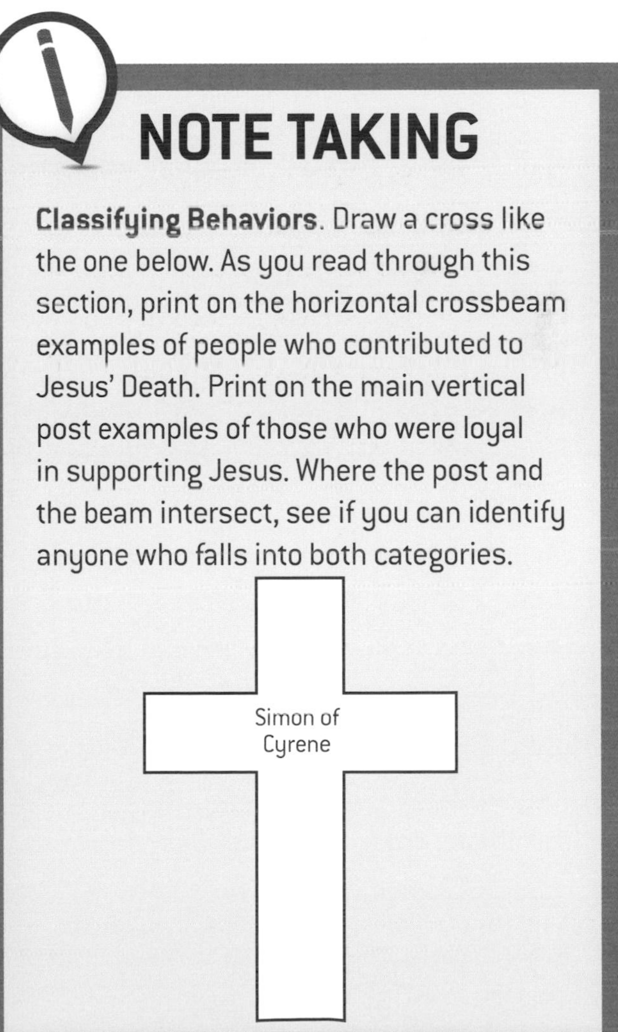

NOTE TAKING

Classifying Behaviors. Draw a cross like the one below. As you read through this section, print on the horizontal crossbeam examples of people who contributed to Jesus' Death. Print on the main vertical post examples of those who were loyal in supporting Jesus. Where the post and the beam intersect, see if you can identify anyone who falls into both categories.

Jesus' response outraged the religious leaders. The high priest accused Jesus of committing the sin of **blasphemy**, punishable by death under Jewish law. Others present spit on Jesus, struck, slapped, and mocked him, saying, "Prophesy for us, Messiah: who is it that struck you?" (Mt 26:68).

During Jesus' appearance before the Sanhedrin, Peter was out in the courtyard. As Jesus had predicted, he three times denied knowing Jesus. When the cock crowed, Peter remembered what Jesus had said. He immediately repented of his grave sin and wept bitterly (see Mt 26:69–75).

Jesus Goes before Pilate

Although the Jews ruled themselves to some extent, under the Roman laws of occupation, only the Roman prefect, a military or civic officer, could give the death penalty, and only for nonreligious crimes. Pontius Pilate would never have executed Jesus based on the Sanhedrin's religious charge of blasphemy, so they told Pilate that Jesus was guilty of a secular crime, namely *sedition*, the challenging of the emperor's authority. Sedition was also a capital offense, made clear by the crowds crying out, "If you release him, you are not a Friend of Caesar. Everyone who makes himself a king opposes Caesar" (Jn 19:12).

The first-century Jewish historian Josephus portrayed Pontius Pilate as arrogant and cruel. He related that Pilate once unleashed his soldiers, dressed as civilians, to beat Jewish citizens who protested Pilate's use of the Temple treasury to build an aqueduct. The Gospels portray Pilate as cynical: Pilate knew that Jesus was innocent, yet he failed to follow his conscience. Jesus accepted Pilate's charge addressed in the form of a question that he was king of the Jews (see Mt 27:11). Pilate's scheme to save Jesus' life by invoking a Passover custom of freeing a prisoner backfired when the people chose Barabbas instead of Jesus. When he asked the crowd what he should do with Jesus, the crowd cried, "Let him be crucified!" (Mt 27:22). Pilate then caved in to the demand of the crowd and handed Jesus over to the Roman soldiers to be scourged and crucified.

blasphemy Any thought, word, or act that expresses hatred or contempt for Christ, God, the Church, saints, or holy things.

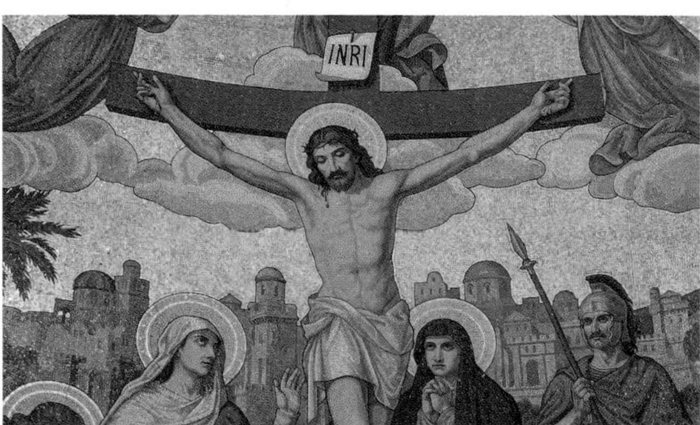

Jesus Dies by Crucifixion

The Roman soldiers scourged Jesus before making him walk to his Crucifixion. They mocked Jesus, stripped him of his clothing, and dressed him in a scarlet military cloak. They crowned him with thorns and put a reed in his right hand. Kneeling before him, they scornfully said, "Hail, King of the Jews!" (Mt 27:29). They spit on him in utter contempt and led him off to the site of crucifixion.

Although some sort of beating was common for people about to undergo Roman capital punishment, Jesus seems to have received the harsher type of these beatings. He may have been hit repeatedly with multiple leather whips with metal balls and sharp objects at the ends of them. Sometimes the Romans scourged prisoners almost to the point of death. Jesus' scourging likely put him close to a state of shock. The beatings so weakened Jesus that

The Stations of the Cross

The Stations of the Cross is a devotional and also a sacramental. The Stations of the Cross are individual images hung on the interior walls of most Catholic churches depicting fourteen steps along Jesus' Way of the Cross in Jerusalem, called "Via Dolorosa" (literally, "Way of Grief") in Latin. Praying the Stations of the Cross means meditation on each of the following scenes:

1. Jesus is condemned to death.
2. Jesus takes up his Cross.
3. Jesus falls the first time.
4. Jesus meets his mother.
5. Simon of Cyrene helps Jesus carry his Cross.
6. Veronica wipes the face of Jesus.
7. Jesus falls the second time.
8. Jesus consoles the women of Jerusalem.
9. Jesus falls the third time.
10. Jesus is stripped of his garments.
11. Jesus is nailed to the Cross.
12. Jesus dies on the Cross.
13. Jesus is taken down from the Cross.
14. Jesus is laid in the tomb.

Some churches also include a fifteenth station, the Resurrection of the Lord.

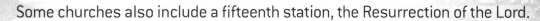

a passerby, Simon of Cyrene, had to help him carry the horizontal crossbeam. (The vertical beam was already at the site of crucifixion.)

The soldiers nailed Jesus to his Cross at about noon on Friday. Crucifixion resulted in a horrible death, usually by dehydration, loss of blood, shock, and suffocation. The Roman emperor Constantine finally banned crucifixion as a form of capital punishment in the fourth century AD.

Matthew's Gospel records that some people who passed by Jesus' Cross mocked him, asking him where his God had gone and why he could not save himself. The Romans had Jesus crucified between two revolutionaries who were truly guilty of sedition. Their presence highlighted Jesus' innocence. Both men taunted Jesus. Luke's Gospel, however, reports that one of these criminals rebuked his fellow criminal and asked Jesus to remember him when he entered his Kingdom. Jesus reassured him that they would both be in paradise that very day (see Lk 23:39–43).

Darkness descended on the land from noon until three in the afternoon, the time of Jesus' Death. His last words were "My God, my God, why have you forsaken me?" (Mt 27:46). Jesus' addressing his Father as "God" represents his utter agony as a human being who cries out to his God for help. Failing to recognize that Jesus was reciting the first line of Psalm 22 in Aramaic (*Eli, Eli, lama sabachthani?*), observers mistakenly thought that Jesus was calling on the prophet Elijah for help.

At the moment of Jesus' Death, the veil of the Temple's sanctuary split in two. This symbolized that the days of the Old Covenant had ended. Jesus' Death initiated the New Covenant by removing the barrier separating humans from God.

Matthew 27:51b–53 describes the occurrence of certain signs that were prophesied to take place when God's Kingdom came in its fullness. Drawing on the prophet Ezekiel's vision of the dry bones (see Ez 37:1–14), Matthew shows that Jesus' Death launched a new stage in history, a stage offering the possibility of the resurrection of the dead. Matthew's Gospel goes on to report that the Roman centurion and his men standing watch over Jesus greatly feared the events they witnessed and immediately understood their significance. They proclaimed, "Truly, this was the Son of God!" (Mt 27:54). Ironically, it was these Gentiles, not Jesus' closest followers, who recognized his true identity at the moment of his Death.

Not everyone abandoned Jesus at his Crucifixion. Matthew's Gospel states that many women were present, looking on from a distance. Among them were Mary Magdalene; Mary, the mother of James and Joseph; and the mother of the sons of Zebedee (that is, the disciples James and John). The Gospel of John reports that Mary, the Blessed Mother, stood beneath the Cross with the **Beloved Disciple**, likely John, and with some other women. All these disciples were witnesses to Jesus' Death (see Mt 27:55–56, Jn 19:25–26).

Beloved Disciple The "disciple whom Jesus loved," referenced several times in John's Gospel. Church Father St. Irenaeus attributed the Gospel of John to the Beloved Disciple. Church Tradition identified this John as one of the Apostles, the one who rested his head on Jesus' chest during the Last Supper (see Jn 21:20).

Take Up YOUR CROSS

How can you participate in the Paschal Mystery of Christ?

Jesus told his disciples, "Whoever wishes to come after me must deny himself, take up his cross, and follow me" (Mt 16:24). Jesus shows you the way, and he wants you to walk in his footsteps. You do this by trying to discern what God wants you to do and then following the path he shows you. This includes offering up any sufferings and disappointments that come your way—joining them to the sufferings of Jesus. Your model is the Blessed Mother who, as she stood beneath the Cross, quietly endured the death of her beloved Son. As St. Rose of Lima once said, "Apart from the Cross there is no other ladder by which we may get to heaven."

ASSIGNMENT

Imagine standing under the Cross at the time of Jesus' Crucifixion. You are an interested bystander who had heard Jesus teaching in the Temple. You think he is a very special person. You look at him suffering on the Cross. He looks down from the Cross into your eyes. You look at him. He looks at you. Write a prayer to Jesus telling him what you feel and think about his sacrifice on the Cross *for you*. Tell him of your love for him.

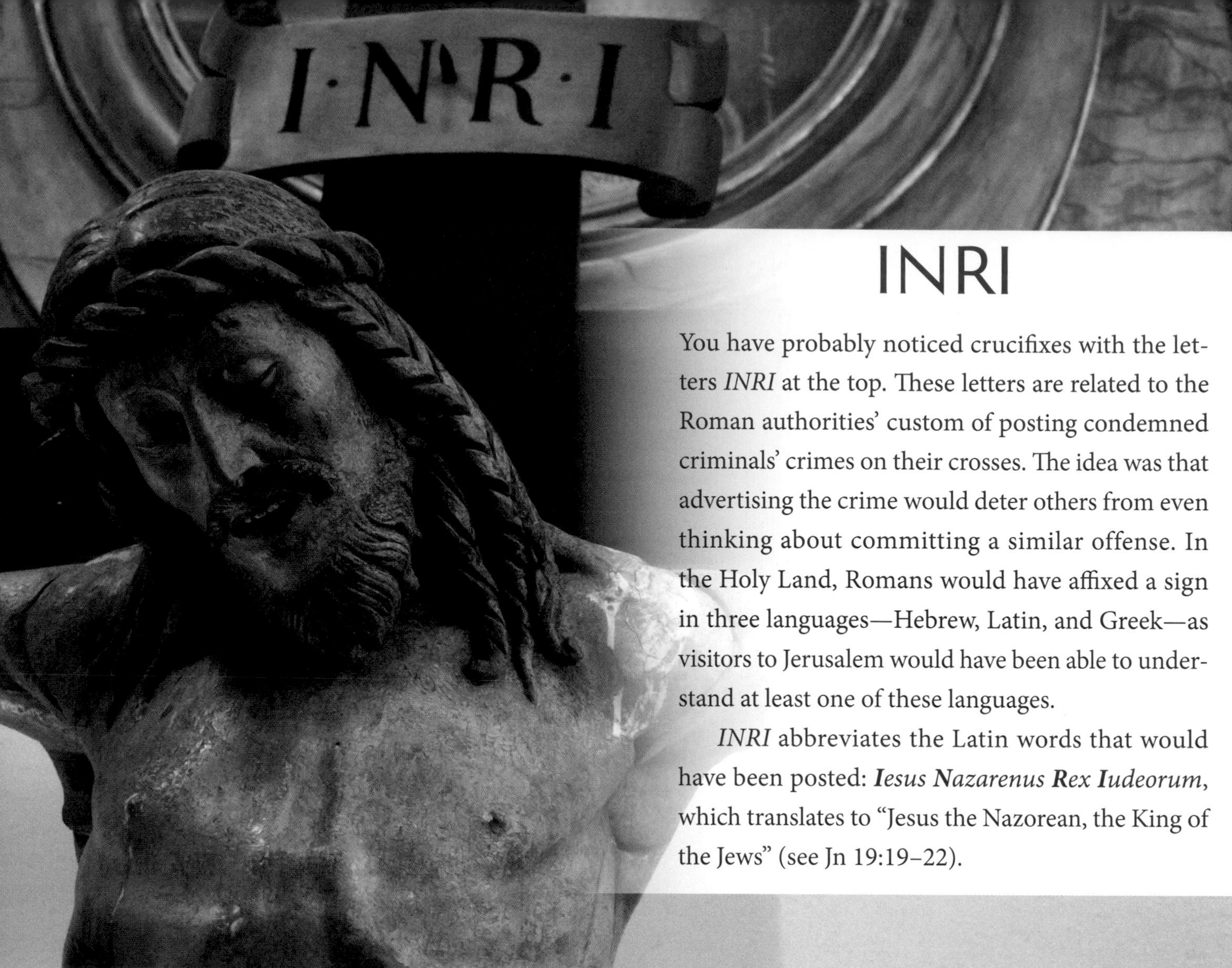

INRI

You have probably noticed crucifixes with the letters *INRI* at the top. These letters are related to the Roman authorities' custom of posting condemned criminals' crimes on their crosses. The idea was that advertising the crime would deter others from even thinking about committing a similar offense. In the Holy Land, Romans would have affixed a sign in three languages—Hebrew, Latin, and Greek—as visitors to Jerusalem would have been able to understand at least one of these languages.

INRI abbreviates the Latin words that would have been posted: ***I**esus **N**azarenus **R**ex **I**udeorum*, which translates to "Jesus the Nazorean, the King of the Jews" (see Jn 19:19–22).

Jesus Is Buried in a Sealed Tomb

Joseph of Arimathea was a wealthy disciple of Jesus. The Gospels of Mark and Luke identify him as a member of the Sanhedrin, but as one who did not approve of the council's condemnation of Jesus. Pilate released Jesus' body to Joseph because he was completely sure that Jesus was dead. Joseph wrapped Jesus' body in a clean linen cloth and placed it in a new tomb in the rock. He did this hurriedly late on Friday afternoon since the Sabbath began at sundown. After the tomb was sealed, Mary Magdalene and another Mary remained sitting, mourning Jesus' Death, in front of the tomb.

Matthew's Gospel is the only one that mentions that certain priests and Pharisees petitioned Pilate to post a guard at the tomb to prevent Jesus' disciples from stealing his body and claiming that he rose from the dead. Pilate refused their request, so the Pharisees posted their own guards. This interesting point reveals that Jesus' opponents, nonbelievers, knew that he was dead and could identify the place of his burial. This is important because after Jesus' Resurrection, nonbelievers could never produce Jesus' body, even though they knew where he was buried.

The Gospels Share Common Elements of the Passion Narrative

In summary, though the evangelists agree on the essential details of the passion narrative, they emphasize different parts. Each of the passion narratives includes the following elements:

- Jesus' arrest
- his questioning by the high priest
- Jesus' trials before the Sanhedrin and Pontius Pilate
- his condemnation
- Jesus' Crucifixion
- his Death
- his burial

Take some time to read the individual passion narratives. You will encounter passages and details that are unique to each of the Gospel writers.

SECTION ASSESSMENT

NOTE TAKING

Use the image you made to help you complete the following items.

1. Name three adjectives that describe those who contributed to Jesus' Death.
2. What do people who were loyal to Jesus at the time of his Passion and Death have in common?

COMPREHENSION

3. For which sin did the high priest convict Jesus?
4. For which crime did Pontius Pilate convict Jesus?
5. Who helped Jesus carry the horizontal beam of the Cross?
6. How did Roman crucifixions kill a person?
7. To whom did Pilate release Jesus' body for burial?
8. Name three elements of the passion narratives that appear in all four Gospels.

CRITICAL ANALYSIS

9. Aside from the fact that their sins were quite different, what do you think made Judas (see pages 165–166) and Peter respond so differently when they realized what they had done to Jesus?
10. Why do you think Jesus quoted Psalm 22, asking why his Father was forsaking him, while on the Cross?

REFLECTION

11. Imagine that you were with Jesus in the Garden of Gethsemane. How do you think you would have acted?

SECTION 3

Christ's Death Redeems the World

MAIN IDEA

Christ's Death, part of the Paschal Mystery, is an act of love that is central to God's eternal plan and to your salvation. Christ died for the salvation of all, and all bear responsibility for his Death.

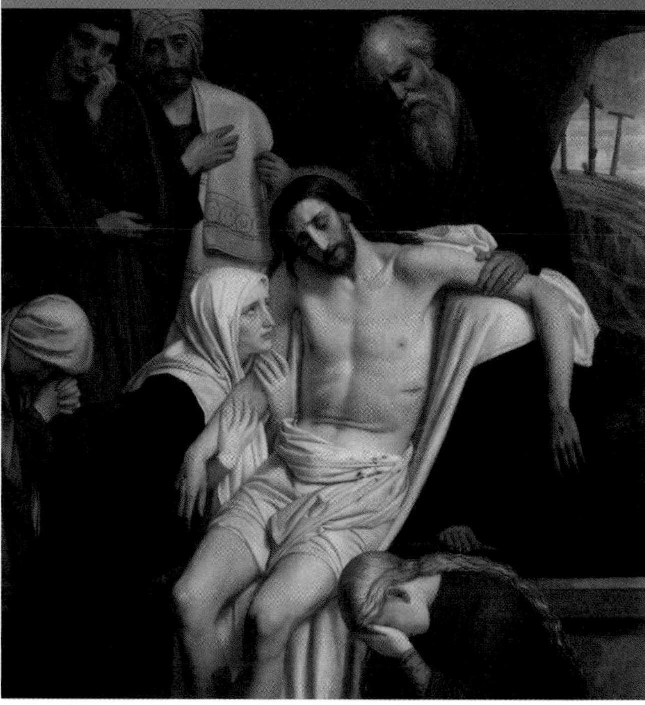

The Paschal Mystery of Jesus Christ, including his redemptive Death on the Cross and his Resurrection, is the high point of human history. It was not the result of chance but was part of the mystery of God's plan of salvation, promised to humanity immediately after the Original Sin of the first man and woman.

Although the events of Jesus' saving Passion, Death, and Resurrection were part of the Father's plan, God the Father did not manipulate the individuals responsible for Jesus' Death in any way; they freely chose to crucify him. Because God the Father does not experience time as humans do, he knew beforehand how each person involved in the events leading up to and including Jesus' Crucifixion would respond to his free offer of grace and the free actions of Jesus. Though God had the power to stop these events, he did not, because they were necessary for his plan of salvation.

These mysteries of the Father's plan of salvation are uncovered in Sacred Scripture. Isaiah 53 prophesied a Suffering Servant who bears the infirmities of all and endures the suffering of all. St. Paul

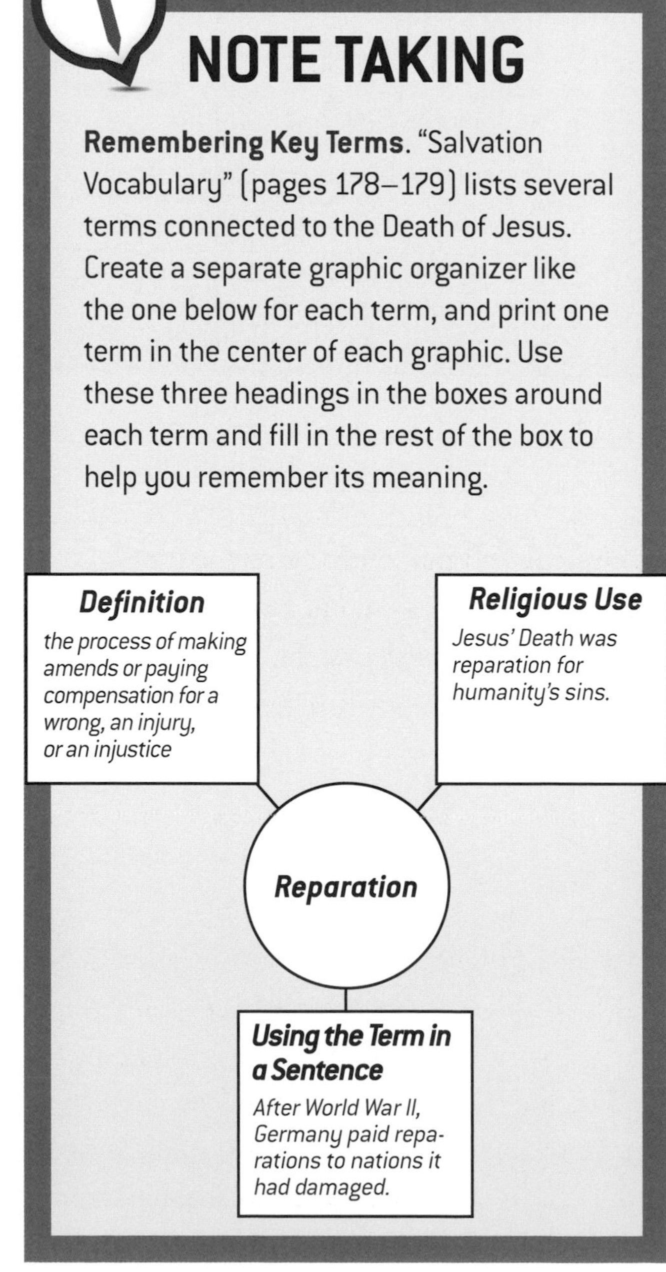

NOTE TAKING

Remembering Key Terms. "Salvation Vocabulary" (pages 178–179) lists several terms connected to the Death of Jesus. Create a separate graphic organizer like the one below for each term, and print one term in the center of each graphic. Use these three headings in the boxes around each term and fill in the rest of the box to help you remember its meaning.

Definition
the process of making amends or paying compensation for a wrong, an injury, or an injustice
Religious Use
Jesus' Death was reparation for humanity's sins.
Reparation
Using the Term in a Sentence
After World War II, Germany paid reparations to nations it had damaged.

Jesus teaching disciples while on the road to Emmaus.

professed that "Christ died for our sins in accordance with the scriptures" (1 Cor 15:3). After his Resurrection, when he appeared to his disciples on the road to Emmaus, Jesus showed them how his Death and Resurrection were recorded in Scripture:

> He said to them, "These are my words that I spoke to you while I was still with you, that everything written about me in the law of Moses and in the prophets and psalms must be fulfilled." Then he opened their minds to understand the scriptures. And he said to them, "Thus it is written that the Messiah would suffer and rise from the dead on the third day and that repentance, for the forgiveness of sins, would be preached in his name to all the nations, beginning from Jerusalem. You are witnesses of these things." (Lk 24:44–48)

Because Jesus is truly God and truly man, he was able to bridge the gap between the Father and humans in a unique way. He was able to bear the full weight of human sinfulness and death and be an expiation for sin. Through his Death and Resurrection, he justified humanity and reconciled people with God. Importantly, he invites you to share in his achievement on the Cross and in his Resurrection through the sacramental life of the Church, especially the Holy Eucharist.

Jesus Freely Embraced the Father's Plan to Redeem Humanity

The Three Divine Persons of the Blessed Trinity do not act separately but instead work together in loving communion. Jesus, the Son of God and Second Person of the Blessed Trinity, did not become man to achieve his own goals or his own agenda. Rather, he came to do his Father's will.

Jesus embraced his Father's plan of salvation. He said, "My food is to do the will of the one who sent me and to finish his work" (Jn 4:34). Jesus' whole life, including even the smallest elements, was an act of redemption as well as a Revelation of the Father. Even when he was in agony in the garden hours before his arrest, he still expressed the desire to accomplish his Father's will. As John the Baptist testified, Jesus was the Suffering Servant who bore the sins of his people. He was the Paschal Lamb, the symbol of Israel's redemption at the first Passover. An early Christian hymn quoted in the Letter to the Philippians states that Christ "emptied himself taking the form of a slave . . . he humbled himself, becoming obedient to death, even death on a cross" (Phil 2:7, 8).

Recall from the first chapters of Genesis that the punishment for sin is death, since the disobedience of Adam and Eve caused the loss of original holiness and original justice for themselves and their descendants. By sending his own Son as a slave to a fallen humanity, God the Father made his sinless Son to *be sin* so that he could restore humanity's righteousness. Of course, Jesus did not experience human sin himself. Instead, he stood in solidarity with sinful humans.

Salvation Vocabulary

People use several terms and phrases to describe why Jesus died and the effects of his Death. Most of them are ordinary words that become theological when applied to the Paschal Mystery, but several of them have multiple meanings. It is therefore important to learn how the terms work theologically. (See the Note Taking prompt on page 176 for an assignment connected with this feature.)

- **Reparation** is the process of making amends or paying compensation for a wrong, an injury, or an injustice. For example, a student who is guilty of defacing school property may pay the school back for items damaged and also do some janitorial work at the school in reparation. Jesus made amends for the wrongs perpetrated by humanity through his own suffering on the Cross and his Death. Christ was put to death for the sins of the world and was raised for the justification of humankind.
- **Atonement** is nearly a synonym for reparation, but it has a more serious connotation. Reparation emphasizes healing the relationship that was broken by an offense, whereas atonement emphasizes making right the offense by paying the just penalty. Think of how the word *atone* is used today: "The teen convicted of driving under the influence and injuring a pedestrian must atone by going to high schools and telling his story to other teens." Jesus atoned for the sin of the world, both Original Sin and all personal sin, by paying the penalty that human beings deserve for their offenses against God, other people, and the world. The eternal Son of God emptied himself of his power and glory to offer himself as an atonement for disobedience, sin, and death; by being obedient to the Father even to the point of Death on the Cross, he atoned for your sins (cf. Phil 2:5–9). "Jesus accomplished the substitution of the suffering Servant, who 'makes himself an *offering for sin*,' when 'he bore the sin of many'" (*CCC*, 615, quoting Is 53:10, 11).

- **Expiation** is a synonym for reparation or atonement that comes from a Latin verb meaning "to atone for." Expiation involves putting right an offense against truth or justice. The First Letter of John says, "In this is love: not that we have loved God, but that he loved us and sent his Son as expiation for our sins" (1 Jn 4:10). Expiation emphasizes that God was reconciling the world to himself in Christ's humanity (cf. Rom 3:25, 2 Cor 5:19).

- **Satisfaction** is "an act whereby the sinner makes amends for sin, especially in reparation to God for offenses against him" (*CCC*, Glossary). For example, if you purposely damaged a neighbor's mailbox, you would not only apologize but also you would satisfy your neighbor by repairing the mailbox or paying for a new one. Jesus not only pays for our wrongdoing but also repairs our relationship with God by being obedient to the Father as the New Adam.

- **Redemption** is the process of buying back or freeing a person by paying a ransom or removing the person's obligation by payment. You may be most familiar with the term in the context of redeeming a special offer or coupon for merchandise. When you take your paper or digital coupon to the store, the checker lessens the amount you are obliged to pay for the item. However, if you do not use the coupon, it goes unredeemed. Jesus redeemed or *paid the ransom for* humans to release them from sin's imprisonment by dying on the Cross. In this case, Jesus did not merely lessen your obligation; he paid in full the debt that we allowed in payment for sin.

- **Ransom** is both a noun and a verb. As a noun, *ransom* might be money paid to free a person who has been captured or kidnapped. *To ransom* is to pay the money. The plots of modern films are often based on the storyline of a victim whose kidnappers demand a ransom before they will release their captive. Because humanity was captive to sin, Jesus ransomed human beings through his Death on the Cross.

- **Sacrifice** is the name for a ritual offering made to God by a priest on behalf of the people as a sign of adoration, gratitude, supplication, and communion. In the case of Christ's Death on the Cross, Jesus was both the priest *and* the sacrifice: he offered himself on behalf of the people. God the Father allowed his Son to suffer and die because Jesus' sacrifice destroyed the power of sin and restored humans to friendship with God.

- **Justification** in this case means to be made holy, just, and acceptable before God. Justification means not only the remission of your sins but also your sanctification and renewal through God's grace. Justification follows upon God's merciful initiative of offering forgiveness in Baptism; it reconciles you with God, frees you from enslavement to sin, and heals you.

Jesus' Death in the Context of Salvation History

Even after sin entered the world, God did not abandon humans. He designed a plan by which he would reveal his love and forgiveness to the world in stages that would culminate in the Person and mission of the Incarnate Word, Jesus Christ. The entire history of God's progressive Revelation of himself and of the promise of redemption is called *salvation history*, because it describes God's gracious work in the world for the salvation of humankind, leading up to Jesus Christ.

Each stage in salvation history foreshadowed the fulfillment of God's work in the Paschal Mystery. The Father sent his Son to descend to the depths of the earth and human experience (cf. Jn 1:14, Phil 2:5–11, 1 Jn 1) and to become "in the likeness of sinful flesh" (Rom 8:3). The perfect sacrifice for the sins of humankind was Christ's Death on the Cross. By this sacrifice, Christ accomplished the redemption of the world. The sacrifice of Christ is commemorated and mysteriously made present in the Eucharistic sacrifice of the Church (see *CCC*, 1357, 1544).

The Father Sent His Son to Save Humanity Out of Love

Because of his love for the people he created, God wanted to regain the close relationship with humanity that he had originally planned before Original Sin created a chasm between him and human beings. No one person or sacrifice offered by humanity was capable of repaying to God the debt of Original Sin and all of the personal sins that followed. God needed to intervene personally in human history in order to heal the ravages caused by sin.

Out of love, God the Father sent his Son to earth to be that sacrificial offering that would pay the debt for humanity and close the chasm between humans and God. Christ's sacrifice was a complete gift to the world. Jesus, who was perfectly suited to be the instrument of God's love, was obedient and offered his Death as a gift to his Father and to all people. Christ's Death is both the Paschal sacrifice of human redemption and the sacrifice of the New Covenant that restores humans to communion with God.

Jesus' Sacrificial Death Restored You to Communion with God

Jesus' Death and Resurrection provide humans with two primary gifts:

1. By his Death, Christ liberates you from sin.
2. By his Resurrection, he opens for you the way to a new life as a son or daughter of God.

Jesus' Death and Resurrection not only erase the debt of Original Sin and death but also offer you a share in God's own heart and life that far exceeds anything Adam and Eve could have imagined.

Who Is Responsible for Jesus' Death?

Part of understanding Jesus' Paschal Mystery is understanding the responsibility and guilt humans themselves had in conspiring to put him to death. Listed next are some of the steps leading to Jesus' Death and the culpability of some of the individuals and groups involved.

Crucified under Pontius Pilate

Specifically, the Roman charge against Jesus was that he was "the King of the Jews." Ironically, Jesus truly

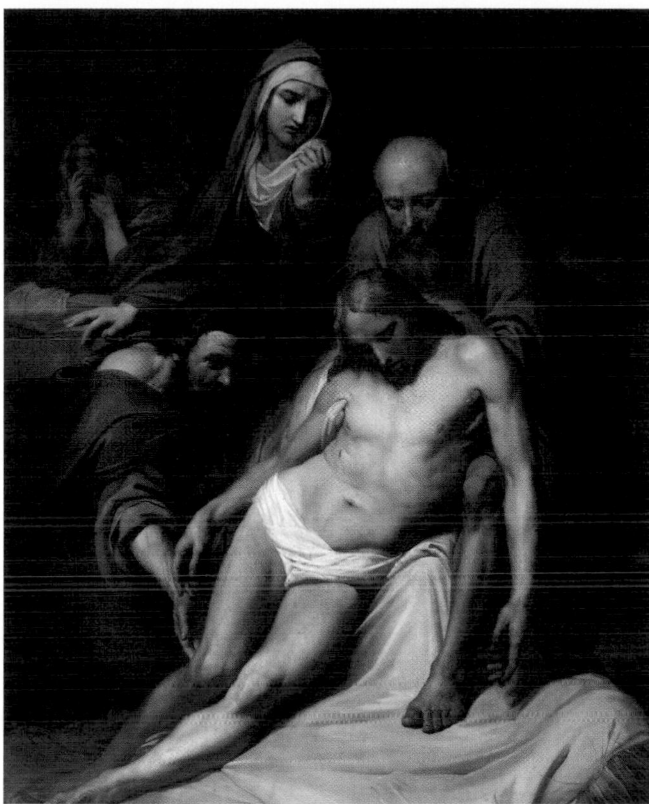

Jesus was executed under the order of Pontius Pilate.

was the King of the Jews, the Messiah whom the Jews were awaiting. However, Jesus' rule was not one of political or military power but one of humble service. Both Pilate and the Jewish leaders who opposed Jesus viewed him as a threat to Roman authority and to the relatively peaceful relations the Jewish authorities had with Roman occupation forces. So Pilate dealt with Jesus the way Romans dealt with all potential revolutionaries—by executing him.

Ultimately, then, the one person responsible for Jesus' Death was Pontius Pilate, the Roman prefect of Judea, Samaria, and Idumea from AD 26 to 36. With the cooperation of some religious authorities in Jerusalem, Pilate sentenced Jesus to death, probably in April of AD 30. The Jewish writer Philo described Pilate as "corrupt, violent, abusive, and cruel." The Gospels suggest that Pilate thought Jesus was probably innocent of the charge brought against him. However, he violated his conscience and did the politically expedient thing by having Jesus executed.

The Role of Jewish Officials in Jesus' Death

Jesus was a popular teacher whose popularity irritated some of the Jewish officials of his day. Furthermore, though he was not a trained rabbi, he spoke with authority on points of the Law, and ordinary people listened to him.

Although many religious leaders felt threatened by Jesus, the Pharisees Nicodemus and Joseph of Arimathea were his secret disciples, and there was additional dissent among other leaders about how to handle his popularity. Some of the religious leaders feared that Jesus would draw the ire of the Roman authorities on the Jews if his disciples were associated with the Jews. It made sense to some that one person's death could save the whole people.

A tipping point in Jesus' condemnation came shortly before his Passion, when he predicted that the temple of his body would be destroyed and rebuilt in three days (see Jn 2:14–24). Certain witnesses who heard this teaching interpreted Jesus' prediction as an attack on the Jerusalem Temple, even claiming that Jesus was involved in revolutionary activity. Jesus' actual behavior did not support such a belief. Jesus had always honored the Temple. He was presented there forty days after his birth, and he taught there at the age of twelve. In addition, Jesus traveled to the Temple in Jerusalem to celebrate the Passover feast. In his public life, he taught in the Temple precincts during certain Jewish feasts.

However, the chief priest, Joseph Caiaphas, and members of the Sanhedrin had an economic and religious interest in the Temple. They too feared a rebellion. They wanted the peaceful status quo that kept them in power and did not want the Romans

The crowd denouncing Jesus before Pontius Pilate, who condemned Jesus to death even though he believed Jesus to be innocent.

to have any excuse for clamping down on a rebellion with repressive measures. So they brought the charge of sedition to Pilate. Coupled with this charge was another that, to many of them, seemed outrageous and blasphemous—Jesus' claim to be the "Messiah, the son of the Blessed One" (Mk 14:61).

Certain Jewish officials wanted Jesus out of their way for several reasons. His *association with sinners*, his *exorcisms*, his *teachings on dietary and ritual purity laws*, his *teaching with unique authority*, his *claims to be the Messiah*, his *forgiving of sin*, and his *claim to be Lord of the Sabbath* all led the chief priest and members of the Sanhedrin to feel justified in turning Jesus over to Pilate for execution.

All People Bear Responsibility for Jesus' Death

Tragically, in the past, some have blamed the Jewish people as a whole for the Death of Jesus. The complex trial of Jesus shows that only a few Jewish officials provoked Pilate to put Jesus to death. The false belief that all Jews are responsible arose in part from the cry of the crowd recorded in the Gospel of Matthew: "His blood be upon us and upon our children!" (27:25). The Second Vatican Council strongly condemned that false belief:

> What happened in his passion cannot be charged against all the Jews, without distinction, then alive, nor against the Jews of today. . . . The Jews should not be presented as rejected or accursed by God, as if this followed from the Holy Scriptures. (*Nostra Aetate*, 4–5)

In a way, sinners from all times crucified Jesus, yet he redeemed sinners of all times too. It might also seem strange that people who lived before *and* after Jesus would really bear responsibility for his

Death. The *Catechism of the Catholic Church* teaches the following:

> We must regard as guilty all those who continue to relapse into their sins. Since our sins made the Lord Christ suffer the torment of the cross, those who plunge themselves into disorders and crimes crucify the Son of God anew in their hearts (for he is in them) and hold him up to contempt. And it can be seen that our crime in this case is greater in us than in the Jews. As for them, according to the witness of the Apostle, "None of the rulers of this age understood this; for if they had, they would not have crucified the Lord of glory." We, however, profess to know him. And when we deny him by our deeds, we in some way seem to lay violent hands on him. (*CCC*, 598)

The eternal Son of God was sent into the world to bear the sin of the world. He could only do this as God. Only God could bear such a mission. By becoming flesh as a human being and by taking the sin of the world upon himself, Jesus knew and loved each person who has ever lived, and he gave himself up for all people. The cry from Matthew 27:25 highlights the responsibility that all of humanity bears for the Death of Jesus.

SECTION ASSESSMENT

NOTE TAKING

Use the organizer you made to help you complete the following items.

1. What is the difference between *reparation* and *atonement*, as in the atonement for sin made by Jesus?
2. Use the word *ransom* in a sentence about what Jesus did for humanity.

COMPREHENSION

3. What is the high point of human history?
4. How were Jesus Christ's Death and Resurrection part of God's plan for salvation?
5. What were the two Roman charges against Jesus?
6. Who is ultimately responsible for Jesus' Death?
7. Why did Joseph Caiaphas and members of the Sanhedrin value the status quo?

CRITICAL ANALYSIS

8. How do you know that Christ's sacrifice was a total gift of love?
9. What do you find ironic about the concern that Jesus would destroy the Jerusalem Temple?
10. How has a misunderstanding of Matthew 27:25 been used as an excuse to persecute others in Christianity's history?

Section Summaries

Focus Question

How did Jesus' Death on the Cross bring about your salvation?
Complete one of the following:

Create an artistic rendition of any of the key moments in the Gospels discussed in this chapter: Jesus' entrance into Jerusalem, the Last Supper, Jesus' agony in the garden, Jesus' arrest, his trial before Pilate, the Way of the Cross, Jesus' Crucifixion, his being taken down from the Cross, or Jesus' burial in the tomb. Choose any art medium you are comfortable with. Scan or videotape your work, and deliver it to your teacher both electronically and as a hard copy or live presentation.

Find a piece of liturgical music or a hymn that you think effectively conveys the truth that Jesus saved you through his Death. In a one-page report, compare and contrast this song with a second song that you think is less effective.

Identify a person you have heard of or met who you think does God's work to save others. This person can "save" in an overtly religious way or through another role such as coach, counselor, teacher, or parent. Compare this person's ministry with Jesus' saving life and Death.

INTRODUCTION (PAGES 157–159)

Dying for Love

Many people sacrifice themselves for loved ones and strangers in part because their worldview values self-sacrifice based on a view of God as love. They know that God loves all people and gives them the infinite value of being made in his image. To sacrifice your life for something or someone is to give your life an ultimate worth. This insight tells us something about how much God loves us, because God gave up his own life for us in Jesus Christ.

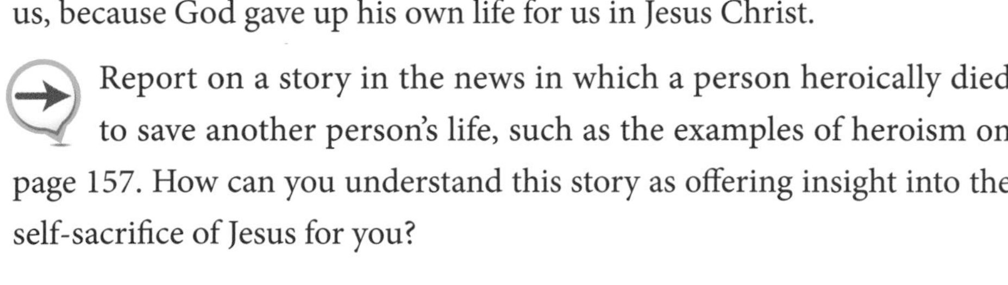

Report on a story in the news in which a person heroically died to save another person's life, such as the examples of heroism on page 157. How can you understand this story as offering insight into the self-sacrifice of Jesus for you?

SECTION 1 (PAGES 160–168)

The Events Leading Up to Jesus' Passion

The events that led up to Jesus' Passion and Death are very significant for understanding the meaning of his Passion and Death. They highlight the wide range of human responses to Jesus, from acceptance and love to scorn and denial. Jews initially welcomed Jesus when he entered Jerusalem. Then Jesus rebuked the moneychangers for using the Temple as something other than a place of prayer. The Jewish leaders made plans to arrest him. Likewise, Judas made plans to betray Jesus; he did so while Jesus prayed in the garden after Jesus and his disciples celebrated the Last Supper.

Imagine that you were one of his disciples during the events leading up to Jesus' Passion and Death. Using "tweets" of 140 characters or fewer, narrate these events, including your own perspective if possible. Write at least five tweets.

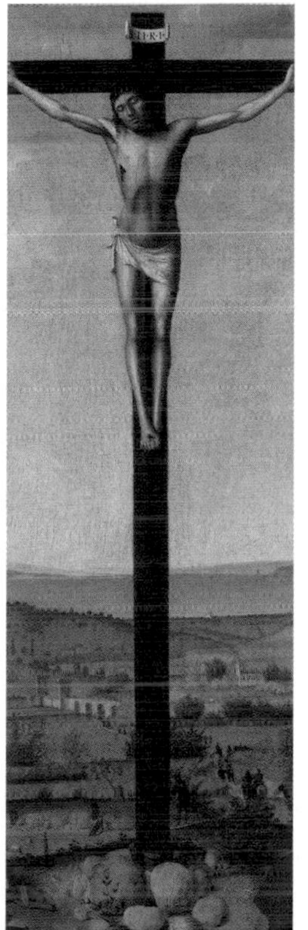

SECTION 2 (PAGES 169–175)

Jesus' Passion and Death

Some Jewish leaders and Pontius Pilate unjustly condemned Jesus to face an agonizing death on the Cross. His Passion and Death are the saving acts of redemption. When Jesus was brought before the Sanhedrin, religious leaders introduced false evidence and testimony to convict Jesus of blasphemy. Pontius Pilate convicted Jesus based on the crowd's demands rather than on Jesus' guilt. Jesus was scourged terribly, needed Simon of Cyrene's help to carry the horizontal beam of his Cross to his execution, and suffered before he gave up his spirit. Several women, including the Blessed Mother, and John, the Beloved Disciple, remained with Jesus to the end. Joseph of Arimathea then buried Jesus in his own tomb.

When people are suffering in some way, they often need help from a person such as Simon of Cyrene to make it through. Write about a character from a novel, movie, or real-life experience who steps up and shoulders a great deal of someone's burden to help them successfully navigate a difficult time.

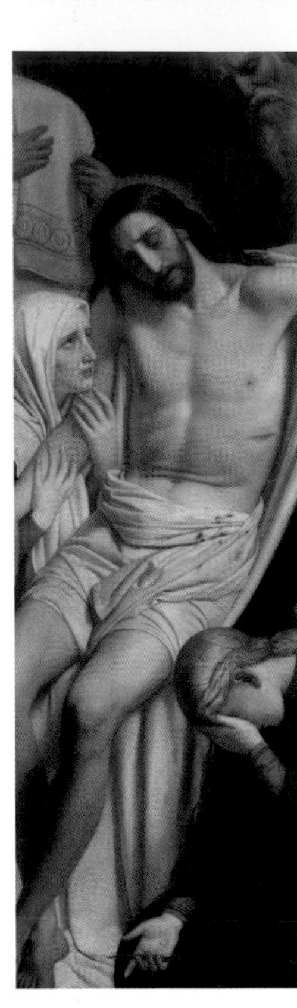

SECTION 3 (PAGES 176–183)

Christ's Death Redeems the World

Jesus' redeeming Death is an act of love that is central to God's plan and to your salvation. Jesus' Death was part of God's plan from the beginning, and Jesus embraced his mission freely. The Father sent his Son into the world to become a human being and to take the burden of our sin upon himself. As the eternal Son of God, Jesus' mission was to reveal the Father's love for the world and to restore humanity's righteousness with God, because the punishment for Original Sin had been death. Jesus' Death and Resurrection not only liberated humanity from sin and death but also opened up the way for people to a new life as sons and daughters of God. While Judas, Pilate, and the Sanhedrin played a historical role in the Death of Jesus, their degree of responsibility is known to God alone. All sinners are the authors of Christ's Passion and Death.

Print the names of each of the sorrowful mysteries of the Rosary (pages 362–363). Under each mystery, write a short prayer or reflection.

Chapter Assignments

Choose and complete at least one of the following three assignments to assess your understanding of the material in this chapter.

1. Redactive Critical Analysis of the Passion Narratives

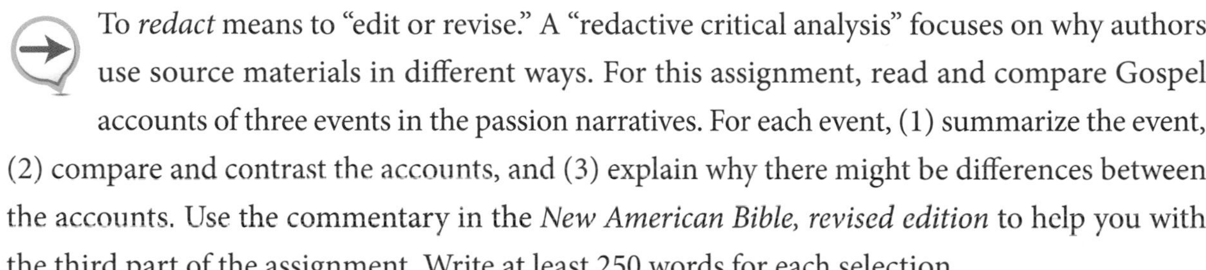

To *redact* means to "edit or revise." A "redactive critical analysis" focuses on why authors use source materials in different ways. For this assignment, read and compare Gospel accounts of three events in the passion narratives. For each event, (1) summarize the event, (2) compare and contrast the accounts, and (3) explain why there might be differences between the accounts. Use the commentary in the *New American Bible, revised edition* to help you with the third part of the assignment. Write at least 250 words for each selection.

- Selection 1: Prediction of Peter's Denial

  Read and compare: Matthew 26:34, 69–75; Mark 14:30, 66–72; Luke 22:34, 54–62; and John 13:38; 18:15–18, 25–27.

  Clue: Why the difference in the number of times the cock crows?

- Selection 2: Taking Up the Sword

  Read and compare: Matthew 26:51–54; Mark 14:46–49; Luke 22:49–51; and John 18:10–11

  Clues: In each Gospel, who cuts off the servant's ear, and how does Jesus respond?

- Selection 3: The Last Words of Jesus

  Read and compare: Matthew 27:46 (same as Mark 15:34); Luke 23:46; and John 19:30

  Clues: Why does Luke quote a different passage from the psalms? What theological meaning do you suppose the last words of Jesus recorded in the Gospel of John have?

2. Jesus on Trial

Develop and write arguments for the prosecution and defense as if you were putting Jesus on trial in a court of law. To prepare for both sides of the case, read the following passages:

- Arrest of Jesus (Mk 14:43–52)
- Jesus before the Sanhedrin (Mk 14:53–65)
- Jesus before Pilate (Mk 15:1–15, Lk 23:1–5, Jn 18:28–40)

Write a one- to two-page report that details the prosecution's case against Jesus. Possible accusations might include the threat to tear down the Temple, blasphemy, claiming to be king, misleading the people on payment of taxes, and instigating riots. Draw additional evidence from other accounts in the Gospels, such as Jesus' "violation" of Sabbath laws and disturbing of the peace.

Then write a one- to two-page report that rebuts the prosecution's case and argues in support of Jesus' innocence. Answer the charges one by one, citing appropriate Scripture passages.

Optional: Work on this exercise with a partner. Each of you will take a different side in the case. Argue the case in front of your teacher and/or your classmates.

3. Reflection on Classical Works Describing the Passion

Many classical musical compositions and works of art depict the events and emotions of Christ's Passion. Research and cite two or three examples from either or both genres for this assignment. For each example, do the following:

- Look up a visual and/or audio representation of the classical work online.
- As part of your report, share a link to the website(s) you explored.
- Write one paragraph about the artist or composer.
- Write one paragraph about the history and background of the creation of the work (including date and place of creation).
- Write one paragraph about how the work connects with the Passion of Christ (include representative lyrics if applicable).
- Write two paragraphs of personal reflection on the work. What do you like about it? How does it speak to you about Christ's Passion? What new insight on Christ's Passion has viewing or listening to this work given you?

Faithful Disciple

St. José Luis Sánchez del Río

José Luis Sánchez del Río was born in 1913, the third in a family of four children. After receiving the Eucharist for the first time, José became more serious about his faith. At age fourteen, José wanted to become a *Cristero*, a soldier fighting for *Cristo Rey* ("Christ the King") against the Mexican government, which was violently persecuting the Catholic Church at that time. Though he was initially rejected because of his age, his persistence and desire finally convinced one commander to use him as a general's flag bearer and bugler.

St. José Luis Sánchez del Río

In a battle with government forces, a bullet killed his general's horse, and José immediately offered the general his own horse. The government soldiers then captured José and an older friend, Lazarus. Thinking that they could force these younger Cristeros to abandon their cause, the soldiers departed from their usual practice of shooting Cristeros or hanging them from trees in the square or on telephone poles.

The federal general offered the boys escape if they would enlist in the government troops, but José said, "Death before that. I am your enemy. Shoot me!" The general transferred the two young men to a prison near their village where the federal deputy happened to be José's godfather. The man tried to persuade José to renounce his cause and pursue other opportunities, but José refused. Meanwhile, Lazarus was eventually able to escape, and he rejoined the Cristeros. José was put back in prison and sentenced to death.

José was marched out to his death. The soldiers leading the way also tried to force José to renounce Christ. They beat his feet until the skin came off and made him walk barefoot over cobblestones to a grave that had been prepared for him. They gave him blows with a machete. They told him that if he publicly said "Death to Christ the King," they would spare his life. He responded, "I will never give in. *Viva Cristo Rey*! *Viva la Virgen de Guadalupe*!" When they reached his grave, the soldiers began stabbing him with bayonets, but he only cried louder, "*Viva Cristo Rey*!" The captain was so enraged that he simply shot José in the head so that he fell into his grave. Those who witnessed the execution believed that only Christ could have given José such courage.

St. José Luis Sánchez del Río was only one of many Mexican martyrs from this time period. He died on February 10, 1928. Pope Benedict XVI declared him a martyr and beatified him on November 20, 2005. Pope Francis canonized him on October 16, 2016.

(Margaret Galitzin, "José Sánchez del Rio, Martyr for Christ the King," review of *For Greater Glory*, Tradition in Action website, June 18, 2012; Christopher Check, "¡Viva Cristo Rey!," *Catholic Answers Magazine*, October 28, 2011.)

Reading Comprehension

1. When José was growing up, what was the relationship between the Mexican government and the Catholic Church?
2. What was the origin of the word *Cristero*?
3. Why did the Mexican soldiers not kill José and Lazarus right away?
4. Why did St. José frustrate the soldiers?

Writing Task

- Describe St. José Luis Sánchez del Río's courage. Explain how a martyr's death can energize people who share his or her views.

Explaining the Faith

Why would God the Father allow Jesus, his only begotten Son, to suffer and die?

Simply put, God the Father permitted the suffering and Death of Jesus Christ, his only begotten Son, because of his immense love for humans. God's love invites all people to live eternally with him in heaven. Through his Passion and Death, Jesus shows you the depth of the Father's love that overcomes evil, sin, and death.

Because of the sin of Adam and Eve, all people are born with a wounded human nature. Original Sin deprives humans of original holiness and original justice. It has wounded the natural powers proper to human nature. It subjects people to ignorance, suffering, and death, and it inclines people to sin (see *CCC*, 405). Humans required redemption because they could not pay the debt from Original Sin themselves.

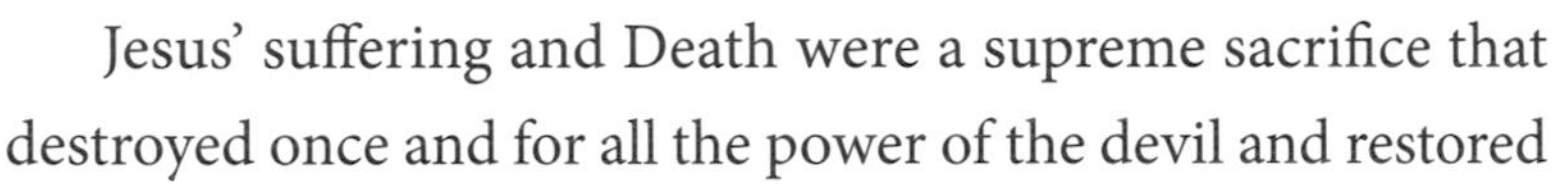

Jesus' suffering and Death were a supreme sacrifice that destroyed once and for all the power of the devil and restored your friendship with God. Out of love for his Father and all human beings, whom his Father wants to save, Jesus freely accepted his Passion and Death. The *Catechism of the Catholic Church* puts it this way:

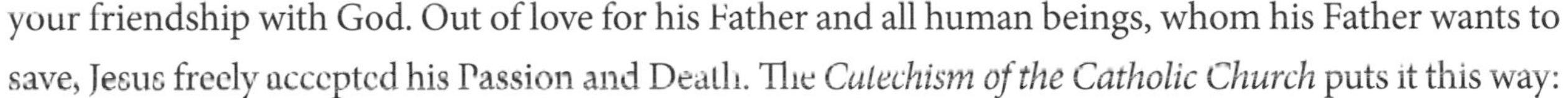

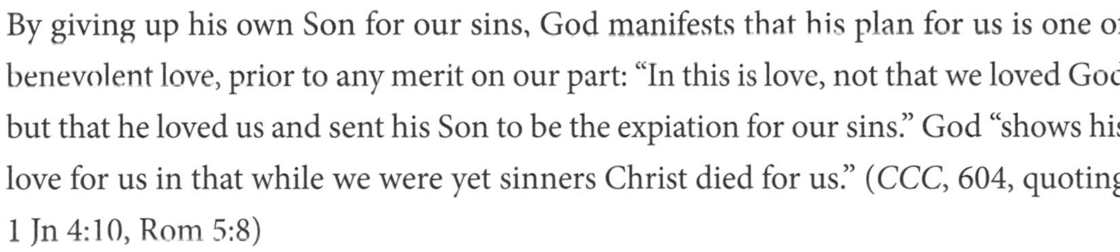

> By giving up his own Son for our sins, God manifests that his plan for us is one of benevolent love, prior to any merit on our part: "In this is love, not that we loved God but that he loved us and sent his Son to be the expiation for our sins." God "shows his love for us in that while we were yet sinners Christ died for us." (*CCC*, 604, quoting 1 Jn 4:10, Rom 5:8)

One final point: when you reflect on the terrible sufferings and Death Jesus endured on your behalf, you begin to understand the seriousness and gravity of sin and its horrible consequences. The Paschal Mystery of Jesus' Passion, Death, and Resurrection has destroyed the worst effect of sin—death—by opening the gates of heaven to you and promising you a participation in his Resurrection and a life of eternal joy with the Blessed Trinity. The Father allowed his Son to make this sacrifice simply out of his and his Son's immense love for each individual person. God has created each and every person, and he wants not even one person to be lost.

Further Research

- Write two paragraphs answering the following question: What makes Christ's sacrifice on the Cross unique? See paragraph 614 of the *Catechism of the Catholic Church*.

Prayer

Prayer to Our Lady of Guadalupe

Our Lady of Guadalupe,
Mystical Rose,
make intercession for holy Church,
protect the sovereign Pontiff,
help all those who invoke you in their necessities,
and since you are the ever Virgin Mary
and Mother of the true God,
obtain for us from your most holy Son
the grace of keeping our faith,
of sweet hope in the midst of the bitterness of life,
of burning charity, and the precious gift
of final perseverance.
Amen.
—Traditional

6

THE RESURRECTION OF JESUS CHRIST

LOVE and LIFE

Kate Ogg gave birth to twins twenty-seven weeks into her pregnancy. The doctors delivered little Emily successfully, but after spending twenty minutes trying to get her son, Jamie, to breathe, they declared him dead.

His mother unwrapped Jamie and held him against her skin and near her husband, David, in order that they could both say goodbye. As they stroked and talked to him, he began seemingly to gasp for air, a movement the doctor called a reflex. But after two hours, the baby began to breathe normally, opened his eyes, and even grasped his mother's finger. Kate put some breast milk on her finger, and Jamie accepted it.

Kate Ogg had saved her son's life using what some call "kangaroo care," a technique that received this name because it resembles the way female kangaroos hold their babies in pouches. Skin-to-skin contact with the mother releases oxytocin, a bonding hormone that affects the newborn's brain and can make a newborn's heartbeat become more regular. It is possible that the Oggs' son was born with an irregular heartbeat. In most cases, premature, at-risk, and unresponsive babies are rushed off to intensive care; however, in some cases, returning the baby to the mother, whose heartbeat, smell, and voice he or she knows, can be more beneficial. Moms can also effectively monitor their tiny babies' body temperatures.

While kangaroo care is appropriate with some newborn babies, it does not resurrect the dead. Baby Jamie was not born dead and did not actually die at any time before he started to breathe. To his parents, though, it felt that way. "We feel so fortunate," said David Ogg. "We're the luckiest people in the world."

(Mail Foreign Service, "Miracle Mum Brings Premature Baby Son Back to Life with Two Hours of Loving Cuddles after Doctors Pronounce Him Dead," *Daily Mail Online*, August 27, 2010.)

FOCUS QUESTION

How does the **ESSENTIAL CHRISTIAN** message—**"JESUS IS RISEN!"**—change your life?

Chapter Overview

Introduction The Fundamental Truth of Faith

Section 1 Death Defeated and Promise Fulfilled

Section 2 The Resurrection Accounts in the Four Gospels

Section 3 The Glorification of Jesus Christ

INTRODUCTION

The Fundamental Truth of Faith

MAIN IDEA

The Resurrection of Jesus Christ turned the despair of Christ's disciples into hope and helped them to better understand God's plan.

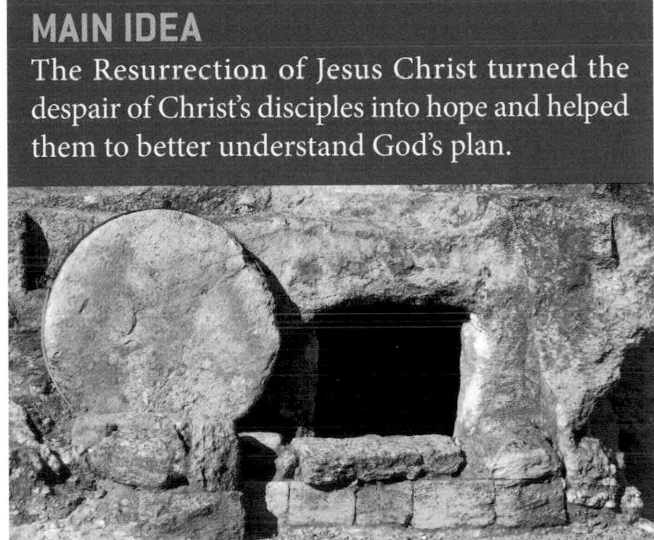

Imagine the sorrow that Kate and David Ogg experienced when they first heard that their son had not made it and then their immense joy when he showed definite signs of life! Something similar yet even more marvelous happened after the Crucifixion of Jesus Christ.

The disciples and Jesus' other followers were frightened and likely felt abandoned and defeated by the death of their good friend and teacher whom they loved. They believed he was the Messiah. Then, suddenly, Jesus was dead—rejected by the authorities, abandoned even by his friends, and executed as a common criminal. Yet the story was not over. Two days later, on the first Easter Sunday, Christ rose from the dead! What Jesus had been born to do was now complete. God's work was now done. His Resurrection spelled victory for humanity—victory over Satan, victory over sin, and victory over death.

The Resurrection of Jesus is a fundamental truth of your faith in Christ. Had this simple yet profoundly earth-shattering event not happened, the Gospels would not have been written. The Resurrection of Jesus forms the heart of the *kerygma*—that is, the essential message of your faith. If Jesus has not been raised from the dead, then your faith is useless. St. Paul put it this way:

> And if Christ has not been raised, then empty [too] is our preaching; empty, too, your faith. . . . If Christ has not been raised, your faith is vain; you are still in your sins. Then those who have fallen asleep in Christ have perished. If for this life only we have hoped in Christ, we are the most pitiable people of all. (1 Cor 15:14, 17–19)

This chapter explores the scriptural details of the Resurrection, including the significance of Christ's Resurrection for you in the mystery of redemption.

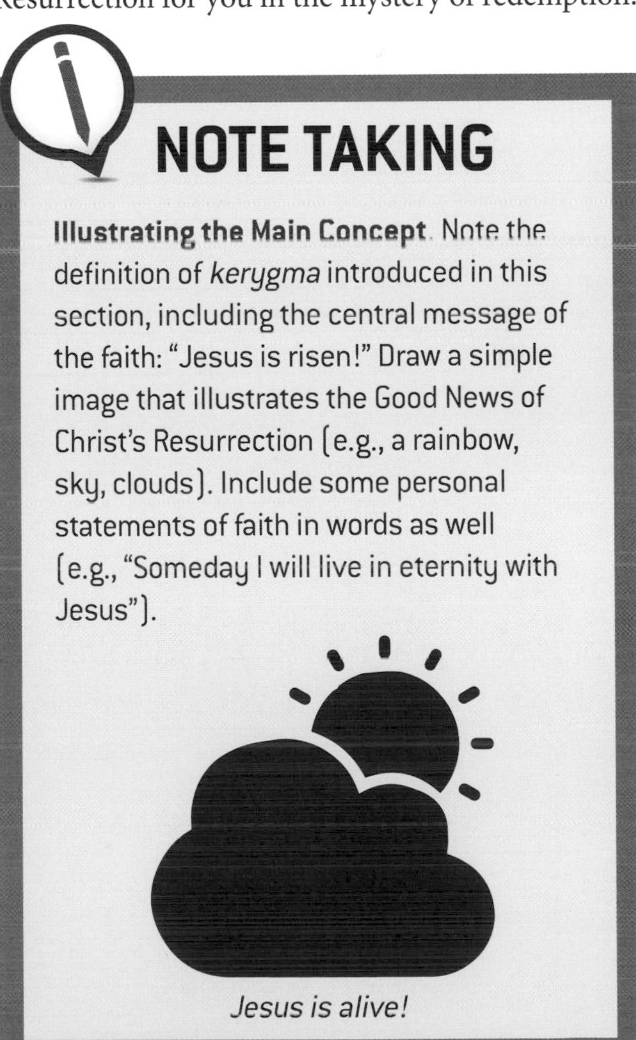

NOTE TAKING

Illustrating the Main Concept. Note the definition of *kerygma* introduced in this section, including the central message of the faith: "Jesus is risen!" Draw a simple image that illustrates the Good News of Christ's Resurrection (e.g., a rainbow, sky, clouds). Include some personal statements of faith in words as well (e.g., "Someday I will live in eternity with Jesus").

Jesus is alive!

Essentials of Your Faith

The word *kerygma* comes from the Greek meaning "proclamation, announcement, preaching." The kerygma contains the basic message of Christianity about Jesus. The heart of the kerygma is the Resurrection of Jesus. According to the New Testament, some of the essential elements of the kerygma in the early Church were the following:

- God's promises foretold by the prophets have now been fulfilled through Jesus Christ.
- God has exalted his Son, Jesus Christ, at his right hand.
- The Holy Spirit is present in the Church and is the sign of Christ's present power and glory.
- Christ will come again, at which time the messianic age will reach its fulfillment.
- Because all of this is true, you should repent of your sins, be baptized, and receive the Holy Spirit.

kerygma A Greek word for "proclamation," the core teaching about Jesus Christ as Savior and Lord. It is the basic Christian message that Jesus of Nazareth died and was raised from the dead by God the Father for the forgiveness of sins.

ASSIGNMENT

Many elements of the kerygma can be found in the sermons of St. Peter that are recorded in the Acts of the Apostles. Read Peter's sermon in Acts 2:14–41. Make notes of the verses in this passage from Acts that correspond to the various kerygmatic statements listed here.

SECTION ASSESSMENT

NOTE TAKING

Use the illustration you created to help you answer the following questions.

1. How does your illustration express the impact that the Resurrection had on early Christianity?
2. How does your illustration reflect your own belief in the kerygmatic statement "He is risen!"?

COMPREHENSION

3. How did the disciples and Jesus' other followers initially feel after Jesus died?
4. Finish this sentence: "If Christ has not been raised . . ."

REFLECTION

5. Explain St. Paul's words: "If for this life only we have hoped in Christ, we are the most pitiable people of all" (1 Cor 15:19).

SECTION 1

Death Defeated and Promise Fulfilled

MAIN IDEA

Christ's Resurrection, part of the Paschal Mystery, has both historical and transcendent dimensions.

Jesus did really die like all people do. But while in the grave, Jesus' body was preserved from corruption because his human soul and body were still the Divine Person of the Son. The Apostles' Creed (see page 354) professes that Christ's soul went to the abode of the dead (*Sheol* in Hebrew, *Hades* in Greek, *hell* in English). There he proclaimed the Good News of salvation to the just who were awaiting the Redeemer.

In hell, there is separation from God so that souls cannot see him. Until Jesus descended there after his Death, this was true for both the just and the damned, those who had lived upright lives and those who had lived evil ones. Jesus did not go there to free the damned but to free the just people. Their situation was not identical: the damned remained unable to see God. The holy souls "awaited their Savior in Abraham's bosom" (*CCC*, 633). Jesus' proclamation of the Gospel to the just who had died meant that he had spread his Word to people of all previous times and all places.

Jesus explained that "no one can enter a strong man's house to plunder his property unless he first ties up the strong man. Then he can plunder his house. Amen I say to you, all sins and all blasphemies that people utter will be forgiven them" (Mk 3:27–28). By his Death, descent into Hades, and Resurrection, Jesus has "bound the strong man"—Satan—and has destroyed his power (see 1 Jn 3:8), rendering powerless "the one who has the power of death" (Heb 2:14). As St. Paul writes, "[the Father] delivered us from the power of darkness, and transferred us to

NOTE TAKING

Classifying Information. Create a note-taking graphic organizer like the one below. As you read through this section, list examples of how the Resurrection is both historical and transcendent on the appropriate side of the graph.

Historical	*Empty Tomb*
Transcendent	

This Greek Orthodox icon depicts Jesus raising the dead from their graves as part of his Resurrection.

the kingdom of his beloved Son, in whom we have redemption, the forgiveness of sins" (Col 1:13–14).

Jesus' descent into hell is related to his rising from the dead. As the First Letter of Peter points out, "For this is why the gospel was preached even to the dead that, though condemned in the flesh in human estimation, they might live in the spirit in the estimation of God" (1 Pt 4:6).

Then, on Easter Sunday, the most important event in salvation history took place.

The Resurrection and the Paschal Mystery

Recall that the Paschal Mystery refers to Christ's Passion, Death, and Resurrection. These events are inseparable. *Paschal* refers to the Passover, Christ's passing through death to new life. It is a *mystery* in the sense that the salvation won by Jesus Christ is a visible sign of the invisible action that God accomplished on your behalf.

Jesus is the **Paschal Lamb** whose Death leads to his Resurrection and to salvation for all humanity. His Resurrection means that redemption is accomplished and the promise of salvation fulfilled. Beginning at Baptism, when you participate in Christ's Paschal Mystery, you die to sin's power over you and to the influence of Satan. You also receive grace in this life and eternal life with the Blessed Trinity in heaven. Jesus' Death and Resurrection have defeated sin. This means that your **soul** will survive physical death and your body will rise again at the **Last Judgment**.

Paschal Lamb The lamb slaughtered by the Israelites in preparation for the Passover. God instructed the Israelites, while they were enslaved in Egypt, to sprinkle the blood of a lamb on their doorposts, which the angel of death saw and "passed over." They were instructed also to eat the lamb and to commemorate this event (the Passover), which signified their preservation from death and their liberation from captivity. In the New Testament, Jesus is recognized as the Lamb of God, who takes away the sin of the world by shedding his blood. By his blood, death passes us over. In the Eucharist we celebrate and share in the new Passover in his Body and Blood.

soul "The spiritual principle of human beings" (*CCC*, Glossary). The soul and body together form one human nature. The soul does not die with the body. It is eternal and will be reunited with the body in the final resurrection.

Last Judgment Christ's judgment of the living and the dead at his return at the end of time. All human beings will appear in their own bodies before Christ's tribunal to render an account of their deeds. The Last Judgment will reveal that God's justice triumphs over all the injustices committed by his creatures and that God's love is stronger than death. After the Last Judgment, the Kingdom of God will come in its fullness, in which the righteous will reign forever with Christ, glorified in body and soul, and the universe itself will be renewed.

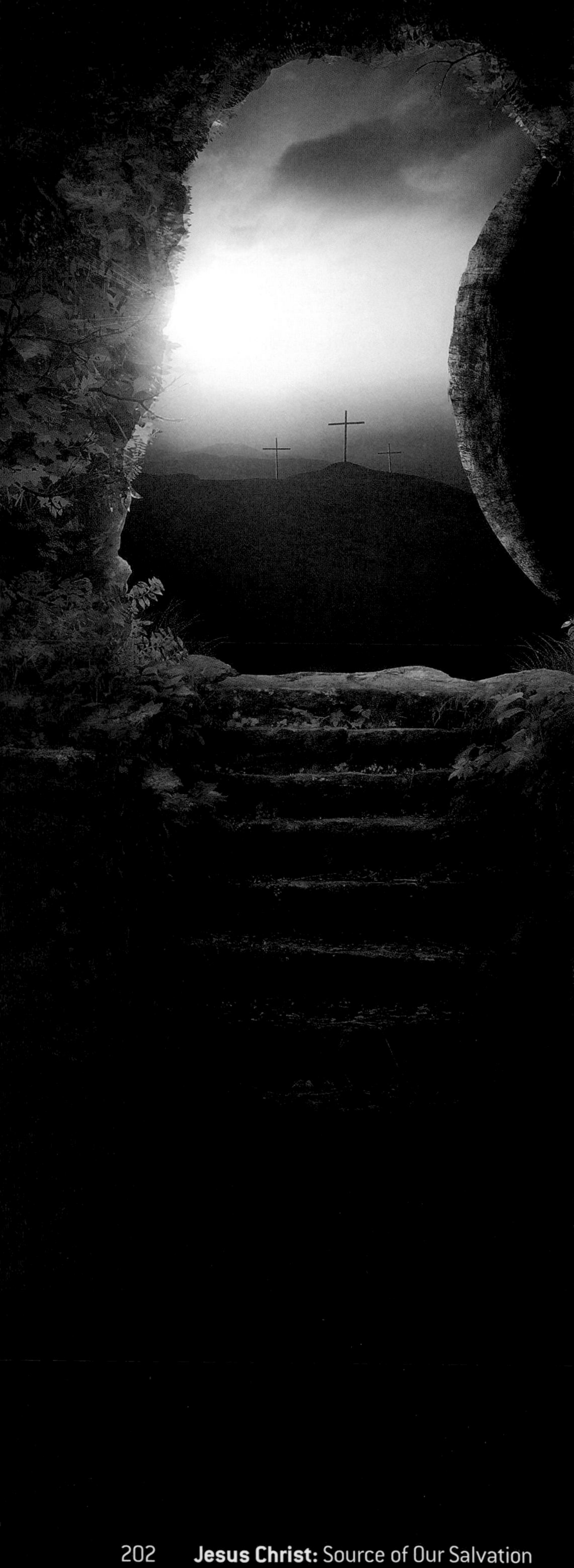

The Resurrection Was a Historical Event

Christ's Resurrection was a *historical* event that occurred in a definite place at a specific time. It is supported by facts, connected with the statements of witnesses—real-life people, both those who were friends and those who were enemies of Jesus.

The disciples were not expecting Jesus' Resurrection. In fact, they were heartbroken, saddened, and afraid after his Crucifixion. They were in hiding in Jerusalem, fearful that they too might be arrested and executed. The Resurrection of Jesus totally changed the frightened disciples into zealous preachers of the Gospel of Jesus Christ.

The empty tomb—reported in each Gospel—is one of the signs that Jesus rose from the dead. Neither Jesus' friends nor his enemies ever claimed to have found Jesus' body. No one ever proved that his corpse was stolen. Recall that after Jesus' Death, Joseph of Arimathea—a member of the Sanhedrin and a secret disciple of Jesus—sought permission from Pontius Pilate to take the body of Jesus down from the Cross and bury him in a new grave that Joseph owned, near the site of Jesus' Crucifixion. Matthew 27:62–66 verifies that Pilate permitted some of Jesus' opponents to post guards at Jesus' tomb as they were afraid that his disciples would steal his body. The inability of the guards to account for Jesus' disappearance is proof that the tomb was empty and that no one had come to remove the body from it.

But the empty tomb does not of itself prove that Jesus rose from the dead. In fact, some disciples were skeptical, simply refusing to believe when told the tomb was empty. Even seeing it empty for themselves did not cause all of them to believe that Jesus had actually risen from the dead. Nevertheless, the empty tomb is a concrete historical marker. It points toward belief that the Father brought his Son back to life, as had been promised by Jesus himself.

More definitive are multiple reports that the risen Jesus was seen by various people. Mary Magdalene and the women who came to finish anointing Jesus' body were the first to see him; they then brought the message to the disciples. Next, Jesus appeared to the disciples. Simon Peter was able to convey the truth that Jesus rose from the dead. As witnesses of the Risen Jesus, the disciples, especially Peter, formed the foundation for the Church.

The appearance of the Risen Jesus did not immediately turn all of his disciples into believers. When Jesus appeared to the eleven on Easter, he had to scold them for being hard-hearted. Some disciples initially thought that Jesus could be a ghost, and others could not get their heads around the idea of the Resurrection. The growth of the faith of the disciples from their direct experience of the Risen Christ is evidence that the disciples did not make Jesus' Resurrection up.

The Resurrection Was a Transcendent Event

All of these details reveal that the Resurrection was a real, verifiable historical event. The Resurrection of Jesus is also a *transcendent* event: one that extends beyond history and a common understanding of space and time. The Resurrection can be described as transcendent in part because no Gospel account reports anyone witnessing it. No one actually saw how Jesus' earthly body transformed into a risen or glorified body.

Jesus appears to his Apostles in the Upper Room after the Resurrection.

The other part of why Jesus' Resurrection is described as a transcendent event is that it has meaning not only for the life of Jesus but for every human person. As Jesus took the sin of the world upon himself—a task that only a Divine Person can bear—so also did Jesus, in his Resurrection, offer newness of life to the whole world. It is only because the eternal Son of God is a Divine Person bearing a human nature that his Passion, Death, and Resurrection has meaning for the whole world. Jesus offered himself for every single person individually; his offer of loving mercy extends to every single human being.

At his Resurrection, Jesus was fully restored to life: "In his risen body he passes from the state of death to another life beyond time and space" (*CCC*, 646). The Holy Spirit transformed Jesus' body at his Resurrection, giving it "the glorious state of Lordship" (*CCC*, 648). Jesus' human body was gloriously transfigured, filled with the Holy Spirit into an incorrupt, immortal body.

Like normal human bodies, Jesus' glorified body could be seen and touched by others. Jesus even shared a meal with his disciples (see Jn 21:1–14). He did these things to prove to his disciples that they were not seeing a ghost. Ghosts do not eat meals with their living friends! But Jesus' glorified body had certain qualities that transcend ordinary life. Unlike the body of Lazarus, whom Jesus raised and who did die again, Jesus' glorified body would never again die. It was immortal and eternal, possessing supernatural qualities. Jesus' risen body could appear wherever he wished, whenever he wished. For example, Jesus materialized in the Upper Room by passing through a closed door (see Jn 20:19).

The unique characteristics of Jesus' resurrected body and the way he can become present—Body, Blood, soul, and divinity—where he wills are witnessed notably in the Eucharist. His Body is fully transfigured by his self-sacrifice into an offering of love, which you receive in the form of bread and wine. His Body now becomes a living sign of God's redemptive love and the communion that you will one day share with God after your own resurrection.

SECTION ASSESSMENT

NOTE TAKING

Use the graphic organizer you made to help you complete the following question.

1. Imagine that you have been asked to explain to students in a second-grade religious education class how Jesus' Resurrection was both a historical and a transcendent occurrence. Write an outline summarizing what you would say.

VOCABULARY

2. What does it mean to say that Jesus is the *Paschal Lamb*?
3. Define *soul*.
4. What will occur at the Last Judgment?

COMPREHENSION

5. Where did Jesus' soul go after his Death?
6. Which souls did Jesus encounter in hell, and which did he free?
7. What are two pieces of evidence that the Resurrection was a real, historical event?
8. What were different responses the disciples had to the news of the Resurrection?
9. How did Jesus' risen body resemble and differ from his body prior to the Crucifixion?

REFLECTION

10. What is more important to you: historical or transcendent evidence of Jesus' Resurrection? Explain.
11. Describe your own faith that Jesus is indeed risen.

SECTION 2

The Resurrection Accounts in the Four Gospels

MAIN IDEA
Relying on different accounts of what happened, the four Gospel writers all included the essential elements of Jesus' Resurrection.

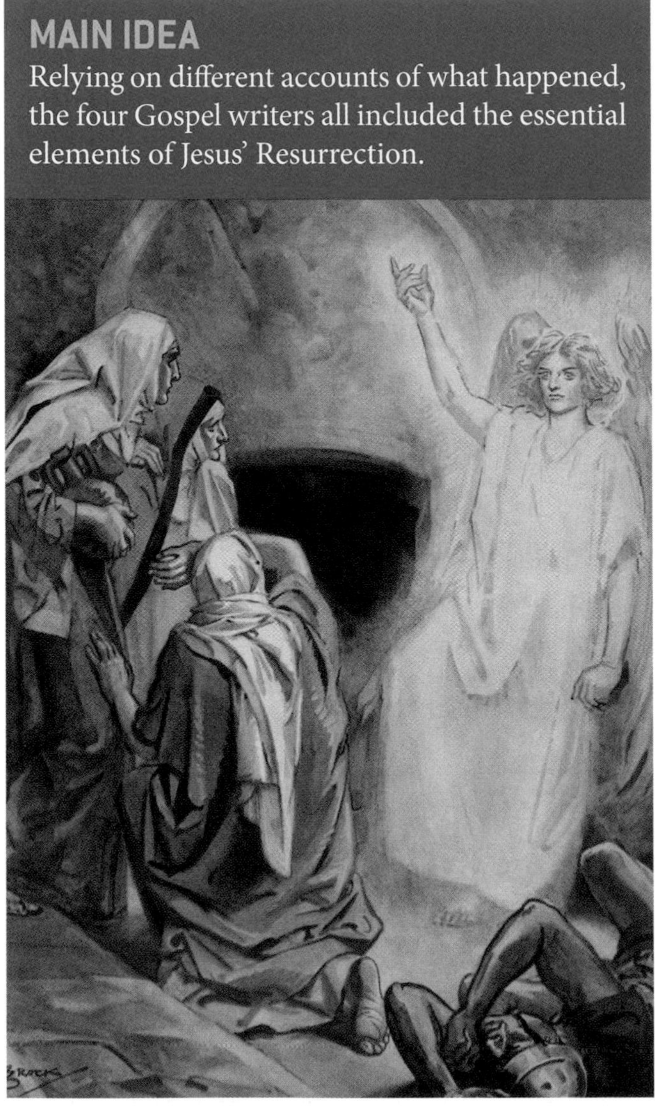

The passages discussed in this section are the main events of the Resurrection accounts in the four Gospels. These narratives, drawing from various eyewitness accounts, share evidence of Jesus' Resurrection. Make sure to keep a Bible with you while completing the reading for this section. Read the Gospel passage cited in each heading prior to reading the textbook material.

The Resurrection in Matthew's Gospel (Mt 28)

Recall that Matthew wrote his Gospel for a Jewish community that had decided to follow Jesus and that was eager to emphasize the continuity between the Old Testament and Jesus. Except for the first eight verses of this Resurrection account, which are similar to Mark 16:1–8, this material is unique to Matthew's Gospel.

Women Find the Empty Tomb (Mt 28:1–8)

Mary Magdalene and "the other Mary" know exactly where Jesus is buried. When they arrive at his grave, there is an earthquake, and they meet an angel, who rolls back the stone in front of the tomb. While the guards posted by the Jewish leaders become "like dead men," the angel speaks to the women. The angel tells the women not to be afraid because Jesus has been raised from the dead as he said. The angel asks the women to inspect the empty tomb and then report to the disciples that Jesus has been raised from the dead and that the disciples should go to Galilee to meet him.

Jesus Appears to the Women (Mt 28:9–10)

The two women encounter Jesus on their way to speak to his disciples. This encounter resembles a passage from John's Gospel (20:17): in both accounts, the women touch Jesus—in Matthew by embracing his feet—and then receive his command to tell his brothers to leave Jerusalem, the place where he was rejected, and go to Galilee, where he will meet them.

The Report of the Guards (Mt 28:11–15)

Only Matthew's Gospel tells why the Pharisees and chief priests posted guards at Jesus'

NOTE TAKING

Compare and Contrast. Create a table like the one below. From your reading of this text section and the Gospel passages it references, list the Gospel passages that mention each of the following events associated with Jesus' Resurrection. You will need to read all of the Gospel accounts in order to complete the table.

Event	Matthew	Mark	Luke	John
A woman or women find the empty tomb.	*28:1–8*	*16:1–8*	*24:1–8*	*20:1–2*
Peter and/or the Beloved Disciple run to the tomb.				
Jesus appears to a woman or women.				
Guards report to the authorities.				
Jesus meets two disciples on the road to Emmaus.				
Jesus appears to the eleven on Easter Sunday evening.				
Just prior to his Ascension, Jesus commissions the Eleven to preach the Gospel.				
Jesus speaks his last words before his Ascension.				
Jesus appears to seven disciples at the Sea of Tiberias.				

tomb—because of their fear that Jesus' body would be stolen. When the guards report to the religious leaders what actually happened, the leaders give them bribes to say that Jesus' disciples stole his body from the tomb. Jesus' foes did not doubt that Jesus' body was gone from the tomb, but they did not believe he was raised from the dead. Therefore, they circulated the story that "his disciples came by night and stole him while [the guards] were asleep" (Mt 28:13).

This passage reveals the disagreement between Jews who did not believe in Jesus and those who did.

After his Resurrection, Jesus appeared to the disciples and proved to them that he had risen.

Both groups believed that Jesus was no longer in the tomb, but they disagreed as to the reason why.

Jesus Appears to the Eleven before His Ascension (Mt 28:16–20)

The very last verses of Matthew's Gospel contain the commissioning of Jesus' disciples. Matthew indicates that at least some of the disciples were struggling to believe that he had risen from the dead. However, like the women, they quickly worship Jesus along with their doubts once they see him.

Jesus tells them, "All power in heaven and on earth has been given to me" (Mt 28:18). Jesus then commissions the Eleven to go out to people of all nations of the world to make them disciples. With this *Great Commission*, he "sends them forth," which in Greek is expressed by the verb *apostolein*, the origin of the word *apostle*. Recall that *apostle* literally means "one who was sent forth." The eleven disciples are now Apostles. (Remember that with Judas's death, the Twelve became eleven. Later, in Acts 1:15–26, Matthias is selected to take Judas's place as the twelfth.) As Apostles, they were to preach the Gospel, teach the commandments, and baptize "in the name of the Father, and of the Son, and of the holy Spirit" (Mt 28:19).

The Resurrection in Mark's Gospel (Mk 16)

Mark is by far the most succinct Gospel. It was likely written for a Gentile Christian community that was experiencing suffering. The inspired author has traditionally been thought to be a disciple of Peter named John Mark, who may have been an eyewitness to several events recorded in the Gospel. Because it is the shortest Gospel and since Matthew's and Luke's Gospels seem to quote some of its material, Mark's Gospel may have been the first written Gospel, dating to approximately AD 65 to 70, though this is only a theory. The

Resurrection account in Mark's Gospel is likewise short. In fact, it comes to an abrupt end in Mark 16:8.

After Mark 16:8, two alternative endings are offered. The so-called "shorter ending," the second half of Mark 16:20 that is presented in brackets, appears immediately after Mark 16:8 in some manuscripts. This shorter ending tells how the women did eventually report to Peter and the other disciples and gives Jesus' commission to preach the Gospel from east to west. The longer ending to the Gospel (Mk 16:9–20a) offers much more detail. It includes appearances of Jesus to Mary Magdalene, to two disciples, and to the eleven disciples, as well as an account of the Ascension. The Church has traditionally accepted Mark 16:9–20b as part of the canon, and it was defined as such at the Council of Trent.

Women Find the Empty Tomb (Mk 16:1–8)

Mary Magdalene; Mary, the mother of James; and Salome go to the tomb to anoint Jesus' body. When they arrive, the large stone sealing the tomb has been rolled back. A young man clothed in white greets them. The women are "utterly amazed." The young man says, "Do not be amazed! You seek Jesus of Nazareth, the crucified. He has been raised; he is not here. Behold, the place where they laid him" (Mk 16:6). The angel further instructs the women to tell Peter and the disciples to go meet Jesus in Galilee where they will see him, as Jesus himself has told them. "Then they went out and fled from the tomb, seized with trembling and bewilderment. They said nothing to anyone, for they were afraid" (Mk 16:8).

The Gospel's ending at Mark 16:8, though abrupt, is consistent with the rest of the Gospel, in which his disciples continually misunderstand Jesus. Consider the brilliance in this shorter ending: Mark challenges you, the reader, to do what the women failed to do. You are called to share, without fear or confusion, the Good News that Jesus is risen. Mark asks you to carry on the work of discipleship.

Appearances of Jesus (Mk 16:9–20a)

The examples in Mark's longer ending are similar to those from the other Gospels, especially Luke, from which they were probably taken.

Jesus' first appearance is to Mary Magdalene (Mk 16:9–11), "out of whom he had driven seven demons." When she tells the disciples she has seen the Risen Jesus, they do not believe her. Note the similarity between the scene with the Risen Jesus and Mary Magdalene in this passage and that in Luke 24:10–11.

Jesus next appears to two disciples on a country road (Mk 16:12–13). These disciples report what they saw to the others, but they also are not believed. Note how this incident compares to Jesus' appearance to the disciples on the road to Emmaus in Luke 24:13–35.

Jesus' third appearance is to the eleven disciples (Mk 16:14–18). As with the commissioning of the disciples in Matthew's Gospel, Jesus appears to them at a meal. He rebukes them for not believing the reports of others who had seen him. He then instructs them to go into the whole world and proclaim the Gospel.

Jesus' Ascension (16:19–20a) occupies the last verses of Mark's Gospel and parallels the report of Jesus' Ascension in Luke 24:50–53.

The Resurrection in Luke's Gospel (Lk 24)

Luke's Gospel, written by a Gentile Christian for an audience of Gentile Christians, is the third synoptic Gospel. The Resurrection narrative in Luke consists of five main sections:

1. Jesus appears to the women at the empty tomb (24:1–12)
2. Jesus appears to two disciples on the way to Emmaus (24:13–35)
3. Jesus appears to the disciples in Jerusalem (24:36–43)
4. Jesus' final instructions (24:44–49)
5. Jesus' Ascension (24:50–53)

Details on the three appearances of the Risen Jesus follow. Jesus' appearance prior to his Ascension to heaven is the subject of Section 3.

Jesus Appears to the Women at the Tomb (Lk 24:1–12)

Like the Gospels of Matthew and Mark, Luke's Gospel tells of women who go to the tomb on Sunday, the first day of the week. They find the tomb empty and are met by two men in dazzling garments. The two men ask, "Why do you seek the living one among the dead?" (Lk 24:5). The angels also help the women remember that Jesus had told them about his Resurrection. Notice that women—Mary Magdalene, Joanna, and Mary, the mother of James—rather than men become the first evangelists by telling the disciples what they learned at the tomb.

At first, the disciples think that the women are talking nonsense, but they go nevertheless to check out their story. Peter runs to the tomb to see for himself the empty shelf on which Jesus' body had rested. He finds there only the burial cloths and returns home amazed at what has happened.

Jesus Appears on the Road to Emmaus (Lk 24:13–35)

Two disciples, one named Cleopas, are going to the village of Emmaus, some distance outside of Jerusalem. On the road, Jesus joins them, though the disciples are prevented from recognizing him, and Jesus asks them what they have been discussing. (Notice how consistently the Gospel writers emphasize that the Risen Jesus was transformed.) They tell their new companion about the recent events that transpired in Jerusalem, including the strange report of the women who were visited by angels and their account of the empty tomb.

The Risen Lord then explains to these disciples the scriptural prophecies about how the Messiah had to suffer before he entered into his glory. When they arrive at the village, the two men urge their companion to stay with them for the evening. While he is with them at the table, he takes bread, says the blessing, breaks it, and gives it to them. Then the disciples recognize Jesus. They say, "Were not our hearts burning [within us] while he spoke to us on the way and opened the scriptures to us?" (Lk 24:32). This encounter with Jesus makes them turn around and return to Jerusalem, where they tell the Eleven that Jesus appeared to them. But they also learn that Jesus has already appeared to Peter: "The Lord has truly been raised and has appeared to Simon!" (Lk 24:34).

The Emmaus account includes some of the rich themes that Luke developed in his Gospel: journey, faith and vision, and hospitality to the stranger. Luke closes this account by pointing out that Jesus was made known "in the breaking of the bread" (Lk 24:35). This is a reference to the Eucharist.

Jesus Appears to the Disciples in Jerusalem (Lk 24:36–49)

Immediately after the disciples from Emmaus report what they had experienced to the other disciples, Jesus appears in their midst and greets them: "Peace be with you" (Lk 24:36). The disciples are startled, thinking they might be seeing a ghost. But Jesus assures them he is not a ghost, showing them his wounded hands and feet, inviting them to touch him, and eating a piece of baked fish. This passage shows that Jesus' risen body, though transformed, is not separate from his former human body. Otherwise, he would no longer have the marks of crucifixion.

The Lord then opens his disciples' minds to understand what the Scriptures had foretold: the suffering of the Messiah and his Resurrection on the third day. He tells the disciples that they are to be witnesses to all that he has said and done and that their task has only begun. He cautions them to wait until they "are clothed with power from on high" (Lk 24:49), a reference to the descent of the Holy Spirit, which would occur at Pentecost.

The Resurrection in John's Gospel (Jn 20–21)

John's Gospel devotes two chapters to Jesus' Resurrection and post-Resurrection appearances: John 20 and 21. John 20 is a series of single episodes in which Jesus reveals his glory and confers the Spirit. John 21 is labeled an "epilogue" to the Gospel, even though the chapter appears to have been part of the Gospel before its initial publication. The text of John 21 is written in Luke's Greek style and varies enough from the rest of the Gospel, suggesting that it perhaps had a different author.

The Empty Tomb (Jn 20:1–10)

All the Gospels agree that Mary Magdalene went to the tomb on the first day of the week, in the morning. Only in John's Gospel does Mary go and report the empty tomb to Peter and "the other disciple whom Jesus loved" (Jn 20:2). She thinks someone has taken Jesus' body. Peter and the Beloved Disciple run to the tomb to see for themselves. They arrive and see the discarded burial garments. The Beloved Disciple allows Peter to enter the tomb first. With only minimal proof of Jesus' Resurrection, they believe, even though they do not fully understand that Jesus had to rise from the dead.

Jesus Appears to Mary Magdalene (Jn 20:11–18)

Mary stays at the tomb after Peter and the Beloved Disciple depart. She weeps and looks into the tomb, where she sees two angels. When they ask why she is weeping, Mary says, "They have taken my Lord, and I don't know where they laid him" (Jn 20:13). After saying this, she turns and sees Jesus, at first thinking he is the gardener. (It seems that even Jesus' friends had some difficulty recognizing him. He was like himself prior to his Death but also very different.)

When Jesus addresses Mary by name, however, she recognizes him and calls him *Rabbouni* ("Master"). This echoes the parable of the Good Shepherd in John's Gospel: the sheep, his followers, recognize his voice (see Jn 10:1–18). Mary then tries to hold Jesus, but the Lord tells her not to cling to him because he has not yet ascended to his Father. The Lord instructs Mary to go and tell Jesus' brothers (not biological brothers but spiritual brothers because they were reborn from the Father's Spirit) that she has seen Jesus and to deliver this message: "I am going to my Father and your Father, to my God and your God" (Jn 20:17). She does as he asks.

Jesus Appears to the Disciples (Jn 20:19–23)

On Sunday evening, Jesus appears in the room where the disciples are staying. He mysteriously appears in their midst even though the doors are locked (the disciples were hiding in fear of the authorities). Jesus wishes them peace, shows them his wounds, and commissions them to continue his work: "As the Father has sent me, so I send you" (Jn 20:21). In John's Gospel, it is in this room on Easter Sunday that Jesus gives his disciples the gift of the Holy Spirit and the authority to forgive sins in his name.

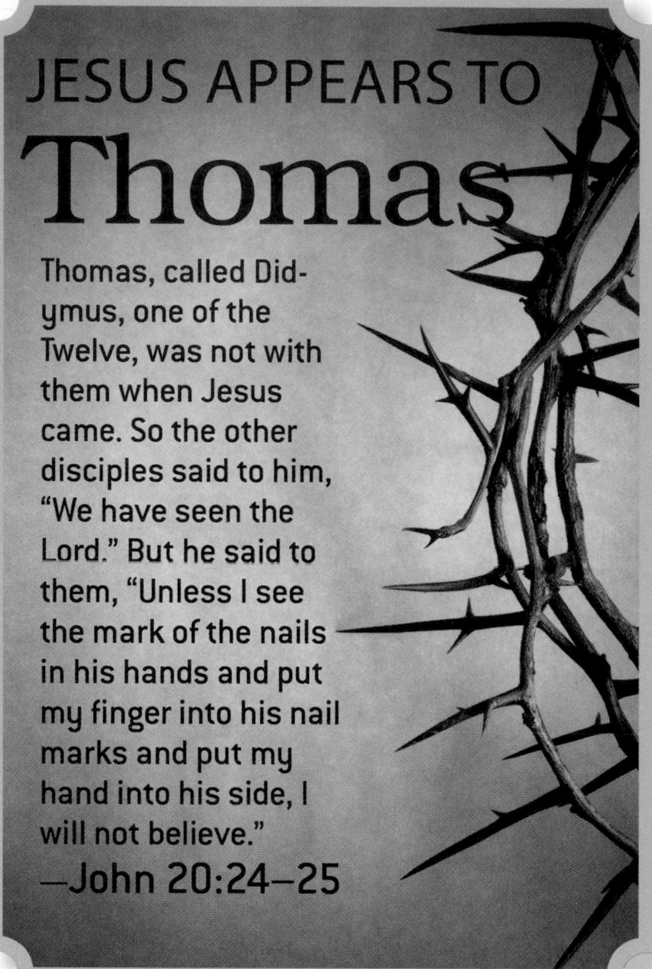

JESUS APPEARS TO
Thomas
Thomas, called Didymus, one of the Twelve, was not with them when Jesus came. So the other disciples said to him, "We have seen the Lord." But he said to them, "Unless I see the mark of the nails in his hands and put my finger into his nail marks and put my hand into his side, I will not believe."
—John 20:24–25

Jesus Appears to the Disciples a Second Time (Jn 20:24–29)

The disciple Thomas was not present when Jesus appeared to the others, so he does not believe in the Resurrection. A week later, the Lord once again appears behind the locked doors; he offers peace to his disciples and invites Thomas to put his fingers in Jesus' wounds so that he would believe. Thomas cries out the great act of faith that every Christian must say: "My Lord and my God!" (Jn 20:28). Jesus replies to the doubting Thomas, and to all Christians, "Blessed are those who have not seen and have believed" (Jn 20:29).

View over the Sea of Galilee in Israel.

These verses lead to what many scholars think is the original ending of the Gospel of John (20:30–31), in which the evangelist states that Jesus performed many other signs not recorded in the Gospel and that the signs that were recorded were written for one purpose—that you "may [come to] believe that Jesus is the Messiah, the Son of God, and that through this belief you may have life in his name" (Jn 20:31).

Jesus Appears to Seven Disciples (Jn 21:1–14)

The opening passage of John 21 details Jesus' appearance to seven disciples at the Sea of Tiberias, another name for the Sea of Galilee. This incident gives the impression that it was the Lord's first appearance to the disciples because they had returned to their occupation as fishermen rather than going out to preach the Good News of Jesus Christ. The men have been out all night in the boat but caught nothing. At dawn, Jesus stands on the shore. He instructs them to cast their net over the right side of the boat. They obey him, and their catch is so great (153 large fish) that they cannot pull it into the boat.

The Beloved Disciple is the first to recognize Jesus. He tells Peter, who then impetuously jumps into the water and runs to the shore. When the rest of the disciples arrive with the catch, Jesus cooks breakfast, providing them with fish and bread. Once again, it is the Lord who serves his disciples.

What does this Gospel passage mean for Christians today? It talks about a large catch of fish, symbolizing that the Apostles, with Peter as their leader, will be fishers of people, bringing the whole world to Christ. Further, the Apostles recognize Jesus in the course of a meal as the host who provides them with the fish and bread. This echoes the Eucharist, where believers recognize and receive the Lord.

The Risen Lord's Dialogue with Peter (Jn 21:15–22)

After breakfast, the scene turns to an interchange between Jesus and Peter. Jesus asks, "Simon, son of John, do you love me more than these?" (Jn 21:15). Peter's threefold responses of *yes* are like a reversal of his three denials at the time of Jesus' trial. Jesus uses the most intimate Greek word for "love," *agape*, in this passage. When Peter responds to Jesus, "Yes,

The crossed keys in the coat of arms of the Holy See symbolize the keys of the Kingdom of Heaven to St. Peter.

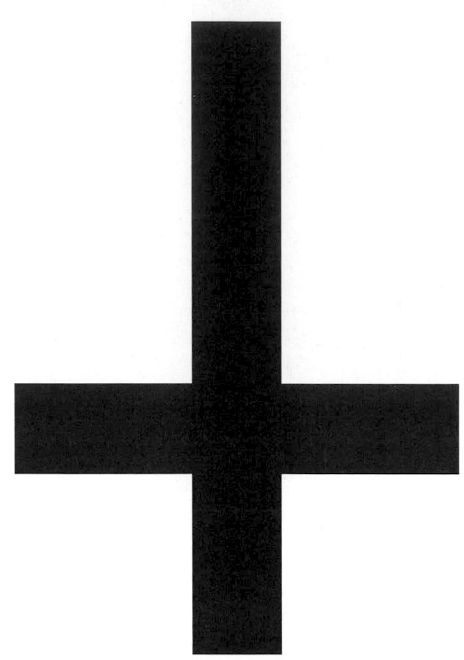

Origen of Alexandria related the tradition that St. Peter was crucified upside down because he was unworthy to be crucified in the same manner as Christ.

Lord, you know that I love you," the Gospel records his word for "love" as the Greek *phile*, meaning love for a friend. Jesus repeats to Simon, "*Agapais me?*" Peter responds, "*Philo se.*" The third time Jesus says, "Simon, son of John, *phileis me?*" One meaning of this exchange is that Jesus will accept whatever love Peter (and you) can give.

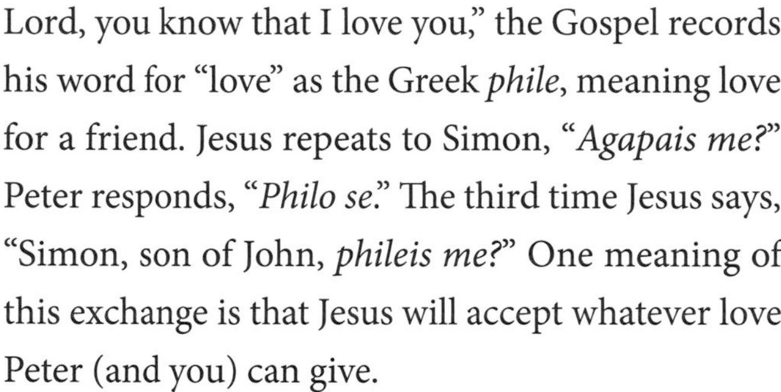

In this exchange, as in his directive in Matthew 16:18, the Lord establishes Peter as the leader of the Church by telling Peter to feed his sheep. Thus, Peter will be the pastor (or shepherd) who leads and guides the Church in serving others in love. Jesus had previously taught about the nature of the Good Shepherd, one who was willing to lay down his life for his flock (see Jn 10:1–18). This is what Jesus himself did for the sake of the salvation of humankind. Later, according to long-held tradition, Peter himself was also crucified under the emperor Nero. He followed Jesus in laying down his life for his friends.

The exchange between Peter and Jesus ends when Peter turns and sees the Beloved Disciple. He asks the Lord what will happen to the Beloved Disciple. Jesus responds: "What if I want him to remain until I come?" (Jn 21:22). Some in the community for which John's Gospel was written might have misinterpreted Jesus, thinking that the Beloved Disciple would not die before the Lord returned again.

Consider the different significance of the question, however, if the Beloved Disciple—who was the probable eyewitness source for the Gospel of John—had already died at the time chapter 21 was written. Some early Christians believed that Jesus would return before the Apostles died. But with the deaths of the Apostles, the Church moved forward to a new day and new era while continuing to await in joyful anticipation the glorious return and appearance of Jesus Christ as judge of the living and the dead at the end of time.

Ultimately, the important points are that John's testimony was reliable and true and that the Gospel was written to tell the Good News of salvation.

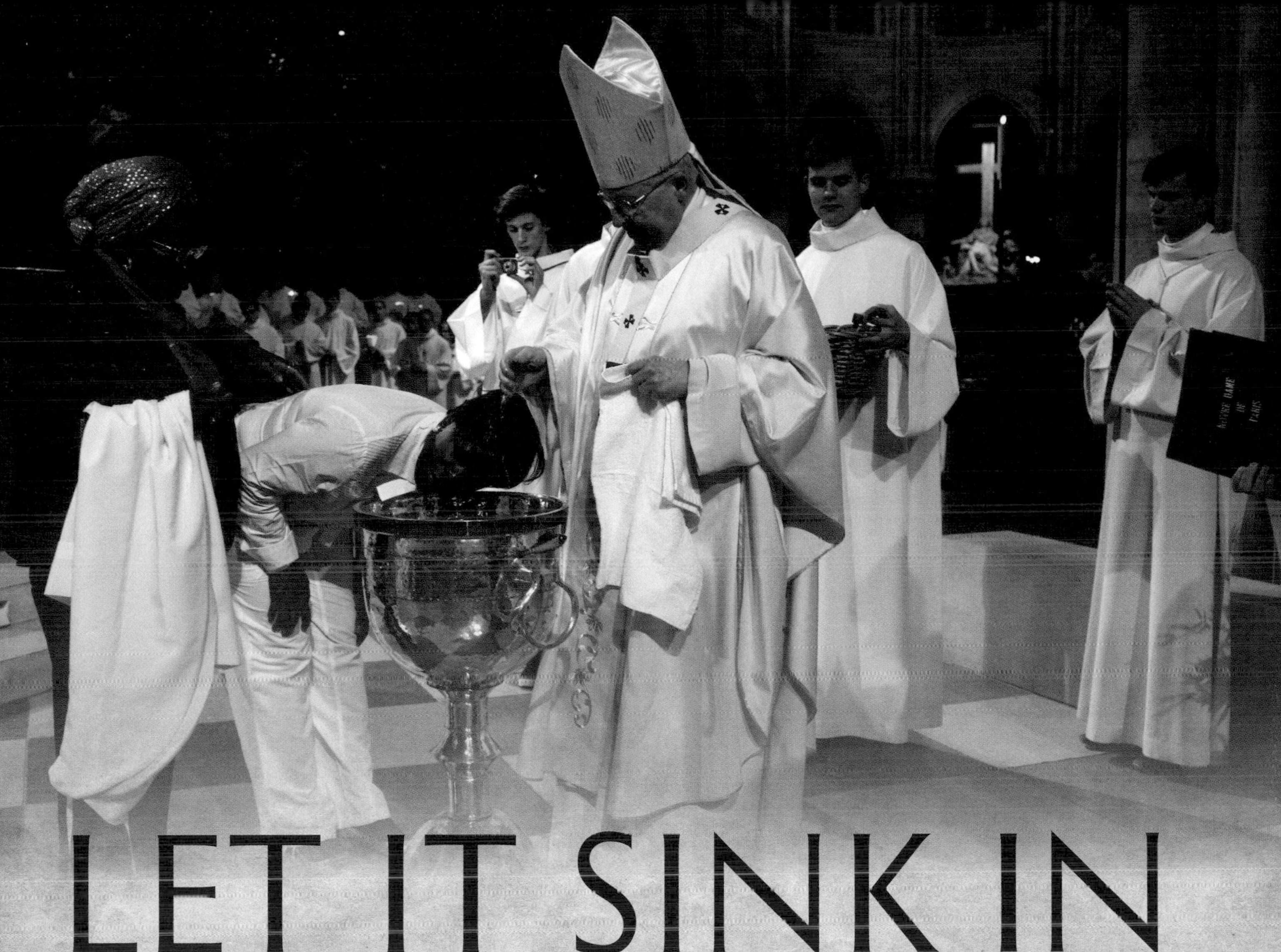

LET IT SINK IN

Consider these points of saving significance of Christ's Resurrection for your own life:

1. The Resurrection fulfilled God's promises after the Fall and throughout the Old Testament that he would not abandon humankind.
2. The Resurrection confirms the truth of Christmas Day: God entered the world to bring about the salvation of humanity.
3. The Resurrection validates all of Christ's works and teachings. It is the fulfillment of all of the promises Jesus made during his time on earth.
4. The Resurrection of Christ is the source of your own resurrection to eternal life.

Your participation in the mystery of Christ's redemption, won through his Resurrection, begins now. Not limited by time and space, the Risen Lord lives and reigns forever. As a member of Christ's Body, you can find Jesus in the Church, in your brothers and sisters who have likewise been baptized in his name.

You can participate in the mystery of Jesus' redemption through the sacramental life of the Church. Christ instituted the Seven Sacraments as powerful signs of his living, ongoing presence and love. By the power of the Holy Spirit, the Lord comes to you at Baptism, conforming you to his own dying and rising, and initiating you into the Church. In the Sacrament of Confirmation, the Holy Spirit strengthens you with spiritual gifts to live a Christlike life. In the Sacrament of Penance, you experience the Lord's forgiveness, just as countless people did who met him during his earthly life. He welcomes you back into the family the way the loving father did in the parable of the prodigal son (see Lk 15:11–32). In the Sacrament of the Anointing of the Sick, you experience the healing touch of the Lord in stressful times of illness. And in the Sacraments of Holy Orders and Matrimony, Christ comes to you to help you live a loving life of service to build up the People of God.

In a most special way, Jesus Christ is alive in the Holy Eucharist, which is "the heart and the summit of the Christian life, for in it Christ associates his Church and all her members with his sacrifice of praise and thanksgiving offered once for all on the cross to his Father" (*CCC*, 1407). The Eucharist contains your Paschal sacrifice, who is Christ himself. By his sacrifice he pours out the graces of salvation on the Church.

Take some time to let the Good News that Jesus is risen sink into the source of all your thoughts and actions. Ask yourself, "What does Christ's Resurrection really mean for me?" Next consider these answers: Practically speaking, Christ's Resurrection means you will live forever. Time and space will never have control of you. You will never again be burdened with sickness, disease, pain, and suffering. Because Christ is raised from the dead, and because you are united to Christ, you can live knowing that you will one day be reunited with your family members and friends who have already died. This truly is great news.

Looking at the Four Gospel Accounts Together

Putting all of the information together from the four Resurrection accounts, it is clear that there are some differences between them.

The differences can be explained by remembering that the Gospels were handed down originally through oral tradition. Think about powerful events—whether positive or negative—and consider whether people usually tell about these events in the same way. The Gospel writers made no attempt to mask their differences or to make their narratives consistent. This inconsistency ironically supports the position that there were valid, true experiences behind the various accounts. The early witnesses knew exactly what happened—what they saw, what Jesus said, how their hearts burned with love for him—and they refused to change anything in their testimony.

- The Resurrection took place early in the morning on the first day of the week.
- Women were present at the tomb. Mary Magdalene is mentioned in each account. There were also "messengers" at the tomb who told the women to tell the disciples what they witnessed.
- The empty tomb was important to the Resurrection accounts. It was an essential sign of Christ's Resurrection, a first step in acknowledging God's work in bringing the Son back to life. It corroborates that something happened. The enemies of the early Christians were never able to produce Jesus' corpse, though they probably tried to do so.

Jesus appeared to his disciples—including Mary Magdalene, Peter, and the others. They were transformed by his appearance from being afraid to being bold witnesses of the Gospel.

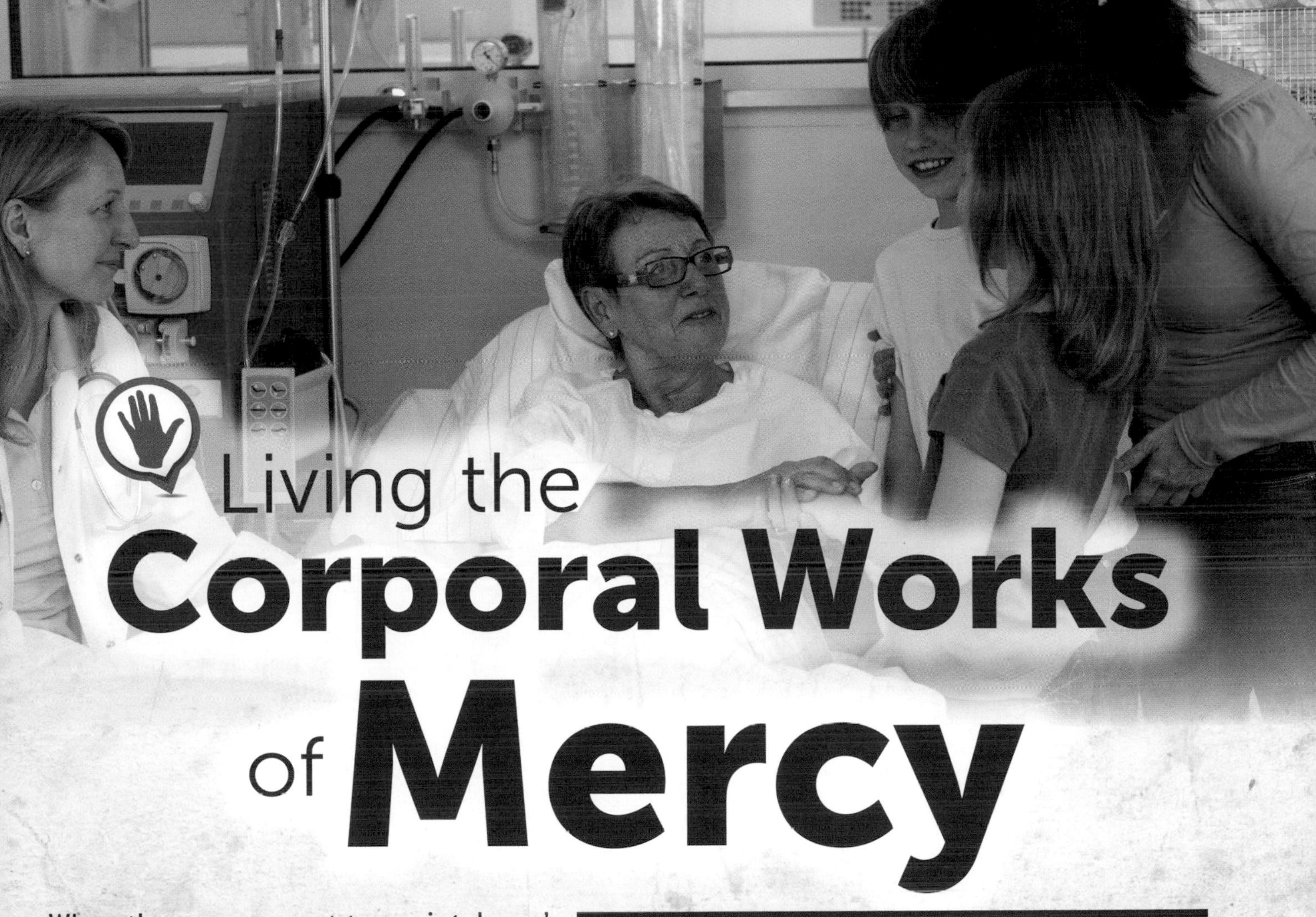

Living the Corporal Works of Mercy

When the women went to anoint Jesus' body, they were engaging in an act of mercy, showing respect to a person's human remains. All Christians are called to engage in the corporal works of mercy, traditionally listed as follows:

The Corporal Works of Mercy

1. Feed the hungry.
2. Give drink to the thirsty.
3. Clothe the naked.
4. Shelter the homeless.
5. Visit the sick.
6. Visit those in prison.
7. Bury the dead.

ASSIGNMENT

Resolve to do one of the following works of mercy in the coming week:

1. Volunteer at a homeless shelter.
2. Collect canned goods for a food bank.
3. Hold a clothing drive at school for the St. Vincent de Paul Society.
4. Collect toiletries for a shelter for abuse survivors.
5. Visit a sick relative, neighbor, or friend.
6. Send a get-well card to a sick friend.
7. Collect magazines to distribute to patients in the hospital.
8. Visit a recently bereaved neighbor or friend.

After you have completed the work of mercy, write a one-paragraph summary of your experience.

SECTION ASSESSMENT

NOTE TAKING

Without referring to your notes, complete the following true-false items. When you are finished, check your answers against your completed table.

1. True or False: The Gospel of Luke is the only Gospel in which Jesus does not appear to the women at the tomb.
2. True or False: Peter and the Beloved Disciple run to the tomb in both Matthew's and Mark's Gospels.
3. True or False: In Mark's Gospel, the authorities report the empty tomb.

COMPREHENSION

4. What natural event occurred when the women visited Jesus' tomb in Matthew's Gospel?
5. How did the women feel after their encounter with the angel in Matthew's Gospel?
6. How did the Jewish religious leaders in Matthew's Gospel deal with the fact that Jesus' body was no longer in the tomb even though the tomb had been guarded?
7. In Matthew's Gospel, what did Jesus commission his disciples to do?
8. How did the disciples on the road to Emmaus in Luke's Gospel recognize Jesus?
9. How did Jesus refer to the coming descent of the Holy Spirit on the disciples?
10. How does Jesus' appearance to the seven disciples in John's Gospel give the impression that it was his first appearance to them?
11. In John 21, who recognizes Jesus first from the boat, and who jumps out of the boat to go see him?
12. How did the Apostles' deaths initiate a new era among some early Christians?

CRITICAL ANALYSIS

13. How do the differences in the Resurrection narratives actually speak in favor of their historical value?
14. How do you understand Mark 16:17–18, in which Jesus says that baptized believers are able to drive out demons, speak new languages, handle snakes, drink poison, and cure the sick?
15. Why do you think Thomas refused to believe his fellow disciples about Jesus' appearance?

REFLECTION

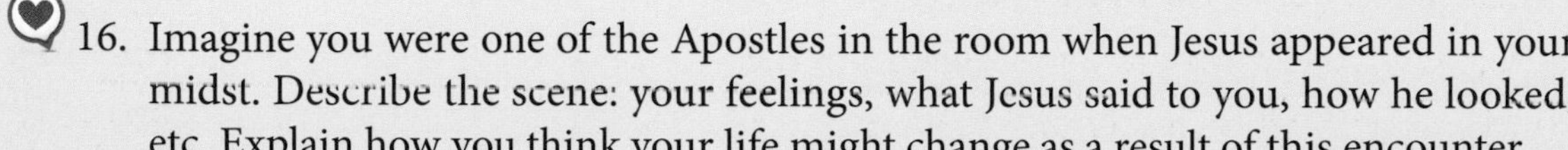

16. Imagine you were one of the Apostles in the room when Jesus appeared in your midst. Describe the scene: your feelings, what Jesus said to you, how he looked, etc. Explain how you think your life might change as a result of this encounter.

SECTION 3

The Glorification of Jesus Christ

MAIN IDEA

The Glorification of Christ culminates in the sending of the Holy Spirit at Pentecost.

Though the focus of this chapter is Jesus Christ's Resurrection, the Resurrection should always be considered as part of the Paschal Mystery, the saving action of Christ that comprises Jesus' Death (Good Friday), his descent to the dead (Holy Saturday), and his Glorification. Jesus' Glorification consists of the Resurrection (Easter Sunday); his Ascension into heaven (forty days after Easter); and Pentecost (fifty days after Easter), when the Apostles and Mary gathered in the Upper Room in Jerusalem, received an outpouring of the Holy Spirit, and began the Church.

The **Ascension** of Jesus refers to the time when he stopped appearing to the disciples in visible form and his glorified body took its rightful place in heaven at the right hand of the Father. Jesus' body was glorified at the moment of his Resurrection, as proved by the supernatural qualities it manifested (see pages 203–204). But during his appearances to his disciples, which took place over forty days, his glory remained partially hidden under the appearance of ordinary humanity. His "final apparition ends with the irreversible entry of his humanity into divine glory, symbolized by the cloud and by heaven, where he is seated from that time forward at God's right hand" (*CCC*, 659).

Ascension Jesus' passage from this world into divine glory in God's heavenly domain forty days after his Resurrection. It is from this domain that Jesus will come again.

NOTE TAKING

Defining Main Concepts. Create a graphic organizer like the one below. In each of the boxes at the right, name one of the parts of the Paschal Mystery and give its definition in your own words. In the boxes labeled "Ascension" and "Pentecost," add definitions of each term.

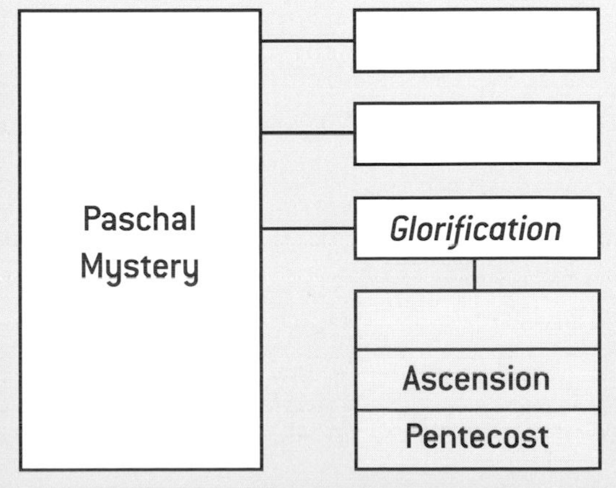

The Ascension indicates that there is a difference between the glory of the Risen Christ on earth after the Resurrection and the glory of "Christ exalted to his Father's right hand" (*CCC*, 660). It makes sense that people could not really perceive Jesus' full glory on earth. Being seated "at the right hand of the Father" means that Christ now glorifies the Father as the Incarnate Son of God. He continuously intercedes for you and all others with the Father and prepares a place for you with him in heaven.

Just as Jesus had come down from the Father, he returned to the Father in the Ascension. Clearly, no regular human being could rise up to the heavens alone. Only Christ could do this. His Paschal Mystery gives human beings access to heaven. You can feel confident that you too will go where Jesus has gone before you.

Consider for a moment the similarities and differences between Jesus' being lifted onto the Cross and his being lifted to heaven by his Ascension. He said, "And when I am lifted up from the earth, I will draw everyone to myself" (Jn 12:32). Jesus is the *only* High Priest of the New Covenant, in contrast to the many priests of the Mosaic covenant honored in the Temple in Jerusalem. Though Jesus inaugurated the Kingdom of God through his works and teaching on earth, at the Father's right hand he has the glory and dominion of that Kingdom, a Kingdom that will never pass away.

Mary Leads the Way to Heaven

The Ascension of Jesus is a reminder that your rightful home is heaven and that you live in the hope that you may one day follow him there. Your model for Christlike human living is the Blessed Mother, the Mother of Christ the Redeemer and of the Church.

Mary was united to her Son from the very moment of his conception, when he was physically within her body, until his Death on the Cross, when she stood near him, in union with him spiritually. After Jesus' Ascension, Mary prayed for the early Church community and asked the Holy Spirit to come upon them. She will continue to intercede for humans for all time. In this role, Mary is known as Advocate, Helper, Benefactress, and Mediatrix.

When her earthly life was over, Mary, who was still free from all stain of Original Sin, was taken up body and soul into heavenly glory, where the Lord exalted her and made her Queen of Heaven. This event is known as the **Assumption** of the Blessed Virgin. Her Assumption "is a singular participation in her Son's Resurrection and an anticipation of the resurrection of other Christians" (*CCC*, 966). Pope Pius XII declared the Assumption of Mary a dogma of the Church on November 1, 1950. The Church does not definitively teach whether Mary was taken into heaven without experiencing death or taken there after she died.

In heaven, she has not ceased to assist in human salvation. She advocates on your behalf and acts as Benefactress and Mediatrix with her Son, the true Mediator. Although people appropriately venerate or honor Mary because of her holiness, she always points to Jesus. When you know Mary, you know Jesus.

Assumption The Church dogma that teaches that the Blessed Mother was taken body and soul into heaven when her earthly life was over. The Feast of the Assumption is on August 15 and is a holy day of obligation.

The Holy Spirit descends on the twelve Apostles and Mary, the Mother of God, on Pentecost in this painting by El Greco.

The Paschal Mystery Culminates in the Coming of the Holy Spirit

Though Jesus Christ entered the sanctuary of heaven once and for all, he did not abandon the people among whom he lived. When Jesus tells his disciples during the Last Supper that he will return to the Father, he tells them that it is better that he goes, "for if I do not go, the Advocate will not come to you. But if I go, I will send him to you" (Jn 16:7). He also says, "When the Advocate comes whom I will send you from the Father, the Spirit of truth that proceeds from the Father, he will testify to me" (Jn 15:26).

Jesus' words show the Trinitarian ordering to salvation. The Son reveals and embodies the Father's love; the Son makes the Father present. The Spirit reveals and embodies the Son; the Spirit makes the Son present. This is why St. Paul writes that "no one can say 'Jesus is Lord,' except by the holy Spirit" (1 Cor 12:3). When he ascended into glory at the right hand of the Father, Jesus fulfilled his promise to be with the Church forever (see Mt 28:20b) by sending *his* Spirit, through whom "the love of God has been poured out into our hearts" (Rom 5:5), to the Church. It is because of the Holy Spirit that he can tell his disciples: "As the Father has sent me, so I send you" (Jn 20:21).

Jesus sent the Spirit so that all he accomplished—his victory over sin and death and his life entirely given in obedience to the Father—may be accomplished in the Church and, through the Church, in the world. Christ is the firstborn and the head of the new creation; through the work of the Spirit, you follow Christ and become transformed into him as part of the new creation. The divine plan accomplished in the Church by the Spirit entails "the communion of saints, the forgiveness of sins, the resurrection of the body, and life everlasting" (see the Apostles' Creed on page 354).

On **Pentecost** Sunday, the Holy Spirit descended on the Apostles and gave them the power and courage to preach the Good News that Jesus Christ had risen from the dead and is Lord of the universe. So filled with the power of the Holy Spirit were Peter and the Apostles that some thought they were drunk, although it was still early in the morning. The Apostles were filled with the Holy Spirit and a charisma that empowered them to preach. People understood them even though many did not speak their language (see Acts 2:1–13).

Peter, the one who denied Jesus three times, became a bold and courageous witness for Christ. Inspired and empowered by the Holy Spirit, he preached to the Jewish people who had come to Jerusalem for the Pentecost feast. He recounted the history of salvation and the life of Jesus Christ, proclaiming the meaning of Christ's Death and Resurrection. He amazed the crowd with his preaching. Three thousand people converted to Jesus Christ on the first Pentecost. They were baptized and received the Holy Spirit (see Acts 2:14–41).

The Holy Spirit enabled the Apostles to understand more clearly Jesus' significance and the totality of the Paschal Mystery. They came to believe that Jesus Christ is truly the Lord, the Savior, the Son of God who is the Second Divine Person of the Trinity. The Holy Spirit was also fully revealed at Pentecost. He bestows divine life on the Church's members and makes them partakers of the divine nature. By joining you to the Risen Lord Jesus Christ, the Holy Spirit makes it possible for you to live holiness of life and to put Jesus' moral and spiritual teaching into practice.

Never forget that the Good News of Christ's Resurrection is the promise of your own resurrection. This means that death is not the final chapter of your life. You will not cease to exist after your physical death. You will not come back as a reincarnated being. Christ's Paschal Mystery—his Passion, Death, and Resurrection—offers you the opportunity for salvation and redemption. While remaining aware that your choices in this life may lead you toward a time of purification (Purgatory) or even eternal separation from God (hell) after death, it is better to look forward in confidence to your own resurrection, when God will call you to himself, reunite your soul to your own glorified body, and give you a life of eternal happiness.

Pentecost The day fifty days after Easter when the Holy Spirit descended on the Apostles and gave them the power to preach with conviction the message that Jesus is risen and is Lord of the universe. The Church celebrates Pentecost every year as the beginning of the new "age of the Church," when Christ lives and acts in and with his Church through the outpouring of the Holy Spirit.

SECTION ASSESSMENT

NOTE TAKING

Use the graphic organizer you created to help you complete the following items.

1. What occurred at the Ascension?
2. Describe the events of Pentecost.

COMPREHENSION

3. What is the relationship between Jesus and the Kingdom of God?
4. How did the arrival of the Holy Spirit change the Apostles?

CRITICAL ANALYSIS

5. How was the Risen Christ on earth different from "Christ exalted to his Father's right hand"?
6. Compare and contrast the symbolism of the lifting of Jesus on the Cross and the lifting of Jesus in the Ascension.
7. Compare and contrast Jesus' Ascension with Mary's Assumption.

Section Summaries

Focus Question

How does the essential Christian message—"Jesus is risen!"—change your life?

Complete one of the following:

→ Interview two practicing Catholics, one adult and one teenager. Ask them, "How essential to your Christian faith is the fact that Jesus rose from the dead?" Write a report summarizing what they said.

→ Imagine that you were one of the disciples who met the Risen Jesus on the way to Emmaus. Imagine further that Jesus asked to come to your house for dinner. Write two or three paragraphs describing the type of faith in him that he would find present in your home.

→ Create a list of five points you would use to convince someone in your age group to believe in Christ. Draw from some of the points used by Peter in Acts 2:14–39.

INTRODUCTION (PAGES 197–199)

The Fundamental Truth of Faith

The Resurrection is the fundamental truth of your faith in Christ. The Resurrection of Jesus Christ invigorated his early followers and was the basis for the growth of the Church. Consider how distraught Jesus' followers must have been after the Crucifixion and how relieved they were to encounter him in his glorified, risen body. But Jesus' actions affected more than simply his earthly friends. He had conquered evil, Satan, and death.

→ Look online for a video of a mother, father, husband, son, or daughter returning home from a military deployment to surprised loved ones. Briefly describe the occasion. Tell how the joy of a loved one's safe return from military service resembles the joy of the Resurrection.

SECTION 1 (PAGES 200–205)

Death Defeated and Promise Fulfilled

Jesus' Resurrection has both historical and transcendent dimensions. Jesus really did experience death in the way all humans do. Yet his risen body, though recognizable to those who knew him, was also transcendent. He could appear to them through locked doors, for example. Many people encountered the Risen Jesus. Jesus' Resurrection did not magically change his disciples. They came to understand the Resurrection in different ways in light of their encounter with the Risen Lord. The Resurrection event, the central piece of the Christian kerygma, was the core of the Good News that those disciples would share near and far.

Cite two pieces of evidence that Jesus' Resurrection is a historical event. What does it mean to say that the Resurrection is also a transcendent event?

SECTION 2 (PAGES 206–218)

The Resurrection Accounts in the Four Gospels

The four Gospel writers included the essential elements of Jesus' Resurrection, relying on different accounts of what happened. A unique feature in Matthew's Gospel is the description of the guards posted outside Jesus' tomb after his Death. Matthew's Gospel ends with Jesus commissioning the disciples. In Mark's Resurrection account, the women at the tomb are more fearful and the disciples less trusting. Mark's original ending is abrupt, with the women at the tomb not returning to share the Good News of the Resurrection with the other disciples. Luke's Gospel, written for Gentile Christians, contains Jesus' appearance to two disciples on the road to Emmaus. In John's Gospel, Jesus gives the Eleven the gift of the Holy Spirit and the authority to forgive sins. The incident of the disciple Thomas's doubting the report of Jesus' appearance to the other disciples is also unique to John's Gospel. Finally, only John's Gospel contains the appearance of Jesus to the disciples while they are fishing; Jesus and Peter then talk, and Jesus asks Peter to reassure him three times that he loves him.

How do the differences in the Resurrection accounts of the Gospels help you to appreciate their validity?

SECTION 3 (PAGES 219–224)

The Glorification of Jesus Christ

The Glorification of Christ—that is, the events beginning with his Resurrection and concluding with the coming of the Holy Spirit at Pentecost—completes the Paschal Mystery. While Jesus appeared to his followers in a glorified body, his Ascension meant that he would be further glorified in heaven where he now sits at the right hand of his Father. Only Jesus could go to heaven by his own power. Though no longer physically present in a human body, Jesus continues to be present to the Church through the gift of the Holy Spirit, primarily through the sacraments and especially through the Sacrament of the Holy Eucharist. The Paschal Mystery is the basis for Christianity and for your own salvation. The Resurrection, particularly, is significant because it affirms Christ's teachings and works, shows that Jesus fulfills Old Testament promises, confirms the truth of the Incarnation, accomplishes human salvation, gives you new life, makes you part of God's family, and is the source of your own resurrection.

Read and outline paragraphs 651–655 of the *Catechism of the Catholic Church*, "The Meaning and Saving Significance of the Resurrection."

Chapter Assignments

Choose and complete at least one of the three assignments assessing your understanding of the material in this chapter.

1. Who Is Jesus?

While she was recovering in a hospital in Rome in 1983, St. Teresa of Calcutta (Mother Teresa) wrote down these thoughts and feelings about who Jesus was to her. Read and reflect on St. Teresa of Calcutta's list.

> Jesus is the Word made flesh.
> Jesus is the Victim offered for your sins on the Cross.
> Jesus is the Word—to be spoken.
> Jesus is the Truth—to be told.
> Jesus is the Way—to be walked.
> Jesus is the Light—to be lit.
> Jesus is the Life—to be lived.
> Jesus is the Love—to be loved.
> Jesus is the Hungry—to be fed.
> Jesus is the Homeless—to be taken in.
> Jesus is the Lonely—to be loved.
> Jesus is the Unwanted—to be wanted.
> Jesus is the Little One—to embrace him.
> Jesus is the Old—to be served.
> Jesus is my God.
> Jesus is my only Love.
> Jesus is my Everything.

Write your own series of ten statements of who Jesus is to you, perhaps in a similar style. Put each statement on a separate multimedia slide. Then do the following:

- Illustrate two of your statements with a photo, either one of your own or one taken by someone else.
- For another two of the statements, include the first names of people you know who bring Jesus to life according to the statements and one sentence to tell why or how.
- Tell how you will serve Jesus based on another two of the statements. Add captions with some practical information: for example, "This week I will share the truth of Jesus by assisting a class of second graders as they prepare for First Communion" or "I will spend two hours with my grandmother, helping her with chores and listening to her wisdom."

- For another two of the statements, include the text of Scripture passages that illustrate them.
- For the remaining two statements, tell how you encounter those images of Jesus when you celebrate the sacraments.

Compose your own prayer of thanksgiving to Jesus. Include the prayer on the final slide of your presentation.

2. Artistic Renditions of the Ascension

Read the Scripture accounts of Jesus' Ascension into heaven in Mark 16:19, Luke 24:50–53, and Acts 1:6–11. Make a list of as many details as you can gather from all three accounts (time, place, witnesses), including how the Ascension was described.

Online, find two artistic renditions of the Ascension. Display these digitally or as print copies attached to a two-page report. For each rendition of the Ascension, answer the following questions:

- Which elements from the biblical accounts are in the rendition?
- Did the artist add other elements to the scene? How well did these additions "fit" with the biblical accounts? Do they change the tone or feel of the story?
- How does the rendition convey a sense of holiness to you?
- What do you think the artist wants to emphasize to you as a viewer about the event? How successful is the artist in doing so?

In a concluding paragraph, tell how you imagine Jesus' Ascension. *Optional*: Draw your own image of the Ascension.

3. Reporting on the Assumption of Mary into Heaven

Write a two-page report on the Assumption of Mary into heaven. Include the following information:

- A summary of the belief
- The origins of this belief from the early Church
- A history of how the belief has been celebrated in various times and places
- Background on Pope Pius XII's November 1, 1950, declaration of the Assumption of Mary into heaven as Church dogma, including references to the infallible statement *Munificentissimus Deus*.

Faithful Disciple

Bl. Giuseppe Puglisi

On May 25, 2013, Pope Francis celebrated the beatification of the priest known as "Don Pino," Fr. Giuseppe Puglisi. The celebration occurred in Palermo, Sicily, where just twenty years earlier, Puglisi had been assassinated on the steps of his church by a single bullet fired at close range. Four members of the local organized-crime family that controlled the neighborhood were eventually convicted of his murder. Puglisi had preached against the Mafia for years prior to his assassination.

Bl. Giuseppe Puglisi

While Puglisi's story may seem unique, in fact thousands of Christians around the world are killed each year for speaking up for their Christian faith. Puglisi had dedicated his life to convincing the young people in his violent neighborhood that there were better options than joining with organized crime. He wanted society in Sicily to be free of the Mafia's political influence.

In the 1960s, Puglisi was a young priest in Godrano, a village twenty-five miles outside of Palermo. Upon his arrival, he learned that fifteen people had died in connection with a feud between two rival Mafia groups. (Only one hundred people lived in the village.) He began to encourage the community to join in small faith groups to read and pray the Bible together and to contemplate ways to change their lives from evil to good. He offered many opportunities for his parishioners to celebrate the Sacrament of Penance.

Puglisi was assigned pastor of San Gaetano Church in a rough Palermo neighborhood in 1990. He took a further stand against the Mafia, refusing to take their money for feast days and forbidding Mafia dons from processing at the head of parades. He encouraged young people to stay in school. He provided places for them to play soccer, and he asked several boys at risk to become altar servers. Puglisi continued to preach against violence at Sunday Mass, attracting increasingly large numbers of Sicilians who appreciated that someone was taking a stand against the culture of organized crime.

Puglisi knew that his life was constantly in danger, but his philosophy stemmed from his faith and from the question, "And what if somebody did something?" At the age of fifty-six, he was killed by a paid assassin in front of his church on September 15, 1993. His beatification reminds Catholics that martyrdom today involves Christians being killed both for their religious beliefs and for challenging injustices.

Traditionally, the Church has recognized martyrs only if they were killed because of hatred of the faith (*in odium fidei*). Fr. Puglisi is a martyr who died because of hatred of virtue and truth (*in odium virtutis et veritatis*) like St. John the Baptist, who was killed because he challenged the morality of King Herod's choices. As with John the Baptist, the virtue and truth that Puglisi advocated came from his faith in Jesus Christ and his loyalty to the Church. Ironically and sadly, he was killed by people who also considered themselves Catholics.

The beatification of Fr. Puglisi is a strong statement against organized crime and for authentically living the faith in Christ, no matter the risks and hardships, even to the point of martyrdom.

Reading Comprehension

1. Why did Fr. Giuseppe Puglisi attract the attention of organized-crime leaders?
2. What first motivated Fr. Puglisi to take a stand against the Mafia?
3. How was Fr. Puglisi murdered?
4. What type of martyr is Fr. Puglisi?

Writing Task

- Fr. Puglisi was motivated by asking, "And what if somebody did something?" Name a situation in your community that would benefit from a positive answer to that question. How might you participate in a solution?

Explaining the Faith

Why are followers of Jesus Christ sometimes so willing to make sacrifices and to accept pain and suffering, especially in witness to Christ and their faith?

Jesus Christ's followers are willing to accept great hardships in this life because the promises and rewards of faith are connected with a Christian's willingness to live his or her life in the same way that Jesus lived his. That Jesus' suffering and Death led to his Resurrection and Ascension teaches you to look beyond earthly suffering to the promise of eternal life in heaven. In imitation of Christ, Christians take up the crosses of their own challenges, pain, and suffering. The rewards of doing so are many, both in this world and in the next:

- Accepting suffering cultivates the virtue of *fortitude*, which strengthens your resolve to pursue the good even in difficult circumstances. This virtue enables you to conquer even the fear of death. In addition to being a virtue, fortitude is a gift of the Holy Spirit.
- Christians do not find suffering to be meaningless. Uniting your suffering with that of Jesus enables you to participate in the saving work of Jesus. Suffering and sacrifice can also help you move toward heaven. Suffering serves as reparation for your sins.
- Following Christ in the midst of suffering may be difficult in this passing world, but Christians look beyond this life to eternal life in heaven.
- Accepting pain and suffering in this world is acknowledgment that Christ accompanies and strengthens you as you undergo suffering. Suffering allows you to become more Christlike.

Suffering is a result of Original Sin. It is impossible to avoid in life, but suffering with Christ gives meaning to your suffering by purifying you and helping to save others. Christ will strengthen you to undergo suffering and thereby to become more like him.

Further Research

- St. Alphonsus Liguori wrote, "Say always, 'My beloved and despised Redeemer, how sweet it is to suffer for you.' If you embrace all things in life as coming from the hand of God, and even embrace death to fulfill his holy will, assuredly you will die a saint." Research and write about the words of another saint who suggests the benefits of "offering up" one's sufferings on behalf of Christ and his redemptive work.

Prayer

Do Not Fear, for I Have Redeemed You

But now, thus says the Lord,
who created you, Jacob, and formed you, Israel:
Do not fear, for I have redeemed you;
I have called you by name: you are mine.
When you pass through waters, I will be with you;
through rivers, you shall not be swept away.
When you walk through fire, you shall not be burned,
nor will flames consume you.
For I, the Lord, am your God,
the Holy One of Israel, your savior.
I give Egypt as ransom for you,
Ethiopia and Seba in exchange for you.
Because you are precious in my eyes
and honored, and I love you.
—Isaiah 43:1–4a

7 REDEMPTION THROUGH THE PASCHAL MYSTERY

COMING HOME AGAIN

In almost any survey of religious preference, Catholicism polls as the largest religious denomination in the United States. However, more people identify as "lapsed Catholics" or "fallen-away Catholics"—that is, baptized Catholics who have stopped going to Mass and participating in the sacraments—than as members of the second-largest religious denomination.

Personal stories can explain why people choose to leave the Church and, just as important, why many choose to return home to the Church. Consider the story of Melanie Rigney, who stopped going to church after her first boyfriend broke up with her just before her sixteenth birthday.

"I was coming home from babysitting one night and decided to stop in the church because I was heartbroken and I wanted to talk to God," Rigney recalled. "The church was all locked up. . . . I sat in the parking lot and said to God, 'I needed you. Where were you?'"

After that, Rigney stopped going to church. No one asked her why.

Years later, after the breakup of her marriage to a non-practicing Lutheran man, Rigney noticed that her friends who prayed were better able to cope with life's ups and downs. She sought the help of a therapist, who eventually suggested she try going to St. Charles Borromeo Church in Arlington, Virginia.

This time when she walked up to the church, the doors were unlocked. She stepped in, sat in the sanctuary, and decided to give the Catholic Church—and God—a second chance. Melanie Rigney began attending St. Charles Borromeo Church. On Christmas Day in 2005, she received Holy Communion for the first time in thirty-three years. "I cried all the way down the aisle," she said.

(Katie Baher, "Former Catholics Return to the Church," *Arlington Catholic Herald,* November 19, 2013.)

FOCUS QUESTION

What does the **PASCHAL MYSTERY** have to do with **ETERNAL LIFE**?

Chapter Overview

INTRODUCTION

Staying Close to God

MAIN IDEA

With forgiveness and compassion, God welcomes everyone into his saving presence and home in his eternal Kingdom.

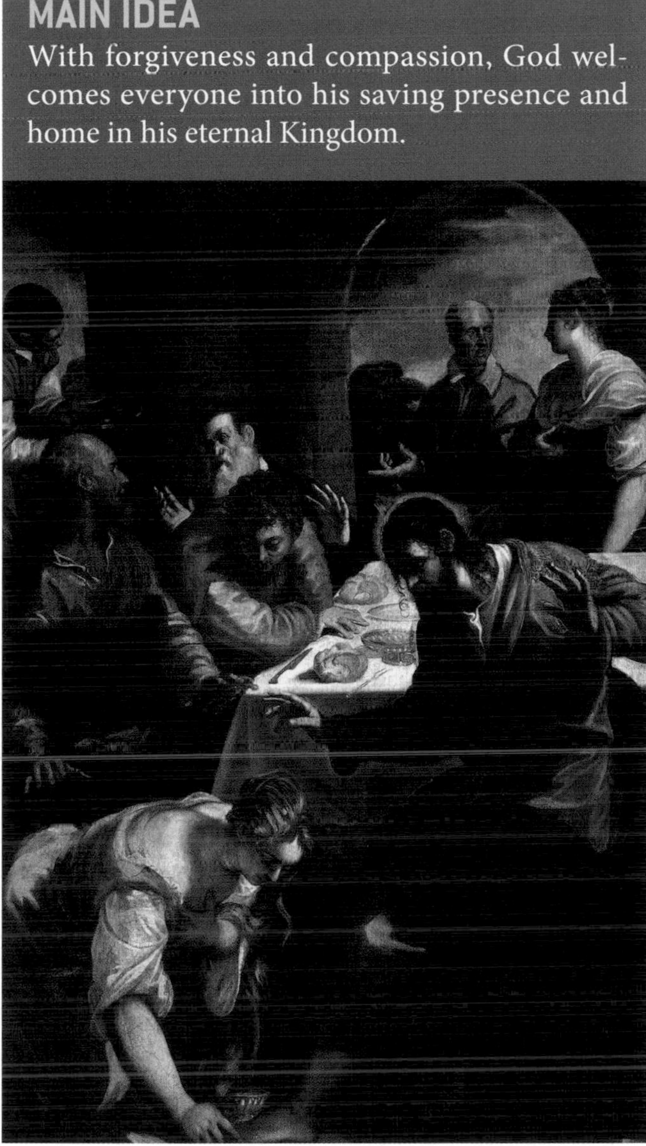

In his parables, other teachings, and his own action of forgiveness, Jesus revealed the true nature of God: a loving Father who cares deeply for his children and will do anything to nourish, teach, and save them. As the example of Melanie Rigney points to, God will do anything to welcome home those who are lost and apart from him.

Jesus wants everyone to be open to God and to the coming of God's Kingdom into their lives. Openness to God and his Kingdom requires faith, a wholehearted acceptance of Jesus, his message, and his example. The first chapter of the Gospel of Mark sums up Jesus' message: "This is the time of fulfillment. The kingdom of God is at hand. Repent, and believe in the gospel" (Mk 1:15).

Repentance means a change of mind and heart, a turning away from sin so that you can be open to Jesus and his message. This means that you must give up what is keeping you from God—fighting and complaining, senseless competition against others, making gods out of pleasure or material possessions, ignoring others and their needs, and so forth. Instead, you can stay close to God and his Kingdom by practicing the virtues of service, peace, harmony, and love for God above everything and for your neighbor as yourself.

NOTE TAKING

Identifying Examples. The section lists several examples of things a person should give up as well as several virtues or qualities to develop in order to have a better relationship with God. Create a chart like the one below. In the appropriate column, write things you should subtract or add in your life in order to improve your relationship with God.

Improving My Relationship with God

Remove	Add
Fighting and complaining	*Peace and harmony*

Celebrating God's Loving Compassion in the Sacraments

Forgiveness is central to Jesus' message. He wants all people, those who call themselves his followers and those who think of themselves as apart from him, to live by the words of the Lord's Prayer: "Forgive us our debts, as we forgive our debtors" (Mt 6:12). No matter how or why or to what degree a person considers himself or herself apart from God, he is there to forgive and welcome the person back. The most powerful example of God's forgiving love occurred at the Crucifixion of Christ. In the midst of excruciating pain, Jesus cried out: "Father, forgive them, they know not what they do" (Lk 23:34). Even at his Death, Christ prayed to his Father to forgive those who had fallen away from a relationship with God to the extent that they sought his Death.

You might understand why it is essential for a person to remain close to God while living in this world. But why must a person also remain in, or be reconnected with, the Church? In fact, Christ, the Gospel, and the Church are all deeply connected. It is in and through the Church that Christ's saving work of redemption is not only made known but also made present through the sacramental life of the Church. St. Joan of Arc (see pages 267–268) explained it this way: "About Jesus Christ and the Church, I simply know they are one thing and we shouldn't complicate the matter."

The Church is the Body of Christ continued in the world, empowered and enlivened by the Holy Spirit. The sacraments are God's loving grace reaching down into the depths of human experience, offering people concrete encounters with his love. You participate in the mystery of redemption through the sacramental life of the Church, especially the Holy

Eucharist. In the sacraments, people can encounter God's compassion and love concretely, manifested right before them. This is why many who have fallen away from the practice of faith—even though they may have been hurt by someone or something in the Church—typically feel a great sense of forgiveness, compassion, and love when they return to the practice of the sacraments. It is in the sacraments—all of them—that God's compassion is celebrated:

> By the sacraments of rebirth, Christians have become "children of God," "partakers of the divine nature." Coming to see in the faith their new dignity, Christians are called to lead henceforth a life "worthy of the gospel of Christ." They are made capable of doing so by the grace of Christ and the gifts of his Spirit, which they receive through the sacraments

and through prayer" (*CCC*, 1692, quoting 2 Pt 1:4 and Phil 1:27).

In previous chapters, you have learned about the saving events of Christ's Paschal Mystery. It is his work of redemption—whereby through his Death he destroyed your death and through his rising he restored you to the possibility of eternal life—that forms the core teaching of this course. The lesson—how you can participate in Christ's saving work and enjoy the fruits of eternal life with him after your life on earth is over—is more important than any other being taught. This chapter highlights how the sacraments make present the Paschal Mystery of Christ. Also, you will be introduced to **eschatology**, the study of the last things that await you at your own death: judgment; resurrection of the body; and Purgatory, heaven, or hell.

eschatology The study of, and teaching about, the last things: death, judgment, heaven, Purgatory, hell, the Second Coming of Christ, and the resurrection of the body.

SECTION ASSESSMENT

NOTE TAKING

Use the chart you created to help you answer the following question.

1. If you could provide one piece of advice to someone who is seeking to renew his or her relationship with God and the Church, what would you say?

VOCABULARY

2. Define *eschatology*.

COMPREHENSION

3. How do Jesus' words from the first chapter of the Gospel of Mark summarize his message?
4. What is the most powerful example of God's willingness to forgive any sinner or sin?

REFLECTION

5. What do you think St. Joan of Arc meant by equating Jesus with the Church?

SECTION 1

Your Participation in the Paschal Mystery

MAIN IDEA
The Paschal Mystery is a living event that you participate in through the sacraments; you can structure your life around it.

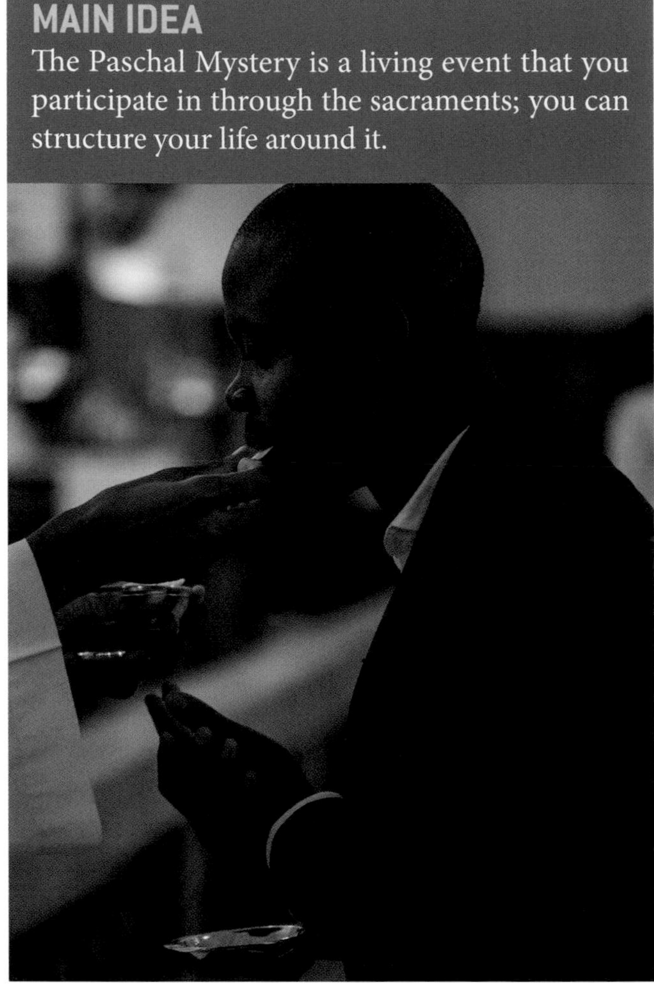

Christ's work of redemption is accomplished through the Paschal Mystery—his Passion, Death, and Resurrection—and this work is communicated, celebrated, and continued today in and through the Church. The Paschal Mystery is celebrated and made present in the liturgy of the Church, and its saving effects are communicated in the sacraments, especially the Eucharist.

The sacraments are efficacious signs of grace, instituted by Christ and entrusted to the Church, by which divine life is dispensed to us. The sacraments are God's love and mercy—his loving grace—poured into time and space so that you can encounter God concretely in your life. It is the mission of the Holy Spirit to make Jesus Christ and his Paschal Mystery present in the Church through the sacraments and to prepare believers to encounter Christ in them. Your celebration of the sacraments is a share in the life of the Trinity and a foretaste of your participation in the *heavenly liturgy*—a great eternal feast and gathering with all of God's People.

The Holy Spirit Guides Your Participation in the Paschal Mystery

If the goal of the heavenly liturgy—of heaven itself—is to adore, praise, and glorify the Father, Son, and Holy Spirit and to be in loving communion with others (namely, the Father, the Son, and the Holy Spirit and all of the angels and saints), then does it not stand to reason that your preparation for the heavenly liturgy would also take place in relation to

NOTE TAKING

Summarizing the Text. After you read the section, write three different sentences that summarize the content. Use at least one of the following verbs in each of your sentences:

- communicate
- participate
- celebrate
- dispense
- receive
- prepare
- guide

St. Teresa of Calcutta cared for mothers and children in a special way.

others, rather than alone? The poet John Milton once wrote, "Loneliness is the first thing which God's eye named not good." St. Teresa of Calcutta said, "The most terrible poverty is loneliness, and the feeling of being unloved." At the Last Supper, Christ himself promised:

> And I will ask the Father, and he will give you another Advocate to be with you always, the Spirit of truth, which the world cannot accept, because it neither sees nor knows it. But you know it, because it remains with you, and will be in you. I will not leave you orphans; I will come to you. (Jn 14:16–18)

The Church does not have a mission apart from Christ and the Holy Spirit. Rather, the Church spreads the mystery of living in communion with the Blessed Trinity:

> By virtue of our Baptism, the first sacrament of the faith, the Holy Spirit in the Church communicates to us, intimately and personally, the life that originates in the Father and is offered to us in the Son. (*CCC*, 683)

Living the Paschal Mystery

With the help of the Holy Spirit, through the sacraments, you receive God's help and strength to structure your life around the Paschal Mystery. The Holy Eucharist in a special way commemorates the Paschal Mystery by celebrating Jesus' sacrifice and Resurrection and his exalted place at the Father's right hand. The Eucharist also helps you to participate in the Paschal Mystery by giving you the Lord himself in Holy Communion; it is the Risen Lord, who is poured into your heart through the Holy Spirit. God enables you to build up your ability to love others by pouring Christ's love into your heart, empowering you with divine grace, and allowing you to look ahead to a time when you will gather with others in a heavenly banquet to celebrate God's goodness and love forever.

Jesus calls you to live the Paschal Mystery now in your daily life by *lifelong conversion*—that is, giving up sin and self-centeredness and embracing a God-centered and holy life while reaching out in love to others. In the Scriptures, Jesus says, "As I have loved you, so you also should love one another" (Jn 13:34). By the Holy Spirit that dwells in your heart, the Triune God infuses the virtues of faith, hope, and love into your soul so that you can live in relationship with him and love others and him with a love that he himself has given you. These virtues prepare you to live in communion with the Blessed Trinity and the angels and saints in heaven for eternity. The Holy Spirit enables and guides you to do the following:

- live the Beatitudes (see pages 357–358) and the Christian virtues
- recognize sin in your life and turn away from it
- love God above all things and your neighbor as yourself for the love of God

Your participation in the Paschal Mystery begins at Baptism, the first sacrament. Baptism is the "door" that gives access to the other sacraments and to Christian life itself.

SECTION ASSESSMENT

NOTE TAKING

Use the notes you made to help you complete the following items.

1. How does the Church communicate the saving events of Christ's Paschal Mystery?
2. How do you participate in the Paschal Mystery?

COMPREHENSION

3. What is the goal of the heavenly liturgy?
4. How did Jesus make sure that people do not have to prepare for heaven alone?
5. How does the Holy Eucharist help a person participate in the Paschal Mystery?

REFLECTION

6. "Jesus calls you to live the Paschal Mystery now in your daily life by lifelong conversion." Name three things you can do this week to live out this statement.

SECTION 2

Living Your Baptismal Call

MAIN IDEA
The graces and effects of the Sacrament of Baptism and the Sacrament of Confirmation help you to live a Christian life and strive for the goal of reaching heaven.

Baptism, the first Sacrament of Initiation, offers you purification from your sins and new birth in the Holy Spirit. Not only is Baptism the door or point of entry into a life of faith but it also provides the graces necessary to build your life in Christ and to model your life after his. You may have just received, or have begun preparing for, the Sacrament of Confirmation. This sacrament perfects baptismal grace; it is the sacrament that gives you the Holy Spirit to lead your growth as a child of God, incorporate you more deeply into Christ, strengthen your bond with the Church, and align you more closely with the Church's mission. Confirmation helps you to bear witness to the Christian faith in what you say and do. The effect of Confirmation is a full outpouring of the Holy Spirit. Your choice to follow God is yours and solely yours; God does not remove your freedom. Rather, he offers you the grace to strengthen you and free you to answer his loving call.

Baptismal Anointing Highlights Your Human Dignity

The sacred chrism you were anointed with at Baptism signifies your reception of the gift of the Holy

NOTE TAKING

Applying Main Themes. In your notebook, create a graphic organizer like the one below. As you read the section, for each of the elements from the Rite of Baptism, (1) tell its effects and (2) tell how its effects can help you live a Christian life.

Chrism	→	*reception of the gift of the Holy Spirit*	→	*incorporates you into Christ*
White Garment	→		→	
Water	→		→	

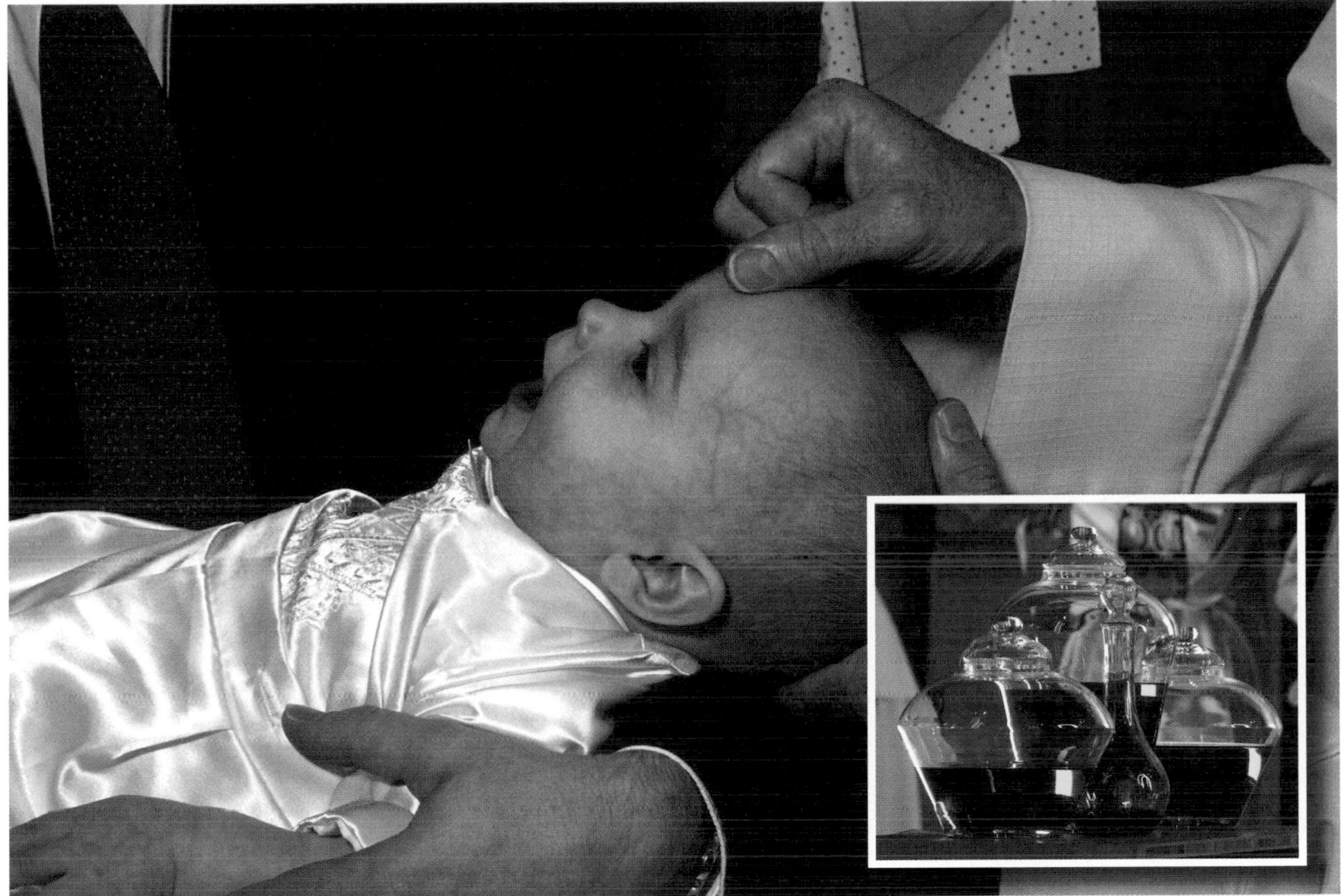

Spirit and your incorporation into Christ. This anointing prepared you to live a Christian life. In the homily he gave at an annual Chrism Mass, where sacred oils are consecrated for use throughout the year, Pope Benedict XVI explained, "Kings and priests are anointed with oil, which is thus a sign of dignity and responsibility, and likewise of the strength that comes from God. . . . A further aspect of the symbolism of oil is that it strengthens for battle" (Homily, April 1, 2010).

Anointing with oil also highlighted your human dignity and your responsibility to live like Christ. As a baptized person, you are a permanent member of the Body of Christ. The sacrament is *indelible*, which means that it cannot be removed. You are part of a global communion of believers who are called to contribute to building up the Church and renewing the world. You never need to feel isolated in your life as one of Christ's disciples: you belong to God and to the Church. You can feel at home when you visit any Catholic parish or community in the world. The only way you can separate yourself from the Church is by your own intention, either through **mortal sin** or a public renunciation of the Catholic faith.

mortal sin A grave infraction of the law of God—in which you turn away from God—that destroys the divine life (*sanctifying grace*) in the soul of the sinner. For a sin to be mortal, three conditions must be present: the sin itself must be grave (serious), you must have had full knowledge of the evil of the act, and you must have fully consented to the act. Your degree of responsibility for an act may be diminished or nullified by ignorance, duress, fear, or other psychological or social factors.

You Have Been Saved in the Waters of Baptism

Baptism brings about your salvation. The effect of Baptism, called *baptismal grace*, is a rich new reality that includes forgiveness of Original Sin and all personal sins, birth into a new life as a child of God, unification with Christ as a member of his Body, and transformation into a temple of the Holy Spirit. In Baptism, we receive **sanctifying grace** and the **grace of justification**. In the words of St. Paul, "So whoever is in Christ is a new creation: the old things have passed away; behold, new things have come. And all this is from God, who has reconciled us to himself through Christ" (2 Cor 5:17–18). Yet the inclination to sin, or **concupiscence**, remains. The sanctifying grace offered in Baptism helps you to overcome the inclination to sin, and this grace carries the following effects:

- It enables you to believe in God, hope in him, and love him through the theological virtues (see pages 288–293).
- It gives you the power to live and act under the Holy Spirit and through the **Gifts of the Holy Spirit**.
- It allows you to grow in goodness through the moral virtues.

Baptism is birth into the new life in Christ. Believers who have remained faithful to the demands of their Baptism until the end will be able to depart this life in the expectation of the blessed vision of God and in the hope of the resurrection. Baptism, therefore, does not remove your freedom to accept or reject God but rather increases your freedom. You must choose to use the baptismal grace given to you to live as a disciple of Jesus. Given that concupiscence remains after Baptism, you must wrestle with it and boldly resist it by the grace of Jesus Christ. You are summoned to spiritual battle (see *CCC*, 405).

Just prior to his death, Moses delivered a speech to the Israelites, explaining the essential choice that every person in every time and place must make:

> See, I have today set before you life and good, death and evil. If you obey the commandments of the LORD, your God, which I am giving you today, loving the LORD, your God, and walking in his ways, and keeping his commandments, statutes and ordinances, you will live and grow numerous, and the LORD, your God, will bless you in the land you are entering to possess. If, however, your heart turns away and you do not obey, but are led astray and bow down to other gods and serve them, I tell you today that you will certainly perish; you will not have a long life on the land which you are crossing the Jordan to enter and possess. I call heaven and

sanctifying grace The grace, or gift of God's friendship, that heals fallen human nature and gives you a share in the divine life of the Blessed Trinity. A habitual, supernatural gift, it makes you perfect, holy, and Christlike (see *CCC*, 2000).

grace of justification The gracious action of God that frees you from sin and communicates "the righteousness of God through faith in Jesus Christ" (Rom 3:22). Justification is not only the remission of sins but also the sanctification and renewal of your inner self so that you can receive his graces, live them in your life through the theological virtues, and grow in your relationship with God.

concupiscence "Human appetites or desires which remain disordered due to the temporal consequences of Original Sin, which remain even after Baptism, and which produce an inclination to sin" (*CCC*, Glossary).

Gifts of the Holy Spirit Outpourings of God's gifts to help you live a Christian life. The traditional seven Gifts of the Holy Spirit are wisdom, understanding, counsel, fortitude, knowledge, piety, and fear of the Lord.

> earth today to witness against you. I have set before you life and death, the blessing and the curse. Choose life, then, that you and your descendants may live. (Dt 30:15–19)

In this speech, Moses equates good behavior with life itself because to grow closer to God is to grow closer to the source of life. Conversely, to turn away from God is to turn away from the source of life and toward death. The white garment in which you were dressed at Baptism is a symbol of purity and holiness and a reminder to resist sin. You are called to wear the white garment unstained into everlasting life. This task involves asking God for daily help to grow in holiness and for the strength to seek recourse in the Sacrament of Penance and Reconciliation for the times when you, like anyone else, commit sin.

Buried with Christ

The Catholic funeral rite and the Sacrament of Baptism are related. At the start of a funeral, the priest sprinkles the body with holy water, just as once occurred at Baptism. The essential rite of Baptism is the triple immersion or pouring of the candidate's head with blessed water. Referring to Romans 6:4, he may pray using these or similar words:

> In the waters of Baptism, N. died with Christ and rose with him to new life. May he/she now share with him in eternal glory. (*Rite of Funerals*, 38)

Through Baptism, you share in the Death of Christ and escape the eternal punishment of sin. Your own resurrection still lies in the future. But because this gift has been promised to you, the thought of living forever in heaven can help draw you away from sin. As St. Paul put it, "What then shall we say? Shall we persist in sin that grace may abound? Of course not! How can we who died to sin yet live in it?" (Rom 6:1–2).

Live in God's Mercy and Keep Your Eye on Your Goal

By living faithfully, avoiding sin, and choosing good actions, you participate in the saving works of Christ: the Paschal Mystery of his Passion, Death,

Stay Close to Jesus

At your Baptism, the priest or deacon put his hands on your ears and mouth and said, "May he (the Lord) soon touch your ears to receive his Word and your mouth to proclaim his faith." Note that you were to both receive his Word and proclaim his faith. How do you do this? Strive to love Jesus as he loves you. Attach yourself to Jesus, and walk in love, following his example. Keep in mind the commandments to love God and neighbor. Know the Ten Commandments (see page 357) and Beatitudes (see pages 357–358), and consider them key guidelines for following Jesus. Also, incorporate the following ideas into your life:

- Strive to allow God the Father to perfect your character in a way that pleases him.
- Acknowledge that you are a sinner and cannot save yourself, and realize that God forgives you and loves you no matter what.
- Listen for the guidance of the Holy Spirit when you are about to make decisions, especially important ones.
- Practice the **evangelical counsels**: chastity, poverty, and obedience—characteristics of the New Law that Christ gave his disciples. While these evangelical counsels are professed by Catholics in **consecrated life**, they are also appropriate for lay Catholics.

Chastity is a moral virtue that helps you integrate your sexuality appropriately into your life. For a single layperson, chastity may require learning self-mastery. Living married life chastely means being faithful to your husband or wife. Chastity is also connected to friendship, the type of friendship Jesus extends to human beings. Poverty relates to living simply and being a good steward of your time, talent, and treasure, using them wisely in God's service. Obedience can mean upholding God's laws or following Church teachings. Obedience also obliges children to obey their parents.

You are extraordinary. You are a member of the Body of Christ. You have been rescued from the forces of darkness. You are a temple of the Holy Spirit, who helps you to pray and prompts you to do good. The Holy Spirit renews you spiritually so that you can live as a "child of the light." The Holy Spirit can help you live a life worthy of the Gospel of Christ.

evangelical counsels Vows of personal poverty, chastity understood as lifelong celibacy, and obedience to the demands of the community professed by those entering the consecrated life.

consecrated life "A permanent state of life recognized by the Church, entered freely in response to the call of Christ to perfection, and characterized by the profession of the evangelical counsels of poverty, chastity, and obedience" (CCC, Glossary).

REFLECTION

- For each of the ideas listed above, write one sentence telling how you might practically apply the idea to your own life. Then add two more ideas or guidelines to the list for staying close to Jesus.

and Resurrection. If you do stray from your life as a Catholic, you should never forget that you will always be able to turn back to the merciful Lord and ask his forgiveness in order to get back on the path to eternal happiness. The Church will always be a welcoming home. Pope Francis spoke of God's mercy this way:

> Ah! Brothers and sisters, God's face is the face of a merciful father who is always patient. Have you thought about God's patience, the patience he has with each one of us? That is his mercy. He always has patience, patience with us, he understands us. He waits for us, he does not tire of forgiving us if we are able to return to him with a contrite heart. "Great is God's mercy," says the Psalm. (Angelus, March 17, 2013)

The baptismal liturgy makes it clear that your goal in life is heaven. St. Paul wrote about the Christian life in terms of a race. Near the end of his life, he wrote:

> For I am already being poured out like a libation, and the time of my departure is at hand. I have competed well; I have finished the race; I have kept the faith. From now on the crown of righteousness awaits me, which the Lord, the just judge, will award to me on that day, and not only to me, but to all who have longed for his appearance. (2 Tm 4:6–8)

Legendary baseball player Yogi Berra, known for his humorous quotations, once observed, "You've got to be careful if you don't know where you are going, because you might not get there." Another time he cautioned, "If you don't know where you are going, you'll wind up somewhere else." The point is clear: if you do not have a well-planned, positive goal in life, wrong turns can lead you to be a person you do not want to be. There is no goal more worthwhile than getting to heaven. So take to heart the advice of St. Francis de Sales: "Resolve henceforth to keep heaven before your mind, to be ready to forgo everything that can hinder you or cause you to stray on your journey there."

SECTION ASSESSMENT

NOTE TAKING

Use the graphic organizer you created to help you respond to the following item.

1. Explain one concrete way the effects of the Sacrament of Baptism help you to incorporate the Paschal Mystery of Christ into your life.

VOCABULARY

2. Define *sanctifying grace.*
3. Name the seven *Gifts of the Holy Spirit.*
4. Explain how a teenager can practice each of the three evangelical counsels.

COMPREHENSION

5. What does it mean to say that the Sacrament of Baptism is *indelible*?
6. What are the effects of sanctifying grace in Baptism?
7. How are the Rite of Baptism and the Catholic funeral rite related?
8. What does Moses say are the opposites of good and life?

CRITICAL ANALYSIS

9. Pope Benedict XVI used the analogy of a battle to describe the Christian life. What do you think he meant?
10. St. Paul equated Christian life with running a race. How would you describe your path: focused on the finish, plodding along, off course, or something else? Explain.

REFLECTION

11. What factors help you to feel at home in a church community?

SECTION 3

The Last Things: Christian Death and the Resurrection of the Body

MAIN IDEA

Your eternal destination is determined by your own deeds on earth, which will be judged fairly in a particular judgment by Christ immediately after your death. After Christ comes again in glory at the end of the world, your body will be resurrected and united with your soul, and the Last Judgment will take place.

Your life is measured by time. You grow, change, and become older. You likely realize that your time on earth is limited and so is the opportunity to live your life fully. One day in the future, you will die.

Death is defined as the separation of your immortal soul from your body. Death is natural: it does not contradict the laws of nature. However, death was not a part of God's original plan for humanity. The separation of body and soul is the price humans have paid for Original Sin, or as St. Paul wrote, "the wages of sin is death" (Rom 6:23). But humans have an innate sense of the immortality they lost because of sin. Venerable Archbishop Fulton J. Sheen, well known on television in the middle of the twentieth century, put it this way:

> Animals die, and so do humans, but the difference is that humans know they must die. By that very fact, we humans surmount death, we get above it, we transcend it, look at it, survey it, and thus stand outside it. This very act is a dim foreshadowing of immortality. Our mortality is frightening to us largely because we can contemplate immortality, and we have a dim suspicion that we have lost the immortality that once belonged to us. (*Peace of Soul*)

After sin entered the world, death has the final word on human existence. Death marked the final threshold of human meaning. Humans lived beyond the grave but without the vision of God; beyond death, there was no light, only darkness. Then, through the Paschal Mystery, Christ conquered death. Now what gives human existence its ultimate meaning is no longer death but God's love, which conquers even death.

Death, as previously noted, is the result of sin. But Christ was sinless. He entered voluntarily into death's jaws, allowing death to swallow him up as an innocent victim. In doing so, he transformed death. He made it so that death no longer has the final word on human meaning or existence. Rather, by dying out of love for humanity and out of obedience to his

Father, though he was innocent, he took on the death that belonged to all people. By his Resurrection, he showed that love is greater than death and that death cannot contain his love. He showed that the Father's love for humans as seen in the Son's self-sacrifice has the final word on human meaning and existence. Christ has conquered death. Through Baptism, you conquer death, too, by becoming united to Christ so that you share in his Death on the Cross and in his glorious Resurrection.

This section addresses what happens to you after you die as a baptized disciple of Christ (your particular judgment, the resurrection of your body, and the Last or General Judgment) as well as the existence, purposes, and characteristics of heaven, Purgatory, and hell.

Death Is Inevitable

Eternal life in heaven is God's desire for you. But given the realities of sin and death, the only path to heaven is through death. Christians do not believe in reincarnation after death. Rather, this one life that you have been given is uniquely yours and endowed with a special dignity. God calls you *in this life* and at *every moment* of your existence in this life to receive his gracious call. This also means that this lifetime is your only opportunity to accept and live God's grace of redemption. Your fate after death is determined by God and is based on your faith and your way of life. This statement has two profound implications for how you should view your own life:

- First, you must see your entire life as heading toward your death. Death is inevitable. It is the temporal punishment everyone must pay for sin.

NOTE TAKING

Depicting Sequence. In your notebook, draw and label pictures to depict what happens at death, particular judgment, and the Last or General Judgment. For particular judgment, add images of heaven, Purgatory, and hell, indicating the three possible outcomes of particular judgment. Some examples are below.

DEATH

PARTICULAR JUDGMENT

LAST OR GENERAL JUDGMENT

This means that each day is a gift, and with each day you have a unique opportunity to love God above all things and your neighbor as yourself.

- Second, by Baptism you are united to Christ. This means that as you approach your death, you are also approaching unity with Christ on the Cross. The promise of your Baptism is that, if you are faithful to your baptismal commitments until the end, then when you face death, you will face it united with Christ. Your death will be a share in Christ's Death, so that you may also share in his Resurrection. For not even death can separate you from the love of God in Jesus Christ (see Rom 8:38–39).

With this in mind, the Church's liturgy describes death not as an end but as a change in dwelling place:

> Indeed for your faithful, Lord,
> life is changed not ended,
> and, when this earthly dwelling turns to dust,
> an eternal dwelling is made ready for them
> in heaven. (*Roman Missal*, Preface I for the Dead)

Not only did Jesus conquer death for himself and for all those who are united to him in faith and love but he also showed you how to face death. In the Garden of Gethsemane, anxious about his own impending Death, Jesus prayed: "Abba, Father, all things are possible to you. Take this cup away from me, but not what I will but what you will" (Mk 14:36). Jesus' words describe his final act of total self-giving to the Father. In faith, at the time of your own death, you can imitate Jesus and say, "Father, into your hands I commend my spirit" (Lk 23:46).

Because of Christ, your death will have a positive meaning. As a Christian, you hope that you will rise on the "last day" with Christ in all his glory. You hope that you will live forever with Jesus and with all who have followed him. Remember, through the sacramental life of the Church, the Paschal Mystery becomes your mystery, and your whole life must be understood as living the Paschal Mystery. Your Baptism initiates you into this mystery, and you share in it most fully in the Eucharist.

Death is a difficult thing to think about and discuss. Death brings sadness for those left on earth who miss a person who has died. Understanding death from God's perspective can help to ease the sadness. In death, God is calling you to be with him.

After souls have been purified in Purgatory, they join the saints in heaven and see God face-to-face.

For those who are baptized, death is our singular, unique, and individual opportunity to share in Christ's Cross, in the hope of sharing in his Resurrection. Seeing death this way, some people, especially those who are older or suffering, may look forward to death because they want to be united with Christ in the happiness and joy of heaven. Even at your age, it is important to realize that life is a gift that can be taken from you at any moment. So you must nourish your relationship with God, so that when you die, you are united to the love of God in Christ and remain so united into eternity.

The Particular Judgment

Eternal life begins immediately after death, when your soul is separated from your human body. Your soul will remain separate from your body until the Last or General Judgment (see pages 259–260). But before that, you will meet a *particular judgment* based on how you lived your life in imitation of Christ and the Gospel. This is a judgment very particular to you as an individual. It will determine whether you go to heaven immediately, need purification in Purgatory, or suffer the punishments of hell and eternal damnation. St. Paul wrote, "For we must all appear before the judgment seat of Christ, so that each one may receive recompense, according to what he did in the body, whether good or evil" (2 Cor 5:10).

Jesus himself referred to particular judgment in the parable of the rich man and Lazarus (see Lk 16:19–31 and the image on page 252). Because he did not feed the starving Lazarus, the rich man suffered the fires of Hades. In contrast, the good man Lazarus went to a peaceful resting place.

If you live a life faithful to the Gospel's demands, then you have nothing to fear when you die. God is a God of justice and mercy. His judgment is based on how you answered his call of loving mercy and whether you worshipped and loved him above all things and loved your neighbor as yourself. At your particular judgment, God is not out to trick you. There will be no surprises. Christ will judge you fairly according to your own free decisions to accept or refuse the grace of his redemption and to live a life of discipleship that includes practicing the virtues of faith, hope, and love.

St. María Guadalupe García Zavala (1878–1963), known as Mother Lupita, was the Mexican founder of the Servants of St. Margaret Mary and of the Poor. As she lay dying, her doctor asked her, "How are you doing, Mother Lupita?" She replied, comfortably, "I'm walking toward heaven." Your goal is to live your life so that you can approach your own death with the same attitude.

Reflection: RIP

RIP is an abbreviation for the short Latin prayer, *Requiescat in pace* ("May he/she rest in peace").

Perhaps you have also seen a print of a medieval painting of a monk at his desk, contemplating the skull sitting on it and what it represents. The artist may also have added the words *Sic transit gloria mundi* ("Thus passes the glory of the world"). The skull reminds you that you have only a brief time to act in life. Time speeds quickly by. What the world finds important may not be so in God's eyes.

ASSIGNMENT

Let this Latin prayer help you reflect on your own life. What would you like to do with your life? Write an obituary notice for yourself that would appear in a daily newspaper several decades from now. Include the following details:

- Your name and age
- Cause of death
- Occupation
- Loved ones left behind
- Major accomplishments
- Unfinished tasks
- Epitaph on gravestone

In your journal, write an entry describing five personal qualities you could offer to Jesus at your particular judgment that show how you have lived a Christian life. Write a detailed plan to help you practice these qualities in the next two weeks. At the end of the two weeks, write a one-paragraph reflection evaluating your progress.

Heaven

If you die in God's friendship and grace and you are perfectly purified, you will receive the reward of perfect eternal happiness. Living with Jesus Christ forever, you will be blessed with the **beatific vision**, where you will see God face-to-face, as he really is, and contemplate his heavenly glory. Perfect life with the Blessed Trinity, the Blessed Mother, and all the angels and saints (including your relatives and friends who have lived God-centered lives) is called *heaven*. In heaven, God "will wipe every tear from [your] eyes, and there shall be no more death or mourning, wailing or pain, [for] the old order has passed away" (Rv 21:4).

Of course, it is Jesus' Death and Resurrection that have opened heaven to you. In heaven, you will have perfect communion with Christ, though you will keep your true, individual identity. You will continue to fulfill God's will in heaven and will reign with Christ Jesus forever.

The pleasures and happiness in store for you in heaven are beyond human imagination. Scripture uses images such as a wedding feast, light, life, peace, paradise, the Father's house, and the heavenly Jerusalem to describe the joy and experience of eternal happiness and communion with God in heaven.

Purgatory

Purgatory is the name the Church gives to the final purification of those who die in God's grace and friendship but who need purification or cleansing to achieve the holiness necessary to enter heaven. From her beginnings, the Church has honored the memory of the dead and offered prayers in solidarity

In heaven, the pains that afflict us on earth, both large and small, will be gone.

with those who have died, especially during the celebration of the Eucharist. Other acts, such as helping the poor and works of penance, can be offered up for someone who is in Purgatory as well.

Catholic belief in the existence of Purgatory is based on biblical passages such as 2 Maccabees 12:39–46, which encourages those who are living to pray for the dead so that they may be released from their sins. In addition, Church Tradition has interpreted certain passages (see 1 Cor 3:15, 1 Pt 1:7) as referring to a place of a "cleansing fire" after death.

The doctrine of Purgatory and the process of purification make sense. To embrace an all-loving God, you must be free of any imperfection in your own capacity to love. Only a person who, before

beatific vision Seeing God "face-to-face" in heaven; the source of eternal happiness and final union with the Triune God for all eternity.

Purgatory The state of purification that takes place after death for those who need to be made clean and holy before meeting the all-holy God in heaven.

death, has been cleansed of sin or any punishment due for sins is pure enough to embrace an all-loving God completely and is thus ready for heaven. Sometimes, this cleansing can only be completed after death. It is both a joyful and a painful process. Those in Purgatory are happy that heaven awaits them, but the process of purgation might entail burning with sorrow and shame over sin and great difficulty in giving up selfish attachments. However, when their purgation is complete, their suffering will end as they enter the bliss of heaven.

Hell

By definition, hell is eternal separation from God brought on by deliberate mortal sin. Its principal punishment is separation from the loving God who created you. God created every person in his image and placed a desire for himself within every human heart, so that our deepest yearnings for love, life, joy, and happiness can only be fulfilled in loving and worshipping him. Hell is therefore not only eternal separation from God but also the eternal unfulfillment of our hearts' deepest desire for God.

Sacred Scripture and Sacred Tradition both affirm the existence of hell. For example, Jesus referred several times to *Gehenna*, a Jewish term associated with hell. One example is the parable of the sheep and the goats—a judgment scene at the end of time in which those who fail to love the needy are condemned to hell (see Mt 25:31–46). Jesus talked on other occasions about divine judgment (see Mt 13:41–42) and separation from God because of selfishness, such as in the parable of the rich man and Lazarus (see Lk 16:19–31). Sacred Tradition speaks of the "fires of hell." Those in hell grieve over their eternal punishment, suffer spiritually and physically, and give up all hope of salvation.

God does not send anyone to hell; unrepented mortal sin does. You cannot know who is in hell, because you cannot see the depths of another human's heart. Jesus warns you not to judge others lest you be judged yourself (see Lk 6:37). What you can and should do is pray that all sinners, including yourself, may repent of sin and accept God's love and forgiveness.

The doctrine of hell is related to the belief that God made you truly free. Knowing about hell ahead of time opens your eyes to the wonderful gift of God's love and offers you the opportunity for conversion to using your gifts and talents in God's service. If you try to live with love in your heart and you perform acts of love for God and others, the existence of hell should not frighten you. If you turn away from sin as Christ Jesus calls you to do, then you can trust and believe that he will save you.

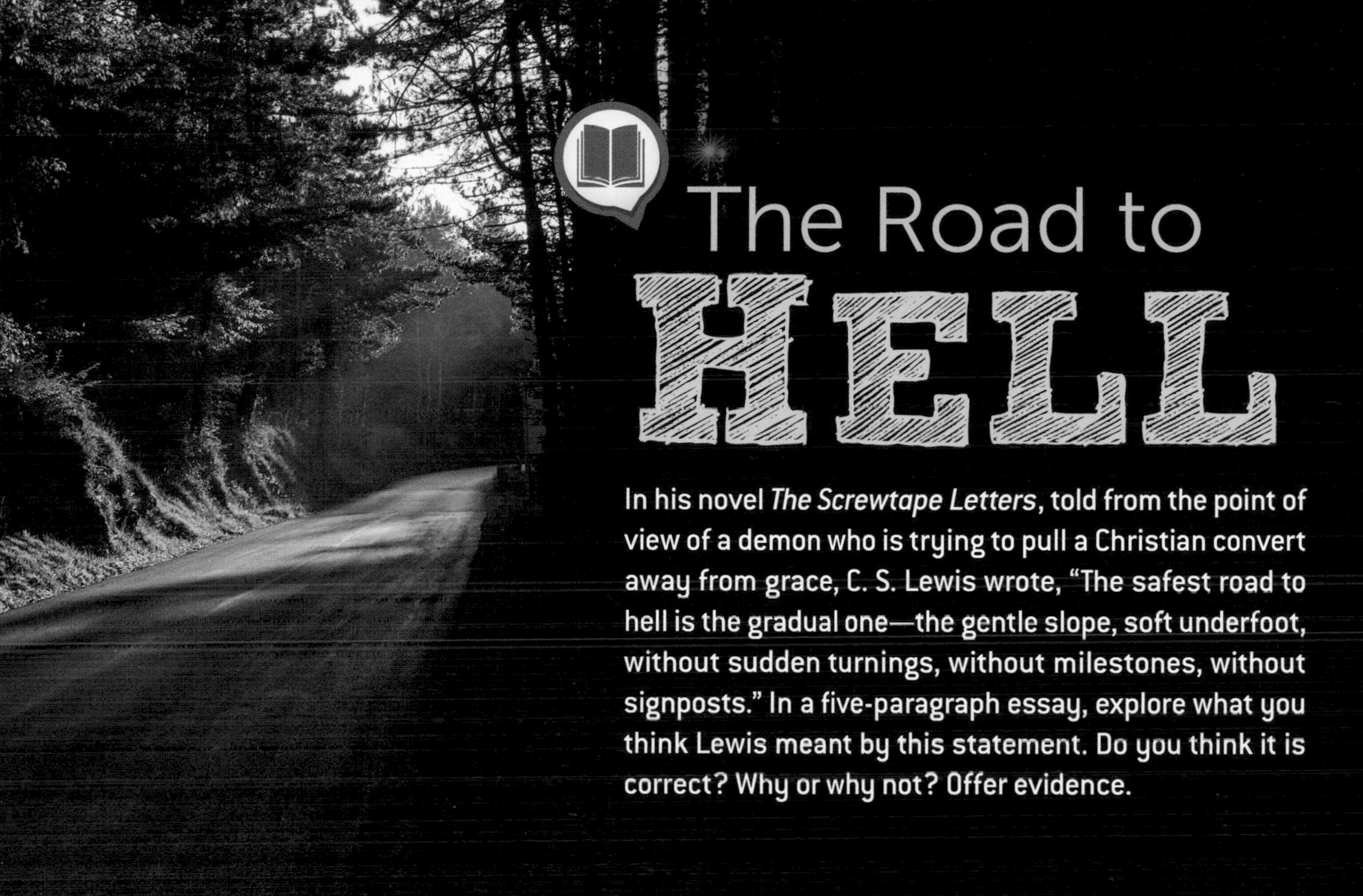

The Road to HELL

In his novel *The Screwtape Letters*, told from the point of view of a demon who is trying to pull a Christian convert away from grace, C. S. Lewis wrote, "The safest road to hell is the gradual one—the gentle slope, soft underfoot, without sudden turnings, without milestones, without signposts." In a five-paragraph essay, explore what you think Lewis meant by this statement. Do you think it is correct? Why or why not? Offer evidence.

The Last or General Judgment

Christians believe that the resurrection of both the just and unjust will come immediately before the Last or General Judgment. On that last day of human history, the risen, glorified Lord will come again. This Second Coming of Christ in glory is also known as the *Parousia* (see page 10), a Greek word that means "presence." Christ, who is truth itself, will lay bare each person's relationship with God:

> The Last Judgment will reveal even to its furthest consequences the good each person has done or failed to do during his earthly life. (*CCC*, 1039)

Jesus, in the presence of all the angels, will separate the sheep (those who lived lovingly toward the poor and marginalized) from the goats (those who lived selfishly and did not attend to people in need) (see Mt 25:31–32). God the Father has given Jesus the role of judge because of the free offering he made of his life for the salvation of all.

As to when this will take place, only the Father knows. When the day does come, however, everyone will see "that God's justice triumphs over all the injustices committed by his creatures and that God's love is stronger than death" (*CCC*, 1040). The followers of Christ look forward to the Last Judgment because on that day their resurrected bodies and souls will reunite. Furthermore, God will transform and restore the entire physical universe. Along with a transformed humanity, "the new heavens and new earth" will share in Christ Jesus' own glory.

Today, you have a glimpse of your future life because Christ has already initiated the Kingdom of God on earth. The Church is the seed and beginning of this Kingdom. The Church "is the Reign of Christ already present in mystery" (*Lumen Gentium*,

3, quoted in *CCC*, 763). In addition to love and faith, the Holy Spirit infuses you with the virtue of hope, which leads you to pray for the coming of the Kingdom of God and to live in a way that is directed toward the Kingdom.

The Resurrection of the Body

"I believe in . . . the resurrection of the body." This is one of the statements you affirm when you profess the Apostles' Creed (see page 354). God created human beings with bodies of flesh. God's Son took on a human body (flesh) in order to redeem it. Furthermore, the "resurrection of the flesh" completes the creation and redemption of the human body.

Early Church Father Tertullian taught that "the flesh is the hinge of salvation" (*On the Resurrection of the Flesh*, 8). The Second Council of Lyons (1272–1274) affirmed the Church's belief "in a true resurrection of the flesh that we now possess" (quoted in *CCC*, 1017). This means that not only will your immortal soul live on after death, but it will also be reunited with your body after the Last Judgment. These interlocking truths about the resurrection of your body and the gift of everlasting life are fundamental Christian beliefs, based on faith in Christ's own Resurrection.

How will this resurrection occur? Recall that at the time of your death, your soul will separate from your human body, but at the Last Judgment, all bodies of the dead will rise, both those who have done good (to heaven) and those who have done evil (to hell).

Consider that the Gospels describe Jesus' body as being the same, yet very different, after his Resurrection. At first, many of his friends had a difficult time recognizing him. Some misidentified him as a ghost or the gardener. Your body will similarly be transformed after death into a spiritual body. Although this mystery is incomprehensible through human reason, faith sheds some light on it. For example, consider the way that ordinary earthly bread and wine become the Body and Blood of Christ at Mass. You have experienced this transformation firsthand, and you have come to believe in its reality. You can apply this experience to the transformation of your body. Christ will raise human bodies and transform them on the last day when he returns. Your resurrected body will be made incorrupt and will rejoin your soul. In talking about that day, Jesus said,

> "Do not be amazed at this, because the hour is coming in which all who are in the tombs will hear his voice and will come out, those who have done good deeds to the resurrection of life, but those who have done wicked deeds to the resurrection of condemnation." (Jn 5:28–29)

Finally, don't forget that through your Baptism, you were already buried with Christ and raised with him in a spiritual sense. Because of your connection to the Body of Christ, you participate at some level in Christ's heavenly life now. Your association with Christ's Body, the Church, means that your physical body has great dignity now and that you should treat it, and others' bodies, accordingly. People who are suffering should receive special attention. When you care for and respect your own body and the bodies of others, you are expressing profound respect and gratitude to a loving God who made you a composite being of body and soul.

SECTION ASSESSMENT

NOTE TAKING

Refer to the labeled pictures you drew to help you complete the following items.

1. Describe the relationship between a person's particular judgment and the Last or General Judgment.
2. Using just one word for each, describe heaven, Purgatory, and hell.

VOCABULARY

3. Define *Purgatory*.
4. What is the term that describes the ability to see God face-to-face, as he really is, and contemplate his heavenly glory?

COMPREHENSION

5. How is the word *dwelling* used in describing Christian death?
6. What will be determined at the particular judgment?
7. When will the Last or General Judgment occur?
8. What gives you a glimpse of your future life in heaven?
9. How does the mystery of the Eucharist help to explain the transformation of the human body into a spiritual body at the Last Judgment?

CRITICAL ANALYSIS

10. Why is it important to be ready for your own death?
11. Why is death natural in one sense but unnatural in terms of faith?

REFLECTION

12. Describe how you should live in order to trust that Christ will save you.
13. Why does your body have great dignity? What is the implication of this truth?

Section Summaries

Focus Question

What does the Paschal Mystery have to do with eternal life?

Complete one of the following:

Jesus said, "Unless a grain of wheat falls to the ground and dies, it remains just a grain of wheat; but if it dies, it produces much fruit" (Jn 12:24). Write two to three paragraphs explaining how these words sum up the Paschal Mystery and your task of incorporating the Paschal Mystery into your life.

St. John Vianney wrote, "You must accept your cross; if you carry it courageously it will carry you to heaven." Create a drawing that explains the meaning of this statement.

Read 1 Thessalonians 4:13–5:11. Write three pieces of good news from this passage that give you hope about your own death and about life after death.

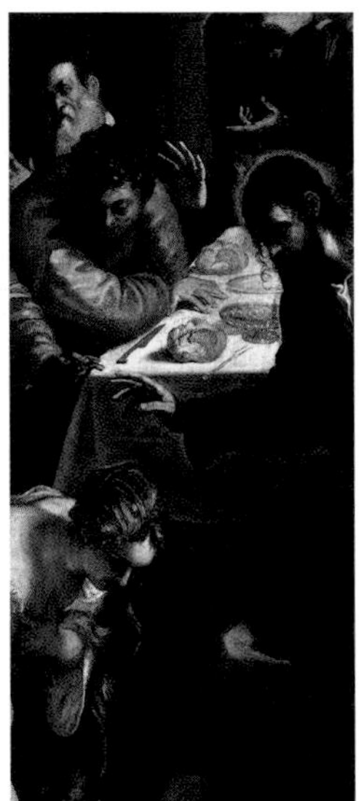

INTRODUCTION (PAGES 237–239)

Staying Close to God

Due to his great love and compassion, God desires that everyone live eternally in his Kingdom. This invitation demands a human response: openness to Jesus and the Gospel, expressed in taking the first step of repentance from sin and then continually expressed in the way you live your life. Forgiveness is central. Participation in the Kingdom begins now, especially through the sacramental life of the Church.

Read the following miracle accounts: water into wine (Jn 2:1–11); Canaanite woman (Mt 15:21–28); and woman with a hemorrhage (Lk 8:43–48). Summarize how each illustrates the theme of conversion.

SECTION 1 (PAGES 240–243)

Your Participation in the Paschal Mystery

It is in the Church that Christ dispenses the gift of salvation: "by this sacrifice, he pours out the graces of salvation on his Body which is the Church" (*CCC*, 1407). Celebration of the sacraments—initially through Baptism and most fully in the Eucharist, the heart and summit of the Church's life—is your opportunity to participate in the Paschal Mystery now. In Baptism, you die with Christ and become alive in him. You receive the outpouring of the Holy Spirit. The Holy Spirit helps you to live out the Beatitudes and Christian virtues, turn away from sin, and put into practice the love of God and neighbor.

Love is the greatest gift of the Holy Spirit (see 1 Cor 13:1–31). Share examples of how you have put each of the following qualities of love into practice at school and among your family and friends: patience, kindness, humility, politeness, and selflessness.

SECTION 2 (PAGES 244–251)

Living Your Baptismal Call

The Sacrament of Baptism not only initiates a person into Christian life but also, through the gift of the Holy Spirit, provides the strength and grace to live as a Christian. Strength, symbolized by oil, is one of the gifts God gives you in Baptism to resist temptation, to selflessly give yourself to God and others, and to grow in holiness in and through the Church. Because of the waters of your Baptism, you have already died and risen with Christ in his Paschal Mystery. The white garment symbolizes the fact that as you rise from the baptismal waters, you "put on Christ" (cf. Rom 13:14). St. Paul wrote of Christian life in terms of a race. Using the graces of Baptism and all the sacraments, you must always keep heaven on your mind and as your goal, just as a runner in a race looks to the finish line.

St. Ambrose wrote, "To the good person to die is gain. The foolish fear death as the greatest of evils, the wise desire it as a rest after labors and the end of ills." What do you think St. Ambrose meant by these words?

SECTION 3 (PAGES 252–261)

The Last Things: Christian Death and the Resurrection of the Body

Because of human freedom, you have the choice to be with God or without him. You know that God did not intend for you to undergo even physical death, but that death is the consequence of sin—that is, of turning away from God as the source of life. Because Jesus, though innocent, took on death for all of humanity, your death has a positive meaning and is the path to eternal life. It is important to be ready for death because we are not guaranteed a long life. After death, you will experience the particular judgment and go to heaven, Purgatory, or hell, depending on your choices in life. At the Last or General Judgment at the end of time, your soul will reunite with your resurrected body. Transformed into a spiritual body, you will live on after death, loving and worshipping God.

Read paragraphs 1023–1029 of the *Catechism of the Catholic Church*. What does this section say about the following: (1) what it means to "live in heaven"; (2) what the life of the blessed in heaven consists of; and (3) the meaning of the beatific vision?

Chapter Assignments

Choose and complete at least one of the three assignments assessing your understanding of the material in this chapter.

1. Interpreting and Recasting the Parable of the Weeds

Read the parable of the weeds (Mt 13:24–30, 36–43). Then complete each of the following steps:

1. Write a two- to three-paragraph interpretation of the parable. What is the message of the parable?
2. Create a list of each of the following symbols in the parable: the field, the sower of the wheat, the good seed, the sower of the weeds, the weeds, the harvest, and the harvester. Write one sentence explaining what each symbol represents.
3. Write your own version of the parable of the weeds in a modern setting. Direct your parable to people your own age. Make sure the message of your version is the same as that of the original.

2. Remembering the Souls in Purgatory

The Catholic Church devotes the entire month of November—particularly the Feast of All Souls on November 2—to praying for the souls in Purgatory. It is important to pray for people you know who have died and who may be in Purgatory. They need your prayers and sacrifices to ease their sufferings and speed up their advancement to heaven.

Do all of the following:

1. Write short biographies of three friends, family members, or acquaintances who have died. Each biography should be two paragraphs in length.
2. Write your own short prayer for the souls in Purgatory, specifically mentioning the people you wrote about.
3. Find and record one quotation written about Purgatory by a saint.
4. The Church suggests, above all, that we should offer Mass for those in Purgatory. Other recommendations are "almsgiving, indulgences, and works of penance undertaken on behalf of the dead" (*CCC*, 1032). Make a list of five different ways (e.g., special prayers, novenas, penances) you can pray and sacrifice for the souls in Purgatory. Write one sentence for each way that explains what it entails.

3. St. Paul Explains the Resurrection of the Body

The new Christians in Corinth raised two objections about the resurrection of the body: one concerning how the body could be raised and the other involving what kind of resurrected body a person would possess. St. Paul answered these objections in 1 Corinthians 15:35–58. Read the passage, and complete each of the items listed below.

- Create a visual image to represent the analogy from agriculture that St. Paul uses to describe what will happen to the human body as it rises from the dead.
- How will the resurrection of the dead take place as described in verses 50 to 54? Answer in one detailed paragraph.
- What is meant by the "sting of death" in verse 56? Answer in two paragraphs referencing Hosea 13:14, Genesis 3:19, and Romans 5:12.
- How do the dead rise? Answer in one detailed paragraph referencing paragraphs 999 and 1000 of the *Catechism of the Catholic Church*.

Faithful Disciple

St. Joan of Arc

St. Joan of Arc was born on a French farm in the small village of Domrémy, near the province of Lorraine, on January 6, 1412. France was in the midst of the Hundred Years' War with England at the time. The English king and the Duke of Burgundy sided against the French heirs to the throne, including the future king, Charles VII, who assumed the title after his older brothers had died in succession.

St. Joan of Arc

When she was thirteen, Joan received visions and heard voices in her head that told her to go the French king and help him regain the throne from the Burgundians. She identified the speakers of the final message to be Sts. Michael, Catherine of Alexandria, and Margaret of Antioch. After much opposition, both from those in the king's court and from the Church, St. Joan was allowed to lead a small army of troops into battle at Orléans on May 8, 1429. She dressed like a man in military armor and clothing and rode a horse into battle. She was seventeen years old.

Although historians do not believe Joan actually fought in the battle, she was wounded. What is known is that Joan's appearance at Orléans led to a change in strategy and almost immediate success for the French. The English halted their siege of Orléans on May 8, 1429, and by July 17 of that year, King Charles VII was crowned at Reims.

During her lifetime, St. Joan of Arc was an international heroine known as the "Maid of Orléans." She inspired many soldiers, and both the French and the English believed that she had supernatural powers. In a later battle, the French Burgundians captured Joan. Since the English and the Burgundians had an alliance of sorts, the Burgundians sold Joan of Arc to the English for a great sum of money.

The English put her in jail. Among other things, she was tried as a heretic for claiming she received direct messages from the saints and for wearing men's clothing. Unfortunately, St. Joan of Arc's help in putting Charles VII on the throne was not significant enough for him to respond in kind: he apparently made no effort to rescue her. According to some sources, her soldiers led barefoot protests on her behalf.

St. Joan of Arc did not receive a fair trial. The court said that Joan's life would be spared if she signed a document denying she received messages from the saints and agreed not to wear men's clothing. As she could not read, Joan likely did not understand these elements of the request. Back in jail, she put on her male clothes to help defend herself from assault. The charge of heresy remained. Joan was also denied many of the options provided to other defendants. She was found guilty and burned at the stake on May 30, 1431.

Thirty years after her death, St. Joan was publicly exonerated of all charges. She had already developed a cult in France of those inspired by her. However, if official state historians had been the only people to record Joan's story, she might never have been canonized. Even Charles VII spoke out against her. Shakespeare portrayed her power as coming from Satan. The French writer and philosopher Voltaire tried to damage her reputation. Luckily, private historians preserved her good name, as did some French literature.

Joan of Arc was canonized in 1920 and declared the patron saint of France.

Reading Comprehension

1. What did the messages from the saints instruct St. Joan of Arc to do?
2. What was St. Joan's objective at the Battle of Orléans?
3. What were the charges brought against St. Joan?
4. How was the truth of St. Joan of Arc's life preserved?

Writing Task

- St. Joan of Arc was called a "relapsed heretic" when she insisted that she did in fact hear saints' voices in her prayers. Because she wouldn't deny this spiritual experience, the secular authorities put her to death. How does her persistence witness to her Christian faith?

Explaining the Faith

What does the Church teach about extraterrestrial life?

Interestingly, the Catholic Church has never made an official statement one way or another about the existence elsewhere in the universe of other intelligent beings. Basically, this is a question for science to answer, not theology. But Catholics can speculate about the theological implications of the possible existence of other intelligent beings in the universe.

First, some Catholic astronomers have commented on the vastness of the universe and how strange it would be if humans were the only intelligent creatures God made. Strange, yes, but that does not prove that there is extraterrestrial intelligent life. So far, none has been discovered.

Second, Jesus Christ is the Word of God spoken once and for all to humanity. Christ is the unique Savior, the Son of God who became man to redeem the world. Although Scripture records the history of human sin and Christ's redemption, it does not record the history of all the civilizations that might exist elsewhere in the universe and whether Jesus saves them. No one knows how God dealt with or deals with them, if in fact they do exist. Christian theology does hold that God would want all of his creatures to share in his Trinitarian love and that his saving plan touches them all in some way. While God's self-Revelation to us in Jesus Christ is directed specifically to the salvation of human beings on earth, it contains claims about the universality and cosmic scope of God's salvific plans and work. The Paschal Mystery has a bearing on created reality, visible and invisible, all that is known and all that is unknown.

Third, the Church teaches that science and religion should not be at odds. If life on other planets were to be discovered, it would simply strengthen Christian belief in a marvelous Creator God who is much greater than you can possibly imagine. Remember that the God who created all things is the same one who freely and graciously chose to save you in Jesus Christ. Ultimately, science (based on God's creation) and religion (based on God's Revelation) cannot disagree because they both derive from the same God who creates and saves.

While most conversations about other life forms focus on material beings who have spirits and exist in time and space as humans do, the Church certainly teaches that God created other creatures that do not live on earth: spiritual, immortal beings called *angels* (and the fallen angels known as *demons*):

> As purely *spiritual* creatures, angels have intelligence and will: They are personal and immortal creatures, surpassing in perfection all visible creatures, as the splendor of their glory bears witness. (*CCC*, 330)

Further Research

- What would the Catholic Church's reaction be if an extraterrestrial showed up on earth? "If, for example, tomorrow an expedition of Martians came, and some of them came to us, here . . . Martians, right? Green, with that long nose and big ears, just like children paint them," Pope Francis wondered out loud in an address he gave in 2014. Research to find out how the pope said that he and the Church would respond.

Prayer

Prayer for the Safety of Soldiers

Almighty and eternal God,
those who take refuge in you will be glad
and forever will shout for joy.
Protect these soldiers as they discharge their duties.
Protect them with the shield of your strength
and keep them safe from all evil and harm.
May the power of your love enable them to return home
in safety, that with all who love them,
they may ever praise you for your loving care.
We ask this through Christ our Lord.
Amen.
—United States Conference of Catholic Bishops

8

DISCIPLESHIP AND HOLINESS THROUGH ONGOING CONVERSION

"IN GOD We TRUST and RIDE"

In the late nineteenth century, many Catholic men took work in factories. The working conditions there were dangerous, and many workers were injured or killed in work-related accidents. Catholic workers also faced prejudice, even from organizations that sponsored life insurance.

How could Catholic men gain insurance benefits without having to denounce their beliefs? Fr. Michael J. McGivney—an assistant pastor at St. Mary's Church in New Haven, Connecticut—came up with an idea. Working with the Connecticut state legislature, he and some of his parishioners helped to charter the Knights of Columbus as a fraternal benefit society in March 1882. Today, the Knights of Columbus have more than fourteen thousand councils and 1.8 million members throughout the world. The order helps families by providing life insurance, financial assistance, and long-term care to those in need.

Knights also work together in service and charity. In 2005, Raymond Medina of Fort Worth, Texas, started a group called Knights on Bikes. The group travels by motorcycle to help brother Knights in need. They also ride in parades, visit nursing homes, and raise money for the needy. There are now thirty Knights on Bikes groups in the United States, Mexico, Canada, and the Philippines.

Mark Cearley, president of the Oklahoma chapter, said, "The Knights on Bikes is a great way for our order to be seen in the public, away from the church, and [to get] more men excited to join our brotherhood." In 2013, Cearley's chapter raised four thousand dollars for the family of fellow Knight Joey Pustajovski after he died in an April 2013 plant explosion in Texas.

The mission and objective of the Knights of Columbus, first envisioned by Fr. McGivney, lives on.

(Mason Beecroft, "'Bike Gang' Aims to Serve Community, Spread Catholic Faith, Values," *Catholic News Service*, August 3, 2013.)

FOCUS QUESTION

What are the **REQUIREMENTS** and **BENEFITS** of being a **DISCIPLE** of **JESUS CHRIST**?

Chapter Overview

INTRODUCTION

Conforming to Christ

MAIN IDEA

Discipleship means conforming yourself to Christ by getting to know him as a friend and by following his teachings and commandments.

The Knights of Columbus connect with one another and minister in their own way—one unique manner of living as disciples of Jesus Christ. Your own life as a disciple will entail conforming yourself to Christ in your own particular way. You can do this through your varied interests. Whatever career or job you later pursue, you can carry it out in a way that is Christlike.

Being a disciple of Christ is a concrete calling. It involves the following:

- adhering to Jesus and accepting his teaching
- converting your heart and life and forming a good conscience
- worshipping and loving God as Jesus taught
- living a sacramental life and a life of prayer
- putting Jesus' oral and spiritual teaching into practice
- serving the poor and marginalized
- taking part in the mission of evangelization
- fulfilling your responsibility for stewardship

To live as a disciple of Christ, you must grow in holiness in and through the Church. Like what the Knights and many other Catholics do, being a disciple will require you to share your faith with others and to care for those most in need. Some general principles of Christian discipleship follow.

Conforming to Christ

Everyone understands what it means to conform to a group. Sometimes people do things against their own beliefs or against morality in order to fit in. Other times, conformity brings benefits; for example, think about how joining a gym could lead you to pick up good habits of fitness and health from other members.

NOTE TAKING

Summarizing Information. After reading this section, print and complete the following sentences in your notes:

- Being a disciple means . . .
- Disciples conform to Christ by . . .
- Disciples grow in friendship with Jesus by . . .
- Two steps for becoming more like Christ are . . .

At World Youth Day 2013 in Rio de Janeiro, Brazil, Pope Francis equated discipleship to being on a team: "Team Jesus." The Pope said:

> Jesus asks you to follow him for life, he asks you to be his disciples, to "play on his team." Most of you love sports! Here in Brazil, as in other countries, football [American soccer] is a national passion. Right? Now, what do players do when they are asked to join a team? They have to train, and to train a lot! The same is true of your lives as the Lord's disciples. St. Paul, describing Christians, tells you: "athletes deny themselves all sorts of things; they do this to win a crown of leaves that withers, but you [to win] a crown that is imperishable" (1 Cor 9:25). Jesus offers you something bigger than the World Cup! Something bigger than the World Cup! Jesus offers you the possibility of a fruitful life, a life of happiness; he also offers you a future with him, an endless future, in eternal life. That is what Jesus offers you. But he asks you to pay admission, and the cost of admission is that you train yourselves "to get in shape," so that you can face every situation in life undaunted, bearing witness to your faith, by talking with him in prayer. . . . Dear young people, be true "athletes of Christ"! (Address at the Prayer Vigil for World Youth Day, July 27, 2013)

The word *disciple* comes from the Latin word for student. As Jesus' student, you come to know him, learn about him, follow his teachings, and take the steps he shows you to attain eternal life. Ironically, if by nature you prefer being a nonconformist, conforming to Christ still fits you, since both Jesus and his disciples are countercultural in many ways.

Those who love God will be conformed to the image of his Son in their way of life. God calls, justifies, and glorifies them. God calls you to live a holy life, to accept and live the grace of redemption, and to remain close to him as a friend.

Friendship with Christ

Friends are incredible gifts in life. Ralph Waldo Emerson said, "The only way to have a friend is to be one." It's nice when you notice that someone else wants to be your friend. Jesus calls you to friendship first. Jesus has already proven his loyalty to you beyond a doubt by dying for you on the Cross.

Jesus' call to friendship is a new way for people to relate to God. In the Old Testament, the biblical authors referred to the great Moses, Joshua, and King David as "servants" or "slaves" of the Lord. Slaves would not have been privy to their masters' plans but would simply have carried out commands. In sharing with them as much as he heard from his Father, Jesus elevated the status of his disciples significantly, bringing them up to his own level by calling them friends. He said:

> This is my commandment: love one another as I love you. No one has greater love than this, to lay down one's life for one's friends. You are my friends if you do what I command you. I no longer call you slaves, because a slave does not know what his master is doing. I have called you friends, because I have told you everything I have heard from my Father. It was not you who chose me, but I who chose you and appointed you to go and bear fruit that will remain, so that whatever you ask the Father in my name he may give you. This I command you: love one another. (Jn 15:12–17)

Being God's friend requires more from you in some ways than being his servant. Instead of simply following a master's clear-cut directions as a servant would, you have to find your path through **discernment**—that is, separating out good from the lie of temptation that appears to be good. Part of discernment is identifying your *charisms* (specific gifts or graces given to you by the Holy Spirit that directly or indirectly benefit the Church). These charisms are given to you to help you live out a Christian life or serve the common good in building up the Church. Another part of discernment is identifying your **vocation**, your calling or destiny in this life.

God calls all persons to a vocation of holiness. He calls the laity to seek the Kingdom of God by engaging in temporal affairs and directing them according to God's will, whereas he calls priests and religious to be dedicated to the service of the Church. You are called to live your vocation in a unique way in response to God's call. It is through your vocation that you receive a unique share in Christ's mission, given to him from the Father. By embracing your vocation, you reflect Christ's own mission of salvation by contributing to building up the Church and renewing the world. It is above all in boldly bearing witness to Jesus Christ by worshipping and loving as he does that you can make a difference in the Church and the world. Uncovering your specific vocation requires discernment, which is supported

discernment A decision-making process that attends to the implications and consequences of an action or choice by prayerfully and meditatively separating out what is truly good from what only appears to be good but is in fact a lie and a temptation.

vocation A word that means "call." God calls all persons to be holy and to be disciples of Jesus Christ. You begin to answer this call by conversion and receiving the Sacraments of Initiation, and you live it out by bringing God's love to others, sharing the Gospel, and seeking the Kingdom of God in everything you do. *Lay vocations* are callings to serve God in the world, and *priestly and religious vocations* are callings to serve God in the Church. Each person is given a unique vocation by which he or she receives a share in Christ's mission of salvation, given to him by the Father.

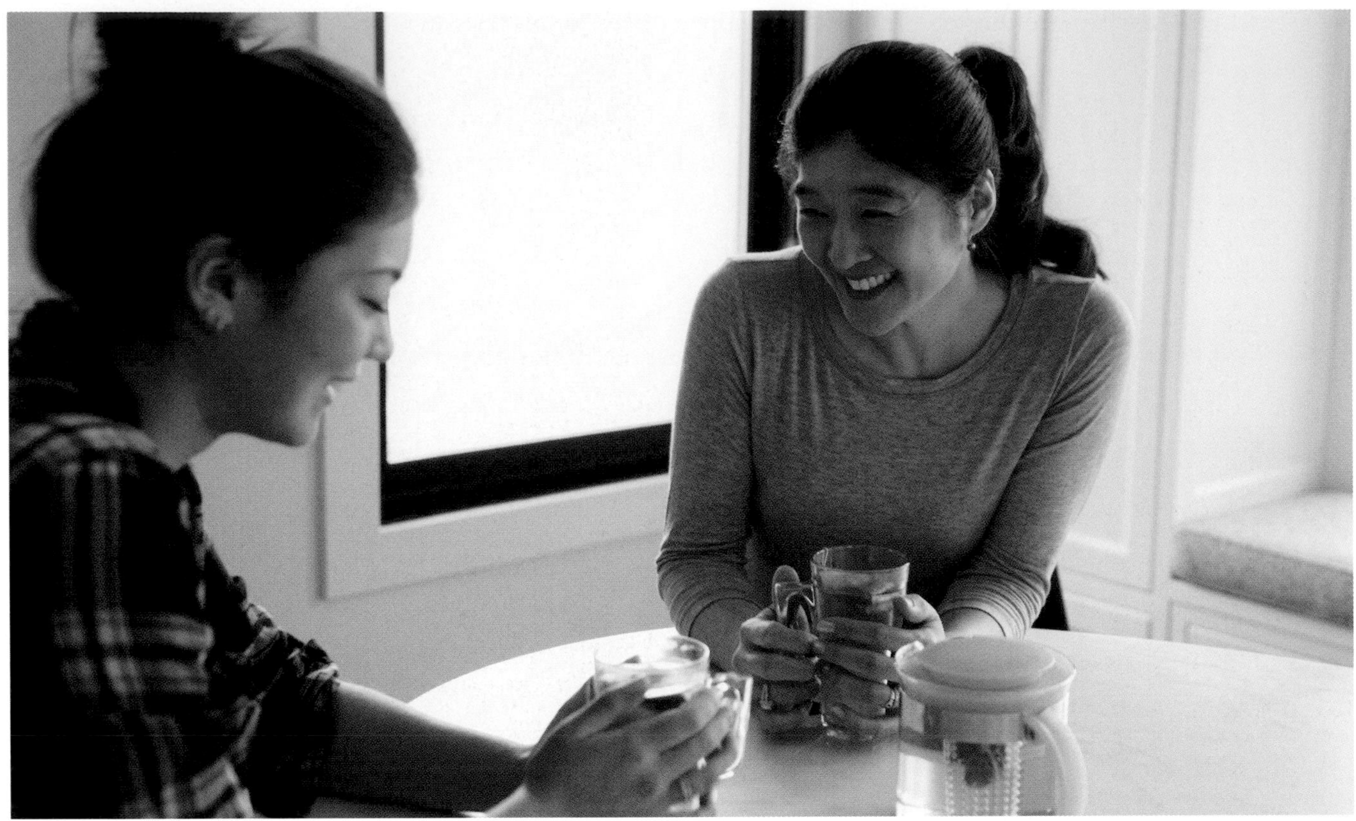

Just like you have to take time to talk with your parents or friends if you want to grow the relationship and let them know what's going on in your life, so too do you need to take time to talk with Jesus.

by frequent prayer and participation in the Mass and other sacraments.

Spending time with Jesus can initially mean a change in inner focus. Everyone talks to themselves throughout the day. Instead of just having a dialogue with yourself, invite Jesus into your thoughts and words so that you can receive his input about whatever issue or situation you are considering. You can update him about your day, your friends, and school or family issues. Exercising is another good time for dialogue with Jesus, especially if you are "unplugged" while you work out. You should also designate focused, quiet parts of the day to spend time with him. You might consider waking up fifteen minutes early and going to a place in your house (other than your bed) where you can concentrate on prayer. Chapter 9 covers several ways of praying.

Becoming like Christ

Jesus taught that his friendship with you is closely related to your obedience to him. Becoming a disciple involves more than listening; it also means following a path that resembles Jesus' own journey. Jesus wants you to take on his mind and heart so that you think and feel as he does. He wants you to use your hands to heal the way he used his. He wants you to worship and love God just as much as he does. He wants you to imitate him and pattern your life on his. You imitate Jesus by loving others and putting your love into action. As you continue, you learn to love more and more the way Jesus loved. St. Paul said, "yet I live, no longer I, but Christ lives in me" (Gal 2:20).

"Becoming like Christ" is not a vague idea for a life devoid of a blueprint. Listening to Jesus' words in the Gospel and studying his behavior and actions reveals a plan for you to follow. This plan can be summarized in two steps:

1. Follow the commandments.

2. Love others.

These steps are explained in the next subsections.

1. Follow the Commandments

Jesus did not abolish the Law of his Jewish ancestors. "I have not come to abolish [the law or the prophets] but to fulfill. . . . Therefore, whoever breaks one of the least of these commandments and teaches others to do so will be called least in the kingdom of heaven" (Mt 5:17b, 19a). Though Jesus never contradicted the old Law, he did challenge religious leaders whose interpretations of the Law were very rigid. Jesus identified the essence of the Law, the Great Commandment: that is,

> You shall love the Lord, your God, with all your heart, with all your soul, and with all your mind. This is the greatest and the first commandment. The second is like it: You shall love your neighbor as yourself. The whole law and the prophets depend on these two commandments. (Mt 22:37–40)

The Ten Commandments (see page 357) explain what loving God and loving your neighbor look like. Jesus expanded further on the commandments in his teaching in the Sermon on the Mount (see Mt 5–7), explaining that as his follower you should love and serve people who are poor, hungry, weeping, and otherwise suffering while you depend on God for all your needs.

An important part of Jesus' teaching is not only to love your friends and those who like you but also to love your enemies and those who do not like you as well. This is a difficult task. It is also difficult not to judge others. Jesus said, "For as you judge, you will be judged, and the measure with which you measure will be measured out to you" (Mt 7:2).

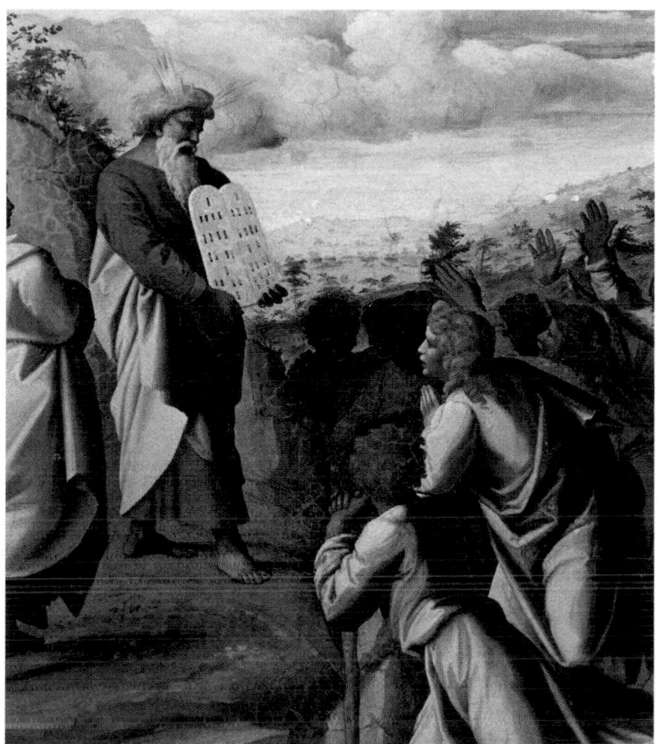

2. Love Others

Recall from Chapter 7 what will happen to you after your death: your judgment and passage to eternal life. In Matthew 25:31–46, Jesus disclosed the criteria he will use when he judges each person after he or she has died. He very clearly explained what it will take to be a "sheep" and go to heaven or a "goat" and end up in hell. There will be no surprises.

Furthermore, Jesus said that you will be judged based on how you have loved others, especially the poor. At the Last Judgment, the questions the Lord will put to you are neither "How popular were you?" nor "How much money did you make?" nor "What were your grades?" nor "How good an athlete were you?" but "*How did you take care of those in need—your brothers and sisters?*" This will be the one, true way of judging what kind of disciple you are. Revisit Jesus' criteria from the Gospel of Matthew:

> Then the king will say to those on his right, "Come, you who are blessed by my Father. Inherit the kingdom prepared for you from

> the foundation of the world. For I was hungry and you gave me food, I was thirsty and you gave me drink, a stranger and you welcomed me, naked and you clothed me, ill and you cared for me, in prison and you visited me." Then the righteous will answer him and say, "Lord, when did we see you hungry and feed you, or thirsty and give you drink? When did we see you a stranger and welcome you, or naked and clothe you? When did we see you ill or in prison, and visit you?" And the king will say to them in reply, "Amen, I say to you, whatever you did for one of these least brothers of mine, you did for me." (Mt 25:34–40)

Jesus is so clear about the need to take care of the "least of these" that you should not be at all surprised when your life is assessed accordingly. When a teacher provides you with a copy of the test to study from so that you know exactly what is expected, you have more than a fair opportunity to prepare and do well.

Recall also from the discussion of the last things from Chapter 7 that it is important to keep your goal of heaven in front of you. St. Francis of Assisi, in his "Letter to the Rulers of People," reminds you:

> Keep a clear eye toward life's end. Do not forget your purpose and destiny as God's creature. What you are in his sight is what you are and nothing more. Remember that when you leave this earth, you can take with you nothing that you have received—fading symbols of honor, trappings of power—but only what you have given: a full heart enriched by honest service, love, sacrifice, and courage.

Conforming yourself to Christ means acting more and more like him. It really does boil down to love of God and love of neighbor. The First Letter to John teaches:

> We love because he first loved us. If anyone says, "I love God," but hates his brother, he is a liar; for whoever does not love a brother whom he has seen cannot love God whom he has not seen. This is the commandment we have from him: whoever loves God must also love his brother. (1 Jn 4:19–21)

An easy formula summarizing the meaning of discipleship is this:

discipleship=
LOVE

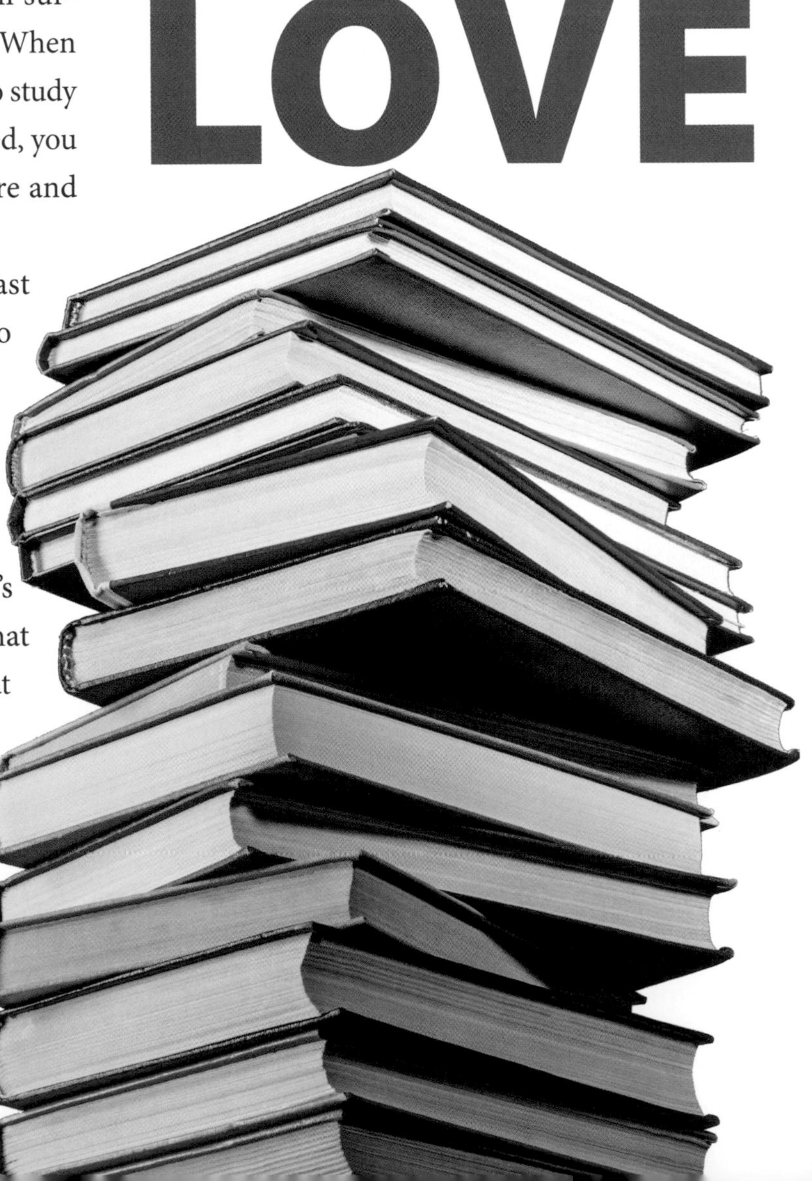

SECTION ASSESSMENT

NOTE TAKING

Use the sentences you wrote to help you complete the following item.

1. In your own words, explain the meaning of *discipleship*.

VOCABULARY

2. What does the Latin origin of the word *disciple* mean?
3. What does the process of *discernment* have to do with your being a disciple of Christ?

COMPREHENSION

4. How did Pope Francis describe "conforming to Christ"?
5. What reward does Jesus offer to those who love him, follow him, and do what he asks?
6. What did Jesus say about the Law of his Jewish ancestors?
7. What did Jesus identify as the essence of the old Law?
8. What are the criteria for judgment Jesus outlined in Matthew 25:31–36?

CRITICAL ANALYSIS

9. What are the primary ways you and your classmates seek to belong or conform?
10. Why does being a friend of Jesus carry more responsibility than being his servant would?
11. Which do you find more difficult: to love your enemies or to avoid judgment of others? Explain.

REFLECTION

12. Outline your personal plan to spend more time with Jesus in friendship.
13. How would you train to be part of "Team Jesus"?

SECTION 1

Conversion and Spiritual Growth

MAIN IDEA

Spiritual growth involves a conversion—that is, a radical reorientation away from sin, evil, and selfishness and toward God and service to others.

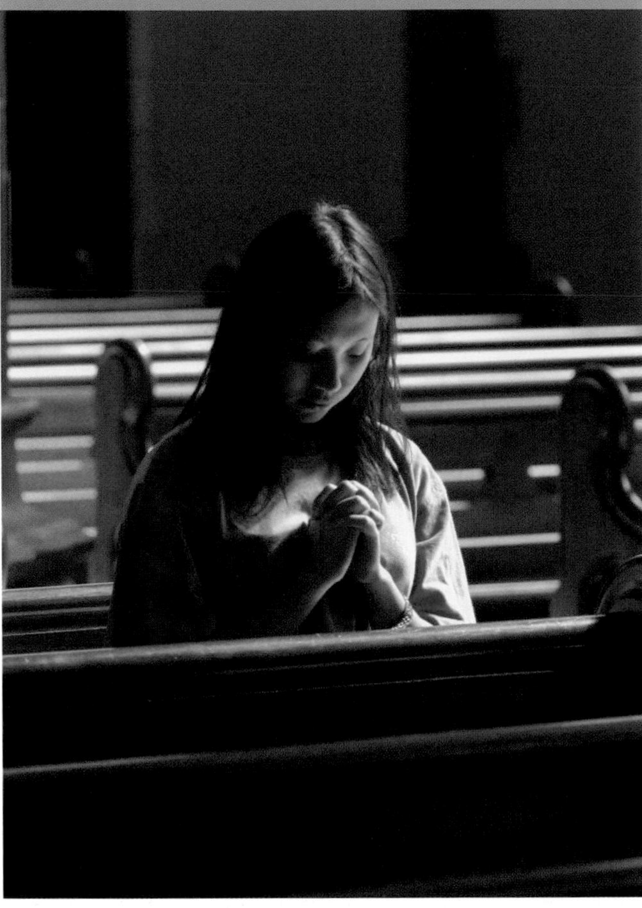

You can think of **conversion** and discipleship as more than just a new way of life. The root of the word *conversion* is "change." Conversion describes the *ongoing* spiritual change a person needs to go through in order to return to God—in other words, to become more Christlike. Jesus calls you to conversion.

conversion A radical reorientation away from sin, evil, and selfishness and toward God and service to others. This change of heart is a central element of Christ's preaching, of the Church's ministry of evangelization, and of the Sacrament of Penance and Reconciliation.

All Christians should be asking themselves how they can *continue* to become more like Christ. You will notice that conversion can seem a bit paradoxical. You must shift your focus from self to others while at the same time spending more time reflecting on your interior life. The Holy Spirit and grace, especially the grace you receive by living a sacramental life and a life of prayer, enable you to grow in holiness of life through ongoing conversion. An element essential for growing in holiness and sustaining ongoing conversion is attention to your interior life through reflection and self-examination. (These functions are aided by interiority and introspection.) You will learn in this subsection more about both shifting your focus to others and strengthening your interior life so that you can continue to become a more complete disciple of Christ.

NOTE TAKING

Categorizing Actions. Draw a graphic organizer like the one below. After you read the section, fill in both the inner and outer circles to show how focusing on both your relationships with others and your interior life can make you a better disciple of Jesus.

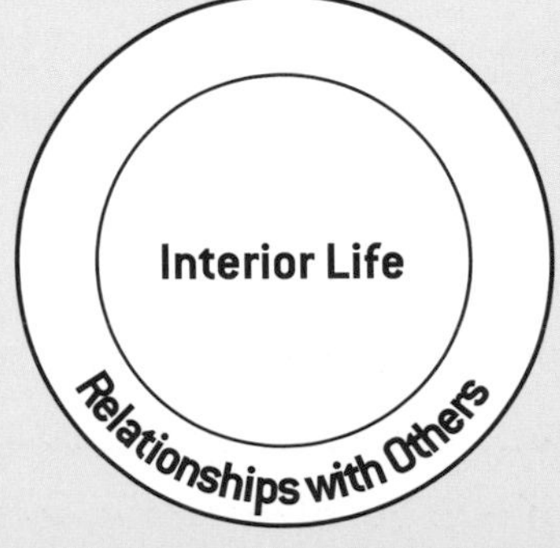

Focusing on Others before Self

In the parable of the sheep and the goats (see Mt 25:31–46), Jesus pointed out the supreme importance of focusing on the needs of others. Here are some ways you can do so:

- Instead of simply worrying about your own sustenance, share food and drink with those who are hungry and thirsty.
- Instead of concerning yourself merely with how you fit in and belong, welcome strangers whom you encounter.
- Instead of being preoccupied with how you dress, make sure those who really need clothing for warmth and comfort have some.
- In addition to taking care of your own health, care for those who are sick and visit them.
- Since you are blessed with freedom, contribute to a prison ministry for those who are incarcerated and need support.

By helping and caring for those who need it, you are actually helping and caring for Jesus. This means that you can look for, and find, Jesus among people who are in need. Befriending Jesus means befriending these people in need, too. Jesus was selfless; conversion means growing in selflessness as well.

Deepening Your Interior Encounter with Christ

You have an interior need to reform and renew your life in Christ. Your interior life is really the life of your soul. Pope John Paul II explained one reason why the inner life of the soul is so important. He said that Christians are often tempted to "act and plan" and do things on their own without the cooperation of God's grace. "But it is fatal to forget that 'without Christ we can do nothing' (cf. Jn 15:5)" (*Novo Millennio Ineunte*, 38).

Deepening your encounter with Christ in this way requires spending time paying attention to your own thoughts and feelings. As you know, the culture does not promote this type of quiet reflection. People often overschedule their days and stay on the Internet and other media while tuning out their interior life. Or they just never stop to think about deeper spiritual things or to pray.

It is within your soul that you have the ability to encounter Christ and build a personal friendship with him, much as you would with a human friend. You can talk with him, listen to him, spend time with him, feel loved by him, and express love for him. You can listen to his voice and let it form your conscience. *Conscience* can be defined as a person's most secret and core sanctuary that helps to discern between good and evil and "moves them at the appropriate moment to do good and to avoid evil" (*CCC*, Glossary). This type of interior reflection enables you to learn where God is leading you. Chapter 9 discusses different types of prayer you can use to begin a relationship with God or build on the one you have already begun to develop.

FORMING *Your* CONSCIENCE

You can form a good conscience according to the guidance of Sacred Scripture and the Sacred Tradition of the Church; the Holy Spirit offers you his grace as well. Forming your conscience properly requires effort, but it is also a key step for growing in holiness and discipleship. Until recently, you may not have been fully responsible for your conscience, but now you are old enough to take full responsibility for forming your conscience as well as nurturing your own spiritual growth. If you face a decision that is unfamiliar, you need to pray, learn more about the Church's teaching, read relevant Scripture, or consult with someone in your family or parish as a spiritual mentor.

A poorly formed conscience can result from listening to attitudes that are not Christlike—attitudes such as sexism, racism, using emotional or physical violence to solve problems, or pursuing financial success at all costs. Learn to be aware of these attitudes and to avoid them whenever you can.

Even when you have a well-formed conscience, you need to use human reason in moral decision-making. *Human reason* is the God-given power by which you can know God and the natural law written on your heart. *Natural law* is the light of understanding that God put in you so that you can discover what is good and what is evil. The Ten Commandments, for example, do not directly or explicitly legislate every moral action. Still, you do not get a free pass to do as you please if your moral dilemma is not directly covered by a commandment. When you use human reason, you take a similar commandment or Jesus' teaching and determine how it would apply in your situation. For example, human reason helps you see that cheating on a test is a form of stealing, a violation of the Seventh Commandment.

Rationalization is not the same as reasoning. When you rationalize, you use lesser values to talk yourself into thinking an action is right even though your conscience tells you it is wrong. For example, you might say that cheating is not lying because lying pertains to words rather than doing something, such as cheating on a test. Or you might say that because "everyone" cheats, cheating is not really wrong. These reasons do not hold up to authentic reasoning or logic. When you rationalize, you try to persuade yourself that such bad reasons make sense.

In the human soul, *free will*—the capacity to choose among alternatives, for the purpose of choosing the good—is an important partner to human reason. While reason makes you capable of understanding what is good, free will allows you to *choose* the good. Without free will, your human reason would be of no use to you. Personal choices help you become the kind of person God calls you to be. Choices become habits, and habits become character. By making good choices and avoiding bad ones, you can form good habits, and with good habits, you can develop a good character.

You can also learn from your mistakes—times when you used your free will improperly. Your choices shape the life you want to live. Although parents and culture influence you, free will enables you to rise above heredity and environment when you must. For example, free will makes it possible for a person raised by racially prejudiced parents to rise above that experience and choose to live without prejudice. Most importantly, you can call on the Holy Spirit to enable you to do good and give you the grace to follow through.

Persevering in Self-Examination

Once you have become accustomed to reflecting on your interior life and have begun to pray, you will likely want to examine yourself and assess how well you have been living a Christlike life. Self-examination is often imperfect. Sometimes you are aware of a sinful quality that is glaringly obvious and needs to change, perhaps because the behavior hurts yourself or others. Other times, it may take years for you to recognize sinful behavior or tendencies that block God out of your life. Ask for Christ's help. With sincerity, effort, frequent prayer, and the grace of the sacraments, you can examine yourself deeply and grow to be more Christlike in all aspects of your life. Thomas Merton, a twentieth-century Trappist monk and author, offers encouragement for persevering in the process of self-examination.

Merton's message is that God is pleased when you reflect on him, his mercy, and his message. The desire to please God does in fact please him.

My Lord God,

I have no idea where I am going. I do not see the road ahead of me. I cannot know for certain where it will end. Nor do I really know myself, and the fact that I think that I am following your will does not mean that I am actually doing so. But I believe that the desire to please you does in fact please you. And I hope I have that desire in all that I am doing. I hope that I will never do anything apart from that desire. And I know that if I do this you will lead me by the right road though I may know nothing about it. Therefore will I trust you always though I may seem to be lost and in the shadow of death. I will not fear, for you are ever with me, and you will never leave me to face my perils alone.

—Thomas Merton, *Thoughts in Solitude*, 1956

SECTION ASSESSMENT

NOTE TAKING

Use the graphic organizer you created to help you complete the following items.

1. How do you deepen your interior life and draw closer to Christ?
2. Name an action you performed for another that has helped you to recognize Christ's presence.

COMPREHENSION

3. What does conversion involve for a disciple of Christ?
4. What is the meaning of *interior life*?
5. Why must a person with a well-formed conscience still depend on human reason?
6. How does the Holy Spirit help in moral decision-making?

CRITICAL ANALYSIS

7. Explain what it means that you can find Jesus among people who are in need.
8. Why do you think modern American culture does not promote time for reflection?
9. How can human friendship give you insight into your relationship with God?
10. Why is self-examination an imperfect process?

REFLECTION

11. Give an example of *rationalization* in a moral argument.
12. What is your impression of Thomas Merton's words about seeking God's will?

SECTION 2

Called to Virtue and Holiness

MAIN IDEA
Faith, hope, and charity (love) are essential virtues for growing in holiness and for following Christ more closely.

You know that, to be a disciple of Christ, you must also live a holy life. In doing so, you build up the Church, of which you are a member. All Christians are called to holiness. Consider in more detail what this means for your life.

The words *holy* and *holiness* originally referred to God. In the Old Testament, to be holy meant to be separated from the ordinary, everyday world. God is holy in the sense that he is wholly other than creation, perfectly good, and totally separated from evil and sin. When people, places, or things are described as being holy, it is because they are related to God. God is the source of all holiness because he alone is truly holy—that is, all good and separate from all evil.

All of the aspects of discipleship discussed in the previous sections are means of becoming holy. Practicing the virtues of faith, hope, and charity is a concrete way to grow in holiness. Take some time to review the definition of a **virtue**. In general, "a virtue is an habitual and firm disposition to do the good" (*CCC*, 1803). Virtues enable you to perform good acts and to give the best of yourself, empowering

virtue A firm, stable, and habitual disposition of your intellect and will that regulates your actions, directs your passions, and guides your conduct according to reason and faith.

NOTE TAKING

Applying Lessons. Create a graphic organizer like the one below. Print the three theological virtues—faith, hope, and charity (love)—at the points of the triangle. From information gleaned in this section, jot down inside the triangle several practical things you can do to incorporate these virtues into your own life.

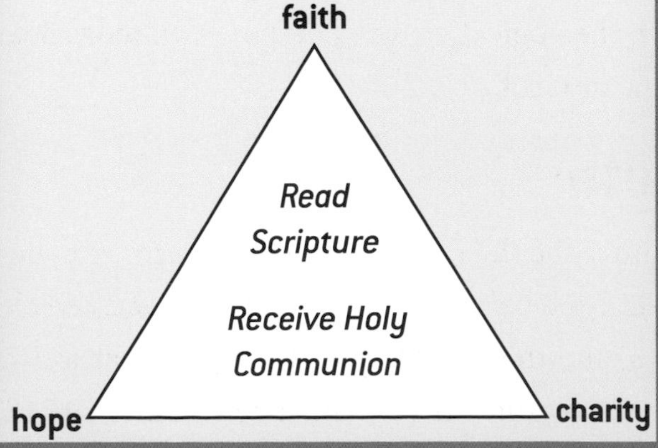

you to become who God wants you to be. Practicing virtues helps you to be more like Jesus Christ.

The *theological virtues*—faith, hope, and charity (love)—are gifts that God gives you to participate in his own divine nature and to lead a moral life. God infuses these virtues into your soul at Baptism, making it possible for you to relate to the Blessed Trinity.

GOD himself is the **origin**, **motive**, and **object** of the **THEOLOGICAL VIRTUES**.

Among other things, this means that faith, hope, and charity are the foundations of Christian moral living, informing and giving life to all of the other virtues. God gives you the theological virtues so that you can act like one of his children and gain eternal life. By putting these virtues into practice, you can grow in holiness and learn to live a Christlike life. Each theological virtue is discussed in more detail in the next subsections.

Faith

"Faith is the theological virtue by which we believe in God and believe all that he has said and revealed to us, and that the Holy Church proposes for our belief, because he is truth itself" (CCC, 1814). Faith makes it possible for you to commit yourself totally to God. Because faith is central to the Christian life, it must be a *living* faith that shows itself in concrete acts. According to the Letter of James, "For just as a body without a spirit is dead, so also faith without works is dead" (Jas 2:26). This means that a person who professes faith in God will necessarily do good things. If the person does not do good things, it is not faith that the person has.

A person's faith must also be connected to hope and love. As a disciple, you must profess your faith, bear witness to it, and spread the Good News of salvation in Jesus Christ to others, even if it leads to suffering. You can strengthen your faith in these ways:

- *Pray.* You can ask the Lord to make your faith stronger, much like the father of the son suffering from convulsions in Mark 9:24: "I do believe, help my unbelief!"

- *Read Scripture.* Reading, studying, and praying with the Bible brings you closer to God and his Word. Listen to the Scriptures proclaimed at Mass and the priest's or deacon's reflections on them in the homily. At the dismissal, you are encouraged to take the Gospel out into the world.

- *Celebrate the sacraments.* The sacraments themselves celebrate the mysteries of your faith, especially the Paschal Mystery. Participation in the Sacrament of Penance can remind you of Christ's compassionate and forgiving love. Receiving the Lord in Holy Communion nourishes and strengthens your faith.

- ***Study your faith.*** Studying and deepening your understanding of the faith is a lifelong process. One concrete task you can undertake is to review summaries of faith such as the Apostles' Creed and Nicene Creed, learning more about what each statement means.

- ***Draw on the faith of friends.*** Choose friends and companions who share your commitment to God and the Church. Their practice of Christian virtues will help you resist temptations and practice the virtues yourself. Join with peers who participate in youth groups, retreats, pilgrimages, service projects, and faith rallies.

- ***Put your faith into action.*** Keep your faith alive by being Christ for others. An excellent way of doing this is to practice the corporal and the spiritual works of mercy (see page 358).

Hope

The *Catechism of the Catholic Church* defines hope this way: "Hope is the theological virtue by which we desire the kingdom of heaven and eternal life as our happiness, placing our trust in Christ's promises and relying not on our own strength, but on the help of the grace of the Holy Spirit" (*CCC*, 1817).

God has placed the desire for happiness in your heart, and the virtue of hope purifies your human activity so that it is oriented toward eternal life with God. Hope helps you in many ways:

- Hope keeps you from discouragement.
- Hope sustains you when you feel abandoned.
- Hope opens your heart to expect happiness in eternal life.
- Hope preserves you from selfishness.
- Hope leads you to the happiness that flows from love.

Pope Francis believes that hope is a wonderful virtue for young people:

> Why do I like being with young people? Because you have the promise of hope in your heart. You are bearers of hope. It is true that you live in the present but you are looking towards the future . . . you are architects of the future, artisans of the future. Now—and this is a joy for you—it is a beautiful thing to walk towards the future with dreams and with many beautiful things. And it's also your responsibility. Become artisans of the future. When they say to me: "But, Father, what difficult times these are. . . . Look, we cannot do anything!" What do you mean you cannot do anything? Then I explain that we can do a lot! (Address to Young People from the Italian Diocese of Piacenza-Bobbio, August 28, 2013)

The patriarch Abraham is a model of hope as well as of faith. God called him and promised him that he would be blessed. Abraham believed God even when the circumstances of his life challenged his hope. Jesus' own life is a model of hope. For example, as he was suffering on the Cross, Jesus prayed to his Father to take his spirit (see Lk 23:46). Hope can give you joy even in the midst of trials. Prayer, especially the Our Father, nourishes hope.

As a Christian, you can believe and hope that good does triumph over evil, that eternal life awaits you on the other side of death, and that every wrong will be righted. In hope, the Church prays that all people achieve eternal salvation.

Pope Francis on the Theological Virtues

At World Youth Day in Rio de Janeiro, Brazil, in 2013, Pope Francis shared these thoughts about the theological virtues with the young people present:

> I say to each one of you, **"put on faith,"** and life will take on a new flavor, life will have a compass to show you the way; **"put on hope,"** and every one of your days will be enlightened and your horizon will no longer be dark, but luminous; **"put on love,"** and your life will be like a house built on rock, your journey will be joyful, because you will find many friends to journey with you. Put on faith, put on hope, put on love! All together: **"Put on faith," "put on hope," "put on love."** (Homily for the Welcoming Ceremony for World Youth Day, July 25, 2013)

REFLECTION

Write your responses to the following:

- **What appeals to you about the pope's words?**
- **What question would you like to ask Pope Francis based on this quotation?**
- **Write a prayer, poem, or short reflection titled "Put on the Virtues." Draw from the words of Pope Francis in your work.**

Charity

St. Paul declared that charity, or love, is the greatest of the three theological virtues (see 1 Cor 13:13). St. Thomas Aquinas echoed this, calling love the "mother of all virtues." The *Catechism of the Catholic Church* teaches that "charity is the theological virtue by which we love God above all things for his own sake, and our neighbor as ourselves for the love of God" (*CCC*, 1822). Charity is the soul of the holiness to which God calls you. Charity, or love, is the calling that includes all other vocations.

God's very nature is love. As God's adopted child, you are called to a holy relationship with him that resembles the relationship among the Three Persons of the Trinity. The First Letter of John describes this goal:

> Beloved, let us love one another, because love is of God; everyone who loves is begotten by God and knows God. Whoever is without love does not know God, for God is love. In this way the love of God was revealed to us: God sent his only Son into the world so that we might have life through him. In this is love: not that we have loved God, but that he loved us and sent his Son as expiation for our sins. Beloved, if God so loved us, we also must love one another. No one has ever seen God. Yet, if we love one another, God remains in us, and his love is brought to perfection in us.
>
> This is how we know that we remain in him and he in us, that he has given us of his Spirit. Moreover, we have seen and testify that the Father sent his Son as savior of the world. Whoever acknowledges that Jesus is the Son of God, God remains in him and he in God. We have come to know and to believe in the love God has for us.
>
> God is love, and whoever remains in love remains in God and God in him. (1 Jn 4:7–16)

You also learn these characteristics of love from other places in the New Testament. For example:

- Jesus made love the new commandment (see Jn 13:34).
- Jesus acted lovingly toward the disciples and taught them that they should love one another in the same way (see Jn 15:9, 12).
- Living in love means that you keep the Ten Commandments (see Mt 22:37–40).
- Love includes loving your enemies, children, and the poor (see Lk 10:27–37).
- For actions to mean anything, you must accomplish them in love. St. Paul wrote, "If I speak in human and angelic tongues but do not have love, I am a resounding gong or a clashing cymbal" (1 Cor 13:1). He went on to describe several characteristics of love:

  > Love is patient, love is kind. It is not jealous, [love] is not pompous, it is not inflated, it is not rude, it does not seek its own interests, it is not quick-tempered, it does not brood over injury, it does not rejoice over wrongdoing but rejoices with the truth. It bears all things, believes all things, hopes all things, endures all things. Love never fails. (1 Cor 13:4–8)

- Love animates and inspires you to practice the other virtues and binds the virtues together in perfect harmony. Love is the goal of the other virtues (see Col 3:14).
- Living a good life inspired by love enables you to be God's son or daughter rather than a slave who turns away from evil out of fear of punishment (see 1 Jn 4:18–19).

The virtue of charity enables you to follow Christ's injunction to love even your enemies. It helps you practice all the other virtues and supports "and purifies our human ability to love, and raises it to the supernatural perfection of divine love" (*CCC*, 1827). In today's world, many people distort the true meaning of love—for example, by claiming that unbridled sexual passion (lust) is love. But lust is not love. The virtue of charity—true love, which has its source in God himself—is self-giving. Jesus Christ, the perfect exemplar of love, teaches by his words and deeds that charity has the following attributes:

- *Obedience.* Jesus' will was perfectly attuned to his Father's. Love means obeying Jesus' commands.
- *Reverence.* Love involves respecting and valuing the absolute goodness of God and the goodness of other people made in his image and likeness.
- *Sacrifice.* Love requires commitment: walking the extra mile and never giving up on God, other people, or oneself. Spiritual disciplines such as fasting, prayer, and sharing with the poor increase love in your heart.

Charity has many fruits or benefits, including joy, peace, and mercy. It is generous and reciprocal. It leads to friendship and communion with others. Christ's love is ever-present to you. By recognizing the many dimensions of love, you are better able to respond to it.

Seven Steps to HolinesS

There are no *easy* steps to becoming holy. But there are ways you can progress in holiness. An important way is to remain close to Jesus. This is the most worthwhile task. Briefly review these seven steps for remaining close to Jesus and growing in holiness.

1. **Follow Jesus, your model** (see *CCC*, 520). You can learn what it means to be fully human by examining the life of Jesus and imitating his humble acceptance of his Father's will. Following Jesus includes adherence to his teaching. It includes conversion of heart and life and the formation of your conscience in conformity to Christ. You can also look to Jesus as your model for how you worship and love God.

2. **Make time and space for interior reflection and self-examination** (*CCC*, 1779). Oftentimes you are not able to hear the voice of your conscience because you are too busy. You need to develop your interiority and ability to engage in introspection in order to form your conscience and to more clearly hear its voice.

Accept sacrifice (see *CCC*, 618). Jesus calls on his disciples to "take up [their] cross[es] and follow [him]" (Mt 16:24). You take up your cross whenever you strive to do the right thing, especially in the face of ridicule and criticism. Jesus is united to you, inviting you to share in offering the Paschal Mystery to all people.

Allow the Holy Spirit to guide you. The Spirit showers on you the gifts that help you grow in holiness. You become more Christlike when you use these gifts and cooperate with all the other graces that come from the Holy Spirit.

Remain aware of the Father's presence (see *CCC*, 1693). You are constantly in the presence of God, whether you consciously think of it or not. Jesus always lived in the sight of his Father and always did what was pleasing to him. He invites you to do the same. Imagine how you would strive to do your best if you remained aware that you are always in the presence of God the Father.

Love God, and love your neighbor. Observe the Ten Commandments, live the Beatitudes, and put into practice Jesus' Great Commandment (see page 279). Your personal response to God's call, his offer of loving forgiveness, and his grace are all shown in your way of life.

Pray and participate in the sacraments. Spending time with Jesus in prayer can nourish your relationship with him (see Chapter 9). Christ instituted the sacraments to extend his love and grace to you. The "sacrament of sacraments" is the Eucharist, which holds center stage in the life of Catholics (see *CCC*, 1324–1325). Receiving Jesus in Holy Communion intimately unites you with him. It also gives you life through the Holy Spirit, separates you from sin, brings you into union with other members of Christ's Body, and commits you to look at the needs of the poor. Frequent reception of your Lord in the Eucharist is a prime way for Catholics to grow in holiness. You should attend Mass every Sunday and holy day of obligation, according to one of the precepts of the Church.

SECTION ASSESSMENT

NOTE TAKING

Use the graphic organizer you created to help you complete the following item.

1. Write one paragraph that summarizes your plan to incorporate the theological virtues—faith, hope, and charity—into your life.

VOCABULARY

2. Define *virtue.*

COMPREHENSION

3. According to St. Paul, which is the greatest of the three theological virtues?
4. How are virtue and holiness related?
5. How is Abraham a model of hope?
6. What are three fruits or benefits of love?

CRITICAL ANALYSIS

7. Pope Francis described your generation as "artisans of the future." What do you think he meant?
8. What does it mean to say that "love is the goal of the other virtues"?
9. How is lust a distortion of the true meaning of love?

REFLECTION

10. Write a brief description of a person who models the connection between faith and works laid out in James 2:26.
11. Describe a situation in your own life in which love required sacrifice.

SECTION 3

The Call to Evangelization and Stewardship

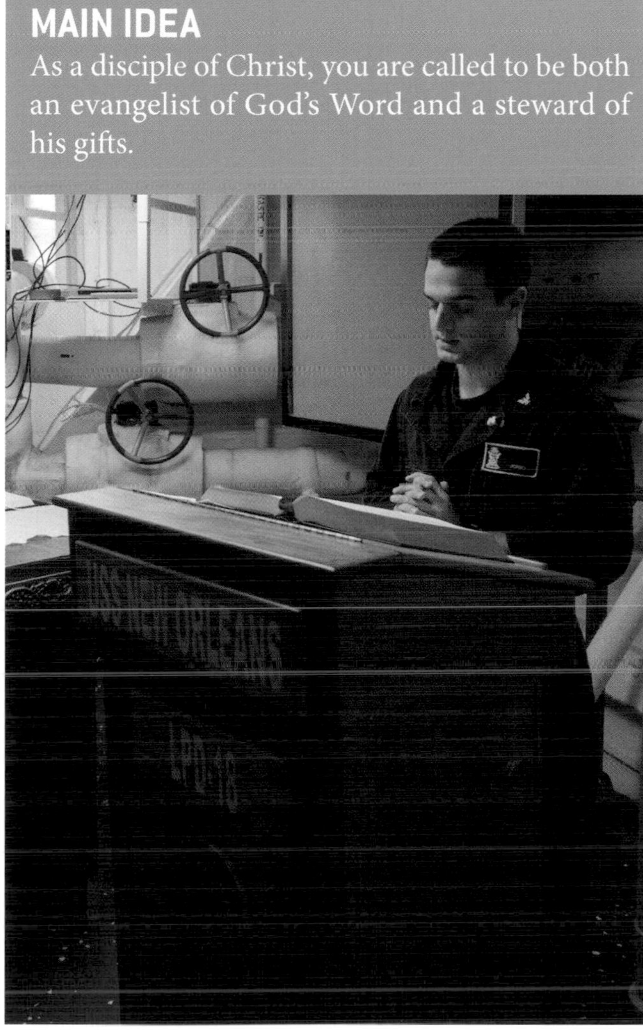

MAIN IDEA

As a disciple of Christ, you are called to be both an evangelist of God's Word and a steward of his gifts.

Another essential element of discipleship is **evangelization**. After Christ accomplished his work of gaining salvation for the world, the Holy Spirit was sent to his disciples so that they might continue what he began. It is now your mission to go out and make disciples of all (see Mt 28:19–20). To do so, you must be a good steward of your own God-given talents and gifts. These essential elements of discipleship are explored in this subsection.

Evangelize through Words

A disciple must do more than simply keep the faith. A disciple must also profess it, bear witness to it with confidence, and spread it. In 2007, Pope Benedict XVI challenged Catholic youth with these words:

> I send you out . . . on the great mission of evangelizing young men and women who have gone astray in the world like sheep without a shepherd. *Be apostles of youth.* Invite them to walk with you, to have the same experience of faith, hope, and love; to encounter Jesus so that they may feel truly loved, accepted, able to realize their full potential. May they too discover the sure

evangelization The proclamation of Christ and the Good News of the Gospel by your words and the way that you live, in fulfillment of Christ's command. Evangelization involves proclaiming the Gospel in such a way that people's hearts and lives are changed.

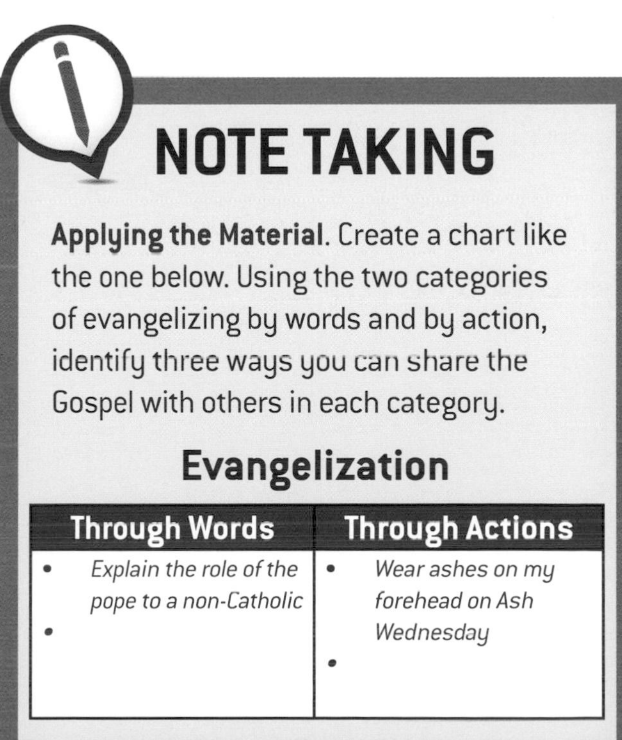

NOTE TAKING

Applying the Material. Create a chart like the one below. Using the two categories of evangelizing by words and by action, identify three ways you can share the Gospel with others in each category.

Evangelization

Through Words	Through Actions
• *Explain the role of the pope to a non-Catholic* •	• *Wear ashes on my forehead on Ash Wednesday* •

ways of the commandments, and, by following them, come to God. (Address to Youth in São Paulo, Brazil, May 10, 2007)

As a teen, you have insight into the lives of your peers and can share your faith with them in a way that adults cannot. In fact, your witness to faith might carry more power and meaning to some teens than an adult's witness would. You can evangelize in many ways:

- Know your Catholic faith so that you are able to explain it. Learn where to find answers to tough questions. Read the Bible on a regular basis. Familiarize yourself with the *Catechism of the Catholic Church*, and use it to find answers to your questions.
- Invite a friend who does not attend Mass regularly to come to Mass with you. Evangelizing involves reaching out not only to non-Catholics but also to lukewarm or nonpracticing Catholics.
- In talking with others about sensitive issues (for example, abortion), do not be afraid to share Church teaching on the subject. Sometimes people have never heard the truth about moral issues. You can be a witness to the truth.
- When asked why you act the way you do, say that your Catholic faith inspires you to live a Christ-like life.

Evangelize through Action

Consider the way St. Francis of Assisi approached evangelization on one occasion. St. Francis asked one of his young monks to join him to go into the town to preach. The young monk was thrilled to be chosen to accompany Francis and joined him enthusiastically. They walked through the main streets, turned into alleys, and made their way into the outlying huts, eventually working their way back to the monastery. As they approached the gate,

the young monk reminded the great saint, "But, Father, you have forgotten. You went to town to preach."

Francis replied, "You have preached. You are preaching while you are walking. Many people saw you and observed your behavior. It was thus that you have preached your morning sermon. It is of no use to walk anywhere to preach unless you preach everywhere you walk." This story may remind you of a quotation often attributed to St. Francis: "Preach the Gospel always, and if necessary use words."

Your daily actions, too, can be an occasion of evangelization. You evangelize in simple ways daily by smiling at classmates you pass in the hall, complimenting others on achievements, offering to pray for someone with a sick family member, tutoring a fellow student, offering someone a ride home, reflecting a positive attitude, and so forth.

You also evangelize through action when you pray in public (perhaps before a meal), when you participate in service opportunities offered by your school and parish, and when you model selflessness and care for others. Yet another way to bring the Gospel to others is to respect the gift of marriage by practicing the virtue of chastity. You can live a powerful witness of sacrifice, self-control, and patience in Christ's name when you choose a chaste life.

The Responsibility of Stewardship

Responsibility is a key term to help you understand stewardship. A *steward* is a person who takes care of something as his or her own, when ultimately it belongs to someone else. You are a steward of any gifts you have been given in this life—money, talents, time, and more. As a disciple of Jesus, you are called to stewardship because everything you have is a gift from God, and God wants you to share what you have been given with others.

In a 2007 pastoral letter, *Stewardship and Teenagers: The Challenge of Being a Disciple*, the United States Conference of Catholic Bishops listed four practical ways for you to be a better disciple of Christ through responsible stewardship:

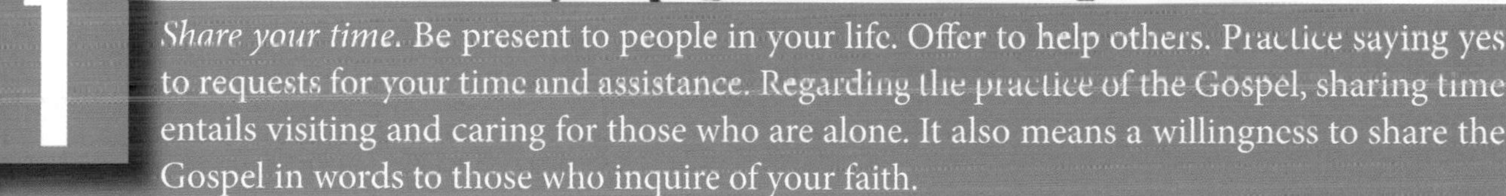

1. *Share your time.* Be present to people in your life. Offer to help others. Practice saying yes to requests for your time and assistance. Regarding the practice of the Gospel, sharing time entails visiting and caring for those who are alone. It also means a willingness to share the Gospel in words to those who inquire of your faith.

2. *Share your talents.* No one else can do exactly what you do. Whether it be singing, cooking, or playing sports, your talents are for sharing with others. When used generously, the good your talents provide is immeasurable. At your parish, seek opportunities to use your talents. You might participate or become a leader of a youth ministry or peer mentoring program. You might participate in a parish fundraiser. You might assist in a religious education program for younger students. There are many opportunities that correspond with your talents.

3. *Share your treasure.* Sharing your money with a charitable cause that lifts up the Church and those in need now at your age will help you grow in a lifelong habit of generosity. Certainly you should contribute a share of your money to your parish. Also research other Church-sponsored charities that depend on the financial support of Catholics to fund their ministries. Identify one or two items from your weekly expenses (e.g., fast food, entertainment, clothing) that you might be able to eliminate or reduce in order to be able to share some of your money with others.

Share your tradition. Embrace the rites and sacraments of the Church as beautiful gifts of God to be appreciated, loved, and shared. Besides inviting a friend to go to Mass with you, pray for others who are not at Mass for whatever reason. Also, consider in more depth the lifelong vocation that will best help you to live as a disciple of Christ. Whatever this call, it will require the ultimate gift of yourself—through marriage and family life or through the priesthood or consecrated life.

Jesus is your guide, model, and friend in the life of discipleship. Praying to and maintaining your friendship with him can help you find and live out your vocation to be a good steward. Meeting Jesus in the Sacrament of Penance gives you the graces to start anew when you have fallen short. In addition, learning the Church's social teaching and her powerful message of respect for all life is one more way to live as a faithful steward and disciple of Jesus Christ.

Reporting on **Stewardship**

Read and outline in a one-page report the summary of the United States Conference of Catholic Bishops' statement on stewardship, found at www.usccb.org.

SECTION ASSESSMENT

NOTE TAKING

Use the chart you created to help you complete the following questions.

1. In what way have you been most effective in spreading the Gospel message?
2. How can you improve in sharing the Good News with others?

VOCABULARY

3. Write a sentence that includes the term *evangelization* and explains its meaning.

COMPREHENSION

4. What four methods of stewardship did the United States Conference of Catholic Bishops recommend?
5. Why is *responsibility* a key term related to stewardship?

CRITICAL ANALYSIS

6. Do you agree that teens can evangelize one another better than adults can evangelize teens? Explain.
7. What did St. Francis mean when he said "Preach the Gospel always, and if necessary use words"?

REFLECTION

8. How can you share the Church's teaching on chastity by your words *and* actions?

Section Summaries

Focus Question

What are the requirements and benefits of being a disciple of Jesus Christ?

Complete one of the following:

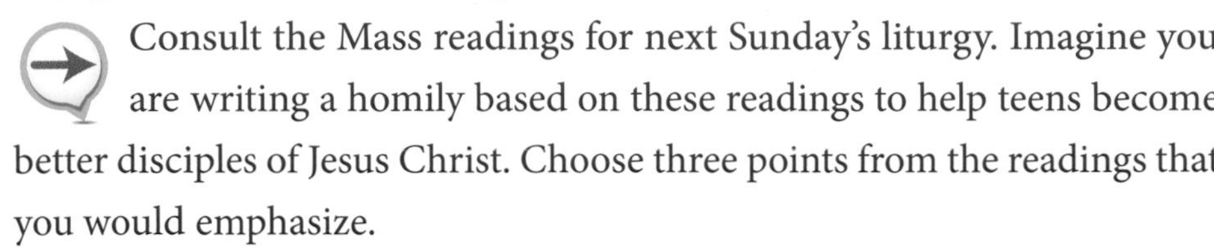

Consult the Mass readings for next Sunday's liturgy. Imagine you are writing a homily based on these readings to help teens become better disciples of Jesus Christ. Choose three points from the readings that you would emphasize.

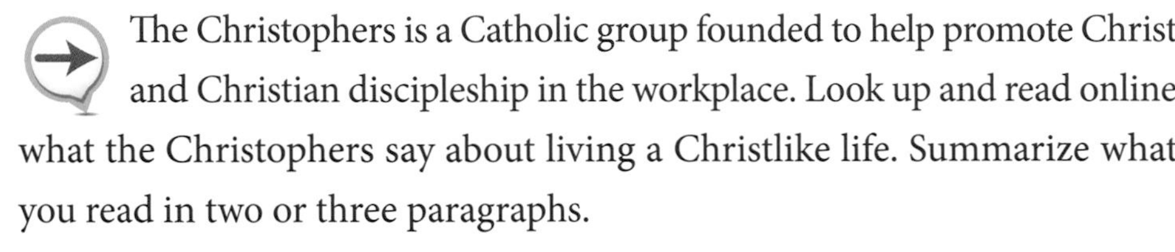

The Christophers is a Catholic group founded to help promote Christ and Christian discipleship in the workplace. Look up and read online what the Christophers say about living a Christlike life. Summarize what you read in two or three paragraphs.

List three Gospel passages where Jesus describes a requirement of discipleship (e.g., Mk 8:34–38) and three Gospel passages that describe the benefits of being a disciple of Jesus (e.g., Mt 19:28–30).

INTRODUCTION (PAGES 275–281)

Conforming to Christ

Discipleship requires you to conform yourself to Christ by getting to know him as a friend and by following his commands. While discipleship explains your relationship with Christ, holiness describes your inner transformation as you move toward God, who is holy. Christ has elevated you from the status of servant to the status of friend. Jesus wants you to become more and more like him in your feelings, thoughts, and actions. The "blueprint" for becoming like Christ is following the commandments and loving others. The Ten Commandments are important guidelines for how to love God and others, expanded further by Jesus when he taught the Beatitudes. In Matthew 25, Jesus explains the criteria by which he will judge who has shown Christian love. Ultimately, Jesus wants you to imitate him in loving God and others.

Write a three- to four-paragraph essay explaining your plan for becoming part of "Team Jesus."

SECTION 1 (PAGES 282–287)

Conversion and Spiritual Growth

Spiritual growth involves lifelong conversion—that is, a radical orientation away from sin, evil, and selfishness toward God and to service of others. Conversion is an ongoing process for all Christians, not simply a one-time embrace of a new life. Conversion calls you to focus more on others than on yourself. Spiritual growth occurs in the path toward perfection and holiness, which includes developing your sense of interiority, your ability to form and examine your conscience, your capacity for introspection and ongoing conversion, and your commitment to worship and love as Christ does. The formation of your conscience to better discern and make moral decisions must be sustained by the sacramental life of the Church, prayer, and Sacred Scripture and Sacred Tradition.

St. Gregory of Nyssa said, "The person who climbs never stops going from beginning to beginning, through beginnings that have no end. He never stops desiring what he already knows." Write a paragraph explaining how this quotation relates to spiritual conversion.

SECTION 2 (PAGES 288–296)

Called to Virtue and Holiness

Holiness and discipleship go hand in hand. The word *holy* originally referred to God. People, places, and things all measure their holiness in relation to God. Living a virtuous life is a way to grow in holiness. A virtue is a habitual disposition to do the good. The theological virtues—faith, hope, and charity—are essential virtues for discipleship and gifts that God gives you to participate in his own divine nature and to lead a moral life. Faith makes it possible for you to commit yourself completely to God. Hope keeps you focused on your goal of eternal life with God. Love is the greatest virtue of the three because love determines whether you are with God or against him. God is love.

Write a brief report on the life of a saint you admire, focusing on how he or she modeled in a heroic way one of the theological virtues—faith, hope, or charity.

SECTION 3 (PAGES 297–301)

The Call to Evangelization and Stewardship

Jesus commanded his followers to share the Good News by word and example. Evangelization is crucial to being a disciple because it means obeying one of Jesus' commands. St. Francis said, "Preach the Gospel always, and if necessary use words." Stewardship is another element of discipleship. Everything you have—money, talents, and time—is a gift from God to be shared with others, especially those who are most in need.

Read Luke 12:13–21, the parable of the rich fool. What does this parable teach about how a person can truly become rich before God?

Chapter Assignments

Choose and complete at least one of the three assignments assessing your understanding of the material in this chapter.

1. Who Are the Knights of Columbus, and What Do They Do?

Complete a three-page research report on the Knights of Columbus. Look up the national website for the organization. Include at least three of these elements in your report:

- history of the Knights of Columbus
- information on the canonization process for Ven. Michael J. McGivney
- membership information (e.g., requirements for becoming a Knight, initiation process, degrees of knighthood)
- information on two charitable services supported by the Knights of Columbus
- information about the Columbian Squires
- an interview with the Grand Knight from a Knights of Columbus council in your area (ask, "How did you become Grand Knight? What does this position require?")

2. Storyboard Depiction and Conclusion of the Story of the Rich Young Man

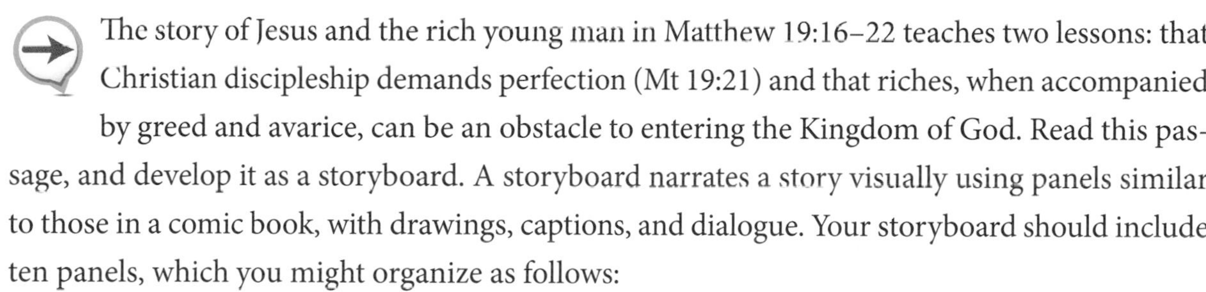

The story of Jesus and the rich young man in Matthew 19:16–22 teaches two lessons: that Christian discipleship demands perfection (Mt 19:21) and that riches, when accompanied by greed and avarice, can be an obstacle to entering the Kingdom of God. Read this passage, and develop it as a storyboard. A storyboard narrates a story visually using panels similar to those in a comic book, with drawings, captions, and dialogue. Your storyboard should include ten panels, which you might organize as follows:

- three panels that depict the conversation between Jesus and the rich young man (see Mt 19:16–22).
- three panels that depict the follow-up conversation Jesus had with his disciples, including some of the images he shared (see Mt 19:23–40).
- four panels that depict how you imagine the rich young man's life after he left Jesus. Ask yourself, "Where did he go? What kind of life did he have? Did he ever give up his riches?"

Your panels can be presented as multimedia slides. You may vary the arrangement described above, but you should fill at least ten panels.

3. Growing in Everyday Holiness

Every new day presents many ways you can live out the call to holiness and discipleship. Read through the following list of settings and opportunities to bring Christ to others. For each *setting*, write one paragraph that evaluates how you are doing and how you can improve. Then write a one- to two-page profile of the holiest person you personally know. How does the light of Christ shine through this person? What might you do in your own life to become more like him or her?

At Home

- I readily obey my parents without arguing.
- I am patient with my siblings.
- I volunteer to do chores around the house without being asked.
- I willingly spend time with my family.
- I make it a point to be on time for family meals.

At School

- I am respectful of my teachers and other adults.
- I greet my classmates.
- I try to make new friends.
- I fully participate in the extracurricular activities I have chosen.
- I resist temptations to cheat.

Other

- I carefully listen to others when they speak to me.
- I go to Mass every weekend.
- I pray every day.
- I avoid immoral sites on the Internet.
- I share some of my wealth of time, talents, and money with others, including those who are less fortunate.

Faithful Disciple

Bl. Pier Giorgio Frassati

Named "the man of the eight Beatitudes" by Pope John Paul II at his beatification ceremony in Rome in 1990, Bl. Pier Giorgio Frassati was a joy-filled man who lived only to age twenty-four but who remains a model for bountiful love and service today. Pope John Paul II noted that Bl. Pier Giorgio "bears in himself the grace of the Gospel, the Good News, the joy of Salvation offered to us Christians." His sister said of him, "He represented the finest in Christian youth: pure, happy, enthusiastic about everything that is good and beautiful."

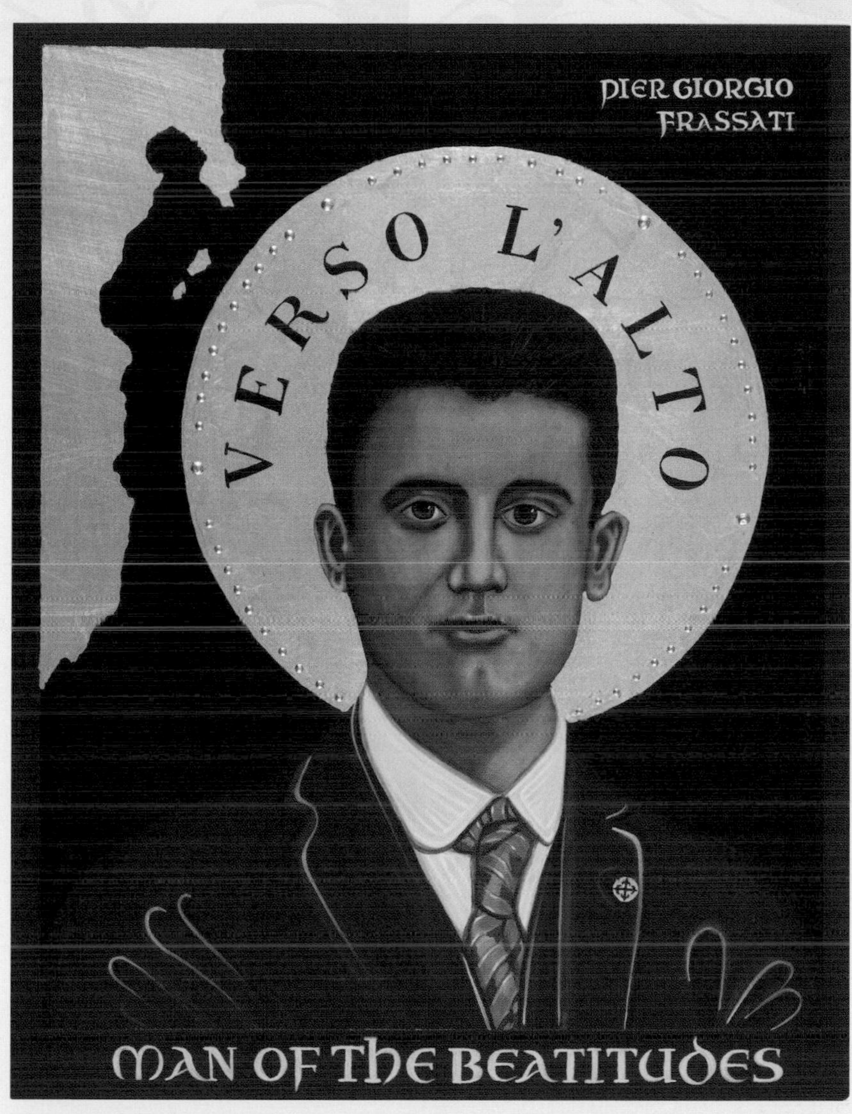

Bl. Pier Giorgio Frassati

Pier Giorgio was born on April 6, 1901, to a wealthy and politically connected family in Turin, Italy. He was an average student but a great athlete and mountain climber. His peers adored him and called him "Terror" because of the practical jokes he played. After high school, he studied mineralogy in an engineering program. He participated in Catholic groups such as the Apostleship of Prayer and the Company of the Most Blessed Sacrament. Both of these groups were known for helping poor people and for promoting Eucharistic Adoration, Marian devotion, and personal chastity.

Pier Giorgio also became active in political groups—such as the Young Catholic Workers, Catholic Action, and Milites Mariae—that ministered to poor people, fought fascism, and put into practice the Church's social teachings. He gave his money to needy people and visited the sick. It was while ministering to the sick that he contracted an acute case of polio that took his life. He died at age twenty-four on July 4, 1925. Bl. Pier Giorgio Frassati offers these words of advice on how to grow in holiness:

> With all the strength of my soul I urge you young people to approach the Communion table as often as you can. Feed on this bread of angels whence you will draw all the energy you need to fight inner battles. Because true happiness, dear friends, does not consist in the pleasures of the world or in earthly things, but in peace of conscience, which you have only if you are pure in heart and mind.

Reading Comprehension

1. What do the descriptions of Bl. Pier Giorgio by Pope John Paul II and Bl. Pier Giorgio's sister have in common?
2. What were Bl. Pier Giorgio's interests?
3. What were some common characteristics of the Catholic groups that Bl. Pier Giorgio participated in?

Writing Task

- Summarize Bl. Pier Giorgio Frassati's advice for how to grow in holiness. Conclude with a sentence that begins, "My personal plan for growing in holiness involves . . ."

Explaining the Faith

Why can't a good outcome justify any means used to accomplish it?

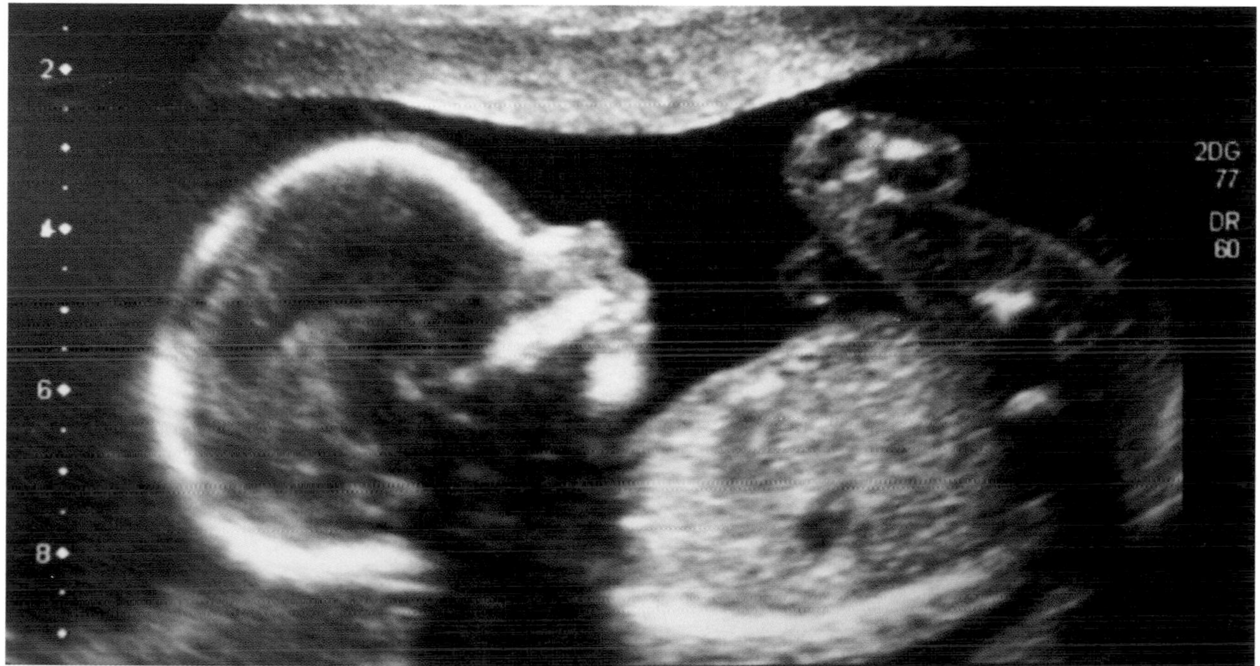

There are those who say the decisive factor in any moral decision is the outcome (the end); if the effect or consequence is good, then that is all that matters. However, this kind of thinking, called *consequentialism*, can ultimately justify any behavior (or means) as long as some good results. For example, it would justify medical experiments on unwilling subjects or the destruction of embryos (unborn human beings) in the course of embryonic stem cell research in the pursuit of finding a cure for certain diseases.

St. Thomas Aquinas clearly taught, following St. Paul in Scripture, that "an evil action cannot be justified by reference to a good intention" (*CCC*, 1759, quoting *Dec. praec.* 6). In other words, the end does not justify the means. One must never do evil so that good may come of it. An action must be good at all stages of its formation and execution. "A *morally good* act requires the goodness of the object, of the end, and of the circumstances together" (*CCC*, 1755).

Further Research

- Name and explain the three sources, or constitutive elements, of the morality of human actions. See paragraphs 1749–1754 of the *Catechism of the Catholic Church*.

Prayer

Prayer to the Holy Spirit

Breathe in me, O Holy Spirit,
that my thoughts may be all holy.
Act in me, O Holy Spirit,
that my work may be all holy.
Draw my heart, O Holy Spirit,
that I love but what is holy.
Strengthen me, O Holy Spirit,
to defend all that is holy.
Guard me, then, O Holy Spirit,
that I always may be holy.
Amen.

—St. Augustine of Hippo

9

DISCIPLESHIP THROUGH PRAYER

SPIRIT-DRIVEN WORK

Over the course of the past decade, parishioners from St. John Vianney Church in Prince Frederick, Maryland, and San Juan Bautista Church in Limay, Nicaragua, have been working together to raise money and build homes for the poorest people of the Limay region. Between 2007 and 2015, the two sister parishes have built more than two hundred new houses, repaired thirty more, built a home for senior citizens, and begun digging wells and building roads for a new subdivision that will eventually have fifty-five more homes.

Fr. Peter Daly, pastor of St. John Vianney, shared the story of cooperation between the parishes: "I think our sister parish relationship is what Pope Francis wants the Church to become: 'a poorer Church for the poor,'" he wrote.

The project began at the urging of Fr. Daly's sister, Maureen, whose neighboring parish was already building homes in Nicaragua. At the time, a small brick house with a dirt floor and metal roof cost $1,800 to build. After Daly gave a homily on the subject and put some photos of the houses on the parish bulletin board, a parishioner slipped him a check for $18,000 and said, "Build ten more."

Now, every six months, St. John Vianney parishioners travel to Limay to meet with a committee from San Juan Bautista. Fr. Daly emphasizes the power of prayer in the experience: "The project is rooted in prayer. Our trips to Nicaragua are like rolling retreats. We pray at every house. We pray morning and evening prayer. We go to Mass every day. We pray the night prayer just after we have an evening beer and discuss the highs and lows of the day. Some people who have gone to Nicaragua say they have never prayed so much in their lives."

(Fr. Peter Daly, "The Holy Spirit Lends a Hand to Sister Parish in Nicaragua," *National Catholic Reporter*, February 11, 2015.)

FOCUS QUESTION

How does PRAYER contribute to your SALVATION?

Chapter Overview

INTRODUCTION
What Is Prayer?

MAIN IDEA
Prayer is defined in many ways, but essentially prayer is your response to God, who seeks you.

Fr. Peter Daly described an experience of almost around-the-clock prayer for anyone participating in his parish's missionary trips to Limay, Nicaragua. He emphasized the power of prayer in helping both parishes achieve their goals.

God always answers prayer. He does so in different ways. He may grant what the person prays for, or he may seem not to answer the prayer for reasons that become clear only with time. As part of his answer, he transforms the person praying by providing the grace of acceptance. God's response to prayer is always loving, intended to guide each person toward eternal salvation.

Prayer is a powerful means to grow in union with Jesus, who instructed his disciples to "pray always without becoming weary" (Lk 18:1). St. Paul followed after Jesus when he instructed Christians to "pray without ceasing" (1 Thes 5:17). St. Frances Cabrini (1850–1917), the first American citizen to be canonized a saint, echoed these words as well:

> We must pray without tiring, for salvation of humankind does not depend on material success; nor on sciences that cloud the intellect. Neither does it depend on arms and human industries, but Jesus alone.

Prayer is a key means to your salvation because it strengthens your relationship with the Blessed Trinity, it lessens the hold that sin has on you, and it protects you from evil.

NOTE TAKING

Naming Definitions. This section provides several definitions of prayer. Choose three that you think best describe prayer, and write them down in a chart like the one below.

Prayer is "the living relationship of the children of God with their Father" (p. 316).

Definitions of Prayer

Prayer is your response to God, who seeks you. The *Catechism of the Catholic Church* defines prayer as "a vital and personal relationship with the living and true God" (*CCC*, 2558). Given God's grandeur, you must approach him with humility.

When you pray, you interact with the Blessed Trinity. You approach your loving Father, who desires only good things for you, which he grants to you through his Son, Jesus Christ. It is the Holy Spirit who enables you to pray. The *Catechism* further defines prayer as "the living relationship of the children of God with their Father who is good beyond measure, with his Son Jesus Christ and with the Holy Spirit" (*CCC*, 2565). Think of prayer, then, as a *relationship*, a coming together with God. When you pray, you become more aware of who you are as an adopted child of your loving Father.

Other great saints provide more insight into the meaning of prayer:

"True prayer is nothing but love." (St. Augustine)

"For me, prayer is a surge of the heart; it is a simple look turned toward heaven, it is a cry of recognition and of love, embracing both trial and joy." (St. Thérèse of Lisieux)

Prayer is a "conversation with God." (St. Clement of Alexandria)

St. Teresa of Ávila spoke of prayer as a journey with the invisible God, a companion who walks next to you along the path of life.

"One who prays aspires first of all to union with God" (Pope Francis).

Just as friendships thrive on conversation, so will your ability to live according to his will be strengthened by regular conversations with God.

How Does Prayer Benefit You?

The most important benefit of prayer is growing in union with the Triune God. Prayer is actually a vital necessity for reaching this goal. If you do not allow the Spirit to lead you, you will fall back into the slavery of sin. Prayer is intimately connected to living a Christian life because it requires love, obedience to the Father's plan, and transformation. Both prayer and action (doing good works, loving others) are essential to the Christian life.

Pope Francis suggested that prayer is a weapon in the struggle against evil as well as a guard against following your own ideology. (An *ideology* is a body of concepts, doctrines, beliefs, or ideas about human life or culture that guides an individual, social movement, institution, class, or large group.) While

Christianity does have beliefs and ideas about how life should be lived, it is fundamentally a relationship with God and not merely a system of ideas. The Pope said:

> In our daily journey, especially in difficulties, in the struggle against evil outside of ourselves and within us, the Lord is not far away, he is at our side; we fight with him beside us, and our weapon is prayer, which makes us feel his presence alongside of us, his mercy, even his help. (Angelus, October 20, 2013)

Pope Francis also warns that without prayer, a Christian can fall into the trap of preferring his or her own way of thinking to the mind of Christ. In his homily at Mass on October 17, 2013, he said that the Christian who does not pray is "arrogant, is proud, is sure of himself. He is not humble. He seeks his own advancement. . . . When a Christian prays, he is not far from the faith; he speaks with Jesus. . . . We ask the Lord for grace, first: never to stop praying to never lose the faith; to remain humble, and so not to become closed, which closes the way to the Lord."

Truly, through prayer, you remain connected with God and stay on the path toward him.

SECTION ASSESSMENT

NOTE TAKING

Use the chart you created to help you complete the following question.

1. Which two definitions of prayer best describe prayer for you? Explain why you chose these two examples.

COMPREHENSION

2. How should you approach God?
3. What does it mean to think of prayer as a relationship?
4. Why is prayer a weapon in the fight against evil?
5. How could Christianity without prayer become an ideology?

REFLECTION

6. Describe what "praying without ceasing" looks like in your life right now.

SECTION 1

Ways You Can Pray

MAIN IDEA

You can pray in multiple ways and on all occasions. Any effort at prayer is prayer itself.

This section introduces many ways to pray, along with some tips on how to overcome challenges and to pray more effectively. Most Catholics learn how to pray from parents, teachers, parish priests, and other believers who inspire them. One of the most important first steps in prayer is to learn to listen to God before you talk with him.

Challenges in Prayer

Praying on a daily basis is challenging for anyone, even the holiest saints. Commitment to and success in prayer suffers both from natural limitations you encounter in other aspects of your life and from moral limitations. You might feel restless one day and completely out of sorts on the next. You have so many things to do in your busy life. You may believe you don't have time to commit to prayer.

Distractions in prayer are normal. Interestingly, distractions can sometimes help you recognize what you might be overly concerned about. You can counteract distractions in many ways. One popular technique is to gaze at a crucifix, holy picture, icon, or lighted candle as you think about God. The battle against distractions requires vigilance. (See also "Dealing with Distractions," pages 320–321.)

NOTE TAKING

Planning and Naming. Draw a weekly planner like the one below. As you read this section, fill out a sample one-week schedule for prayer. Include at least seven different ways, expressions, forms, or practices of prayer. Write your planner in first-person language, and make it a plan that you can follow.

Sunday	Monday	Tuesday	Wednesday	Thursday	Friday	Saturday
				I will spend time with Jesus before the Blessed Sacrament.		

Sometimes distractions can come from your own lack of faith or practice. There is a saying: "Prayer should be your first choice rather than your last resort." Is God only a last resort for you? Do you think you can handle life pretty much on your own most of the time? If so, pray for the gift of humility, which highlights your dependence on God.

In addition to distractions, a person sincerely trying to pray can encounter spiritual dryness or darkness and a feeling that may be experienced as separation from God. But sometimes the experience of spiritual dryness or darkness can be a special occasion that God gives you to share in the suffering of his Son. After her death, the publication of Mother Teresa's letters to spiritual directors revealed her inner dryness and darkness in prayer. As with other great Christians before her, her desire to grow in holiness brought her a special share in the suffering and spiritual darkness experienced by Christ on the Cross when she set out to pray.

Another challenge you might encounter is a feeling of doubt that God hears your prayers. Interestingly, while most people do not worry about whether God hears them when they praise or thank him, they expect immediate results when their prayers are petitions. Be patient with your prayers. God knows what you need. He will answer you in his time and in his way. He is always with you.

Catholics are willing to trust God and approach him in prayer because of his love for them. God's love can be seen in all that he has done for humanity throughout salvation history, culminating in the Paschal Mystery. Prayer is a key part of your own personal connection with God and his plan for your life. Look to Jesus as a model of prayer. Jesus not only models how to pray, but he also prays in and with you. His presence helps your prayer focus on God himself, rather than only on what God can give you.

Getting Started in Daily Prayer

You will need a firm commitment if you want to persevere in prayer. While conversing and communicating with God can be spontaneous and ongoing, you should also *set aside a place and time for prayer.* Consider the following places to pray: your bedroom, a special corner in your house where you might light a **votive candle**, the school chapel or parish church, your car with the radio turned off, or a regular walking route outside where you can focus on prayer. Likewise, remember that it is important to carve out a scheduled part of the day for prayer (e.g., first thing in the morning, last thing at night, before a meal, during a free period at school). Here are three other suggestions for remaining focused and committed to prayer:

1. *Posture.* You can be more alert and relaxed while praying with a suitable posture such as standing, walking, kneeling, sitting upright in a chair, or, like St. Ignatius of Loyola, lying on your back.

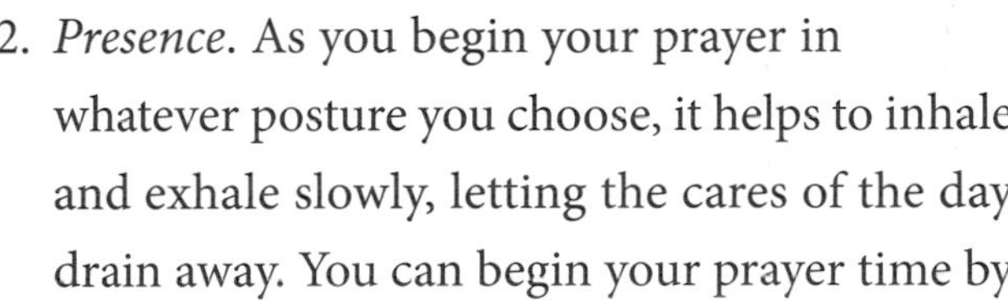

2. *Presence.* As you begin your prayer in whatever posture you choose, it helps to inhale and exhale slowly, letting the cares of the day drain away. You can begin your prayer time by

votive candle A prayer candle typically placed before a statue of Jesus, the Virgin Mary, or a saint and lit for a prayer intention.

recalling a basic truth that cultivates humility and gratitude: God is always present to you; he loves you beyond what you can imagine. You can enter your prayer realizing that the Holy Spirit himself has led you to spend time with God. Being present to God in prayer is itself a prayer.

3. *Persistence.* Amid the distractions of daily life, praying regularly can be a challenge. It is sometimes described as a battle because when you pray, you are fighting against yourself, your surroundings, and Satan, who tries to turn you away from your prayer. Remember the words of St. Pio of Pietrelcina, a beloved Italian priest of the twentieth century: "Prayer is the best weapon you have. It is a key to opening God's heart."

Jesus is pleased with your effort to pray, even if you do become distracted. His love will touch you, despite the restlessness of your mind. Christ offers the gift of the Holy Spirit, who will strengthen you and help you to be more like him.

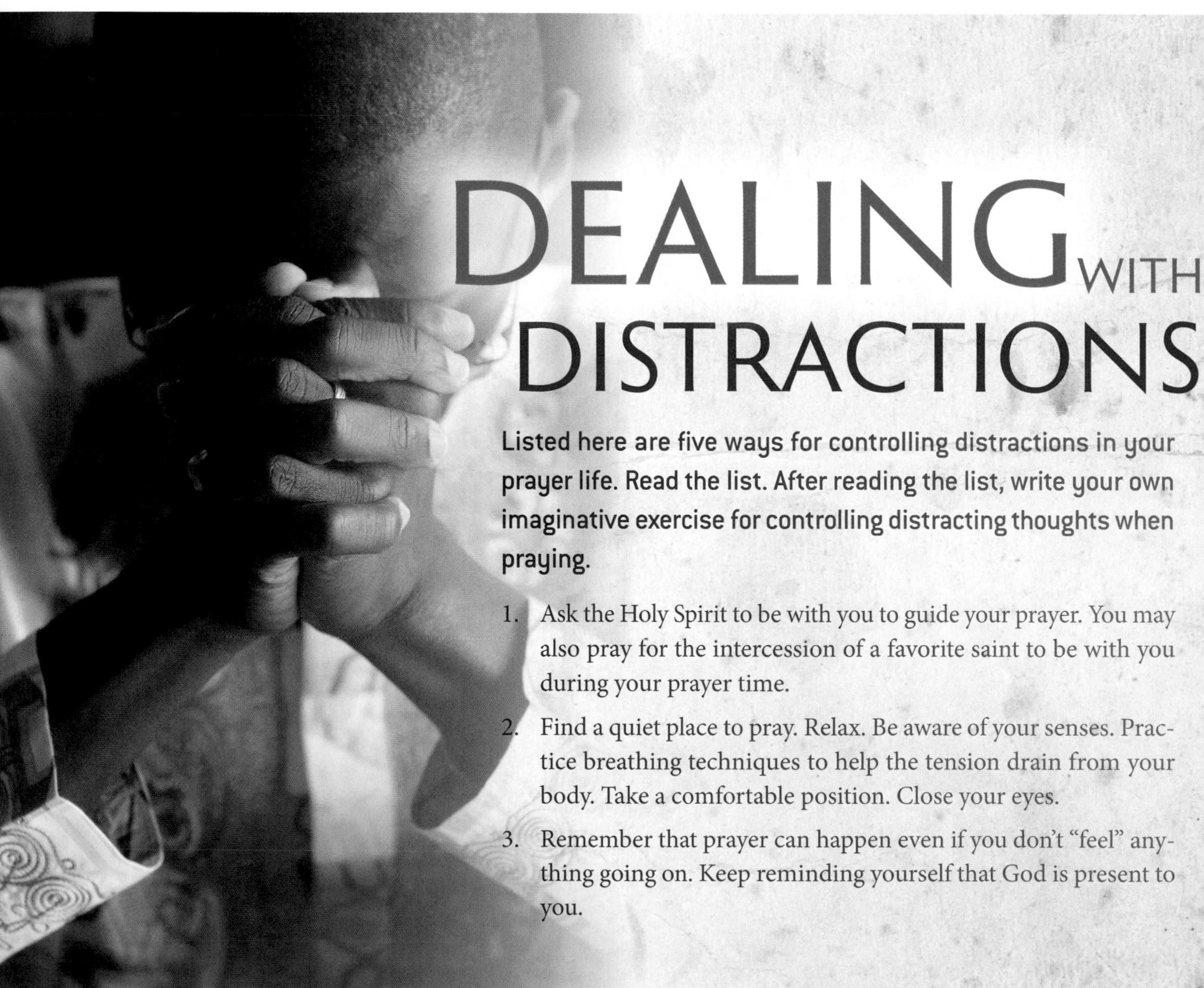

DEALING WITH DISTRACTIONS

Listed here are five ways for controlling distractions in your prayer life. Read the list. After reading the list, write your own imaginative exercise for controlling distracting thoughts when praying.

1. Ask the Holy Spirit to be with you to guide your prayer. You may also pray for the intercession of a favorite saint to be with you during your prayer time.
2. Find a quiet place to pray. Relax. Be aware of your senses. Practice breathing techniques to help the tension drain from your body. Take a comfortable position. Close your eyes.
3. Remember that prayer can happen even if you don't "feel" anything going on. Keep reminding yourself that God is present to you.

Expressions of Prayer

There is a connection between your spiritual life and your physical body. Because humans are both spirit and body, you experience God and pray to him through your body *and* senses. When you slow down and put yourself in God's presence, you hear the Lord speak to you through your intellect, feelings, imagination, will, and memories. In addition, your prayer leads to loving actions that require the body as well.

Christian prayer is heartfelt, expressing itself in three major ways: vocal prayer, meditation, and mental prayer (which may lead to contemplation).

Vocal Prayer

Vocal prayer—using spoken words—is one way to pray. But you must listen to God as well, cherishing moments of silence when you can hear God speak to you. Vocal prayer reflects the union of body and soul, following Christ's example of praying to his Father and teaching the Our Father to his disciples. Vocal

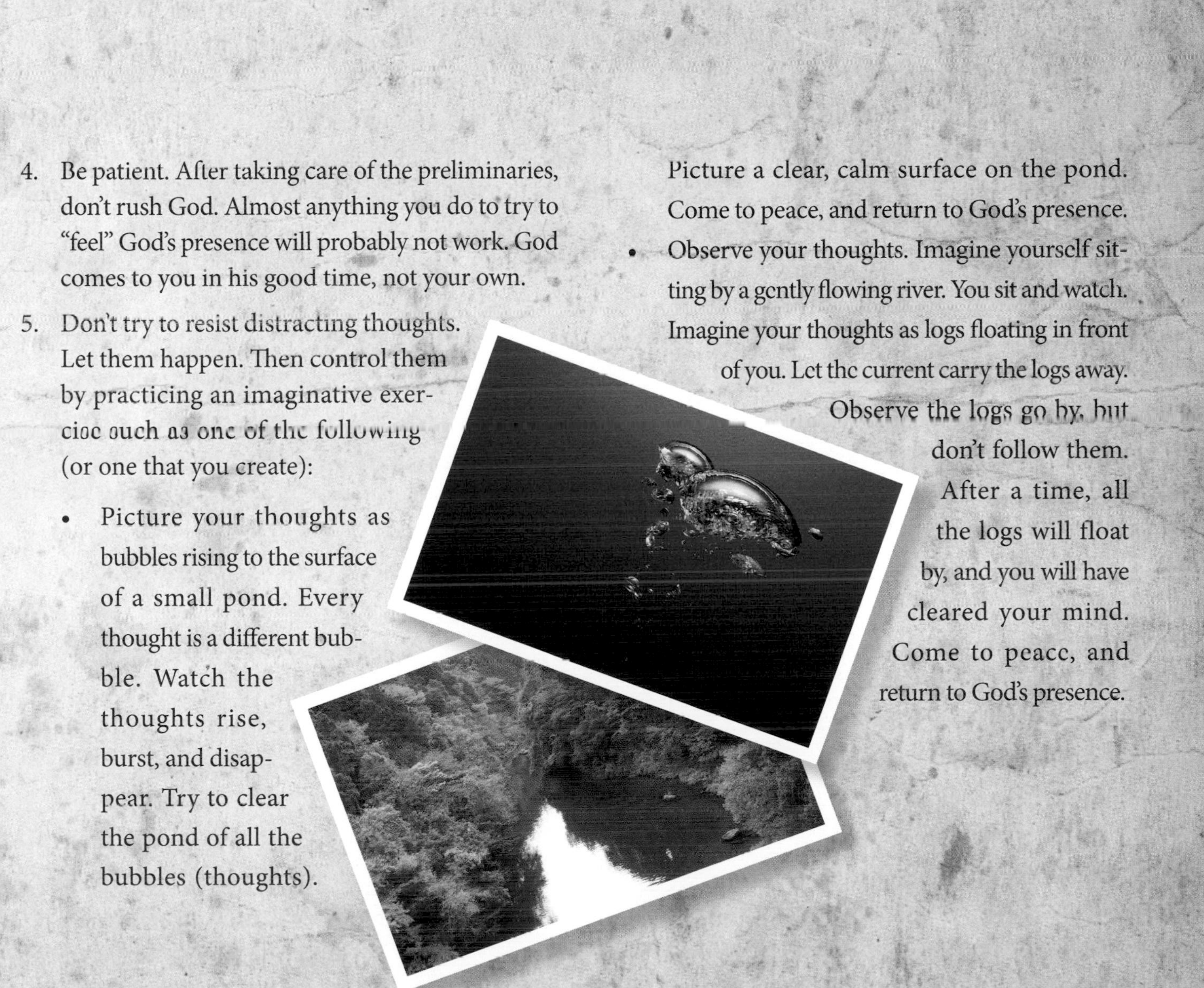

4. Be patient. After taking care of the preliminaries, don't rush God. Almost anything you do to try to "feel" God's presence will probably not work. God comes to you in his good time, not your own.
5. Don't try to resist distracting thoughts. Let them happen. Then control them by practicing an imaginative exercise such as one of the following (or one that you create):
   - Picture your thoughts as bubbles rising to the surface of a small pond. Every thought is a different bubble. Watch the thoughts rise, burst, and disappear. Try to clear the pond of all the bubbles (thoughts). Picture a clear, calm surface on the pond. Come to peace, and return to God's presence.
   - Observe your thoughts. Imagine yourself sitting by a gently flowing river. You sit and watch. Imagine your thoughts as logs floating in front of you. Let the current carry the logs away. Observe the logs go by, but don't follow them. After a time, all the logs will float by, and you will have cleared your mind. Come to peace, and return to God's presence.

prayer is an essential element of the Christian life and is also the most effective prayer for groups. The Church has a rich tradition of vocal prayer. Several examples of prayers meant to be prayed aloud are given on pages 360–362.

Meditation

Meditation is a quest to uncover the "why and how of the Christian life, in order to adhere and respond to what the Lord is asking" (*CCC*, 2705). Because distractions are plentiful, prayerful reflection on a written text—especially on Sacred Scripture but also on writings of the saints or other spiritual writings—can help foster meditation. When you meditate, you "tune in" to God. You use your thoughts, emotions, imagination, and desires to consider God's presence in the world and in your life. When you humbly and prayerfully read, you consider the words' implications for your life. You ask God, "How are you speaking to me through these words?" You then wait for God's response. Regular meditation helps you to become the rich soil described in the parable of the sower (see Mt 13:1–9)—that is, open to spiritual growth.

Mental Prayer and Contemplation

Mental prayer describes inner prayer, rather than prayer based on a text. Mental prayer usually centers directly on Jesus. You might converse with him or reflect on one of the mysteries of his life—for example, his Passion and Crucifixion. While this form of prayer requires steadfast determination, it is also flexible because it does not require any physical tools. It does require that you listen to God. It is possible to pray mentally when riding the bus, exercising, or doing chores around the house.

Some people are able to move, by God's grace, from mental prayer into **contemplative prayer**, or *contemplation*. Contemplation describes a gaze of faith fixed on Jesus. It too is a form of silent, wordless prayer in which you simply rest in the presence of God. However, contemplative prayer is more intense than mental prayer. Entering contemplative prayer resembles your preparation for receiving the Eucharist, when, prompted by the Holy Spirit, you hand yourself over to Christ to be purified and transformed by him. Contemplative prayer is a gift from God and deepens the covenant and communion begun in Baptism, when the Blessed Trinity conforms you to the image and likeness of God.

St. John Vianney, a holy parish priest of eighteenth-century France, told of a simple peasant who experienced contemplative prayer. The peasant sat daily in front of the tabernacle, where the

contemplative prayer Wordless prayer wherein a person's mind and heart rest in God's goodness and majesty.

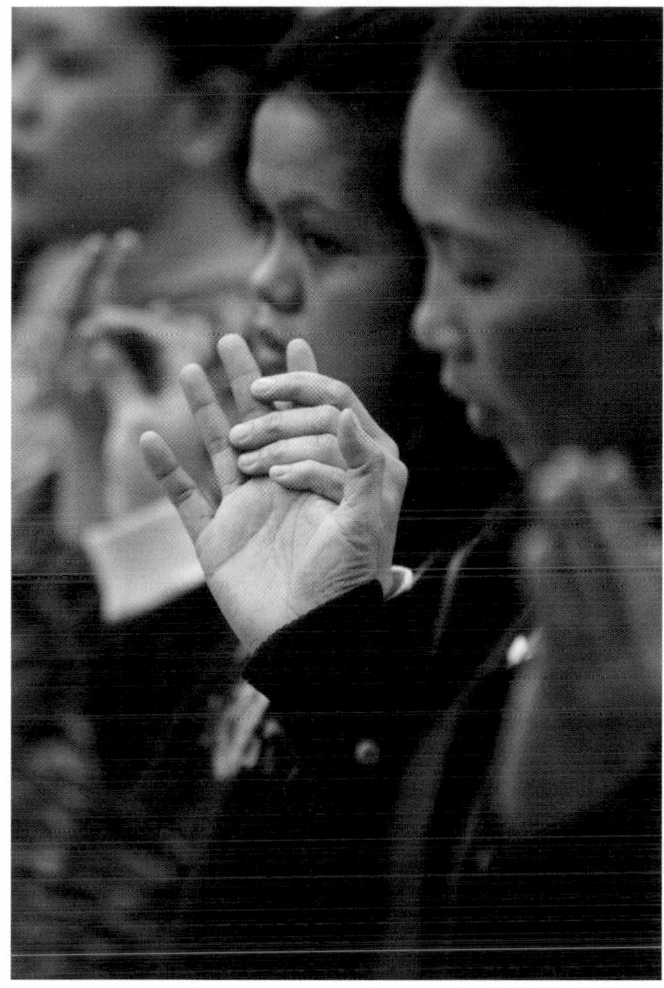

Lord present in the Blessed Sacrament is reserved. He explained, "I look at him and he looks at me." Contemplation requires silence—silent love. In this type of prayer, you seek Christ, give yourself over to the will of the Father, and place yourself under the guidance of the Holy Spirit. When praying this way, you empty your mind of thoughts and images and simply allow God's presence to penetrate your being. You do not have to do anything at all. If you are able to pray this way, you have been given a great gift from God.

Forms of Prayer

There are several forms in which Christians express prayer. The following prayer forms have roots in both Sacred Tradition and Sacred Scripture.

- *Blessing.* God declares his goodness through blessing. He first blessed you by giving you many gifts. When you ask for God's blessing, you ask him to shower grace upon you or others. You respond to God's blessings by thanking him, praising him, and offering yourself to him. This is your blessing of God in return.
- *Adoration.* When you adore God, you humbly acknowledge that he is the loving Creator of everything and that you are his creation. Adoration glorifies God's greatness.
- *Petition.* In petition or supplication, you ask God to provide what you need, either materially or spiritually. By doing so, you communicate your need, as God's creature, for his help. When you ask God for something, your request expresses your desire for the coming of the Kingdom of God, in which God himself satisfies every desire. You glorify Jesus by asking the Father to meet your needs in his name. Because the Holy Spirit helps you to pray, you can ask for the Spirit's guidance and help in formulating your petitions. **Contrition** is a special type of petition in which you ask your merciful Father to forgive your sins. A model of contrition is the tax collector who began his prayer with "O God, be merciful to me a sinner" (Lk 18:13).
- *Intercession.* In prayers of intercession, you pray not for your own interests but for the interests of others, even of those who cause you harm or those you count as enemies. Intercessory prayer is a special form of petition, resembling the prayers Jesus made on his disciples' behalf since he is the one intercessor with the Father on behalf of all people. Intercessory prayer is an example of Christian mercy. Praying for others

contrition Heartfelt sorrow and aversion for sins committed along with the intention of sinning no more. Contrition is the most important act of the penitent and is necessary for receiving the Sacrament of Penance.

at Mass and reciting a Rosary on behalf of others are two examples of intercessory prayer that express Christian compassion and love.

- *Thanksgiving.* Your entire life is a pure gift from God. God deserves your constant thanks, even in difficult circumstances; every event and need can become a thanksgiving offering. Think of the gifts of your life, friends, health, and much more. In truth, every breath you take is an opportunity to thank God. Jesus himself expressed his thankfulness to his Father out loud when he raised Lazarus from the dead (see Jn 11:41–42). The Eucharist (a Greek word that means "to give thanks") is a special prayer of thanksgiving. At Mass, you express your sorrow, ask for forgiveness, and petition God for all the good things you and others need to live your lives fully. When you receive Holy Communion, Christ comes to you and unites you to him and all your Christian brothers and sisters by the power of the Holy Spirit. He allows you to participate in his own thanksgiving to the Father.
- *Praise.* This form of prayer acknowledges that God is God and that he is awesome, not just for what he does but simply for who he is. Prayers of praise are given selflessly. The Scriptures praise God. Many of the psalms praise, adore, and bless God. Those who are already in heaven praise God constantly, as does the Church on earth. The celebration of the Eucharist is the ultimate prayer and sacrifice of praise.

Categorizing Prayer in the Book of Psalms

Read any three psalms, and identify the form of prayer taking place in them. Copy the verses that give evidence for your decision, and write a sentence for each sample explaining how it fits the description of one of the prayer forms listed in this section.

Traditional Catholic Prayer Practices

During the long history of the Church, many different prayer practices have developed. Some practices not previously named are listed below. See the Appendix (pages 360–364) for several additional Catholic prayers and devotions.

Prayer before the Blessed Sacrament

Adoration, or spending some time with your Lord in the **Blessed Sacrament**, is a beloved prayer practice. When you are before the Blessed Sacrament, you can recite short prayers, meditate on a Gospel passage, enter into a conversation with the Lord, or simply sit in his presence, adoring him and thanking him for his many gifts.

Litanies

Litanies contain a series of prayers—both *invocations* (prayers that call on God or saints for something) and responses such as "Hear us" or "Pray for us." Jesus taught you to pray fervently and with perseverance. A **litany** is a popular way to pray because it can help you to remain persistent and focused in prayer. In its Greek root, the word *litany* means "to ask in earnest."

Many parishes celebrate the Forty Hours' Devotion, in which the Blessed Sacrament is exposed continuously and parishioners are invited to spend some time with Jesus in prayer for that amount of time. This prayer devotion begins with a Solemn Mass of Exposition. The forty hours mark the time that Jesus spent in the tomb from his Death to his Resurrection.

Novenas

The word ***novena*** comes from the Latin word for "nine." It refers to the number of days Mary and the Apostles spent in prayer between the Ascension of Jesus and the descent of the Holy Spirit on Pentecost Sunday. Novenas are prayed over nine days, either privately or publicly, to obtain special graces or to petition for particular intentions. People often recite novenas for urgent intentions.

Blessed Sacrament "The name given to the Holy Eucharist, especially the consecrated elements reserved in the tabernacle for adoration, or for the sick" (*CCC*, Glossary).

litany From the Greek word *litaneia*, meaning "prayer or supplication," a form of prayer used in liturgies that includes prayers with responses.

novena From the Latin word for "nine," a set of prayers prayed over nine days in order to obtain special graces or to petition for particular intentions.

Prayer with Icons

An **icon** is a religious image "written" by an artist who seeks to be God's channel, allowing God's spirit to guide his or her brush. When you pray with an icon, you put yourself in the presence of the holy person (e.g., the Blessed Mother) or the religious mystery (e.g., Mary's visitation to Elizabeth) that is portrayed. You gaze at the icon. You might thank the Blessed Mother for giving her child to the world or pray for all expectant mothers.

The Jesus Prayer

Prayers can be short, as brief as one sentence or one word. A famous one-line prayer is the **Jesus Prayer**: "Lord Jesus Christ, Son of God, have mercy on me, a sinner." You express a lot in this short sentence. You acknowledge Jesus' divinity as Lord, Son of God, and Savior, and you acknowledge that you are a sinner and in need of Christ's forgiveness. You can recite the Jesus Prayer repeatedly for any period of time, concentrating on each word as you slowly inhale and exhale. There are many other short sayings that you can use for prayer (e.g., "Help me, Lord Jesus," "Come, Holy Spirit," or "Praise God!").

icon A holy image you gaze at, putting yourself in the presence of the holy person or mystery it portrays.

Jesus Prayer A short, formulaic prayer to Jesus or about Jesus that is said repeatedly. The Jesus Prayer may have originated with the Desert Fathers in the fifth century.

Trying Out Ways to Pray

During the next nine days, try praying using a novena of your choosing (for example, the Novena to St. Joseph). At the end of the novena, write a one-paragraph reflection on the experience. Also, write a three-paragraph report on the history of the novena that you chose.

SECTION ASSESSMENT

NOTE TAKING

Use the planner you created to help you complete the following item.

1. Write a reflection on how you have prayed on two recent days. Make sure to point out the specific expressions, forms, and practices of prayer you used on these days.

VOCABULARY

2. Under what circumstances does a person pray in *contrition*?
3. What are the origins of the *Jesus Prayer*?

COMPREHENSION

4. In addition to talking to God, what is the other important part of prayer?
5. What is the relationship between prayer and your physical body?
6. Name an example of a vocal prayer.
7. Why is mental prayer a more flexible type of prayer than meditation?
8. Distinguish between blessing and adoration.
9. What is the process for praying with an icon?

CRITICAL ANALYSIS

10. Suggest two ways to handle distractions in prayer.

REFLECTION

11. List several special gifts you have been given, then compose your own prayer of thanksgiving.
12. Note the following for your own life:
    - a good place to pray
    - an ideal time to pray
    - a comfortable position in which to pray
    - a good way to remind yourself of God's presence
    - a word or phrase that helps you refocus and handle distractions in prayer

SECTION 2

How to Pray with Scripture

MAIN IDEA

Sacred Scripture offers many examples of faithful people who related to God through prayer. Many Catholic prayers that are prayed both individually and in community come directly from the Bible or are partially based on Sacred Scripture.

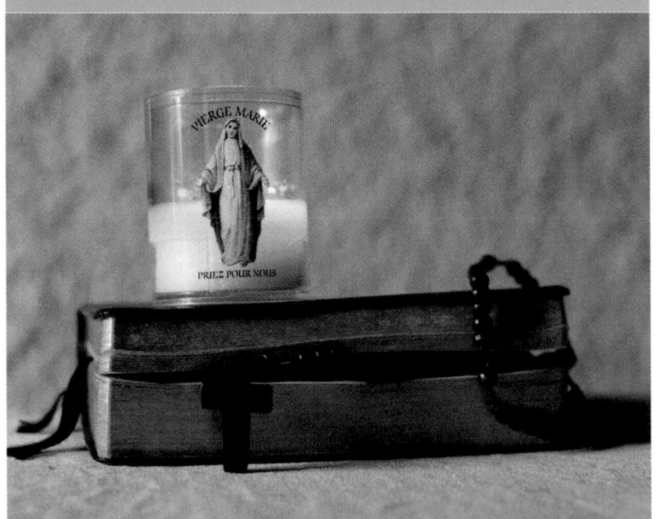

A constant theme in Scripture is that God's relationship with his people occurs through prayer. Prayer leads many figures in the Bible to respond to God's call and obey him. Jesus is the greatest model of prayer, followed by Mary. But both the Old and New Testaments include many other worthy examples of people who cultivated an intimate relationship with God through prayer.

As the examples from Scripture remind you, on the one hand, God constantly seeks out his people. On the other hand, people, though weakened by sin, seek him. Sacred Scripture reveals that God always initiates the process. Prayer takes place when people respond to God's invitation.

You can also pray with Scripture. Scripture is a source and guide for prayer. Scripture is a source in that many prayers come out of the Bible or are partly based on scriptural passages or events. Scripture is a guide in that it presents figures who were models of praying and who taught about prayer.

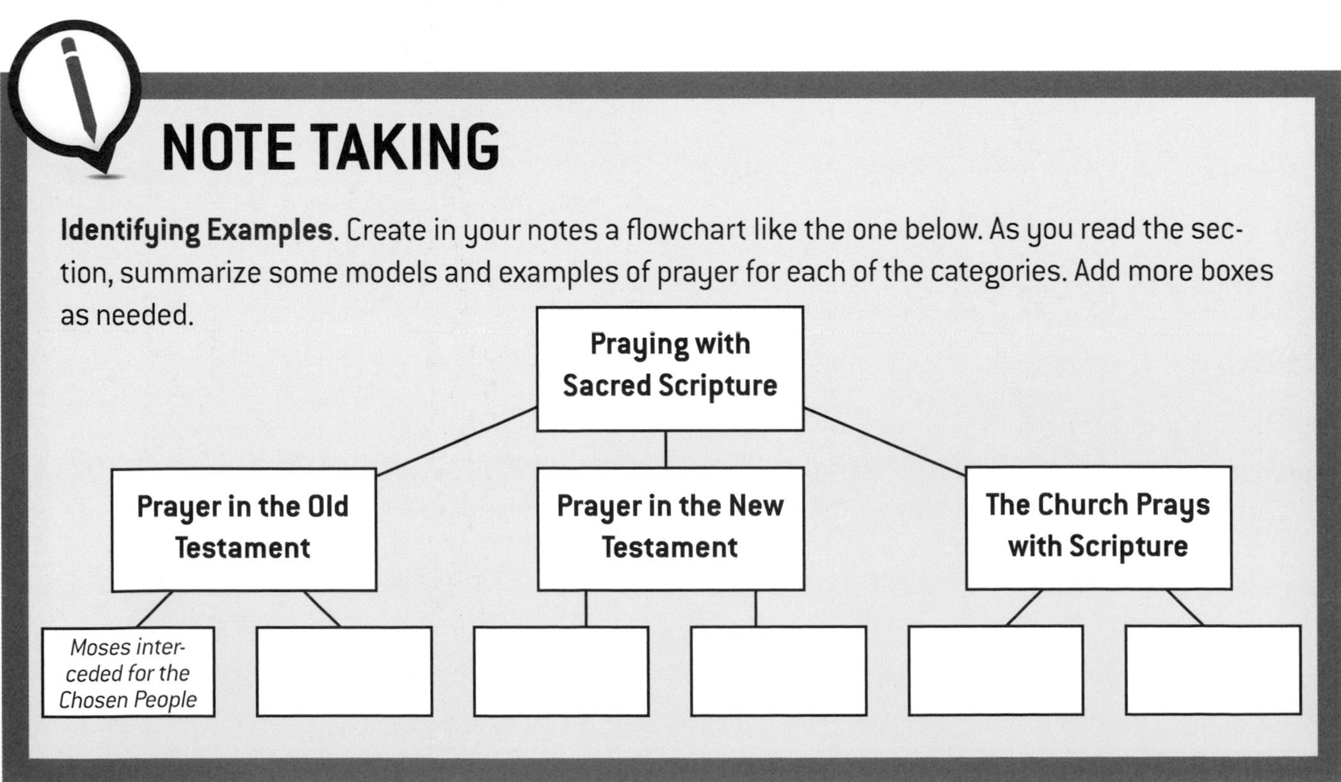

NOTE TAKING

Identifying Examples. Create in your notes a flowchart like the one below. As you read the section, summarize some models and examples of prayer for each of the categories. Add more boxes as needed.

Prayer in the Old Testament

Prayer is bound up in human history because it is a relationship between people and God. Probably the greatest examples of prayer in the Old Testament are the psalms. Inspired by the Holy Spirit, the psalms are marvelous prayers that have comforted and challenged individuals and communities for thousands of years. King David, alone or with other authors, composed the psalms. These prayer-poems, quoted and prayed by Jesus himself, have appeal for all times. Originally sung in the Temple and later in local synagogues and in family and personal settings, the psalms capture human emotions of joy and awe before God's creation, confidence and trust, complaints and sorrows, and thanksgiving and praise. Over time, the psalms were gathered into five books, called the **Psalter**.

The psalms are unique. While the other books of the Old Testament share God's deeds, the psalms are sung to God: they are actual prayers, rather than accounts of prayer, and were written in the same Spirit that inspired God's works. The psalms arose from the prayer-filled life of God's People, extending back to those who first entered into covenant relationships with God.

Models of Prayer in the Old Testament

The Old Testament gives many examples of people who modeled prayer in their intimate communication with God:

Psalter A name for the Book of Psalms or a collection of psalms for liturgical or devotional use.

Noah received God's blessing to "be fertile and multiply and fill the earth" (Gn 9:1).

The patriarch Abraham heard God's voice, responded to his invitation, and obeyed him. Abraham's faith conformed him to the likeness of God in that he was willing to give up his only son when God asked him to (see Gn 22:1–19).

Abraham's grandson Jacob wrestled with an angel before receiving a blessing from him (see Gn 32:23–33).

God initiated the relationship with Moses because he wanted to save the Israelites, with Moses as his messenger. Moses was on intimate terms with God, conversing with him "face to face, as a person speaks to a friend" (Ex 33:11)—a model of contemplative prayer. Moses was a mediator between God and his People and interceded on their behalf with God just as Jesus would later do.

Though a Gentile by birth, Ruth, the grandmother of King David, trusted in God and modeled fidelity in her prayer. After her Jewish husband died, Ruth prayed to remain close to her mother-in-law and the Chosen People: "May the Lord do thus to me, and more, if even death separates me from you!" she promised (Ru 1:17).

Elijah was the "father" of the prophets. His prayer on Mount Carmel, "Answer me, Lord! Answer me" (1 Kgs 18:37), was so powerful that it strengthened the Israelites' faith in the one God. Elijah is the prophet who appeared with Moses at the time of Jesus' Transfiguration. He is a model of a man of faith whose prayers God answered.

Besides composing psalms, King David modeled prayer for his people by praising God and trusting him. David was concerned that God should have a worthy place of worship and eventually left it to his son Solomon to build a Temple that would house the Ark of the Covenant. In response to God's promises to him, David prayed a heartfelt prayer of thanksgiving (see 2 Sm 7:18–29). After his public sin of adultery, David also modeled repentance, admitting, "I have sinned against the Lord" (2 Sm 12:13).

The Old Testament prophets derived great strength from individual prayer. They talked to God, listened to him, interceded for the people, and proclaimed God's Word to their brothers and sisters. The prophet Jeremiah's prayerful relationship with God began when he was very young, when God first commissioned him to share his Word with the people (see Jer 1–6).

Prayer in the New Testament

In the New Testament, contemplating Jesus in prayer and following his instructions on prayer are the best ways for you to grow in your own understanding and practice of prayer. Jesus learned to pray from his parents, Mary and Joseph, and from Jewish tradition. However, Jesus also prayed from his identity as the eternal Son of God. The Gospels record that even at the early age of twelve he sought out a place to be with his heavenly Father in prayer. When his parents found him in the Temple after searching for three days, he told them, "I must be in my Father's house" (Lk 2:49).

There are other inspiring models of prayer in the New Testament. The Blessed Mother and St. Paul, the author of the majority of the New Testament letters, offer both examples of prayerful lives and instruction in prayer.

Jesus Is the Master of Prayer

The Gospels document many instances of Jesus at prayer. After his Baptism in the Jordan River, Jesus went into the desert for forty days to pray in preparation for his ministry (see Mt 4:1–11). He also prayed before selecting the disciples (see Lk 6:12–16). After performing his first miracles of healing, Jesus withdrew to pray, just as he did after performing the miracle of the loaves and fishes (see Mt 14:22–23).

The Transfiguration (see Mk 9:2–8) showed Jesus in dialogue with his Father, Moses, and Elijah. At the Last Supper, Jesus offered the High Priestly Prayer (see Jn 17:1–26), interceding on behalf of all as he invited men and women of all ages to become one with him.

Jesus prayed about his impending Death when he took his disciples to the Garden of Gethsemane. Jesus, like all humans, feared death. Even so, he prayed, "Father, if you are willing, take this cup away from me; still, not my will but yours be done" (Lk 22:42). Jesus' prayer of *petition* to be spared suffering and death led to a prayer of *submission*, of obedience to his Father's will. Jesus even prayed on the Cross (see Lk 23:34).

Jesus taught his disciples how to pray when they asked him. For example, in the Sermon on the Mount, he told them to pray sincerely, confidently, and with forgiveness. He gave them the words of the Lord's Prayer, also known as the Our Father (see page 360). In Luke 11:5–13 he told them to pray constantly and with faith that their prayers would be answered: "I tell you, ask and you will receive; seek and you will find; knock and the door will be opened to you" (Lk 11:9).

PRACTICING SACRED READING

Lectio divina, or "sacred reading" of Scripture, is one component of the Liturgy of the Hours. Through the prayerful reading of God's Word, you can encounter God and allow the Holy Spirit to lead you into deeper union with him.

When you attempt this method of prayer, begin by taking a short Scripture passage, reading it slowly and attentively, and letting your imagination, emotions, memory, desires, and thoughts engage the written text. The following method describes the steps of lectio divina from the Benedictine tradition:

THE STEPS OF LECTIO DIVINA

1. *Reading (lectio).* Select a Bible passage. Read it slowly. Pay attention to each word. If a word or phrase catches your attention, read it to yourself several times.
2. *Thinking (meditatio).* Savor the passage. Read it again. Reflect on it. This time, pay attention to any emotions that may surface. Note the images that arise in your mind. Note any thoughts or memories the passage might call forth from you.
3. *Prayer (oratio).* Consider what the Lord might be saying to you in this passage. Talk to him as you would to a friend. Ask him to show you how to respond to his Word or connect this passage to your daily life.
4. *Contemplation (contemplatio).* Sit in the presence of the Lord. Imagine him looking at you with great love. Rest quietly in his presence. There is no need to think here. Just enjoy your time with him.

lectio divina Literally, "sacred reading." This is a prayerful way to read the Bible or other sacred writings.

Beloved, let us love one another, because love is of God; everyone who loves is begotten by God and knows God. Whoever is without love does not know God, for God is love. In this way the love of God was revealed to us: God sent his only Son into the world so that we might have life through him. In this is love: not that we have loved God, but that he loved us and sent his Son as expiation for our sins. Beloved, if God so loved us, we also must love one another. No one has ever seen God. Yet, if we love one another, God remains in us, and his love is brought to perfection in us. (1 Jn 4:7–12)

5. *Resolution.* Take an insight that you gained from your sacred reading and resolve to apply it to your life. Perhaps it is only a matter of saying a simple prayer of thanks. Perhaps you need to be more patient with someone in your life. Through the power of the Holy Spirit, Christ prays alongside you. You can be confident that your prayers are heard because Jesus constantly intercedes for you.

PRACTICE

Complete both of the following assignments:

1. Find the Gospel reading for today's date (see http://www.usccb.org/bible/readings). Read and pray over the passage using the method outlined above.
2. Using one of the following Scripture passages (their themes are given in parentheses), record some words of the prayer you speak to God or he speaks to you as you practice lectio divina.

ROMANS 12:9–21
("CONQUER EVIL WITH GOOD")

1 CORINTHIANS 12:4–31
("SPIRITUAL GIFTS")

GALATIANS 5:16–26
("LIVE BY THE SPIRIT")

COLOSSIANS 3:12–17
("PUT ON LOVE")

The Blessed Mother and St. Paul Model Prayer

Mary is sometimes called the perfect *Orans* (a Latin word to describe someone who is constantly at prayer) (see CCC, 2679). Mary uttered the beautiful canticle known as the Magnificat (see page 114 and Lk 1:46–55) in praise of God's choosing her to be the Mother of the eternal Son of God. After the Ascension, Mary prayed with the Apostles in the Upper Room (see Acts 1:14). Mary was with Jesus' disciples when the Holy Spirit descended on them, as she was when "they devoted themselves to the teaching of the apostles and to the communal life, to the breaking of the bread and to the prayers" (Acts 2:42).

In her openness to God and to his will, Mary shows you how to cooperate with the graces the Holy Spirit showers on you. Not only should you imitate Mary, but when you pray for her intercession, you should know that you are following the Father's plan of salvation, in which Mary plays an important part. Mary prays for you. Prayer, especially in union with the Blessed Mother, helps you to grow closer to Jesus, your Savior, and to live a life of Christian discipleship.

Prayer was central for all of the early Christians. The Pauline letters reveal that St. Paul was a person of prayer. Paul praised God for blessings bestowed on him and for people who joined him in his ministry. Time and again, Paul petitioned God on behalf of the people who preached the Gospel. He also wrote of his personal relationship with God and how the Lord helped him in tough times. Paul told the early Christians that they should "pray without ceasing" (1 Thes 5:17).

The Church Prays with Sacred Scripture

The Church, of course, encourages you to read Sacred Scripture in order to learn about God and especially about Jesus Christ. But reading Scripture differs significantly from reading your world history book. You want to read Scripture prayerfully, realizing that you can converse with God as you read and listen to him. Reading Scripture this way can lead you into meditation on Scripture.

Praying with Scripture does not only happen at home in your room. You pray with Scripture at Mass and in all the sacraments of the Church. You pray with Scripture when you read the psalms and recite scriptural prayers such as the Our Father. The official daily prayer of the Church—called the **Liturgy of the Hours** or Divine Office—is made up of scriptural prayer, especially from the Book of Psalms.

The Liturgy of the Hours

The Liturgy of the Hours is part of the official set of daily prayers prescribed by the Church, also known as the "public worship" of the Church. The practice of praying the Liturgy of the Hours is based on these two truths: First, the Paschal Mystery permeates and transfigures the various times of each day. Second, praying constantly helps to make the whole day holy. The Liturgy of the Hours is traditionally recited by priests and professed members of religious orders on behalf of the whole Church, but laypeople are also encouraged to pray it. The following are some of the characteristics of this prayer:

- Scriptural prayers, including readings (especially from the Book of Psalms), are at its heart.
- The Liturgy of the Hours provides prayers for each day of the year in each of the three liturgical cycles (A, B, and C).
- Each day follows a pattern of prayer with themes closely tied to the liturgical calendar and feasts of the saints.

Liturgy of the Hours The official daily prayer of the Church; also known as the Divine Office. The Liturgy of the Hours consists of prayers, Scripture, and reflections at regular intervals throughout the day.

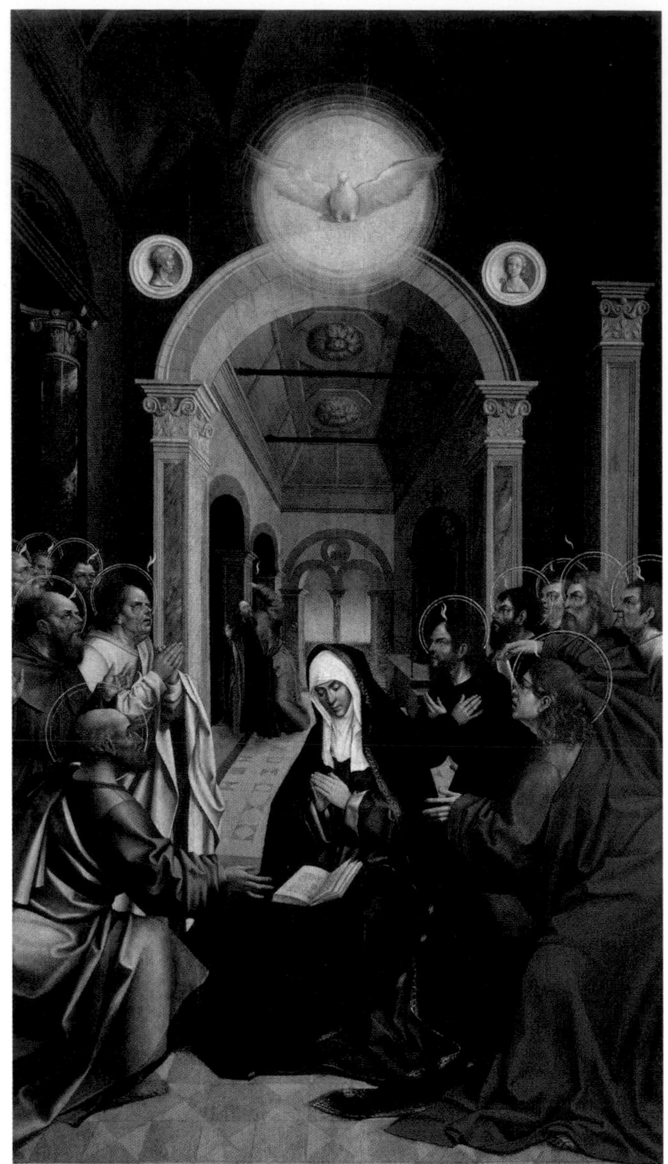

Mary devoted herself to prayer.

- The Liturgy of the Hours is prayed at five periods from early dawn until late at night:
    - The Office of Readings (formerly Matins)
    - Lauds or Morning Prayer
    - Daytime Prayer, which includes prayers traditionally said at three different times of day
    - Vespers or Evening Prayer
    - Compline or Night Prayer

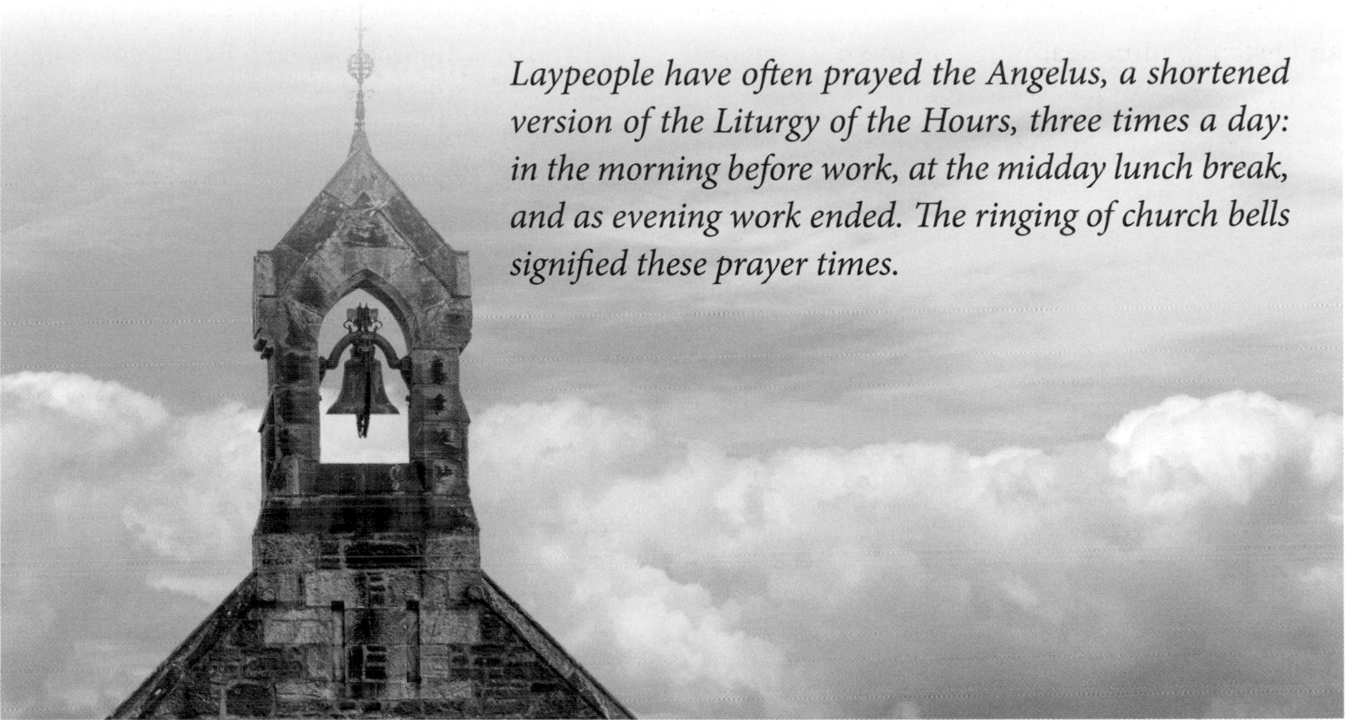

Laypeople have often prayed the Angelus, a shortened version of the Liturgy of the Hours, three times a day: in the morning before work, at the midday lunch break, and as evening work ended. The ringing of church bells signified these prayer times.

SECTION ASSESSMENT

NOTE TAKING

Use the flowchart you created to help you complete the following items.

1. Name two examples of prayer from the Old Testament.
2. Describe the Liturgy of the Hours.

VOCABULARY

3. How does the name *lectio divina* define what this prayer practice is about?
4. Name the five steps of lectio divina.

COMPREHENSION

5. Name an occasion of prayer by King David.
6. Give two examples from the Gospels of Jesus at prayer.
7. What does it mean to describe Mary as "the perfect *Orans*"?
8. For whom did St. Paul petition?

REFLECTION

9. Which prayer practice of the Church were you least familiar with when you began this section? Summarize what you learned about this practice.

SECTION 3

Jesus Teaches His Disciples to Pray

MAIN IDEA

While the Our Father and Hail Mary are both essential Christian prayers, it is the Our Father, emanating from Jesus' response to his disciples' request to "teach us to pray," that is the preeminent Christian prayer.

The Lord's Prayer, the Our Father, holds the preeminent position among all Christian prayers because it was the prayer that Jesus taught his disciples to say when they asked him to teach them to pray (see Lk 11:1). Jesus not only provided the words for this prayer but also sent the Holy Spirit to teach his disciples how to pray it. The Lord's Prayer forms the basis for the Church's understanding of the value of prayer.

From the earliest centuries on, the Lord's Prayer has been used in the liturgy of the Church—in all the sacraments, especially the Eucharist. The communal nature of the Our Father makes it very appropriate in the three Sacraments of Initiation: Baptism, Confirmation, and the Eucharist. The Lord's Prayer marks new birth into the divine life during the Rites of Baptism and Confirmation. In the early Church, the Lord's Prayer was not taught to new Christians until the week after they were baptized. Since it was a prayer of Christian identity, a person could only say it when initiated into the Church.

At Mass, the Our Father is offered as the prayer of the whole Church. It sums up the petitions and intercessions of the priest when he asks the Father to send the Holy Spirit and invites you to get ready to receive Holy Communion. The Our Father is also prayed as part of the Liturgy of the Hours. It is the prayer of a disciple of Jesus Christ.

NOTE TAKING

Connecting the Meaning. Create a chart like the one below. Print the parts of the Our Father (as listed on pages 338–339 of this section) in the first column. In the second column, list the Latin translations of the parts (see the Appendix, page 360). In the third column, write words and short phrases that remind you of the meaning of each petition. Add as many rows as needed.

Petition	Latin Translation	Meaning
Our	*Noster*	*Expresses communal aspect of prayer.*
Father	*Pater*	*I am a child of a loving God.*

Scriptural Context of the Lord's Prayer

The Gospels of Matthew and Luke each record the Lord's Prayer, though their wordings are different and they place the prayer in different settings. Compare the two versions below.

Our Father in heaven,
hallowed be your name,
your kingdom come,
your will be done,
on earth as in heaven.
Give us today our daily bread;
and forgive us our debts,
as we forgive our debtors;
and do not subject us to the final test,
but deliver us from the evil one.
(Mt 6:9–13)

Father, hallowed be your name,
your kingdom come.
Give us each day our daily bread
and forgive us our sins
for we ourselves forgive everyone in debt to us,
and do not subject us to the final test.
(Lk 11:2b–4)

In Matthew's Gospel, the prayer is set as part of Jesus' Sermon on the Mount (see Mt 5–7). The *Catechism of the Catholic Church* explains:

> The Sermon on the Mount is teaching for life, the Our Father is a prayer, but in both the one and the other the Spirit of the Lord gives new form to our . . . lives. Jesus teaches us this new life by his words; he teaches us to ask for it by our prayer. The rightness of our life in him will depend on the rightness of our prayer. (*CCC*, 2764)

The Gospel of Matthew's version of the Lord's Prayer has seven petitions (in contrast to the five petitions in Luke's Gospel). The first three petitions are petitions of praise made directly to God, addressing his name, his Kingdom, and his will. The last four petitions are driven by concerns for the present world, beginning with these requests: "give us," "forgive us," "lead us," and "deliver us."

In Luke's Gospel, Jesus is praying in a quiet place when his disciples come and ask him to teach them to pray "just as John [the Baptist] taught his disciples" (Lk 11:1). In Luke's account, after teaching them the Our Father, Jesus tells the disciples two parables that stress important attitudes you should have when you pray (see Lk 11:5–13). The first parable—of a friend who comes knocking on the door late at night to request bread—makes the point about remaining persistent in prayer. Jesus says, "I tell you, if he does not get up to give him the loaves because of their friendship, he will get up to give him whatever he needs because of his persistence" (Lk 11:8). The second parable explains that, if a human father will give his children what is good for them (in the parable, wholesome food), "how much more will the Father in heaven give the holy Spirit to those who ask him" (Lk 11:13). Both of these parables emphasize themes and petitions similar to those of the Our Father.

Tertullian, a Father of the Church from the second century, called the Lord's Prayer "the summary of the whole Gospel" (*On Prayer*, 1). St. Augustine wrote in the early fifth century, "Run through all the words of the holy prayers [in Scripture] and I do not think that you will find anything in them that is not contained in the Lord's Prayer" (Letter 130, 22).

The infographic on pages 338–339 tells you more about each of the main petitions and phrases of the Lord's Prayer.

UNDERSTANDING THE PARTS OF THE LORD'S PRAYER

OUR

- The collective term "our" shows that this is a communal prayer.
- You are praying in communion with other Christians, and you are addressing God in communion with the Divine Persons of the Blessed Trinity.

FATHER

- Jesus addressed God as "Abba," an Aramaic term for a very familiar form of "Father," something like "Dad." Jesus invites you to call God "Father," implying two very important truths: (1) Jesus' Father is the Father of all, and (2) all people are intimately related to one another as brothers and sisters.
- The use of "Father" to describe God was unique in all of Scripture. Tertullian wrote:

> The expression God the Father had never been revealed to anyone. When Moses himself asked God who he was, he heard another name. The Father's name has been revealed to us in the Son, for the name "Son" implies the new name "Father."

- While other religions, including the Jewish faith, did understand and reference God as Father because he is Creator and "first origin of everything" and due to his "goodness and loving care for all his children" (*CCC*, 238, 239), it was Jesus who "revealed that God is Father in an unheard-of sense: he is Father not only in being Creator; he is eternally Father in relation to his only Son, who is eternally Son only in relation to his Father" (*CCC*, 240).

WHO ART IN HEAVEN

- "In heaven" refers to God's transcendence, his way of being, and his majesty above all his creatures.
- You profess your exile from God in heaven.
- You pray for a conversion of heart and await the day when your heavenly reward will be fully yours.

HALLOWED BE THY NAME

- In the Old Testament, God's name, YHWH or "I AM" (Ex 3:14), underscores the mystery of God.
- Christ's Paschal Mystery and your reception of the Sacrament of Baptism adopt you into God's family and permit you to call God "Father."
- God is the source of all holiness. When you imitate the Son, you are witness to the Father's holiness.

THY KINGDOM COME

- Jesus inaugurated God's Kingdom from the beginning of his earthly ministry through his Passion, Death, Resurrection.
- The seeds of the Kingdom (peace, justice, and service) are now present in the Church. These are also ways you should prepare for the Kingdom.
- However, God's Kingdom is not yet fully established until Jesus comes again at the end of the world.

THY WILL BE DONE ON EARTH AS IT IS IN HEAVEN

- God's will on earth is for you to join your will to his Son's will and to contribute to his ongoing work of salvation by loving others, especially those people most in need. In this way, you can live your vocation to share in Christ's mission to build up the Church and renew the world.
- In summary, to do the Father's will is to love him above all things, and your neighbor as yourself.
- You need the Holy Spirit's help to overcome your own selfishness and strengthen you to live as a disciple of Christ.

GIVE US THIS DAY OUR DAILY BREAD

- When you pray for "bread," you are requesting what bread represents—the material and spiritual goods that are necessary for life: food, shelter, clothing, friendship, love, companionship, and above all Jesus, who is "the bread of life" (Jn 6:35).
- You pray not only for your own needs, but the needs of all, especially those who are hungry and poor. This petition reminds you to share your material blessings with others.
- The petition has a future dimension. In the original Aramaic spoken by Jesus, the word *daily* may also have meant something like "for tomorrow, today." You are also praying for the fullness of God's material and spiritual gifts, which will be yours in heaven. You dare to ask for a foretaste of these gifts today.

AND FORGIVE US OUR TRESPASSES AS WE FORGIVE THOSE WHO TRESPASS AGAINST US

- In praying this petition, you acknowledge you are a sinner in need of God's forgiveness.
- Both Matthew's and Luke's Gospels use the term *debts* instead of *trespasses*, probably indicating a request for forgiveness at the Last Judgment.
- The second part of the petition names the requirement that you must also forgive others. Jesus teaches you by both word and example to refrain from revenge and to forgive those who sin against you.

AND LEAD US NOT INTO TEMPTATION

- Trials, inevitably, will come your way. What you pray for in this petition is that you will have the strength to overcome any difficulties that might steer you away from Christ and his Church.
- The time prior to the end of the world will be one of "great tribulation, such as has not been since the beginning of the world until now, nor ever will be" (Mt 24:21). This petition likely refers literally to being spared from this final test that will occur before the end of the age.
- This petition also asks the Holy Spirit to shower you with gifts such as fortitude, watchfulness, perseverance, and a heart to know the difference between trials that strengthen you spiritually and temptations that lead to sin and death.

BUT DELIVER US FROM EVIL.

- In union with the saints, you ask God to show forth the victory that Christ has already won over Satan. You pray that the Father will deliver you from Satan's snares, including the temptations you encounter in the world.
- You pray for practical removal of evils: of accidents, illness, violence, and natural disasters. You ask God to keep you from any unjust, prejudicial, and selfish actions that will lead you away from him.
- Finally, you pray with the Holy Spirit and all of the Communion of Saints for the Lord's Second Coming, when you and all people will be free from the snares of Satan.

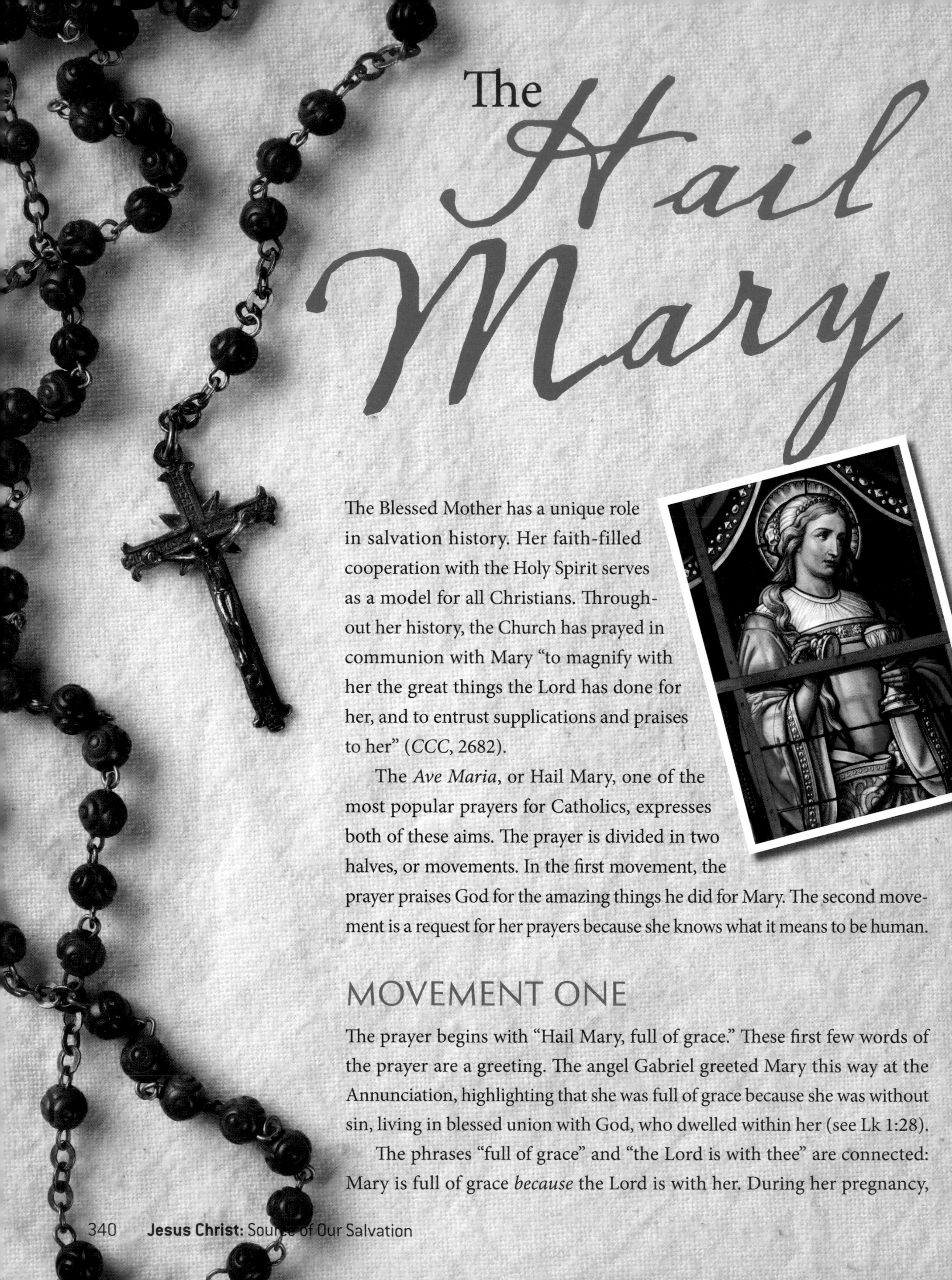

The Hail Mary

The Blessed Mother has a unique role in salvation history. Her faith-filled cooperation with the Holy Spirit serves as a model for all Christians. Throughout her history, the Church has prayed in communion with Mary "to magnify with her the great things the Lord has done for her, and to entrust supplications and praises to her" (*CCC*, 2682).

The *Ave Maria*, or Hail Mary, one of the most popular prayers for Catholics, expresses both of these aims. The prayer is divided in two halves, or movements. In the first movement, the prayer praises God for the amazing things he did for Mary. The second movement is a request for her prayers because she knows what it means to be human.

MOVEMENT ONE

The prayer begins with "Hail Mary, full of grace." These first few words of the prayer are a greeting. The angel Gabriel greeted Mary this way at the Annunciation, highlighting that she was full of grace because she was without sin, living in blessed union with God, who dwelled within her (see Lk 1:28).

The phrases "full of grace" and "the Lord is with thee" are connected: Mary is full of grace *because* the Lord is with her. During her pregnancy,

Jesus was literally *within* her, living in her womb. She had to be graced by God to have such an important role. Her free response was to give herself over completely to God.

Perhaps you remember that it was Mary's cousin Elizabeth who first said, "Most blessed are you among women, and blessed is the fruit of your womb," when Mary came to visit her and both of them were pregnant (Lk 1:42). Elizabeth knew Mary was blessed because her own child, John the Baptist, jumped in Elizabeth's womb when Mary came near. Elizabeth was the first of countless numbers of people in every generation who have called Mary blessed. Mary is blessed because she believed and accepted for herself God's Word to her.

Hail Mary
Hail Mary, full of grace,
the Lord is with thee.
Blessed art thou among women
and blessed is the fruit of thy womb, Jesus.
Holy Mary, Mother of God,
pray for us sinners
now and at the hour of our death.
Amen.
Ave, María, grátia plena,
Dóminus tecum.
Benedícta tu in muliéribus,
et benedíctus fructus ventristui, Iesus.
Sancta María, Mater Dei,
ora pro nobis peccatóribus
nunc et in hora mortis nostræ.
Amen.

MOVEMENT TWO

The prayer continues, "Holy Mary, Mother of God." Mary has the name "Mother of God" because she gave birth to Jesus, the Son of God. As the patriarch Abraham is the father of all believers, Mary is the mother of all the faithful, including every generation of believers who are welcomed and received by her Son, Jesus. Entrusting yourself to Mary's prayer means that you abandon yourself to God's will as she did.

The prayer's closing phrase is "Pray for us sinners, now and at the hour of our death." By saying these words, you acknowledge that you are a sinner (like everyone else) as you reach out to Mary, the Mother of Mercy. You give yourself over to her at this moment (now) and put your death into her hands as well, desiring her presence at your death, as she was present at Jesus' Death. You pray in confidence that Mary will lead you to her Son, Jesus, in paradise.

You have probably had the opportunity to pray the Rosary (see pages 362–364) alone or with others. The Hail Mary is prominent in this prayer practice: you say the prayer fifty-three times in one set of the joyful, luminous, sorrowful, or glorious mysteries. In medieval times, everyday people could not all say the Liturgy of the Hours, so the Rosary became a substitute. For this reason, it was known as "Our Lady's Psalter."

The title "The Lord's Prayer" conveys the truth that Jesus himself gave this prayer to his disciples. Only Jesus could have given his disciples this prayer so that they too could pray to the Father with the boldness of a son or daughter. The Our Father is a prayer of hope and faith in what is to come. The Greek term *parrhesia* is used in the New Testament (see Acts 4:13) to describe "bold speech." *Parrhesia* describes the attitude you are to take in praying the Our Father: simple, straightforward, trusting, assured, bold yet humble, and with the certainty of being loved.

Prayer, especially prayer in union with the Blessed Mother, will always help you grow closer to Jesus and to a life of Christian discipleship: this message serves as a good summary for this chapter and this course. As you continue your studies, may you grow ever closer to the Lord in both knowledge and love. Concerning your future, remember the words of St. Pio of Pietrelcina (1887–1968): "Pray, hope, and don't worry." And take to heart the words of an old Irish blessing:

> May the road rise up to meet you.
> May the wind always be at your back.
> May the sun shine warm upon your face,
> And rains fall soft upon your fields.
> And until we meet again,
> May God hold you in the palm of his hand.
> Amen.

My Daily Bread

Make a list of the "daily bread" you need to live a full, happy, holy, and healthy life. Consider these categories:

- **physical needs**
- **psychological needs**
- **spiritual needs**

ASSIGNMENT

Write a one-paragraph follow-up to your list telling how you can share some of these same things with others, especially those most in need.

SECTION ASSESSMENT

NOTE TAKING

Use the chart you created to help you complete the following items.

1. How does the phrase "who art in heaven" refer to God's transcendence?
2. What desire does "thy kingdom come" express?
3. What is a requirement that arises from praying for "our daily bread"?
4. What does "evil" refer to in the last petition of the Our Father?
5. Translate these Latin phrases from the Our Father: *fiat volúntas Tua*; *Panem nostrum quotidiánum da nobis hódie*; *sed libera nos a malo.*

COMPREHENSION

6. What distinguishes the first three petitions of the Our Father in Matthew's Gospel from the last four petitions?
7. How is the Gospel of Matthew's version of the Our Father similar to and different from the version in the Gospel of Luke?
8. Who first said that Mary was blessed among women, and why?

CRITICAL ANALYSIS

9. Church Father Tertullian said that the Our Father is "the summary of the whole Gospel." Explain what he meant.

REFLECTION

10. What are some concrete ways in which you can hallow God's name?

Section Summaries

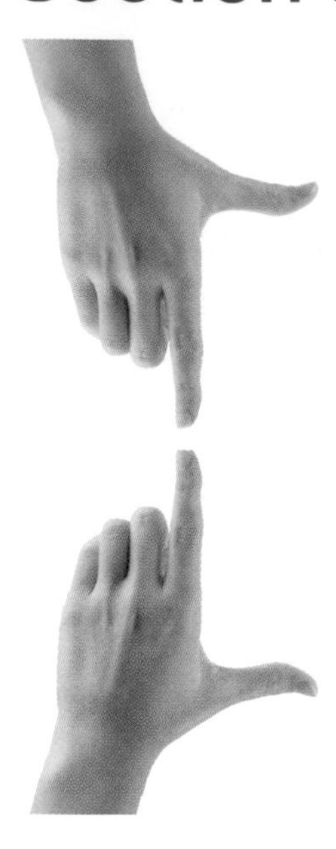

Focus Question

How does prayer contribute to your salvation?

Complete one of the following:

Reread the story "Spirit-Driven Work" on page 313. Locate another news story in which prayer is credited for work accomplished, a goal met, a hardship alleviated, or a blessing gained. Write a three-paragraph summary of the story. Include a quotation from the story about the importance of prayer.

Write three paragraphs telling about a friend, religion teacher, priest, religious, or relative who is a model of prayer for you.

Examine the Act of Contrition on page 362. Explain the meaning of the prayer, sentence by sentence. Also answer: How does this prayer help you to combat sin in your life?

INTRODUCTION (PAGES 315–317)

What Is Prayer?

There are several ways to define prayer. The *Catechism of the Catholic Church* defines prayer as a "vital and personal relationship with the living and true God" (*CCC*, 2558). Prayer is vitally necessary for growth in your relationship with God, for interaction with the Blessed Trinity, and for remaining on the path to eternal salvation. Pope Francis suggested that prayer is a help in avoiding evil and defending against the trap of preferring one's own way of thinking over the example of Christ.

In a discussion with Catholic friends or your parents, ask them to share a time when they felt a prayer was answered and when they felt that God was strengthening them. Write a one-paragraph summary of the discussion.

SECTION 1 (PAGES 318–327)

Ways You Can Pray

You can pray in multiple ways and for various occasions. Finding a particular place to pray, a scheduled period of time, and a prayerful posture can help you pray regularly. Remind yourself that you are in God's presence, try different methods of prayer, and persevere through distractions. Different expressions of prayer include vocal prayer, meditation, and mental prayer. Blessing, adoration, and petition are three of the forms prayer takes. Traditional Catholic prayer practices include Adoration before the Blessed Sacrament, litanies, novenas, icons, and the Jesus Prayer.

On his apostolic visit to the United States in 2008, Pope Benedict XVI posed these questions to young people: "Have we perhaps lost something of the art of listening? Do you leave space to hear God's whisper, calling you forth into goodness?" Write your own response to each of these questions.

SECTION 2 (PAGES 328–335)

How to Pray with Scripture

The Bible not only provides examples of prayerful people, it is also Divine Revelation and thus the subject of prayer. The Book of Psalms is a rich book of prayers that capture joy and awe as well as sorrow and complaints. Moses's face-to-face encounters with God are perhaps the most intimate examples of prayer in the Old Testament. In the New Testament, Jesus provides a model of prayer by his own actions and by giving his followers the Lord's Prayer. The Church prays with Sacred Scripture through the sacraments, a method of sacred reading called *lectio divina*, and the Liturgy of the Hours, the official prayer of the Church.

Read the following Gospel passages that contain Jesus' teachings about prayer. For each, briefly summarize the point he is making: Matthew 5:44, 6:5–8, 18:19–20, 21:21–22; Mark 11:23–25; Luke 11:5–13, 18:1–8, 18:10–14; John 14:13, 15:7.

SECTION 3 (PAGES 336–343)

Jesus Teaches His Disciples to Pray

The Lord's Prayer, or the Our Father, is the preeminent Christian prayer. Jesus himself taught this prayer to his disciples. The Our Father is prayed in the Church's liturgies, all the sacraments, and as part of the Liturgy of the Hours. It is a communal prayer, yet one you can keep on your lips and in your heart each day. Church Father Tertullian called the Our Father the perfect Christian prayer and a "summary of the whole Gospel." As recorded in Matthew's Gospel, the Lord's Prayer has seven petitions—three that glorify God and four that ask him for help. Another important Catholic prayer is the Hail Mary, a prayer that calls on the Blessed Mother for intercession with God.

Translate the Lord's Prayer and transcribe it in a foreign language you are studying.

Chapter Assignments

Choose and complete at least one of the three assignments assessing your understanding of the material in this chapter.

1. Acrostic Prayer

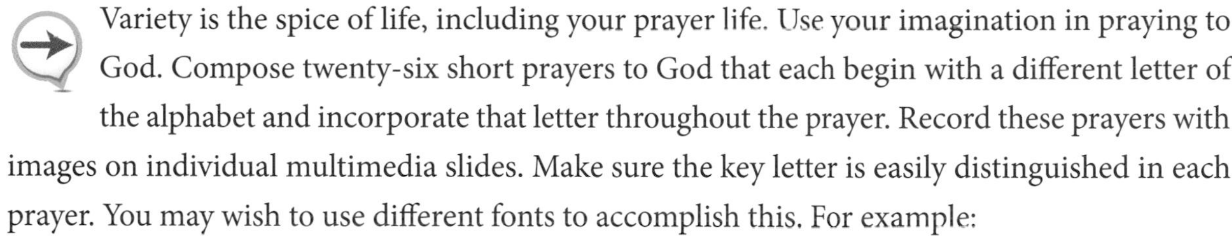

Variety is the spice of life, including your prayer life. Use your imagination in praying to God. Compose twenty-six short prayers to God that each begin with a different letter of the alphabet and incorporate that letter throughout the prayer. Record these prayers with images on individual multimedia slides. Make sure the key letter is easily distinguished in each prayer. You may wish to use different fonts to accomplish this. For example:

A **A**lmighty Father, I **a**dore you. Make me an **a**mbassador of your love.

C **C**hrist, my **c**ompanion, help me to be a worthy **c**hild of your Father. Give me **c**ourage and **c**onviction to **c**arry my **c**ross.

S **S**pirit of God, give me, a **s**inner, **s**trength to live a Christian life.

2. Prayers of Saints and What Saints Say about Prayer

Create a chart in the style of the one below. Fill in each column of the chart for four different saints. In column 1, write a two-paragraph biography of the saint. In column 2, print a prayer or a quotation about prayer written by the saint. In column 3, write one paragraph explaining the meaning of the prayer or the quotation's lesson on prayer. In column 4, write a personal reflection on the saint's words (e.g., how you would apply them to your own life, what words you found inspiring, or your own similar prayer for today).

Name of Saint	Biography	Prayer/ Quotation	Meaning	Personal Reflection
1.				
2.				
3.				
4.				

3. Where to Pray

Complete both parts of this assignment:

- Look up each of the following Gospel passages. Write down the passage and the location it names where Jesus prayed.
    - Luke 5:16
    - Luke 6:12
    - Mark 14:32
    - Matthew 21:12–13
    - Luke 23:34, 46
- Create a pictorial essay showing five places where you pray (e.g., your bedroom, a quiet place in your home, at a park, before the Blessed Sacrament, etc.). Record these places in photos, videos, drawings, or paintings. Include the following information with each image: (1) the name of the location; (2) when you most often pray there; and (3) why it makes a good prayer space. Finally, for each location, compose a prayer that reflects the intentions and form of prayer you most often pray there.

Faithful Disciple

St. Benedict of Nursia

St. Benedict was born in Nursia, a town in Umbria in north central Italy, in AD 480. He was a monk who founded the Benedictine order and is known as the father of Western **monasticism**. Around 520, St. Benedict founded the monastery of Monte Cassino, about eighty miles southeast of Rome. From this community, St. Benedict wrote a famous *rule*, or standard, for monks that would influence the monastic rule for the entire Western Church. The Rule of St. Benedict is still practiced in monastic life today; it also serves as a model for the prayer and spiritual lives of all Christians.

St. Benedict of Nursia

monasticism A way of Christian life that stresses communal worship along with private prayer, silence, poverty, chastity, and obedience.

The history of Monte Cassino and monasticism has roots in the fourth century, in the period after Christianity was legalized by the Roman emperor Constantine and Christians were no longer persecuted and martyred for their faith under Roman law. During that time, Christians began to seek out other intense ways to practice their faith. In every age, there have been Christians who have felt drawn to single-minded devotion to God in prayer, solitude, and communal living. In the early centuries of legal Christianity, some men and women withdrew from everyday life to go to the desert to be alone with God. There they prayed, fasted, read and meditated on the Scriptures, and performed other works of penance and sacrifice. They were known as *hermits*.

Before long, hermits saw advantages in gathering with others to live the same type of lifestyle in community. Monasteries were formed so that these men and women could share the burden of providing for food, shelter, and protection and could then devote more time to prayer.

Benedict attempted to seek a balance among three things: (1) public prayer at set times throughout the day; (2) regular reading and meditation on the Bible; and (3) manual work for the physical support of the whole monastery. Benedict's motto was *Ora et Labora*, "Pray and Work." It remains the practice of the Benedictines today.

By following their rule faithfully, those who live a monastic life grow in deeper union with God. Monastic life also provides a strong statement about God's Kingdom. The witness monks and nuns offer to the world is their dedication to the coming of God's Kingdom without being attached to the passing things of this world. This lifestyle—codified by St. Benedict—should also call you to examine what you are doing and help you to look more seriously at your own level of commitment to God and prayer.

Reading Comprehension

1. What is a name for people who withdrew to the desert to pray and fast?
2. Why were monasteries formed?
3. How did St. Benedict's Rule reflect his motto *Ora et Labora*?

Writing Task

- Research and write a brief history of Monte Cassino from 1944 to the present.

Explaining the Faith

Isn't making sacrifices and putting up with suffering a sign of weakness?

Making sacrifices and putting up with suffering are not signs of weakness but signs of a great deal of courage and strength. Jesus teaches by example about the value of unselfish living and the courage and strength it requires. Living like Jesus, who accepted his Father's will even though it involved suffering, takes grace and personal holiness. Jesus showed through his Paschal Mystery—that is, his Passion, Death, Resurrection—that giving of yourself is the path to eternal life and happiness.

If you want to cope with suffering or forgive someone—especially an enemy—you must pray for inner conversion and grace. Only God can transform your soul so that you can accomplish very difficult tasks such as forgiving another for a serious offense. Jesus teaches us by both word and example to refrain from revenge and to forgive those who hurt or sin against us. The Holy Spirit is able to turn our hurt and injury into compassion for the other person. The Holy Spirit's gift of fortitude gives you courage to speak out or risk rejection as you follow Jesus. In fact, the Holy Spirit provides you with the strength to sacrifice your life if necessary.

Sacrifice, suffering with Christ, and forgiveness are experiences that develop your maturity and make you better able to love God and neighbor. They are signs that love is stronger than evil. They are certainly not signs of weakness.

 Further Research

- Read paragraph 2844 of the *Catechism of the Catholic Church*. What does it say about proper recourse for dealing with an enemy?

Prayer

Suscipe

Take, Lord, and receive all my liberty,
my memory, my understanding,
and my entire will,
all I have and call my own.
You have given all to me.
To you, Lord, I return it.
Everything is yours; do with it what you will.
Give me only your love and your grace;
that is enough for me.
—St. Ignatius of Loyola

APPENDIX
CATHOLIC HANDBOOK for FAITH

Beliefs

From the beginning, the Church expressed and handed on her faith in brief formulas accessible to all. There are early formulas of belief in the New Testament, especially in 1 Corinthians 15. Early Christians continued to develop their understanding of the God who saves in Jesus Christ and in the Church, and they formed professions of faith to pass on for generations. These professions of faith are called creeds because their first word in Latin, credo, *means "I believe." The following three creeds have special importance in the Church. The Apostles' Creed is an early summary of the Apostles' faith. The Nicene Creed expresses the Church's faith in the Trinitarian God who saves in Jesus Christ. It was developed from the Councils of Nicaea (AD 325) and Constantinople (381) and remains the common profession of faith between the Churches of the East and West; it is typically recited at Mass on Sundays. The Chalcedonian Creed (also known as the Symbol of Chalecedon or the Chalcedonian Definition) was issued by the Council of Chalcedon (451). This creed summarized the Church's understanding of the Person of Jesus Christ, rejecting the view that we can no longer distinguish Jesus' divinity from his humanity because they became commingled into one (the notion of a single nature in Christ).*

Apostles' Creed

I believe in God,
the Father almighty,
Creator of heaven and earth,
and in Jesus Christ, his only Son, our Lord,
who was conceived by the Holy Spirit,
born of the Virgin Mary,
suffered under Pontius Pilate,
was crucified, died, and was buried;
he descended into hell;
on the third day he rose again from the dead;
he ascended into heaven,
and is seated at the right hand of God the Father Almighty;
from there he will come to judge the living and the dead.

I believe in the Holy Spirit,
the holy catholic Church,
the communion of saints,
the forgiveness of sins,
the resurrection of the body,
and life everlasting. Amen.

Nicene Creed

I believe in one God,
the Father almighty,
maker of heaven and earth,
of all things visible and invisible.

I believe in one Lord Jesus Christ,
the Only Begotten Son of God,
born of the Father before all ages.
God from God, Light from Light,
true God from true God,
begotten, not made, consubstantial with the Father;
through him all things were made.
For us men and for our salvation
he came down from heaven,

and by the Holy Spirit was incarnate of the Virgin Mary,
and became man.

For our sake he was crucified under Pontius Pilate,
he suffered death and was buried,
and rose again on the third day
in accordance with the Scriptures.
He ascended into heaven
and is seated at the right hand of the Father.
He will come again in glory
to judge the living and the dead
and his kingdom will have no end.

I believe in the Holy Spirit, the Lord, the giver of life,
who proceeds from the Father and the Son,
who with the Father and the Son is adored and glorified,
who has spoken through the prophets.
I believe in one, holy, catholic and apostolic Church.
I confess one baptism for the forgiveness of sins
and I look forward to the resurrection of the dead
and the life of the world to come. Amen.

Chalcedonian Creed

Following therefore the holy Fathers, we unanimously teach to confess one and the same Son, our Lord Jesus Christ, the same perfect in divinity and perfect in humanity, the same truly God and truly man composed of rational soul and body, the same one in being (*homoousios*) with the Father as to the divinity and one in being with us as to the humanity, like unto us in all things but sin (cf. Heb 4:15). The same was begotten from the Father before the ages as to the divinity and in the later days for us and our salvation was born as to his humanity from Mary the Virgin Mother of God.

We confess that one and the same Lord Jesus Christ, the only-begotten Son, must be acknowledged in two natures, without confusion or change, without division or separation. The distinction between the natures was never abolished by their union but rather the character proper to each of the two natures was preserved as they came together in one person (*prosopon*) and one hypostasis. He is not split or divided into two persons, but he is one and the same only-begotten, God the Word, the Lord Jesus Christ, as formerly the prophets and later Jesus Christ himself have taught us about him and has been handed down to us by the Symbol of the Fathers.

Deposit of Faith

Deposit of Faith *refers to both Sacred Tradition and Sacred Scripture handed on from the time of the Apostles, from which the Church draws all that she proposes is revealed by God.*

Relationship between Sacred Scripture and Sacred Tradition

The Church does not derive the revealed truths of God from Sacred Scripture alone. Sacred Tradition hands on God's Word, first given to the Apostles by the Lord and the Holy Spirit, to the successors of the Apostles (the bishops and the pope). Enlightened by the Holy Spirit, these successors faithfully preserve, explain, and spread it to the ends of the earth. The Second Vatican Council Fathers explained the relationship between Sacred Scripture and Sacred Tradition:

> It is clear therefore that, in the supremely wise arrangement of God, Sacred Tradition, Sacred Scripture, and the Magisterium of the Church are so connected and associated that one of them cannot stand without the others. Working together, each in its own way, under the action of the one Holy Spirit, they all contribute effectively to the salvation of souls. (*Dei Verbum*, 10)

Canon of the Bible

There are seventy-three books in the canon of the Bible—that is, the official list of books the Church accepts as divinely inspired: forty-six Old Testament books and twenty-seven New Testament books.

The Old Testament			
The Pentateuch		**The Prophetic Books**	
Genesis	Gn	Isaiah	Is
Exodus	Ex	Jeremiah	Jer
Leviticus	Lv	Lamentations	Lam
Numbers	Nm	Baruch	Bar
Deuteronomy	Dt	Ezekiel	Ez
The Historical Books		Daniel	Dn
Joshua	Jos	Hosea	Hos
Judges	Jgs	Joel	Jl
Ruth	Ru	Amos	Am
1 Samuel	1 Sm	Obadiah	Ob
2 Samuel	2 Sm	Jonah	Jon
1 Kings	1 Kgs	Micah	Mi
2 Kings	2 Kgs	Nahum	Na
1 Chronicles	1 Chr	Habakkuk	Hb
2 Chronicles	2 Chr	Zephaniah	Zep
Ezra	Ezr	Haggai	Hg
Nehemiah	Neh	Zechariah	Zec
Tobit	Tb	Malachi	Mal
Judith	Jdt		
Esther	Est		
1 Maccabees	1 Mc		
2 Maccabees	2 Mc		
The Wisdom Books			
Job	Jb		
Psalms	Ps(s)		
Proverbs	Prv		
Ecclesiastes	Eccl		
Song of Songs	Sg		
Wisdom	Ws		
Sirach	Sir		

The New Testament			
The Gospels		**The Catholic Letters**	
Matthew	Mt	James	Jas
Mark	Mk	1 Peter	1 Pt
Luke	Lk	2 Peter	2 Pt
John	Jn	1 John	1 Jn
		2 John	2 Jn
Acts of the Apostles	Acts	3 John	3 Jn
The New Testament Letters		Jude	Jude
Romans	Rom		
1 Corinthians	1 Cor	Revelation	Rv
2 Corinthians	2 Cor		
Galatians	Gal		
Ephesians	Eph		
Philippians	Phil		
Colossians	Col		
1 Thessalonians	1 Thes		
2 Thessalonians	2 Thes		
1 Timothy	1 Tm		
2 Timothy	2 Tm		
Titus	Ti		
Philemon	Phlm		
Hebrews	Heb		

Moral Teaching

Morality refers to the goodness or evil of human actions. Listed below are several helps the Church offers for making good and moral decisions.

The Ten Commandments

The Ten Commandments are a main source for Christian morality. The Ten Commandments were revealed by God to Moses. Jesus himself acknowledged them. He told the rich young man, "If you wish to enter into life, keep the commandments" (Mt 19:17). Since the time of St. Augustine (fourth century), the Ten Commandments have been used as a source for teaching baptismal candidates.

I. I am the LORD, your God: you shall not have strange gods before me.
II. You shall not take the name of the LORD your God in vain.
III. Remember to keep holy the LORD's day.
IV. Honor your father and your mother.
V. You shall not kill.
VI. You shall not commit adultery.
VII. You shall not steal.
VIII. You shall not bear false witness against your neighbor.
IX. You shall not covet your neighbor's wife.
X. You shall not covet your neighbor's goods.

The Beatitudes

The word *beatitude* means "happiness." Jesus preached the Beatitudes in his Sermon on the Mount (see Mt 5–7). They are:

Blessed are the poor in spirit, for theirs is the kingdom of heaven.

Blessed are they who mourn, for they will be comforted.

Blessed are the meek, for they will inherit the land.
Blessed are they who hunger and thirst for righteousness, for they will be satisfied.
Blessed are the merciful, for they will be shown mercy.
Blessed are the clean of heart, for they will see God.
Blessed are the peacemakers, for they will be called children of God.
Blessed are they who are persecuted for the sake of righteousness, for theirs is the kingdom of heaven. (Mt 5:3–12)

Cardinal Virtues

Virtues (habits that help in leading a moral life) that are acquired by human effort are known as moral or human virtues. Four of these are known as the cardinal virtues, as they form the hinge (*cardinal* comes from the Latin word for "hinge") that connects all the others:

- prudence
- justice
- fortitude
- temperance

Theological Virtues

The theological virtues are the foundation for moral life. They are gifts infused into our souls by God:

- faith
- hope
- charity (love)

Works of Mercy

The works of mercy are charitable actions that remind you how to come to the aid of a neighbor and fulfill his or her bodily and spiritual needs.

Corporal Works of Mercy

1. Feed the hungry.
2. Give drink to the thirsty.
3. Clothe the naked.
4. Visit the imprisoned.
5. Shelter the homeless.
6. Visit the sick.
7. Bury the dead.

Spiritual Works of Mercy

1. Counsel the doubtful.
2. Instruct the ignorant.
3. Admonish sinners.
4. Comfort the afflicted.
5. Forgive offenses.
6. Bear wrongs patiently.
7. Pray for the living and the dead.

Precepts of the Church

The precepts of the Church are basic obligations for all Catholics decreed by laws of the Church. They are intended to guarantee to Catholics the minimum in prayer and moral effort to facilitate their growth in love for God and neighbor.

1. You shall attend Mass on Sundays and on holy days of obligation and rest from servile labor.
2. You shall confess your sins at least once a year.
3. You shall receive the Sacrament of Eucharist at least during the Easter season.
4. You shall observe the days of fasting and abstinence established by the Church.
5. You shall help to provide for the needs of the Church.

Understanding Sin

Being a moral person entails avoiding sin. Sin is an offense against God.

Mortal sin is the most serious kind of sin. Mortal sin destroys or kills a person's relationship with God. For a sin to be mortal, three conditions must exist:

1. The moral object must be of grave or serious matter. Grave matter is specified in the Ten Commandments (e.g., do not kill, do not commit adultery, do not steal, etc.).
2. The person must have full knowledge of the gravity of the sinful action.
3. The person must deliberately consent to the action. It must be a personal choice.

Venial sin is less serious sin. Examples of venial sins are petty jealousy, disobedience, or "borrowing" a small amount of money without the intention of repaying it. Venial sins, when not repented, can lead a person to commit mortal sins.

Vices are bad habits linked to sins. Vices come from particular sins, especially the seven *capital sins*: pride, avarice, envy, wrath, lust, gluttony, and sloth.

Steps for Celebrating the Sacrament of Penance

- Spend some time examining your conscience. Consider your actions and attitudes in each area of your life (e.g., faith, family, school, work, and social relationships). Ask yourself: "Is this area of my life pleasing to God? What needs to be reconciled with God? With others? With myself?"
- Sincerely tell God that you are sorry for your sins. Ask God for forgiveness and for the grace you will need to change what needs changing in your life. Promise God that you will try to live according to his will for you.
- Approach the area for Confession. Wait at an appropriate distance until it is your turn.
- Make the Sign of the Cross with the priest. He may say, "May God, who has enlightened every heart, help you to know your sins and trust in his mercy." You reply, "Amen."
- Confess your sins to the priest. Simply and directly talk to him about the areas of sin in your life that need God's healing touch.
- The priest may talk to you about your life and encourage you to be more faithful to God in the future, and he will impose on you a penance for your sin. The penance corresponds as far as possible with the gravity and nature of the sins committed. It can consist of prayer, offerings, works of mercy, service to neighbor, voluntary self-denial, sacrifices, and patient acceptance of the crosses you must bear. You should continue in acts of penance, prayer, charity, and bearing sufferings of all kinds for the removal of the remaining temporal punishment for sin.
- The priest will ask you to express your contrition or sorrow and to pray an Act of Contrition. Pray an Act of Contrition you have committed to memory. See page 362 for an example.
- The priest will then extend his hands over your head and pray a prayer of absolution for your sins. You respond, "Amen."
- The priest will wish you peace. Thank him and leave.
- Go to a quiet place in the church and pray your prayer of penance. Then spend some time quietly thanking God for the gift of forgiveness.

Prayers

Some common Catholic prayers are listed below. The Latin translation for four of the prayers is included. Latin is the official language of the Church. There are occasions when you may pray in Latin (for example, at a World Youth Day when you are with young people who speak many different languages).

Sign of the Cross

In the name of the Father,
and of the Son,
and of the Holy Spirit. Amen.

In nómine Patris,
et Filii,
et Spíritus Sancti.
Amen.

Our Father

Our Father
who art in heaven,
hallowed be thy name.
Thy kingdom come;
thy will be done on earth as it is in heaven.
Give us this day our daily bread
and forgive us our trespasses
as we forgive those who trespass against us.
And lead us not into temptation,
but deliver us from evil. Amen.

Pater Noster qui es in caelis:
sanctificétur Nomen Tuum;
advéniat Regnum Tuum;
fiat volúntas Tua, sicut in caelo, et in terra.
Panem nostrum quotidiánum da nobis hódie;
et dimítte nobis débita nostra,
sicut et nos dimíttimus debitóribus nostris;
Et ne nos inducas in tentatiónem,
sed libera nos a malo.
Amen.

Glory Be

Glory be to the Father
and to the Son
and to the Holy Spirit,
as it was in the beginning,
is now, and ever shall be,
world without end.
Amen.

Glória Patri
et Fílio
et Spirítui Sancto.
Sicut érat in princípio,
et nunc et semper,
et in saécula saeculórum.
Amen.

Hail Mary

Hail Mary, full of grace,
the Lord is with thee.
Blessed art thou among women
and blessed is the fruit of thy womb, Jesus.
Holy Mary, Mother of God,
pray for us sinners
now and at the hour of our death.
Amen.

Ave, María, grátia plena,
Dóminus tecum.
Benedícta tu in muliéribus,
et benedíctus fructus ventristui, Iesus.
Sancta María, Mater Dei,
ora pro nobis peccatóribus
nunc et in hora mortis nostræ.
Amen.

Memorare

Remember, O most gracious Virgin Mary,
that never was it known
that anyone who fled to thy protection,
implored thy help,
or sought thy intercession was left unaided.

Inspired by this confidence I fly unto thee,
O virgin of virgins, my Mother,
To thee do I come, before thee I stand,
sinful and sorrowful.
O Mother of the Word Incarnate,
despise not my petitions,
but in thy mercy hear and answer me. Amen.

The Angelus

V. The Angel of the Lord declared unto Mary.

R. And she conceived of the Holy Spirit.

Hail Mary.

V. Behold the handmaid of the Lord.

R. Be it done unto me according to thy word.

Hail Mary . . .

V. And the Word was made flesh.

R. And dwelt among us.

Hail Mary . . .

V. Pray for us, O holy Mother of God,

R. That we may be made worthy of the promises of Christ.

Let us pray: Pour forth, we beseech you, O Lord, thy grace into our hearts; that we, to whom the Incarnation of Christ thy Son was made known by the message of an angel, may by his Passion and Cross be brought to the glory of his Resurrection. Through the same Christ our Lord. Amen.

Grace at Meals

Before Meals

Bless us, O Lord,
and these thy gifts,
which we are about to receive from thy bounty,
through Christ our Lord. Amen.

After Meals

We give you thanks, almighty God,
for these and all the gifts
which we have received
from your goodness
through Christ our Lord. Amen.

Guardian Angel Prayer

Angel of God, my guardian dear,
to whom God's love commits me here,
ever this day be at my side,
to light and guard, to rule and guide. Amen.

Prayer for the Faithful Departed

Eternal rest grant unto them, O Lord,
and let perpetual light shine upon them.
May they rest in peace. Amen.

Morning Offering

O Jesus, through the Immaculate Heart of Mary, I offer you my prayers, works, joys, and sufferings of this day in union with the holy sacrifice of the Mass throughout the world. I offer them for all the intentions of your Sacred Heart: the salvation of souls, reparation for sin, and the reunion of all Christians. I offer them for the intentions of our bishops and all Apostles of Prayer and in particular for those recommended by our Holy Father this month. Amen.

Act of Faith

O my God, I firmly believe that you are one God in Three Divine Persons, Father, Son, and Holy Spirit. I believe that your divine

Son became man and died for our sins and that he will come to judge the living and the dead. I believe these all the truths which the Holy Catholic Church teaches because you have revealed them who are eternal truth and wisdom, who can neither deceive nor be deceived. In this faith I intend to live and die. Amen.

Act of Hope

O Lord God, I hope by your grace for the pardon of all my sins and after life here to gain eternal happiness because you have promised it who are infinitely powerful, faithful, kind, and merciful. In this hope I intend to live and die. Amen.

Act of Love

O Lord God, I love you above all things and I love my neighbor for your sake because you are the highest, infinite and perfect good, worthy of all my love. In this love I intend to live and die. Amen.

Act of Contrition

O my God, I am heartily sorry for having offended Thee, and I detest all my sins because of Thy just punishment, but most of all because they offend Thee, my God, who art all good and deserving of all my love. I firmly resolve with the help of Thy grace to sin no more and to avoid the near occasion of sin. Amen.

Devotions

Devotions are external acts of holiness that are not part of the Church's official liturgy but are popular spiritual practices of Catholics through history and today. Catholics have also expressed their piety around the Church's sacramental life through practices like the veneration of relics, visits to churches, pilgrimages, processions, the Stations of the Cross, religious dances, the Rosary, wearing religious medals, and many more. Some popular Catholic devotions are included in this subsection.

The Mysteries of the Rosary

The Joyful Mysteries

1. The Annunciation
2. The Visitation
3. The Nativity
4. The Presentation
5. The Finding in the Temple

The Luminous Mysteries

1. The Baptism of Jesus
2. The Wedding Feast of Cana
3. The Proclamation of the Kingdom, with the Call to Conversion
4. The Transfiguration
5. The Institution of the Eucharist

The Sorrowful Mysteries

1. The Agony in the Garden
2. The Scourging at the Pillar
3. The Crowning with Thorns

4. The Carrying of the Cross
5. The Crucifixion

The Glorious Mysteries

1. The Resurrection
2. The Ascension
3. The Descent of the Holy Spirit
4. The Assumption of Mary
5. The Coronation of Mary Queen of Heaven and Earth

How to Pray the Rosary

Opening

1. Begin on the crucifix and pray the Apostles' Creed.
2. On the first bead, pray the Our Father.
3. On each of the next three beads, pray the Hail Mary. (Some people meditate on the theological virtues of faith, hope, and charity on these beads.)
4. On the fifth bead, pray the Glory Be.

The Body

Each decade (set of ten beads) is organized as follows:

1. On the larger bead that comes before each set of ten, announce the mystery to be prayed (see above), and pray one Our Father.
2. On each of the ten smaller beads, pray one Hail Mary while meditating on the mystery.
3. Pray one Glory Be at the end of the decade. (There is no bead for the Glory Be.)

Conclusion

Pray the following prayer at the end of the Rosary:

Hail, Holy Queen
Hail, holy Queen, Mother of Mercy,
our life, our sweetness, and our hope.
To thee do we cry,
poor banished children of Eve.
To thee do we send up our sighs,
mourning and weeping in this valley of tears.
Turn then, most gracious advocate,
thine eyes of mercy toward us,
and after this our exile,
show unto us the blessed fruit of thy womb, Jesus.
O clement, O loving, O sweet Virgin Mary.

V. Pray for us, O holy Mother of God,

R. That we may be made worthy of the promises of Christ.

Amen.

The Stations of the Cross

The Stations of the Cross is a meditative prayer based on the Passion of Christ. This devotion developed in the Middle Ages as a way to allow the faithful to retrace the last steps of Jesus on his way to Calvary without making the journey to the Holy Land. Most Catholic churches have images or symbols of the Stations depicted on side walls to help Catholics imagine the sufferings of Jesus and focus on the meaning of the Paschal Mystery. Praying the Stations means meditating on each of the following scenes:

1. Jesus is condemned to death.
2. Jesus takes up his Cross.
3. Jesus falls the first time.
4. Jesus meets his Mother.
5. Simon of Cyrene helps Jesus carry his Cross.
6. Veronica wipes the face of Jesus.
7. Jesus falls the second time.
8. Jesus consoles the women of Jerusalem.
9. Jesus falls the third time.
10. Jesus is stripped of his garments.
11. Jesus is nailed to the Cross.
12. Jesus dies on the Cross.
13. Jesus is taken down from the Cross.
14. Jesus is laid in the tomb.

Some churches also include a fifteenth station, the Resurrection of the Lord.

Further Study: Jesus and the Church

Your study of Jesus Christ, from his ancestors in faith to his mission and ministry on earth through the accomplishments of his Paschal Mystery—the source of our salvation—leads to uncovering more about his continuing presence on earth in his Body, the Church. The Catholic Church is instituted by Christ: "The Lord Jesus inaugurated his Church by preaching the Good News, that is, the coming of the Reign of God, promised over the ages in the scriptures" (Lumen Gentium, *5). Christ and his Church together make up the "whole Christ"* (Christus totus)*. Christ is the head; you are a member. St. Joan of Arc, speaking of Jesus and the Church, said, "About Jesus Christ and the Church, I simply know they are one thing and we shouldn't complicate the matter."*

Marks of the Church

1. *The Church is one.*

   The Church remains *one* because of her source: the unity—in the Trinity of the Father, Son, and Holy Spirit—in one God. The Church's unity can never be broken or lost because this foundation is itself unbreakable.

2. *The Church is holy.*

   The Church is *holy* because Jesus, who founded the Church, is holy, and he joined the Church to himself as his Body and gave the Church the gift of the Holy Spirit. Together, Christ and the Church make up the "whole Christ" (*Christus totus* in Latin).

3. *The Church is catholic.*

   The Church is *catholic* ("universal" or "for everyone") in two ways. First, she is catholic because Christ is present in the Church in the fullness of his Body, with the fullness of the means of salvation, the fullness of faith, sacraments, and the ordained ministry that comes from the Apostles. The Church is also catholic because she takes the message of salvation to all people.

4. *The Church is apostolic.*

   The Church's *apostolic* mission comes from Jesus: "Go, therefore, and make disciples of all nations" (Mt 28:19). The Church remains apostolic because she still teaches the same things the Apostles taught. Also, the Church is led by the pope and bishops, who are successors to the Apostles and who help to guide the Church until Jesus returns.

Some Basic Questions about the Church

As you continue your studies, you will be addressing questions and discerning answers to some of the following questions about Jesus, the Church, and all baptized Catholics. Preview the following:

Why do people need organized religion?

God wants you come to him as a member of his family, so he established the Church to accomplish that purpose. Because people are social in nature, they need each other's support and example. Organized religion as practiced in the Catholic Church offers you authentic worship in spirit and truth when you unite yourself with Christ's self-offering at Mass.

Is the Catholic Church really the only true Church?

The very word *catholic* means that the Church strives to reach out and include all people—this is the Church's mission. The Church teaches that "one true religion subsists in the Catholic and Apostolic Church" (*Dignitatis Humanae*, 1), yet it recognizes that holiness can be found and God's will detected in various other Christian and non-Christian communities and in individuals who through no fault of their own have not been exposed to the Catholic Church.

Did Jesus found the Catholic Church?

Yes. The Church was foreshadowed from the world's beginning and prepared for in the Old Testament when God called Abraham. The Church was established by Jesus Christ when he called the disciples with Peter as their head, proclaimed the Gospel, and instituted the sacraments. The Church was born from Christ's self-giving on the Cross. The Church was revealed to the world at Pentecost.

Why is the Church called Roman Catholic?

A simple answer is that the Church is called *Roman* Catholic because of its unity with the pope, the bishop of Rome. It is a term that first came to use about the time of the Great Schism of 1054, which led to the division of Christians between those united to the patriarch of Constantinople and those united to the pope. However, there are many Catholic rites other than Roman that are in union with the pope. Hence, the term *Roman Catholic* is often one used by Christians outside of the Church as a way not to recognize the Catholic Church as the one, true Church.

Why should a person be Catholic?

To be a Catholic is to be a member of the one, true Church of Christ. While elements of truth can be found in other churches and religions, the fullness of the means of salvation subsists in the Catholic Church.

Is the Church necessary for salvation?

The answer to this common question is yes simply because Jesus is necessary for salvation and Jesus remains present in the Church, his Body. Those who know and understand that the Church is the Body of

Christ, yet reject it, are rejecting salvation. However, this also means that those who have never heard of Christ or the Church have not forfeited their chance for salvation.

Epilogue: Straining Forward

"Creation has its own goodness and proper perfection, but it did not spring forth complete from the hands of the Creator" (*CCC*, 302). These words can also apply specifically to you. You are created good, unique, and much loved by God, but you are not yet complete.

However, God does intend for you to be perfect. Jesus said this about you: "So be perfect, just as your heavenly Father is perfect" (Mt 5:48). You are called to a perfection that is yours alone, intended by God in his "proper" creation of you.

It should be comforting to know that God loves and cares for you so much that he has a special plan for your life and guides you to it. This plan is known as divine providence. As the Book of Proverbs teaches:

> Many are the plans of the human heart,
> but it is the decision of the LORD that endures. (Prv 19:21)

Church Father St. Gregory of Nyssa spoke of the soul's journey toward Christ and heavenly perfection as something that you must consistently engage in. When Pope Francis spoke of his "top ten secrets for happiness," first on his list was "live and let live." He expanded on this to say that you should "move forward and let others do the same."

This process of daily attention to divine providence and daily focus on "moving forward" or on what is ahead is referred to in Scriptures as *epektasis*—a Greek word that means an unending "straining forward." St. Paul used this description in his Letter to the Philippians:

> Forgetting what lies behind but straining forward to what lies ahead, I continue my pursuit toward the goal, the prize of God's upward calling, in Christ Jesus. (Phil 3:13b–14)

For you, *epektasis* means moving forward on a daily basis, exercising your spiritual muscles, reaching out to God and others, and straining with hope. You have spent a semester studying the events of the Paschal Mystery—specifically Christ's Passion, Death, and Resurrection—that took place over a period in historical time of just over forty days. It would not be hyperbole to describe these as the most important days in the history of life on earth and, likewise, the most important for your own life as well. These events in the life of Christ form the pattern of how you are to move forward, live your own life, and reach perfection.

Your participation in this same pattern of life—accepting small and large trials and sufferings marks you as a disciple of Christ and keeps you journeying toward fullness of relationship with the Blessed Trinity. Your participation in the Paschal Mystery is celebrated and graced when you go to Mass and receive the Lord in Holy Communion.

Remain faithful to the Lord in all you do. Stay close to his Church, his Body. *Epektasis* begins in this life and extends to the next, for eternity. Thus, even eternal life is part of—not the end of—your journey.

GLOSSARY

Ascension Jesus' passage from this world into divine glory in God's heavenly domain forty days after his Resurrection. It is from this domain that Jesus will come again.

Assumption The Church dogma that teaches that the Blessed Mother was taken body and soul into heaven when her earthly life was over. The Feast of the Assumption is on August 15 and is a holy day of obligation.

beatific vision Seeing God "face-to-face" in heaven; the source of eternal happiness and final union with the Triune God for all eternity.

Beloved Disciple The "disciple whom Jesus loved," referenced several times in John's Gospel. Church Father St. Irenaeus attributed the Gospel of John to the Beloved Disciple. Church Tradition identified this John as one of the Apostles, the one who rested his head on Jesus' chest during the Last Supper (see Jn 21:20).

blasphemy Any thought, word, or act that expresses hatred or contempt for Christ, God, the Church, saints, or holy things.

Blessed Sacrament "The name given to the Holy Eucharist, especially the consecrated elements reserved in the tabernacle for adoration, or for the sick" (*CCC*, Glossary).

catechesis The education of children, adolescents, and adults in the faith of the Church through the teaching of Christian doctrine in an organic and systematic way to make them disciples of Jesus Christ. Those who perform the ministry of catechesis in the Church are called *catechists*.

concupiscence "Human appetites or desires which remain disordered due to the temporal consequences of Original Sin, which remain even after Baptism, and which produce an inclination to sin" (*CCC*, Glossary).

consecrated life "A permanent state of life recognized by the Church, entered freely in response to the call of Christ to perfection, and characterized by the profession of the evangelical counsels of poverty, chastity, and obedience" (*CCC*, Glossary).

contemplative prayer Wordless prayer wherein a person's mind and heart rest in God's goodness and majesty.

contrition Heartfelt sorrow and aversion for sins committed along with the intention of sinning no more. Contrition is the most important act of the penitent and is necessary for receiving the Sacrament of Penance.

conversion A radical reorientation away from sin, evil, and selfishness and toward God and service to others. This change of heart is a central element of Christ's preaching, of the Church's ministry of evangelization, and of the Sacrament of Penance and Reconciliation.

Decalogue Literally, "ten words," it describes the Ten Commandments given by God to Moses.

discernment A decision-making process that attends to the implications and consequences of an action or choice by prayerfully and meditatively separating out what is truly good from what only appears to be good but is in fact a lie and a temptation.

dogma A revealed teaching or set of revealed teachings of Christ proclaimed by the fullest extent of the exercise of the authority of the Church's Magisterium. The faithful are obliged to believe the truths or dogmas contained in Divine Revelation and defined by the Magisterium.

Enuma Elish The Babylonian epic or myth of creation.

Epiphany The *manifestation* to the world of the newborn Christ as Messiah, Son of God, and Savior of the world. The Feast of the Epiphany celebrates the adoration of Jesus by the wise men (Magi) from the East, together with his Baptism in the Jordan River and the wedding feast of Cana in Galilee.

eschatology The study of, and teaching about, the last things: death, judgment, heaven, Purgatory, hell, the Second Coming of Christ, and the resurrection of the body.

etiology An explanation of the cause of something. In the Bible, etiology appears as narrative, typically reaching back to the distant past to describe the core meaning of something that we experience universally. For example, although Genesis attributes the origin of sin to Adam and Eve in the past, it is also an explanation of humanity's rejection of God at all times, even today.

evangelical counsels Vows of personal poverty, chastity understood as lifelong celibacy, and obedience to the demands of the community professed by those entering the consecrated life.

evangelization The proclamation of Christ and the Good News of the Gospel by your words and the way that you live, in fulfillment of Christ's command. Evangelization involves proclaiming the Gospel in such a way that people's hearts and lives are changed.

Gifts of the Holy Spirit Outpourings of God's gifts to help you live a Christian life. The traditional seven Gifts of the Holy Spirit are wisdom, understanding, counsel, fortitude, knowledge, piety, and fear of the Lord.

grace of justification The gracious action of God that frees you from sin and communicates "the righteousness of God through faith in Jesus Christ" (Rom 3:22). Justification is not only the remission of sins but also the sanctification and renewal of your inner self so that you can receive his graces, live them in your life through the theological virtues, and grow in your relationship with God.

guardian angel The name for a messenger with free will and naturally superior intellect to humans. Since the third century, the Church has maintained, though not officially, that all the baptized have guardian angels who personally watch out for them. The Feast of the Guardian Angels is October 2.

high priest In Jewish history, the priest in charge of Temple worship. The high priest shared in the general priestly duties; however, he was the only one allowed to enter the holy of holies, and then only on the Day of Atonement. Jesus is the High Priest of the New Covenant. Christ fulfilled everything that the priesthood of the Old Covenant prefigured (cf. Heb 5:10, 6:20). He offered himself once for all (cf. Heb 10:14) in a perfect sacrifice upon the Cross. His priesthood is made present in a special way in the

Church through the ministerial priesthood, conferred through the Sacrament of Holy Orders.

hosanna A Hebrew word meaning "(O Lord) grant salvation," but the invocation became a shout of joy and welcome.

icon A holy image you gaze at, putting yourself in the presence of the holy person or mystery it portrays.

Immaculate Conception "The dogma proclaimed in Christian Tradition and defined in 1854, that from the first moment of her conception, Mary—by the singular grace of God and by virtue of the merits of Jesus Christ—was preserved immune from original sin" (*CCC*, Glossary).

Jesus Prayer A short, formulaic prayer to Jesus or about Jesus that is said repeatedly. The Jesus Prayer may have originated with the Desert Fathers in the fifth century.

justification God's gracious action freeing a person from sin through faith in Jesus Christ and the Sacrament of Baptism. Justification not only frees a person from sin but also brings sanctification and deep interior renewal.

kerygma A Greek word for "proclamation," the core teaching about Jesus Christ as Savior and Lord. It is the basic Christian message that Jesus of Nazareth died and was raised from the dead by God the Father for the forgiveness of sins.

Last Judgment Christ's judgment of the living and the dead at his return at the end of time. All human beings will appear in their own bodies before Christ's tribunal to render an account of their deeds. The Last Judgment will reveal that God's justice triumphs over all the injustices committed by his creatures and that God's love is stronger than death. After the Last Judgment, the Kingdom of God will come in its fullness, in which the righteous will reign forever with Christ, glorified in body and soul, and the universe itself will be renewed.

lectio divina Literally, "sacred reading." This is a prayerful way to read the Bible or other sacred writings.

litany From the Greek word *litaneia*, meaning "prayer or supplication," a form of prayer used in liturgies that includes prayers with responses.

Liturgy of the Hours The official daily prayer of the Church; also known as the Divine Office. The Liturgy of the Hours consists of prayers, Scripture, and reflections at regular intervals throughout the day.

Magisterium The bishops, in communion with the pope (the successor of St. Peter), who are the living and teaching office of the Church. The Magisterium is entrusted with guarding and handing on the Deposit of Faith and with authentically interpreting God's Revelation, in the forms of both Sacred Scripture and Sacred Tradition.

Magnificat Named for its first word in Latin, the Blessed Virgin Mary's song of praise to the Lord found in Luke's Gospel. It is also known as the Canticle of Mary.

monasticism A way of Christian life that stresses communal worship along with private prayer, silence, poverty, chastity, and obedience.

mortal sin A grave infraction of the law of God—in which you turn away from God—that destroys the divine life (*sanctifying grace*) in the soul of the sinner. For a sin to be mortal, three conditions must be present: the sin itself must be grave (serious), you must have had full knowledge of the evil of the act, and you must have fully consented to the act. Your degree of responsibility for an act may be diminished or nullified by ignorance, duress, fear, or other psychological or social factors.

New Adam A name for Jesus Christ, who, through his obedience in his life and Death, makes amends for the disobedience of the first Adam.

New Covenant The covenant established by God in Jesus Christ to fulfill and perfect the Old Covenant. The New Covenant, also called the Law of the Gospel, is the perfection here on earth of the natural law and the Law of Moses. The New Covenant is the law of love, grace, and freedom. The New Covenant, made in the Blood of Jesus, is the climax of salvation history and is God's eternal covenant with human beings.

novena From the Latin word for "nine," a set of prayers prayed over nine days in order to obtain special graces or to petition for particular intentions.

original holiness and original justice The state of man and woman in paradise before sin. The grace of original holiness was to share in the divine life (see *CCC*, 375). "The inner harmony of the human person, the harmony between man and woman, and finally the harmony between the first couple and all of creation, comprised the state called 'original justice'" (*CCC*, 376). "From [Adam and Eve's] friendship with God flowed the happiness of their existence in paradise" (*CCC*, 384).

Original Sin "The sin by which the first human beings disobeyed the commandment of God, choosing to follow their own will rather than God's will. As a consequence they lost the grace of original holiness, and became subject to the law of death; sin became universally present in the world. Besides the personal sin of Adam and Eve, Original Sin describes the fallen state of human nature which affects every person born into the world, and from which Christ, the 'New Adam,' came to redeem us" (*CCC*, Glossary).

parables Simple images or comparisons that confront the hearer or reader with a radical choice about Jesus' invitation for us to enter the Kingdom of God. Parables are a characteristic feature of the teaching of Jesus.

Parousia The Second Coming of Christ, when the Lord will judge the living and the dead.

Paschal Lamb The lamb slaughtered by the Israelites in preparation for the Passover. God instructed the Israelite people, while they were still enslaved in Egypt, to sprinkle the blood of a lamb on their doorposts, which the angel of death saw and "passed over." They were instructed also to eat the lamb and to commemorate this event (the Passover), which signified their preservation from death and their liberation from captivity. In the New Testament, Jesus is recognized as the Lamb of God, who takes away the sin of the world by shedding his blood. By his blood, death passes us over. In the Eucharist we celebrate and share in the new Passover in his Body and Blood.

passion narratives Four separate accounts of the Passion of Christ in the four Gospels. The passion narratives of the synoptic Gospels follow a similar literary and thematic plan. The passion narrative of John's Gospel provides an independent account of these Paschal events.

Pelagianism The heretical belief that people, because of their natural powers of free will, can lead morally good lives without God's help. Associated with this view is the belief that Original Sin is passed on only through example but is not "contracted" as such. This system of beliefs derives from Pelagius (AD 354–420), who disputed with St. Augustine of Hippo on the question of grace.

Pentecost The day fifty days after Easter when the Holy Spirit descended on the Apostles and gave them the power to preach with conviction the message that Jesus is risen and is Lord of the universe. The Church celebrates Pentecost every year as the beginning of the new "age of the Church," when Christ lives and acts in and with his Church through the outpouring of the Holy Spirit.

philosophy The human attempt to provide rational explanations for why things are the way they are and for how people should conduct their lives.

primeval history The accounts humans have told and recorded about the origins of the earth, humans, other creatures, languages, and cultures.

Psalter A name for the Book of Psalms or a collection of psalms for liturgical or devotional use.

Purgatory The state of purification that takes place after death for those who need to be made clean and holy before meeting the all-holy God in heaven.

Real Presence The Real Presence of Jesus Christ means that he himself is truly present under the appearances of the consecrated bread and wine.

sanctifying grace The grace, or gift of God's friendship, that heals fallen human nature and gives you a share in the divine life of the Blessed Trinity. A habitual, supernatural gift, it makes you perfect, holy, and Christlike (see *CCC*, 2000).

Satan A fallen angel or the devil; the Evil One (see *CCC*, 391, 395, 2851).

soul "The spiritual principle of human beings" (*CCC*, Glossary). The soul and body together form one human nature. The soul does not die with the body. It is eternal and will be reunited with the body in the final resurrection.

synagogues Meeting places for Jews to study and pray.

Transfiguration The glorious transformation of Jesus that manifested his divine identity to Peter, James, and John on a high mountain, probably Mount Tabor. The event, reported in all three synoptic Gospels, also involved the appearance of Moses and Elijah.

typology A method of biblical interpretation in which persons, events, places, or things in the Old Testament are seen to prefigure ones found in the New Testament. The initial one is called a *type*, and its fulfillment is called its *antitype*. By showing how

Old Testament types are fulfilled in God's plan in the Person of Christ, typology points to the unity of God's salvific work.

virtue A firm, stable, and habitual disposition of your intellect and will that regulates your actions, directs your passions, and guides your conduct according to reason and faith.

vocation A word that means "call." God calls all persons to be holy and to be disciples of Jesus Christ. You begin to answer this call by conversion and receiving the Sacraments of Initiation, and you live it out by bringing God's love to others, sharing the Gospel, and seeking the Kingdom of God in everything you do. *Lay vocations* are callings to serve God in the world, and *priestly and religious vocations* are callings to serve God in the Church. Each person is given a unique vocation by which he or she receives a share in Christ's mission of salvation, given to him by the Father.

votive candle A prayer candle typically placed before a statue of Jesus, the Virgin Mary, or a saint and lit for a prayer intention.

SUBJECT INDEX

A

B

C

D

E

F

G

H

I

J

K

L

M

N

O

P

R

S

T

U

V

W

Y

Z

SCRIPTURE INDEX

OLD TESTAMENT

Pentateuch

Historical Books

Wisdom Books

Prophetic Books

NEW TESTAMENT

Gospels

Acts

New Testament Letters

Romans

1 Corinthians

2 Corinthians

Galatians

Ephesians

CATECHISM OF THE CATHOLIC CHURCH INDEX

CHURCH DOCUMENTS INDEX

PHOTO CREDITS

Alamy

p. 1, 5, 23, 49, 55, 65, 69, 75, 92, 94, 96, 100, 107, 108, 117, 119, 124, 125, 132, 138, 146, 147, 158, 160, 161, 165, 169, 172, 177, 181, 185, 185, 195, 200, 201, 204, 206, 215, 220, 226, 235, 238, 240, 241, 242, 245, 247, 254, 258, 263, 273, 275, 278, 283, 291, 297, 302, 304, 313, 318, 319, 323, 325, 328, 329, 330, 331, 336, 340, 341, 345, 346, 351, 367

Associated Press

p. 15, 35, 79, 316

Art Resource

p. 51, 53, 59, 69, 97, 131, 132, 133, 203, 208, 222, 330

Getty Image

p. 3, 8, 10, 13, 18, 22, 25, 27, 30, 31, 31, 32, 34, 35, 36, 40, 43, 45, 48, 50, 52, 53, 57, 60, 64, 66, 77, 79, 81, 84, 86, 88, 93, 98, 101, 103, 104, 106, 107, 111, 113, 114, 120, 121, 122, 126, 126, 127, 129, 142, 143, 147, 152, 153, 155, 157, 158, 158, 164, 170, 173, 174, 176, 178, 180, 182, 184, 186, 191, 192, 197, 202, 210, 212, 213, 214, 215, 216, 217, 221, 225, 232, 233, 244, 245, 250, 252, 253, 255, 256, 257, 259, 263, 264, 271, 277, 280, 282, 285, 286, 288, 292, 293, 294, 295, 298, 299, 299, 300, 303, 309, 310, 315, 319, 321, 322, 324, 326, 329, 330, 332, 333, 335, 340, 341, 342, 344, 353,

iStock photo

p. 6, 7, 11, 47, 68, 171, 248, 269, 276, 294

Rene Martinez Valadez www.mavare100.dibujando.net / **Diocese of Zamora**

p. 189

Super Stock

p. 10, 17, 20, 28, 38, 61, 63, 70, 82, 85, 89, 90, 133, 134, 141, 148, 162, 166, 167, 219, 227, 237, 262, 279, 284, 320, 334

Tracy Christianson www.portraitsofsaints.com

p. 73, 74, 111, 150, 230, 267, 349

Vivian Imbruglia www.sacredimageicons.com

p. 307